ALL THE WAY

ALSO BY MICHAEL FREEDLAND

Jolson
Fred Astaire
Jerome Kern
James Cagney
Shirley MacLaine
Gregory Peck
Jack Lemmon
Dino: The Dean Martin Story
Katharine Hepburn
The Secret Life of Danny Kaye
Dustin: A Biography of Dustin Hoffman
Maurice Chevalier
The Warner Brothers
Sophie: The Story of Sophie Tucker
Irving Berlin (later editions: A Salute To Irving Berlin)
Errol Flynn (in the USA: The Two Lives of Errol Flynn)
So Let's Hear the Applause – The Story of the Jewish Entertainer
The Goldwyn Touch: A Biography of Sam Goldwyn
Leonard Bernstein
Shirley MacLaine
Peter O'Toole
Jane Fonda
Liza With a 'Z'
Kenneth Williams
André Previn
Sean Connery
Music Man

With Morecombe and Wise:
There's No Answer to That

With Walter Scharf:
Composed and Conducted by Walter Scharf

ALL THE WAY

A Biography of *Frank Sinatra*

Michael Freedland

St. Martin's Press ❧ New York

For Beth and Elinor
who have brought such joy

ISBN 0-312-19108-1

First published in Great Britain by Weidenfeld & Nicolson, the
Orion Publishing Group Ltd.

First U.S. Edition

10 9 8 7 6 5 4 3 2 1

CONTENTS

ILLUSTRATIONS

At Grauman's Chinese Theatre, Hollywood.[4]
With Nancy Jnr., Frank Jnr., Barbara Sinatra, Dolly and Tina.[2]
Giving Nancy away on her wedding day.[3]
Frank Sinatra, elder statesman.[2]

Photographs reproduced by kind permission of:

[1] Hoboken Library, New Jersey
[2] Camera Press
[3] Corbis-Bettmann/UPI
[4] Hulton-Getty
[5] Kobal Collection

ACKNOWLEDGEMENTS

I don't think it's ever been harder to compile a list of people whose invaluable help in writing a book is so much appreciated.

The truth of the matter is that more than a hundred people came to my aid with a project I first decided to write some twenty years ago – when Frank Sinatra was still in the full blush of his return from what was laughingly called retirement. But at that time there seemed so much more to say, so much more of his life to live. It was filed as something still to do.

Yet all this time, I was – slowly and more casually at first – researching the project. I met people for other reasons and inevitably the conversation turned to Sinatra. There were documents which came my way and were studied and copied. One of the most important discoveries revealed in this book for the first time had to be stored away literally for years for reasons which will become obvious.

Eventually it all came together in a crescendo of activity and with the huge support of my editor, Ion Trewin, and my agent, Jonathan Lloyd, the work began in earnest. It was a longer, harder and more rewarding process than I could ever have imagined, with scores of new interviews and research in places like the Academy of Motion Picture Arts and Sciences in Los Angeles, the library of the Performing Arts at the Lincoln Center, New York, and the Songwriters Hall of Fame in that city. I wish to thank the numerous people in those institutions who helped me, but it is true to say that no one provided more help than the officials of the city of Hoboken, New Jersey – including the Mayor – who day after day sat with me, answered questions about their town and its most famous former citizen, introduced me to more people and gave me the feel of a place that plays such an important part in this story.

Also, for fairly obvious reasons, a number of the people I have spoken to wanted to talk to me anonymously. In one case, we mutually agreed on a pseudonym, and this is stated in context. In others, conditions of 'non attribution' were insisted upon and I had to agree to this, too. Alas, a number of my early interviewees have since died –

including, and perhaps saddest of all, Juliet Prowse, Sinatra's sometime fiancée who unburdened herself about their relationship for the very first time to me very shortly before her death in 1996. The long taped interview we did in Las Vegas – scene of so much Sinatra activity over the years – has to be one of my most treasured possessions and an archive of incalculable value.

Among those who assisted me so willingly and whom I also warmly thank are: Larry Adler, Paul Anka, the late Jack Benny, Lillian Burns, the late Sammy Cahn, Saul Chaplin, the late Maurice Chevalier, Joan Cohn, Bobby Cohn, Eve Coil, Betty Comden, Ivor Davis, Sally Ogle Davis, the late Sammy Davis, Jr., Leo Deilizzi, George 'Bullets' Durgom, Hilly Elkins, Julius Epstein, Lt. Anthony Falco, the late Ella Fitzgerald, Sidney Furie, Douglas Galloway, Betty Garrett, the late Morton Gould, the late Abel Green, Adolph Green, the late Johnny Green, James Hans, Harold Harris, the late Laurence Harvey, the late Dick Haymes, 'Ida', Paul Jericho, the late Gene Kelly, Evelyn Keyes, Michael Kidd, Howard W. Koch, Teddy Kollek, Stanley Kramer, the late Burton Lane, Eddie Larkin, Ruta Lee, Jerry Lewis, John Marotta, the late Dean Martin, the waiters of Mattheo's, Robert Merrill, the late Lewis Milestone, the late Vincente Minnelli, Hal Needham, Gregory Peck, André Previn, the late Juliet Prowse, the late Richard Quine, David Raksin, Phil Ramone, Robert Rietty, Jack Rose, Anthony Russo, Walter Scharf, Dennis Selinger, McKevin Shaughnessy, Lucille Shavelson, Melville Shavelson, Artie Shaw, Mike Shaw, the late Dinah Shore, George Sidney, Lillian Sidney, David Simon, Jane Simon, Joseph 'Sparky' Spaccavento, Patleo Spaccavento, the late Morris Stoloff, Jonie Taps, Daniel Taradash, Madeleine Taradash, Simon Wiesenthal, Bud Yorkin and the late Fred Zinnemann.

Merle Kessler's help was particularly invaluable and led to much new information.

Last of all, thanks to my wife Sara – for everything.

London, May 1997

PROLOGUE

There never was anyone like Sinatra.

Certainly, there have been other entertainers who have made love to their audiences and earned their adoration in return. There have been other performers who literally bruised their way into the public attention but were so magnetic, so articulate, that any misdemeanours were soon forgiven. There have been showmen who so lived for the spotlight that they then tried to find ways of bottling it all up and taking it away with them. There have been other vocalists whose singing faded along with the colour of their hair and yet who still kept going as though their voices were cut from the same old velvet that had long gone threadbare – simply because paying customers were still being mesmerised.

Only Sinatra was all of those things. Frank Sinatra? The first name has been superfluous ever since they stopped calling him Frankie, which is an immortality of sorts. Francis Albert? That's there to be used by fawning near-celebrities who are afraid of the consequences of addressing him as Ol' Blue Eyes.

So is Sinatra a collection of clichés? Yes, except that he created them – and all of them about himself.

There has to be some secret for a man to sell records by the million, fill the biggest concert venues in the world, make more than a handful of movies which were memorable, and yet still have the reputation and manners of a prizefighter. There had to be an audience out there who defined Sinatra's unique kind of megastardom. Was it simply a question of love? It wasn't a marriage between public and performer, more a sixty-year-old affair – with every episode, from foreplay to the final consummation, performed in front of a microphone.

Everyone in Sinatra's life has been a participant in that affair.

— 1 —

YESTERDAY

Hoboken isn't exactly paradise, even if now they are trying to gentrify it, a word that would have been unknown and totally inexplicable to the people living in this grimy little New Jersey city eight decades ago.

Today, there are flowers in tiny front gardens where once there had only been trashcans. There are pictures on walls where once the sole colour had come from the blood of kids and much older men – the ones who daily had been forced up against the brickwork in the course of being made offers they couldn't possibly refuse.

The ferries still ply the Hudson River to and from Manhattan. These days, you can also take a train and get there in ten minutes. The journey isn't so pleasant in summer, but in the winter when the cold is so bitter that you find yourself envying a hibernating tortoise, those ten minutes are to treasure. This is not a town helped by its climate. Today when virtually every house and apartment has enough radiators to provide warmth in winter and air conditioners to cool the heat of summer, the weather plays less of a part in Hoboken life than once it did. But in the first three decades of the century, existence could be hard in a place where snow comes in November and lasts till March, and the only refuge from the stifling heat of July and August was to dance in the spray of a fire hydrant by day and sleep on a fire escape by night.

Hoboken has always been an insular sort of place. There are still people who have never been further than across the Hudson to New York and at least one man who has never even left New Jersey. Although an urban village, the inhabitants know each other as well as if Hoboken were a farming community in the middle of a Kansas plain; it is a place where, at one time, a couple living in sin would have caused as much of a stir as a country-town librarian taking a secret lover.

Familiarity is bred by size – or at least by the lack of it. From the ferry stop or the train station, take a taxi to anywhere in town and it is always four dollars. Hoboken is still only a mile square, just as it was when Francis Albert Sinatra – all thirteen-and-a-half pounds of him – fought his way into the world and confounded the doctor, the midwife and, not least of all, his twenty-year-old mother, Dolly.

Dolly, born Natalie Catherine Garavente, didn't look big enough to carry a sack of potatoes that heavy. She weighed no more than ninety pounds. No one in the room that day in December 1915 expected her to survive. Everyone thought that the baby with the lacerated earlobe and cheeks – along with a punctured eardrum, the result of being wrenched out of the birth canal with all the finesse of a plumber's mate using a pair of pliers – was dead. In fact, he would have been, had Dolly's mother Rosa, who ran a grocery store, not also been a part-time midwife. She held the baby under the cold-water tap until he screamed.

This was Hoboken in 1915, and the city has changed little over the years, even if today's gentrified population of 30,000, boosted as it is by the commuters taking those ferry trips and train rides, is only half the number it was. The legacy of the past lingers among the few families who still remember the Sinatras – along with the dirt and the squalor and the fights.

Not for nothing was this town the setting for *On the Waterfront*, the 1950s Marlon Brando film of union wars and corruption among the stevedores and longshoremen, a movie which almost might have been remembered as the Frank Sinatra film, a story to come later in this tale of the man who is regarded as Hoboken's favourite son – at least by some. Others have not forgiven him and doubtless never will. For what? For slighting the town of his birth during his greatest years? Or just for being the most successful entertainment figure American ever knew?

Let us begin with his name. Like almost every Frank Sinatra story, there is more than one version. A birth certificate records the arrival on 12 December 1915 of 'Frank Sinestro'. The surname could only have been a misprint. When a new copy was issued more than twenty years later, the name was changed to 'Francis A. Sinatra'. There is no doubt that Sinatra was the family name; but did his parents later wonder whether Francis didn't sound a little nicer than Frank? And the 'A'? Was his middle name always 'Albert'? Or did he copy Harry

Truman and later find something to fit an initial? (In 1976 the matter was made official. The Officer of the Registrar of Vital Statistics issued yet another birth certificate – this time, the name was given as Francis Albert Sinatra.)

The notion that 'Frank' came before 'Francis' is supported by the fact that although the family proudly spoke about naming the child after the saint, his father Marty's dear friend and fellow amateur baseball player Frank Garrick always said the name was in honour of himself. Not only that; Garrick was chosen as the baby's godfather at the christening on 2 April 1916 – appropriately at St Francis's Church in Hoboken.

In these facts, too, there are no more certainties than in anything else concerning Sinatra's early years. According to legend, he was to have been named Martin after his father, Anthony Martin Sinatra – but the priest, having asked for the name of the godfather, got confused and called him Frank. However, it is hard to imagine the Sinatra parents, especially powerful Dolly, allowing something like this to occur. If she had really wanted to call her son Martin, she would surely have corrected the priest.

Opinions also vary about the links between Frank Sinatra and the town of Hoboken. In the City Hall, the local authority has put on a Sinatra tribute exhibition – old photographs, record labels and sleeves and a dozen or more posters recalling the days when Frankie wowed the crowds at the Paramount Theater over the water and only one or two of him performing in Hoboken because Frank didn't come back to his home town once that reputation as Frankie was made.

Upstairs at City Hall, there are other photographs – of Hoboken when the great ocean liners docked there instead of at the more crowded piers of New York itself, of baseball teams, wholly appropriate because this was the nursery of baseball, the first place where the words 'pitcher', 'first base', and 'home run' were ever heard. Today, though, you have to be a local historian to appreciate those things. To know that Hoboken is Frank Sinatra's birthplace is something else. Children are taught about the great entertainer who put their town on the map along with the dates of the signing of the Declaration of Independence and the assassination of Abraham Lincoln. Those with grandparents and great-grandparents with long memories may hear slightly jaundiced tales.

The Mayor, Anthony Russo, certainly finds no cause for anything but tribute to the man he has never met. 'Frank Sinatra,' he told me, 'has a place in this town which is a microcosm of his place in the world.' And you can take that any way you wish. Russo went on, 'There may have been some conflict with some of the people here at the time when his career was blossoming. I think that people may have felt jealousies and that he was perhaps justified in staying away for a while.' Unquestionably, Sinatra had given Hoboken a sense of pride and they rejoiced in his talent. 'But for material things – the things that people do or have given to people or to a city – maybe he hasn't done that. But he didn't need to do it – because he has done so much as an artist.'

On the whole, the older folk in Hoboken remember Dolly Sinatra and her husband Martin a lot better than they remember Frank – and in that order because Dolly wore the trousers in the Sinatra home, while her blue-eyed husband Marty, as everyone knew him, was an inoffensive man who had worked on the docks as a labourer before becoming the local fire-station cook, and, in the early 1930s, was to open a tavern called Marty O'Brien's. The Irish name sounded right but because firemen were not allowed to operate such establishments, the licence was held in Dolly's name. In fact, Marty never seemed to exert much influence at all and it was Dolly who had got him the job as a fireman in the first place. She was a force in the local Democratic Party and her influence with the Fire Department was as strong as it was with the other ward leaders. When she put the idea to one of the local politicians his response was unenthusiastic: 'But Dolly, we don't have an opening.'

'Make an opening,' she replied – and they did. That was Dolly Sinatra. So her husband became one of the few Italians in Hoboken ever to get near to a fire engine. It was not the first time Marty realised that things might have been easier had he been Irish. As a bantam-weight fighter, he boxed under the name he used for his liquor business: Marty O'Brien. His choice of name, then, had been deliberate – and, in the context of Hoboken, wholly appropriate.

It was not easy being Italian, even in Hoboken, a town where a third of the population was made up of the Sinatras' fellow countrymen and which boasted that it provided the best Italian food in America, with its macaroni in particular superior to anything on offer elsewhere. Marty came from Agrigento in Sicily, arriving as a small child with his parents, John and Rosa Sinatra. At least, that is what Nancy Sinatra, Jr., says in her book *Frank Sinatra: An American Legend*. But was that, too, a rewriting of history, like the birth certificates? Every other reference to the early Sinatra lineage says that John (Giovanni?) and Rosa were the names of Dolly's parents and came from outside Genoa. Nancy doesn't name their surname, Garaventes, at all. Why?

Could there be some resentment of the fact that when Dolly and Marty were married at a civil ceremony at the City Hall in Jersey City on St Valentine's Day in 1913, the Garaventes refused to attend? (They were later to relent and a church ceremony was held with both bride and bridegroom dressed suitably for the occasion, she wearing a chic short wedding dress, he a tuxedo and white tie.)

The couple had first met when Dolly's brother Dominic, known always as 'Champ Seger', fought Marty in the boxing ring – in an open-ended contest that would be completed only when one of the participants hit the canvas. Women were not allowed into New Jersey boxing crowds in those days, so Dolly borrowed a pair of Dominic's trousers and an old jacket and nobody was any the wiser. Her voice may have been higher than most men's, but what came out of her mouth wouldn't have let her down. Her language was always choice, to say the least. The evening Dolly met her future husband for the first time was a memorable one. Today, her granddaughter says that the two men fought over the event again and again for years afterwards – both claiming victory that night.

Why the Garaventes were not keen on their daughter linking up with the Sinatras can be traced to the traditions of the Old Country, and a desire, straight out of folklore, to move on once they had seen the Statue of Liberty. Marty's father had worked in a pencil factory and never learned to speak English. The Garaventes were a family of educated craftsmen – Dolly's father was a lithographer – and wanted nothing of any match. In this and in everything else, Dolly won.

She and Marty – he gave his occupation on the marriage certificate as 'athlete' – set up their home in the heart of Hoboken's Little Italy. The five-floor, ten-apartment, cold-water tenement at 415 Monroe Street was about as miserable a spot (but conveniently close to the fire station) as could be imagined, although later press stories made it even more miserable. These described it as so crowded that the family had to go out into the street to gasp for air – air that was polluted by fumes and noise from the docks and the Erie–Lackawanna railroad tracks. The problem with those stories is that the apartment was too far from the docks for a steamboat's horns to be heard, and the railway is more than half a mile away too. But it was bad enough.

In the years following the Sinatra marriage, things began to change in Hoboken. Those piers which saw the luxury liners arrive and depart would, in 1917, be used by GIs going off to France to fight in the First World War. Two years earlier, when Frank was born, the Europe from which most of the city's inhabitants came was already in the midst of the conflict and nothing would ever be the same again.

In 1913 those changes hadn't yet come to affect the ethnic divisions, and to live peaceably in the town, it was important to emphasise them. A few streets away from where the Sinatras lived was Irish territory, the third of a mile famous for providing New York with its policemen. The notion of the Irish cop in his tight blue tunic and distinctive brown helmet, so famous in those early Technicolor Hollywood musicals, was no whim of a screenwriter's imagination; these were the immigrants who not only administered the laws, but made them – because they were the ones who spoke English. Young, strong Irishmen were fitted up with a uniform, given a gun and a 'billy club' and told that they were policemen. They controlled the politics of New York as openly as they did the traffic.

The German third of the population were the wealthy ones. They lived in uptown Hoboken and were concentrated around Hudson Street in particular. These were the people who kept the beer gardens, who were the local merchants, and who ran the vaudeville theatre, the Empire, as well as nearby movie theatres such as the Fabian, the US, the Eureka and the Europa. The fame of the German quarter extended well beyond the square mile. Jerome Kern set his musical *Sweet Adeline* in a Hoboken beer garden.

Even after the world had begun its somersault, each ethnic group kept to its own part of town as surely as if they were second-class citizens confined to ghettos. You didn't venture from Italian Hoboken into the German or Irish sections any more than you would allow your daughter to marry out into another community. 'The Italians were the greenhorns,' restaurateur Joseph Spaccavento, known by everyone in town as 'Sparky', now recalls. 'At one time we couldn't pass through Willow Avenue. The Irish would chase us out.

With the strength of the ethnic divisions came the insults. To every 'Mick' of an Irishman, an Italian was a 'wop', a Jew was a 'kike' or a 'sheeny'. The blacks were 'Niggers' and the other Latins, 'Dagos'. The adult Sinatra would say that even as a child he felt offended by the tag of 'wop'. It was an offence that would rankle forever after. And forever after, he would make the connection with the place where he first heard it – Hoboken.

'There was real hated there,' says another Sinatra contemporary, John Marotta. 'If we went further than Willow Avenue, they'd say, "Get down to Guinea Town where you belong." That's what they called the Italian part of town. It was hatred I couldn't understand.'

On one occasion that hatred hit Frank directly. Ten years old, he was attacked by an Irish gang and added a few more scars to the face already damaged at birth. One story has it that he went to the rescue of a Jewish boy in the neighbourhood, in response to the kindness of a Mrs Goldberg, a friend of his grandmother, who rewarded him with a Star of David medallion which he later backed with a St Christopher. If so, it was the first of many similar attacks by Sinatra on anti-Semitism and other examples of racial prejudice.

'Scarface', other kids called him, not a pleasant way for a child to be introduced to the wider world. But it was to stand him in good stead. When he made what was to become the most important movie of his life, *From Here to Eternity*, he would say of Maggio, the character he played: 'I knew him. I was beaten up with him in Hoboken.'

Not that ethnic mixing didn't occasionally happen and, when it did, Romeo and Juliet could have been set in Hoboken and *West Side Story* removed to west of the Hudson River. Ethnic conflict was always the best excuse for fists to be made and then used. And, sometimes, more than just fists.

The gangs were divided strictly by race – with the best fights between the Italian mobs and the Irish. Ask any of their descendants today who won and the Irish will tell you that they were hands-down victors and the Italians will say they had the winning ways all the time. Over the years, Frank has both spoken of the violence of those days and declared the aggression overplayed. In one of the former moods he said: 'Everyone carried a twelve-inch pipe – and they weren't all studying to be plumbers.'

Despite the glamour that the idea of the street fights lent to later publicity campaigns, this was not in fact Frank Sinatra's way. 'He was a loner,' says Spaccavento, who likes to think that his restaurant, Piccolo's, with its main room devoted to Sinatra posters and pictures, serves the best Italian food in the square mile. 'He had his own ideas, but he didn't go fighting the boys in those days, even though it was a tough neighbourhood. People now like to say they went to school with Frankie and that they went robbing with him. It's all bullshit.'

Others will say they went to church with him. If they did, they, too, will have to have been Italian. For above all else in Hoboken, each ethnic group had its own place of worship. The idea of praying together was no more acceptable than was the notion of fighting on the same side. St Francis's, St Ann's and St Joseph's were where the poor Italian congregations put no more than a nickel in the plate. Our Lady of Grace – forever known as OLG – on the corner of Fourth and Willow – did a little better. Its Irish worshippers, thanks to those regular jobs in the police and local government, were able to be more generous. The Catholic church of the Germans, St Peter and St Paul, like the beer gardens and the theatre on Hudson Street, never had any financial problems.

The part of Monroe Street where the Sinatras lived is still dominated by shrines to the Virgin Mary in front gardens. The Sinatras were good Catholics, but not so good, unlike some of their neighbours, that it dominated their lives. But young Frank was not allowed to escape the customary role of altar boy at the church of the saint after whom he was told he had been named, and throughout his childhood the local priest was as much a feature of his life as in anyone else's family. Congregants listening to the church choir would later be able to say they were the first to hear Frank Sinatra singing in public.

Legends about the life of the young Sinatra have grown over the years, as have the stories about his family, as told both by that family and by other contemporaries. According to your own attitude – or how your own crowd was treated by the Sinatras – you judge Frank and you pronounce verdicts on his family, and always with Dolly in the forefront.

Early on, it was clear that the love Dolly felt for Frank was only matched by his for her. He returned every kiss, every loving gesture, every inclination. They read each other's minds. One of the things he knew while still a child was Dolly's reputation. He may not have known that she was an abortionist – it is extremely unlikely that he did – but he knew about that power, Dolly style. Years later, he would deny that his mother was tough. 'It was the neighbourhood that was tough,' he would say – and he probably meant it.

In the kitchen at Piccolo's restaurant, between rolling the meatballs and checking on the spaghetti stock, Joe Spaccavento and his son Patty – Patleo – still discuss the Dolly Sinatra they remember. Sparky knew Dolly well because, for a tip of 50 cents or a quarter, he used to deliver groceries to her home when she had begun to move up in the world in the late 1930s and lived in the neighbouring town of Weehawken.

By then, she was a well-upholstered woman who walked through what they call the 'main drag' of town, Washington Street, as though she were its queen, and in a way she was – at least in ward three, where she had become the local Democratic Party boss. This was Italian territory – wards one and four were Irish, the second ward was German – so inevitably the ward chief would have to be Italian, too. It would take thirty years for things to change and it was not until 1946 that the Democrats and Republicans formed a 'fusion' party under an Italian Mayor, Fred Di Sappio, with Dolly in its train.

Most women in Hoboken, at the end of the First World War, had jobs of one kind or another – the brighter ones in offices, the others mainly in factories over the river, more than a few simply relying on cleaning and washing for a few cents an hour. Dolly worked as a dipper in a chocolate factory. In other words, she knew how to douse the creams or the hard centres in chocolate and because she was Dolly she knew how to do it better than anyone else. The company were so impressed that, soon after the war, they offered to send her to Paris so that she could train workers there to do the job with equal proficiency. But although she liked the work and would not at all have minded going to France, she didn't want to leave baby Frank totally in the care of her mother. And she had political ambitions, too.

By then, things were changing in Hoboken politics as well. In the 1920s, the idea that an Italian could replace an Irishman as head of the Hoboken equivalent of Tammany Hall was impossible to contemplate. But virtually from when Bernard 'Barney' McFeeley came to power at the beginning of his thirty-year reign as Mayor, at around the time of Frank's birth, Dolly Sinatra was his faithful lieutenant, almost his Italian ambassador. She was a woman of power, never more so than in her own ward.

And, so the stories say, young Frank would come to get his first leg up into show business, through being the son of a power-crazed matriarch, the woman who had worked for years delivering babies as well as votes, who was never crossed – until the day in 1937 when she was convicted of being an abortionist in Hudson County, of which Hoboken was part. Nobody denies that she ended pregnancies as surely as she did the careers of people in Hoboken who dared to risk upsetting her. 'Look,' says Sparky, 'she was a midwife – and sometimes when attending to people accidents happened. She was a powerful woman, but she was a good woman.'

The accidents were undoubtedly frequently on purpose. Nevertheless, a surprising number of Hoboken people share that memory of her. Spaccavento is determined not to blemish Dolly's memory, or at least to bandage over the blemishes uncovered by other people. 'She did wonderful things for a lot of poor people,' he told me. 'When a member of our community got into trouble and had to go to court, who went to speak for him? Dolly. When he couldn't speak English – and these were the days of the immigrants who knew only Italian – who was it who interpreted his case before the judge? Dolly. There weren't any official interpreters in those days.

Her help wasn't simply that of a court official, even an unofficial one. 'When she knew that people didn't have enough money to allow them to eat properly, she got them welfare cheques. She knew how to get them.' People would come to her when they needed coal for their fires or advice on how to deal with a sick child. She sent them baskets of fruit. Dolly didn't actually *ask* for people's votes, but she knew she could get them.

'And who was it who fixed things when an Italian longshoreman got into trouble with his boss and was out of work? Dolly.' The longshoremen on the dock were nearly all Italians. So were the railroad workers, a number from the town of Bari, the part of southern Italy from which so many of today's Hoboken residents hail that it is as though a piece of the 'boot' was sliced off and carried by ship across the Atlantic.

The Sinatras thought of themselves as strictly Italian, but very much as Americans, too – which was why, as Sparky says: 'People misconstrue things about Dolly. If people weren't Italians or even if they weren't in her ward, she'd help them, too.' By all accounts, Marty just let this all happen around him and didn't complain. Even when he was made a captain at the local station, it seems to have been out of deference to his wife's exalted station in town. 'Yeah, I think that's how it happened,' said Sparky.

Dolly had, in fact, decided the time had come for Marty to be shown some respect – not easy in a town like theirs, where being a fireman was respectable and sometimes envied but regarded as a fairly lowly occupation, even so. So Dolly started pressing for an improved rank which she thought would be suitable for *her* status in town. One day there was a phone call. It was the voice of another local politician. 'Dolly,' said the man. 'Congratulations.'

'For what?' she asked.

'*Captain* Sinatra,' he replied.

'Oh, so you finally made him one,' she said sardonically. 'Thank you very much.'

Then she rang the fire station. 'I want to speak to Captain Sinatra,' she said. There was a silence at the other end, one that seemed to say, 'Captain Who?'

'Marty,' the man called out, 'it's your wife, I think she's gone nuts. She asked to talk to *Captain* Sinatra.'

Marty came to the phone. 'Congratulations, *Captain* Sinatra,' Dolly said. It was all he needed to hear. He wanted an improved status as much as Dolly did, but he would never have dreamed of doing anything about it – short of, perhaps, working a bit harder.

That small promotion in a small part of a small town gives a taste of how powerful Dolly was. Having proved that an Italian could break the racial barrier in getting a fireman's job in the first place, she went on to get Marty a new job. In a way, the first task had been the harder one. The fire station until then had been as much an Irish closed shop as the local police headquarters – for much the same reason: the Mayor decided that when there was rescuing to be done, firemen had to be able to communicate in English to the people at the top of burning buildings. The notion that those people could have been German or Italian does not seem to have come into consideration.

Dolly was proud of Marty, particularly in his new uniform. She also knew that if her Frank was going to do well in his chosen career, he had to look the part too. Ever since she had first dressed him in Little Lord Fauntleroy suits – on her mother's insistence; at first, he wore little girl's dresses, quite a thought for Sinatra fans to contemplate – she decided that he was going to be a step above the average youngster from Hoboken. Stories that press agents loved putting about at one time – that Sinatra was a kid from the slums, who pulled himself up by his own bootstraps – are pure fantasy. Not only did Frank always have a shirt for his back; it was a well-stitched, comfortable shirt which Dolly believed suited her own position in life. From earliest childhood, young Frank was dressed better than the other children on the block. 'They were jealous of him, especially the ones with rips in their pants,' says Spaccavento. There are stories that he had a different suit for every day of the week. He was so well dressed from early childhood – he sported a smart fedora at the age of ten – that he was called 'Slacksey', which seemed to mean he was never without a new pair of trousers. And since the only well-dressed people round about were Irish, the nickname took on another dimension. Frank became know as Slacksey O'Brien.

He took it as a compliment. Dolly wanted him to be a gentleman, he would say years later. But a gentleman with a fairly select vocabulary. If she thought she could train him to speak as well as he looked, it would have to be with other people's influence. She couldn't easily leave her ward-meeting language behind. Dollars were bucks and not yet clams, but she was sowing the seeds of what would become Sinatra-speak. Slang was Dolly's only language. When she wanted someone to do something, there was nothing polite about the summons. 'Get your ass over here, you sonofabitch,' she demanded. And the sonofabitch got his ass just where she wanted it.

Frank was not allowed to suffer for his mother's indelicate approach to life. He had bicycles when other boys in the neighbourhood thought themselves lucky to have an orange box with four roller-skate wheels. 'We spoilt the kid,' said one of his uncles thirty years later. Dolly would never be satisfied with anything less than perfection for her boy – as though giving him anything else would somehow reflect on her. She was right. It was all part of the way in which she governed her family as powerfully as she helped run the neighbourhood.

Both parents expected a lot of their only child. Not having brothers and sisters was an unusual situation in itself in Italian families who regarded children as gifts from God and a gift that was not to be underrated. But Dolly's experience with her thirteen-and-a-half-pound baby was not one she was able to repeat. There would never be any more children. As a result, she was as protective of Frank as a mother hen with a new chick. She wanted him to have friends, but only if they were 'suitable', nice clean Italian boys who didn't get themselves into too much trouble.

Dolly saw to it that Frank had a baseball team to play in – because she founded the team herself. The Turks Palace, she called it, and she had uniforms specially made for all the boys. That way, she knew, her son would not only have a group of playmates but a team that he could control. It was like a soccer player always getting the goals, because he owned the ball. It was probably unnecessary – Frank was good with his feet anyway.

Those feet would have been useful had he ever needed to run away from the police, like a number of his friends who would have found it difficult to win Dolly's approval. As Spaccavento remembers: 'Kids would say, "Come on, let's get into that truck or let's pick the Five and Ten Cents store", and Frank wouldn't have anything to do with it. He didn't believe in that.'

Years later, when he had taken upon himself the role of guide to the misguided, Frank embellished his childhood and his role as a juvenile delinquent – one that his contemporaries now say was never his. In the first fan magazine articles, he was quoted as saying: 'We started hooking candy from the corner store. Then little things from the five-and-dime, then change from cash registers and finally we were up to stealing bicycles.'

But even if Frank had ever *wanted* to get into trouble, Dolly was there to see that he had a very limited opportunity of doing so. Instead he swam and played a little basketball, and when he did his fighting he generally had boxing gloves on. Marty was pleased to see him follow his footsteps around a three-roped ring.

Young Frank was good with his hands, too – which was why his parents were convinced he was going to be a civil engineer. 'I did sketches of bridges and tunnels and roads,' he said once. And to that end, the Sinatras decided they were going to send their son to finish his education at the Stevens Institute of Technology (named after John Stevens, the man who invented the first American steam locomotive), Hoboken's pride and joy which it was boasted was second only to MIT.

As a small boy, Frank had progressed from local elementary school to the David E. Rue Junior High, which didn't exactly extend his education – he spent a great deal of time impersonating stars from the new talkies – and then to the A. J. Demarest High School where he enjoyed singing, but little else. He wasn't much interested in schoolwork. 'Homework we never bothered with,' he was quoted as saying years later.

In fact, the only thing that really did hold any attraction for him was singing. At eleven he sang with the school choir as well as in the choir at St Francis's Church. When there were picnics, the high treble Sinatra voice could be heard along with the cries for more lemonade. But all this was not enough for Demarest's Principal, Arthur Stover, who wanted more intellectual prowess from his students and saw no academic future for the boy at all. One day he rang up Marty and told him: 'Get over here and get this boy out of school.' The reason for the expulsion was given officially as 'general rowdiness'.

In fact, young Frank had already heeded that request before it was made. A boy whose mother had bought him a second-hand car when he was fifteen years old was unlikely to take kindly to school discipline. For the best part of a year he had played truant from school; his time there, he later revealed, totalled no more than forty-seven days.

The call from the headmaster worried Marty much more than it did young Frank. 'I knew then I wanted to become a singer,' he said. His father hoped that he would develop other interests. He was impressed with his son's bridge-drawings and agreed that the Stevens Institute was where Frank ought to go. But it didn't happen. Instead, he spent just enough weeks at the Drake Business School to qualify for New Jersey's minimum education requirements and then began a different life altogether.

By now, Frank was more than ever convinced that all he wanted to do was sing – and preferably in a band. When he told his mother about this ambition she threw a shoe at him. The truth of the matter was – and it may not have been a familiar phrase in those days – that in the early thirties Francis Sinatra was, to all intents and purposes, a dropout. Once he realised that his son was not destined for Stevens, Marty refused to speak to him – and, Frank later revealed, did not do so for a year.

It would be another forty years, thanks to a visit to his old haunts with the then President of the United States, Ronald Reagan, before Frank would get his graduation diploma.

Ironically, it was school that convinced Frank to go into show business. As well as singing in the school choir, occasionally, just occasionally, he had been allowed to sing with the school band, too, and these were the happiest of his schooldays. Now he made up his mind that he was going to be the best boy singer Hoboken had ever produced. That was how he was going to make his living. More than that, Frank had discovered the ukulele, the instrument favoured by the young blades of the time when serenading their girls, usually on a dark summer's night in a hidden cove on the nearest beach.

The blame for his taking it all a lot more seriously than might have been expected of a teenage boy could be laid at the door of a young man a decade Frank's senior who had gone from Spokane, Washington, all the way to Hollywood, via a group called the Rhythm boys and the Paul Whiteman orchestra. Sinatra heard a crooner called Crosby sing and decided he wanted to be just like him. Al Jolson had been an even earlier influence, but it was the smooth, easy tones of Harry Lillis Crosby, known for ever as Bing, that Frank knew he wanted to emulate. And not just the tones. 'You'd see Frank standing on street corners wearing a blazer, a sailing cap and smoking a pipe,' John Marotta told me in his Hoboken home.

Marotta is a musician himself (years later he would try – unsuccessfully – to have his fellow townsman join him in the biggest concert Hoboken had ever put on) and looking back more than sixty years, he can only admire the way the young Sinatra set about achieving his aims. 'His middle name should have been Determination, not Albert. He would go anywhere that there was music.'

Frank had the advantage of parents who, by most Italian and Hoboken standards, were rich. Owning the tavern in town increased the Sinatra fortunes even more. As they got richer, so they moved, and each house was always better than the one before. First they settled in Park Avenue, which was not quite as grand as it sounds, and then in Garden Street, Hoboken.

The tavern's success was aided by the end of Prohibition, which seemed to lead to more drinking, not less. Hoboken had seen all that coming. Long before Prohibition was introduced by the Federal Government, it had come to the town on an experimental basis. In 1914, Hoboken was the port of departure of the American soldiers bound for Europe and the Government banned drinking there lest it make the embarking Dough Boys too drunk to concentrate on winning the war and killing the Hun. Nevertheless, it was a regulation that was rarely enforced and ironically, when the Volstead Act became law in 1919, the town turned itself into an unofficial oasis in the midst of the Prohibition desert.

Eventually, when Frank told them that nothing was going to stop him singing for a living, his parents talked it over and Dolly decided that there was no point in throwing any more shoes. His schoolfriends and fellow baseball players laughed at the cheek of it all but others were less encouraging. As Frank said years later: 'There's always someone to spit on your dreams.'

Dolly wasn't about to do that kind of spitting. If Frank didn't succeed it might rebound on her and she was only interested in an idea that would work for them both. If her son was going to sing for a living, she would work as hard to help him as she did to find a stevedore's job for a neighbour's boy. Frank later remembered: 'She loved it. She was the spark for my going into show business. My father joined forces and backed her.' At least, that is what he said on one occasion.

As Spaccavento told me: 'Marty was a really quiet man. She was the boss – and Frankie listened to his mother.' When she said that he could go into show business, he listened more intently than ever. Not that he went straight into the band world. His father wanted to get him off the streets and got him a job as a riveter.

Frank Sinatra was one of the less skilled of the employees at the Teijent and Lang Shipyards. He wasn't actually a riveter, but a riveter's 'catcher'. He was to say later that the guy who threw rivets at him was cockeyed, so he 'couldn't hit a bull in the ass with a bag of rice'. Neither of them lasted in the job long – which suited Frank perfectly, especially when a rivet, white hot, almost hit him on the shoulder. He now got a job unloading crates of books and then worked for a fruit company on one of the piers.

But it didn't do his self-esteem a great deal of good. 'This was a guy with a chip on his shoulder,' recalls Sparky. 'It motivated him a lot – and I think a lot of it had to do with the way Italian people were treated.'

For a while, Frank worked in the dispatch department of the local newspaper, the New Jersey *Observer*, hauling bundles of papers on to the trucks. His mother had decided that the moment had arrived for more pressure to be applied. Frank Garrick, the boy's godfather, who was himself also something of a political wheeler dealer, was the paper's circulation manager. When she thought it appropriate, Garrick, like all the others, was given the Dolly treatment – her son was not beyond saying a word or two himself – and after a conversation that lasted about as long as it would take to sing 'Always', he found young Frank a job on the newspaper.

But neither Frank nor his mother were satisfied with the idea of his humping bundles, even though it did provide him with a weekly paycheque of $11 and also led to a friendship with a photographer – who obliged when Frank, in his best sports jacket, asked him to take his picture, sitting in front of a typewriter, with ticker-tape machines, lamps and telephones in the background. The shot served perfectly for later publicity purposes – the early life of Frank Sinatra, 'when he was a sports reporter'.

Old hands at journalism recall the times they used every conceivable device to get themselves jobs on newspapers, the sort of jobs that would make their careers. Frank had no such journalistic ambitions. It would have been a pointless use of the sort of energy he needed to make his way in show business. Let the hacks write, Sinatra was going to sing.

The photograph, which before long would be handed to George Evans, a budding press agent anxious to make his way every bit as much as was Frank, did wonders for the Sinatra ego. So did promotion of a sort – to the *Observer*'s City room. Frank had read in the paper about two copy boys being killed in a road accident. He immediately applied for one of their jobs and got it – although the stories that have circulated over the last sixty years are almost as much of an exaggeration as the myth that he was a sports reporter. The closest he got to the copy desk was filling the gluepots for the reporters and junior editors.

After two weeks of that, he was out on his ears. It wasn't that he was inept at filling the gluepots, but rather that conflict of interest arose: his interest and that of the editor of the newspaper who couldn't understand who this strange kid was, the one lolling on the desk looking as though he regarded himself as the next Damon Runyon. Had he known that the kid fancied himself as the next Bing Crosby, things might have been a lot easier.

Garrick was offered a choice that seems to have amounted to: 'It's his job or yours', and his godson found himself looking for other work. This was a youngster driven by the kind of ambition about whom Depression-age novelists wrote best-sellers. He was single-minded. What made Frankie Run? The knowledge that there was a much bigger world out there; the self-assurance that anything Bing Crosby could do, he could do, too – and so could Dolly.

'His mother's influence was so strong,' said Johnny Marotta, 'that when she told him he had to look the part to get the work he wanted, he took notice of everything she said.' She bought him another smart jacket and, more important, an open-top car. In 1935 there was no finer passport to success, and Frank managed to persuade a social club on Sixth and Grand Streets to pay him to sing on a Saturday night. Today, the Cat's Meow Club, the place that gave Sinatra his first big chance, is somewhere the older citizens of Hoboken still talk about when discussing the 'good old days'. It was just a start, an occasional song in a place unknown to anyone outside town, but he treated it with all the seriousness he would later reserve for the Sands Hotel at Las Vegas. It was the only way to get on.

That same year, a nine-year-old Joseph Spaccavento heard him sing at the Continental Bar on First and Hudson Streets – dangerously close to the German part of town, although by then old prejudices were beginning to die out. 'He would go round the bars and people seemed to like what they heard.' Another Hoboken restaurateur, Leo Deilizzi, recalls a similar story at the Oval Bar on First and Washington Streets. He has good reason to remember. 'After every show, Frank would come down to my place for a plate of mussels. He also loved my pizza.' Not enough, though, to put on any weight.

'In a bathing suit, when he moved, he looked nude,' Johnny Marotta recalls. 'But it didn't stop the girls in town running after him. He was a flashy guy and like a lot of flashy guys he was a womaniser.' And the women of Hoboken talk about him to this day. One respectable matron still living within the square mile told me: 'I slept with him partly because I was intrigued to find out what a bundle of bones like that could do. It wasn't very much in those days. I imagine he got better.'

Another woman – 'Ida' she says we ought to call her – didn't go that far. 'We'd go on double dates together. He was fun. He would take his ukulele and sing in a voice he thought was wonderful but which we thought was pretty terrible, but we all enjoyed ourselves immensely.' The open sports car he could produce for the occasion didn't do any harm either.

'None of us had cars at all,' Marotta said. 'So who Sinatra was dating week by week was a topic of conversation hereabouts. He was a real show-off.' But, according to Marotta, the voice had a lot to do with his success. 'I don't know what there was about it. Not all good. That's for sure. But when he sang, he ran them over. I wish I knew the secret.'

Another of the places to which Frank went on dates was Palisades Park, a huge Hoboken complex covering ten blocks with pools filled with salt water – 'just like the ocean'. Afterwards, he would take the girls to Leo's Grandezvous for more mussels and pizza. It was a never-changing routine: Palisades Park or wherever he was singing until very late in the evening and then on to eat. 'We used to go to the Fourth and Jefferson Club together,' Leo told me. 'But when he became famous, he stopped coming.'

Frank's friends were, of course, all Italians – like Ralph Bragnola, Joe Apone, who called himself Joe Farmer, Nick Pionbino and Joe Dice. He hung out with them at the clubs and went driving and swimming with them, not worrying about that 'nude' look in his bathing suit. In those days a bathing suit was precisely that – a suit that covered the chest as much as the lower regions. It was a fortunate fashion for Frank while it lasted.

As far as girls were concerned, he worked out a campaign based on the big weekly events for young Hoboken guys and dolls – the school socials. These were not New Jersey versions of high-school proms, but dances where the youngsters would meet, mostly months and sometimes years after they themselves had stopped learning, or pretending they were learning. The school buildings were the only ones that had halls big enough to take the social events.

When Frank arrived with Bragnola or Apone, or any one of the numerous girls he had on his arm in those days, the dancers knew he was going to sing. When he was with Augie Delano, there were other expectations. 'Augie was the one everybody thought was going to make it,' said Johnny Marotta. 'But Frankie was the guy with drive. He would make sure he had a chance to sing. Sometimes, he would insinuate himself with the piano player.'

Now, 'insinuating' himself with the piano player was about the cleverest thing he could have done – if not the most popular. 'He would pester anyone who would let him on the stage. He kept on saying, "Can I sing a song? Can I sing a song?"' And they let him sing – numbers like 'Sweet and Lovely' and 'Blue Moon'. He'd sing into a megaphone, à la Rudy Vallee, or make himself heard without the benefit of any sound equipment at all. 'You didn't have microphones for that kind of hop in those days,' said Marotta. 'They would accommodate him happily at first – and then it became pestering. The bands had their own vocalists, the people who had rehearsed with them. They couldn't stop the dancing to let him sing, so they said no. Then he would go to the piano player and he would say, "OK. What do you want to sing?" So the dancing would stop and he would sing.'

Frank entered amateur contests. He didn't win and he wasn't offered any work as a result. But he didn't get the hook either – that old tradition of vaudeville, the long pole with a hook at the end to drag off those whom the management considered the worst performers. It could only give him hope.

The changes in Hoboken life as well as in his own were by now becoming apparent. Youngsters of Irish and German ancestry were beginning to go to the Italian socials and musicians from other ethnic groups were allowed to perform there. Now the young Frank Sinatra had a much wider audience for what he was sure were his talents.

His friendships helped. His pals were the ice-breakers. They were the first to applaud and cheer, and what they did, others did, too. Says Marotta: 'I can't say that he was particularly generous to those people, even though he was the only one of them with any money. Generosity in those days was not part of the Sinatra take.'

His incursions into the socials were repeated at whatever school was holding the best gig that particular night. Joseph F. Brandt was the one with the best acoustics, which was why bands like those of Lou Gaborini, Frank Fosco and Tommy Giamo – in New Jersey terms, extremely good outfits – liked playing there.

But Frank Sinatra and his megaphone wasn't exactly a welcome sight. 'He carried that megaphone around like it was part of his wardrobe,' says Marotta. The band leaders sensed trouble whenever he appeared. He was about to disrupt their carefully-worked-out programme. They tried to devise ways of keeping him away, but they never could.

'He wasn't that good,' Marotta recalls. 'There were plenty of others who were better than he was. His voice didn't have much power then, but he sang in the known way of singing in those days. I've seen a lot of others try to sing the way he did, but they didn't make his impact. I think his success was as much of a surprise to him as it was to us.'

Like the others, Marotta would have put money (at least the ten cents he might have been able to afford) on Augie Delano making it. And Tony Costello, another Hoboken youngster, too: 'Tony was always thought of as the great singer of Hoboken. He had a beautiful voice – much better than Sinatra in those days.'

Frank always got his way, sometimes, it is now suggested by the less charitable among the citizenry of Hoboken, simply because of who his mother was. They knew who had provided the blazer and cap – to say nothing of the car he drove – a ready passport to the best dates in town.

'He always had a girl with him and they'd drive out to the beach every weekend. They couldn't resist him,' says Marotta. 'It was always a sports car, one with the shed down. He had one after the other, flashy white or cream, at a time when every other car was black.' His influence stretched across the sex barrier, too. 'He was a snappy dresser. Everyone wanted to follow the way he dressed.'

What Frank really wanted them to like him for, however, was his larynx. They all knew the songs he sang – in a pseudo-Crosby voice. That Bing influence was all-powerful. When Crosby appeared at the Loews Theatre in Journal Square, Jersey City, Frank sat through a performance spellbound. Later he tried to see him backstage, but since Crosby had never heard of him, he wasn't allowed past the stage door.

But there were those who persisted in saying they thought Frank had a talent all his own. Sometimes, to his mother's great pleasure, he entertained local chapters of the Democratic Party. And he kept up the ethnic connections, too – by performing for the Hoboken Sicilian Cultural League. The Sinatra parents were big there, so it was right that their son should uphold the country's reputation.

Sometimes, he would also go to Republican events. Dolly was secretly thinking of backing one particular candidate for Mayor, simply because he was Italian. Privately, that was more important to her than his political affiliations, but she couldn't show her enthusiasm in public – if the man lost, she would lose her power. But there was no reason why her boy should absent himself from a chance to meet new people and make more contacts.

What Frank really wanted to do was join a local trio called the Three Flashes, and turn them into a quartet. The three – Patty Prince (real name, Patrick Principe), Jimmy Skelly (James Petrozelli) and Freddie Tamby (Fred Tamburro) – were not convinced. Why should they be? They were doing well enough as far as their own ambitions were concerned. They were all Italians who had grown up together on Sixth Avenue, near the first Sinatra home on Monroe Street. They sang and danced when not working on the docks and didn't need the addition of Frank Sinatra – except that there was the matter of that open sports car which he drove. None of them had enough money to compete with that, and there was the constant problem of moving their instruments from place to place. 'If you have a car to take you and the instruments you don't have to stay in Hoboken,' Frank told them.

He had another trump card up his sleeve. The boy with the mega-phone had gone electronic. The hardest job for any outfit in those days was simply making themselves heard, and Frank had borrowed $65 from his mother to buy a small public address system. With Sinatra aboard, how much easier life could be for the Three Flashes. It was a difficult argument to resist. It seemed that young Sinatra could be a useful person to have along, if only for what they sensed was his business acumen. But he saw himself as more than a driver and certainly more than an ideas man. He had one idea in particular from which he was not going to be deflected. He wanted to sing on stage. There was a magic there which nothing else could provide.

Whether they agreed or simply wanted to be assured of continuing transport facilities, the three succumbed.

The story is that Dolly also helped persuade the Three Flashes to take her son on. What sort of influence she could have used is now open to speculation. Possibly she promised them favours which only someone in her position could offer. Everyone in Hoboken knew about Dolly's power, but she was not about to threaten them. The most she could do was suggest – and, knowing Dolly, probably not so gently – that if they wanted work in the various groups in which she had an interest, they could do worse than agree to what she had in mind. 'She was such a pusher,' recalls Marotta. 'Dolly pestered the boys to take Frank along.'

But history will have to record that it was a useful exercise. One of the places in which the Three Flashes appeared with Frank Sinatra was to play an important part in the Sinatra story – the Rustic Cabin in Englewood Cliffs, although Skelly (so-called because he was a man twice the size of any of the others in the group) maintained that Frank did no more than deliver the three there in his car in the early evening and pick them up again at three the next morning. Later, they let him do the occasional song with them. As Tamburro commented: '[We] knew Frank as a local guy who had his own act singing and we knew he owned a car, so we made a deal … We asked him to drive us and we told him he could sing in exchange.' For his part, Frank recognised the opportunity he potentially had. The trio might just want a driver. He would show how good a singer he could be.

Nobody took much notice of Frank at the time. But they would. It was only a matter of time before the Three Flashes had a new name – the Hoboken Four.

Frank had also met a young dark Italian girl called Nancy.

— 2 —

NANCY (WITH THE
LAUGHING FACE)

Things were happening at what, looking back, seems like breathtaking speed. Quite suddenly, Frank Sinatra was singing more than he was working – the two words were not yet synonymous, although he wished more than anything else for them to be so.

As in all the very best show-business stories, it took a long time for him to become an overnight sensation. The Hoboken Four went round the neighbourhood, playing and singing together in a kind of Ink Spots routine. But they knew they had to try to move on, and there was just one way to do so. This was 1935, the age of radio. No matter what else the Flashes had in mind, Frank Sinatra knew that was where they had to go.

If any of the group's working engagements involved playing at halls which had 'wires' – radio links – that was where he wanted to work. So far, without much success. But he kept hoping, kept trying – and so did Nancy Barbato.

Frank and Nancy had met in 1934, during a summer holiday at the New Jersey resort of Long Branch. They were neighbours. She was seventeen, he was two years older. One night she was sitting on the porch of the house her father Mike had rented, polishing her nails and giving her sister Ella a manicure, while Frank sat on the steps of his Aunt Josie's house on the opposite side of the street – strumming his ukulele. It was a 1930s-style version of the lute-player serenading the maiden on her balcony, too corny for a dime novel, but true. He walked over to talk to her and she offered to give him a manicure, too. They went for a walk and repeated the experience the following evening. Before long, they were dating.

During that same holiday, on the beach at Long Branch, Frank

25

proposed. He said he was being serious. Nancy wasn't so sure, but forty years ago she said he told her: 'We've just got to get married *now*. I'll probably never make more than $25 a week – and I don't want to wait any longer.'

Nancy had gone with him to the Crosby concert at the Loews Theatre in Jersey City. 'I'd like to be just like him,' Frank had said. 'Go ahead,' Nancy retorted. 'You can do it.' He left the theatre that night dazzled by the career prospects which he now thought he had before him and equally enchanted by the prospect of marriage to Nancy. From the start, Miss Barbato found herself on a collision course with Dolly, who had already started combing out prospective brides for the most eligible boy in Hoboken in the way that she had selected members of his baseball team. Some she liked, some she did not – and at least one used her professional services following the kind of night Frank would not normally have described to his mother.

Nancy was not to Dolly's taste at all. A woman who believed that her current social status demanded the holding of receptions for the influential of Hoboken and having the occasion published in the local newspaper, wanted a young woman of status for her son. Had Nancy been the daughter of the Mayor – better still the Governor – she would have been ecstatic. Had she been beautiful enough to be featured, on her son's arm, in the society pages of the New Jersey *Observer*, Dolly would have stifled any resentment she felt. But Nancy was the daughter of a plasterer from Jersey City; hers was not at all the kind of pedigree Dolly thought suitable for her beloved Frank.

Not that the Barbatos were less industrious than her own family. Indeed, Nancy's father was a hard worker, while Frank was largely unemployed. To try to restore the balance, Mike Barbato was persuaded by his daughter to give the youngster a chance. He did, working on a wall Barbato had been hired to plaster. In Frank's hands, it was about the worst-plastered wall known to the American building industry. Secretly, he hoped he would be instantly fired, but Barbato senior kept him on. With words like, 'You either work or you stop seeing my Nancy', Frank felt he had little alternative but to stay with the bucket and brush.

It was persuasive talk and fostered a work ethic which Marty Sinatra, at least, thought worthy of his approval. But Dolly was convinced that Frank should ditch the girl whom she was certain would hold him back – and, by extension, hold her back, too. Nor could she begin to understand the girl's appeal for Frank. Nancy was not overwhelmingly pretty. Pleasantly attractive, yes, but that was not enough. Her figure was not one of those which made women subconsciously take out their tape measures. Worse, this woman had the temerity to give her son advice – and Frank was taking it. If anyone was responsible for Sinatra giving up any other career notions and so concentrate on his singing, it was Nancy.

The competition to get work for Frank was intense, a constant ideological table-tennis match between the two women. Sometimes he pursued his own ideas – like entering the most popular and, therefore, the most important amateur radio show in the country. When Nancy gave her blessing to the idea of Frank and the Three Flashes trying their luck on *Major Bowes and His Original Amateur Hour*, he knew that was where he had to go next. The other three agreed.

Major Edward Bowes was a discoverer of talent. Those who appeared on his programme hoped that the exposure would turn them into stars. It was one of the most popular shows on American radio and one of the cheapest. The performers were lining up to appear and didn't need to be paid, hoping it would be the big break that would make all the difference. Audiences enjoyed what they heard, and waiting to hear who would get the loudest applause had all the tension of a Hitchcock movie. Besides which, there was always the possibility, perhaps the hope, that one competitor on the live shows would lose his nerve while on air and chicken out for everyone to hear.

Bowes was a big bluff bazooka of a man – he always gave the impression of aiming at a target he intended to hit – who liked people to think he was the radio equivalent of their favourite uncle. Nevertheless, cross him and a recipe for disaster was in operation. There were numerous leading artists who, every time they appeared elsewhere, would say they got a start on his show. There were instrumentalists, impersonators and, above all, singers. And not just crooners, as popular singers in those days were largely known: future stars of New York's Metropolitan Opera, like Beverley Sills (then known as Bubbles Silverman) and Robert Merrill got their first break after experiencing the turn of Bowes's 'wheel of fortune'.

There would, however, rarely be anything quite like the effect of having Frank Sinatra on the show. Never before and never again would Bowes have such a hit. Not that it looked that way when Frank and the other three young men appeared at New York's Capitol Theatre on 8 September 1935 for the show broadcast on the NBC network. Neither did the months that followed give any indication that anything really notable was afoot. But, looking back now, it doesn't take long to realise that everything that happened to Sinatra after that evening could be ascribed to Bowes. It was the single event that made him switch from an overenthusiastic, nothing's-going-to-stop-me amateur into a professional who was learning his trade.

The story is that the Three Flashes made one application to appear on the Bowes show and Frank applied to appear on his own. That seemed strange, not least to the Major himself. Possibly the group had already had the first of a series of bust-ups that would dog them in the months ahead. Whatever the reason, Bowes saw through it all, knew that the four had been working together and was not interested in promoting a trio and a solo singer from the same town.

But what to call them? It was Bowes who decided on the Hoboken Four, not exactly a name to set the show-business pulses racing – at least outside of the city of Hoboken or the state of New Jersey. But it suited him perfectly. It sounded parochial and amateur, and he was in the business of turning parochial amateurs into stars, even if, in most cases, they were just stars for a night. He wanted something that could identify the act as a complete ensemble and Hoboken Four had just the right kind of non-professional ring to it. It wouldn't instantly enhance the group's reputation or, seemingly, their chances of national fame, but that wasn't Bowes's concern.

'The wheel of fortune, round and round she goes,' the Major said. 'Where it stops, nobody knows' – 'the dullest opening I ever heard on any radio show,' said Frank almost half a century later. Then Bowes introduced the 'boys'.

He was talking to seemingly four of the shyest, most gauche performers ever to stand in front of a microphone. 'Introduce yourselves,' he said and, one by one, they gave their names and stated what they were currently doing for a living – at least, when they were not out of work. One worked in a silk mill, one was a page and Jimmy had worked in his father's ice-cream parlour. When it came to introducing the newest member of the gang, Frank Sinatra, there was perhaps the first public sense that this was not a four-handed marriage made in heaven. 'This feller here has never worked at all,' said Tamby. Frank laughed uneasily and nervously but instinctively knowing that was what he had to do.

Frank made a plea to end this particular corner of America's intense unemployment problem. 'I'm Frank. We're looking for a job. How about it?' Then he added: 'Everyone that's ever heard us, likes us. We think we're pretty good.'

'Nobody working right now?' asked the genial host.

'No. Not at all.'

The Major laughed again – the kind of bored, let's-get-on-with-it laugh that went well with the kind of jokes he cracked. 'I bet I know your address,' he said. 'Where's that?' one of them asked. 'Care of Jimmy's father's ice-cream parlour.' He could hardly get the words out, so funny did he think the line. He also found a reason for everyone's laughter: 'They seem so happy and everyone else is happy.' Fortunately, he then asked what they were going to sing. They said 'Shine', he said, 'Fine' and then proclaimed: 'We start the dizzy spell of the wheel of fortune ... around and around ...'

Suddenly, the nation outside of New Jersey, thanks to Bowes's coast-to-coast hook-up, heard Frank Sinatra's voice for the first time – in brief solo moments that owed not a little to Bing Crosby and the Rhythm Boys and a great deal to the Mills Brothers, whose arrangement this song originally was. (Indeed Crosby had recorded it with the brothers in 1932.)

The applause told the newly-named Hoboken Four what they wanted to hear. It was a fact confirmed by the 'audiometer' at the end of the show. When the studio audience was boosted by no fewer than 40,000 calls from the listening public – supposedly the biggest response ever scored by an act, but that could have been the word of a publicist, either one working later for Frank or for the radio programme – the boys were left in no doubt that they had won the contest. They were on their way.

To confirm the fact, they were brought back every week for the season, becoming in the process as well known by radio audiences in Hollywood as they were in Hoboken. Not that anyone in Hollywood offered them jobs. But they got into films just the same.

Bowes didn't depend on his radio show for either his fame or his fortune. America knew him because of the broadcasts – and every-where he went, he was introduced as the star of one of the country's most popular radio programmes – but he was also the producer of a series of highly successful vaudeville shows and his own movies. The Hoboken Four made two of those short films for Major Bowes: *The Night Club*, followed smartly by *The Big Minstrel Act*. These were programme-fillers, cast with unknowns – Oliver Hardy made them before he met Stan Laurel, when he worked under the name 'Babe' –

and were particularly useful for matinees when extra 'treats' were offered to attract the customers. The Major Bowes movies did, however, have the distinction of being shown at New York's Radio City Music Hall, the biggest cinema in the world.

In the first of the two pictures, Frank appeared as a waiter. Nothing strange or controversial about that. In the second, following in the footsteps of his first idol, Al Jolson, and a string of other top-line entertainers like Eddie Cantor and George Jessel, he and the other boys appeared in blackface – a fact that would surprise people who know Sinatra for either the gentle love ballads of the forties, the swinging songs of the fifties and sixties, or the belt'em 'New York, New York' numbers of the seventies and eighties. But the man who was to write his epitaph in his own lifetime by saying that he did things 'My Way', really began in serious show business by doing it the way so many others had done it before.

Blackface was a respected theatrical convention. Frank has since said that he did not at the time think he was insulting the black man by wearing burnt cork. None of them did. Everyone knew that these were not blacks on the stage. The white gloves they wore proved it. The white line around their mouths was not so much an extension of their lips as a declaration that they were counterfeit. There was one other important feature: the blackface comedian, particularly when it was Jolson, was the one who got the upper hand when in conflict with the white man, the character in the play who outwitted the wicked plantation owner taking advantage of the poor defenceless parlourmaid.

Bowes also made the group an offer to appear in one of the various vaudeville shows he had touring the country, playing with a top band and being broadcast at the same time. They accepted without so much as having to think twice. For $50 a week each – the sort of income none of them had ever dreamed of earning before – plus meals, the Hoboken Four were booked to appear in the Major's Number 5 show, not necessarily the fifth best, but the one where he needed them most. Altogether there were sixty Bowes acts touring the country in six shows, one on the East Coat, another on the West Coast and four others in between.

The group travelled from one destination to the next either by train or bus, entertaining in the local vaudeville theatre at every stop. They sang the way they had on the air and in their movies. None of them ever thought they could be billed as stars of screen and radio but with a stretch of the imagination that was legitimately what they were – even if the films in which they 'starred' lasted no more than a few minutes and had been shot, not on some vast West Coast lot but in the studios of the Biograph Company in New York's Bronx, a new use for one of the veteran establishments of the silent film era. The combination of films, radio and vaudeville was a heady one.

This was the world that Frank Sinatra and his colleagues from Hoboken entered in the latter part of 1935 and early 1936. Every Sunday night they would check into some cheap theatrical boarding-house where, over the soup passed from the coloratura soprano – a woman who Frank might well have noted looked suspiciously like Dolly – to the 66-year-old comedian who was then asked to carve the roast, the members of the profession in town that night would discuss the parlous state of the theatre, the horrendous work of a certain director and the outrageous behaviour of a group of young hecklers. The Hoboken Four, placed at the end of the table near the salt, as all newcomers to the business were, sat wide-eyed and open-mouthed – when their mouths were not being filled by the soup or the scraps from the roast – listening to those tales and wanting to be part of it themselves.

The following morning they handed their music to the orchestra leader, and began rehearsals for shows in theatres emblazoned with slogans like 'Major Bowes's Amateurs Stopping Here'. Sometimes they appeared for a whole week, sometimes for a couple of days, but the basic routine never changed. They started out at the Auditorium in Des Moines, Iowa, on 15 September 1935 and two days later were at Wichita, Kansas. At the end of the month there was a week at the State Theatre, Los Angeles, sponsored by Standard Brands of California. When the 'cast' posed for a photograph, the Three Flashes, Jimmy, Patty and Fred, were in the front row and Frank was in the back.

In San Diego the group got close to having their booking cancelled. During their rendition of 'Shine', Frank started giggling and couldn't stop. Prince and Skelly were infected, too, and ran off the stage, leaving Tamby to turn the number into a baritone solo and then to apologise to the road manager.

And so the tour went on – into Canada where it took them to Victoria, British Columbia, in November, then on to Vancouver and back to Bellingham, Washington. It was planned to finish in April at Fort Worth, Texas.

Behind it all was their broadcasting. Major Bowes's deputy as musical director of the radio show was the composer Morton Gould, soon to be best known as the writer of *Pavanne* and to become one of the most respected figures in American music. 'I remember Sinatra in those days as being a very exciting talent,' he told me. There was also an excitement in the trouble between the various members of the group – or, to be more precise, between Frank and the others, who were content being part of a team and believing in collective responsibility.

It all came to a head in Spokane, Washington, appropriately perhaps because it was the home town of Bing Crosby, the man whom Frank wanted to emulate even more than Al Jolson. Here Sinatra and Tamby got into a fight and, according to a television biography of Frank, Sinatra punched him to the floor. According to Tamby's stories, told for decades afterwards at Hoboken's Piccolo restaurant, it was he who floored Sinatra. 'He was on the ground for ten minutes,' Tamby liked to recall. Even Prince, he said, took a swipe at him. The skinny kid had found himself a new role – 'as a punchbag.'

'He was hit day after day,' Joe Spaccavento told me. 'To the point that Frank packed his bags and went home.'

That was precisely the outcome Frank wanted. The story around Hoboken at the time, Sparky remembers, was that the row itself had been about Sinatra's having had enough of the vaudeville grind and wanting to go home. The others wanted to stay on the road and they couldn't do it, they thought, without him. He was the one with the voice as well as the car.

It was the end of the Hoboken Four. Talking it over, the other three decided they had to go back too. Soon afterwards, Major Bowes asked Tamby to get the group together again, but Frank wasn't interested and, besides, they had had enough of him. Prince and Skelly found themselves jobs as waiters in the town of Keansburg and didn't want to leave (they had girlfriends there). Before long, Skelly became a longshoreman and Prince worked on the Erie–Lackawanna railroad. Tamby found himself the odd singing job, then became a truck driver. It was the precise reverse of the kind of story Major Bowes liked to tell of his discoveries. But one Frank Sinatra in a lifetime should have been enough to satisfy him.

Dolly and Marty had mixed feelings about it, too. On the one hand, they were glad to have their adored only child with them once more. On the other, the notion that he had apparently failed at the one thing he wanted to do haunted them. One morning at breakfast, Marty put his foot down. Frank had to go out and look for work.

'I remember the moment,' he said in a television interview. 'He told me, "Get out of the house and get a job." I was shocked ... I think the egg was stuck in there about twenty minutes and I couldn't swallow it or get rid of it, in any way. My mother, of course, was nearly in tears, but we agreed that it might be good thing.' He went, taking his suitcase across the Hudson to New York.

It wasn't a successful trip. A few days later, he was back home. Meanwhile, his was not the most popular name in Hoboken. The families of the surviving three members of the Four started saying the kind of things not usually heard about Dolly Sinatra's family at that time. Dolly decided she had to take matters into her own hands. Did Frank still want to sing for a living? It was probably a rhetorical question, but Dolly had ideas of her own and if she were to put those ideas into practice she had to be more sure about that than about anything else.

This was a challenge to Dolly, on two levels. Firstly, she was a mother wanting her son to succeed, indeed to lift himself from the mire of unemployment which was the biggest curse of the age. Secondly, she saw his failure as an affront to her ideas of power. If *she* couldn't get something done for her son, what did that say about her relationship with the world beyond the offices of the local Democratic Party? There was also the other side of that coin: if she *could* find him an opening, her political stock as someone to influence events would be even higher in the second ward of Hoboken than it had been up to then. But it meant her straying into an entirely different industry: the music business.

'She put her weight around with Local 526 of the Musician's Union, to which I later belonged, my local,' said John Marotta. 'You didn't argue with her.' Neither did the proprietor of the Union Club at 600 Hudson Street. She told him that she wanted a job for her boy and a job singing there was his for the asking.

Dolly's power was so well established – she was not only on first-name terms with Hoboken's Mayor McFeeley, but also with Mayor Frank Haig of Jersey City – that it was just assumed she would get her way. But why? 'We took it for granted that there were some mobsters behind her, says Marotta, 'because there had to be some reason for her power, but it was just something we assumed.' Certainly, Marty didn't have a share of it. He now suffered from asthma and was frequently unable to work.

As a result, Frank began to be heard on the radio again, appearing with a local boy, Matty Golizio, who, according to John Marotta, 'played beautiful guitar'. The two got air time whenever they could on the Newark radio station, WAAT, which Hoboken regarded as its own, singing the songs people wanted to hear at the time like Crosby's signature tune, 'Pennies from Heaven', or 'These Foolish Things'. He worked for almost nothing – 70 cents a week for bus fares – although nothing was not what he would have called it. The sheer opportunity to broadcast was all the payment he required. Suddenly, a wider audience was available for Sinatra interpretations of 'How Deep is the Ocean' or 'Body and Soul'.

He was following a hunch that would help both his career and his ego. He knew that radio exposure was the most potent form of advertising he could get. It also did his ego the world of good to know that Nancy, to say nothing of Dolly and Marty, were tuning in and listening to him on the big brown boxes in the corner of their living rooms. Even better than that was the sheer joy in thinking that all those detractors who were spreading the evil words about him were listening, too – to say nothing of the remaining members of the Hoboken Four.

Indeed, there was something sweet about the position Frank found himself in now. It wasn't big business, but as far as the folks back home were concerned, this was big enough. 'The announcer, Jay Stanley, was a pretty good pianist and Frankie along with Matty on guitar had a pretty good trio going,' John Marotta remembers. 'They started to make tracks and become pretty popular. Frankie always made sure that, wherever he performed, he had Matty along with him.'

He knew how to get the music for the trio to perform. Says Marotta: 'He would go to the publishing houses where bands could get free orchestrations. Later he would look through the orchestrations and pull out the piano and guitar parts.'

It all provided good experience, the kind he couldn't get anywhere else – particularly now that he was occasionally appearing on WNEW – one of the big New York stations, the one the critics listened to. After a few weeks, he had an agreement to appear eighteen times a week for the princely sum of $4 a week.

He had begun taking voice lessons from a man named John Quinlan, whose message was simple: other singers with fairly high voices relied on a microphone and made acceptably nice noises; to succeed, Frank Sinatra had to sound different. For the $1 a session Frank paid him, he told him about a bonus that he believed his pupil had to offer: his range which was much wider than that of any other singer. Quinlan emphasised what needed to be done to take advantage of it. There was, for instance, breath control, the importance of Frank holding on to notes long after the other guys had let them go.

Ray Sinatra, his father's cousin, thought he could help, too. Ray was about to become a well-known band leader in his own right. At the time, however, he was playing in the NBC house orchestra. He told his bosses in the music department about this youngster who happened to be a relation, the one with the sweet, high voice and a range that would knock them dead. They gave him a try. For another 70 cents a week, Frank appeared on a daily fifteen-minute show. It was blood money, but the younger Sinatra was willing to spend every drop.

The cheapskate approach of the radio stations seems incredible today. But these were not prime-time enterprises and the networks, even more than the big companies, knew the value of the opportunities they provided for young talent.

The swing era was really swinging now. Ella Fitzgerald had sung about losing her yellow basket and every teenager was singing it. Big bands were never bigger. People were trying to work out whether this was jazz (a 1930s version of ragtime?) or just the latest kind of popular music. It didn't matter. The dance halls were the big centres of entertainment and those joints were, to adopt the phrase of the time, really jumping. Frank Sinatra didn't yet have people copying him, but he was beginning to be close to the centre of where things were happening – thanks to these early expeditions into radio. He was not the only one to benefit. Appearing on the 70-cent show with Frank was a teenager from Tennessee who had just been discovered by Eddie Cantor, a fresh-faced blonde with a voice that sounded as though it came wrapped in silk. Her name was Dinah Shore.

Just a month before her death, when I was researching a television programme about Danny Kaye, she recalled her own beginning and started thinking about the people she knew in those days. Kaye, vibrant, excitable, brilliant was one; Sinatra was the other. 'I'm not going to say I knew he was going to be a huge star,' she told me. 'I was ambitious, but I've never seen anyone so determined to get on. Everything he was asked to do, he did. Give him a chance to make one more programme that he was contracted to do – contracted, that's funny! – and he would kiss the producer who suggested it. He made a good impression and I honestly think he took deliberate steps to be better every time.'

He must have succeeded or he wouldn't have been given the opportunity for those extra programmes. But there were certain other advantages to appearing for nothing on the radio. It meant that Frank's amateur status was not affected. That didn't help his parents' bank balance (he was still living at home) but it did mean that there were opportunities out there that were not available to professionals. Not only could he still qualify for Major Bowes's show; he was also perfect material for *Town Hall Tonight*, the radio show hosted by Fred Allen, one of America's biggest radio stars.

Allen was a dour-faced comedian who before long would become most famous for his on-air competition with Jack Benny, a sort of Hope–Crosby running joke that had radio audiences creasing up for years. But in the late thirties his fame came from his own version of the Major Bowes talent show, although there was little competition involved. The entertainers were on the show because they were amateurs and because Allen thought they provided him with good fodder.

Frank appeared on the show on 12 May 1937, a day when most of the world's attention – and all its newspaper photographers – was focused on London, the scene of the coronation of King George VI. Allen didn't mention the royal event on his programme. He did, though, show great interest in Frank Sinatra, who appeared with a new group, the Four Sharps. 'You have a strange name,' said Allen in one of those remarks that ought to be registered in some kind of show-business hall of fame. 'Are you related to Ray Sinatra?'

Frank told him Ray was his father's cousin and inwardly hoped that the fame of this new up-and-coming band leader would one day be his, too. Allen was kind to his artists. He wanted to know about the Four Sharps. 'You have your own little swing outfit here. How many? Five?'

'Four instrumentalists and myself,' replied Frank, sounding a lot more confident now than on his first 'interrogation' on Major Bowes's show.

Allen continued probing: 'That's rather a small combination for swing music, isn't it?'

'Oh. We make it swing loud, don't worry about that.'

Allen thought it was time for a play on words. 'Oh you do? I suppose the man on the flying trapeze got on all right with swing himself.' Then he asked: 'Does size matter?' He was referring solely to any musical advantage.

'You must be in the mood,' Frank replied, brooking no suggestion of criticism now. 'And we're always in a swinging mood.'

Fred Allen appeared to dismiss him at that. 'Thank you very much for your time, Mr Sinatra,' he said. But that was merely an introduction to the number the Four Sharps and Frank were going to sing. 'Exactly Like You', it was called, and the next day letters were sent via the station to Frank by hundreds of people who said they wanted to sing 'exactly like you'. Frank anticipated that. On the air, he told them; 'Don't swing exactly like me, or you'll be creeping around.' It wasn't quite the Sinatra-speak of future years, but it was coming that way.

Now, though, he needed to be more than just an amateur picking up less than a dollar an appearance. And once more Dolly came into the picture − together with her friends in the Musician's Union. Thanks to them he was back at one of the old haunts of the Three Flashes, the Rustic Cabin. The roadhouse on Route 9W, close to the New Jersey town of Alpine, was more successful now than it had been when Frank first went there as a combination of chauffeur and lifter. It was firmly entrenched as the kind of place which, before the advent of the highways in the 1950s and the various campaigns against driving and drinking which followed later, was a popular nightspot for couples out in the family car. The orchestras there were as important as the drink and the food. And now Frank was singing with one of the best of them, a union band led by Harold Arden. It was all Dolly's doing. Frank had to join the union himself but thanks to her efforts he was seriously in work.

This was the start of a new chapter in his life and, if they did but know it, of American music, too. The Rustic Cabin had a 'wire' − a broadcasting link − and the chance of appearing on that wire was as much an attraction to Frank as he hoped his singing was to the people who came to the roadhouse for a beer, a hamburger or something more substantial. Every night the Cabin was featured on *The WNEW Dance Parade*.

Sinatra's job was not as a performer standing in front of the band but as a singing waiter. He sang, waited on tables and acted as MC. Now he was earning real money − less than he could have got working in the docks, but he no longer had to count his income in cents. He made $15 a week − a figure that was not to change for the next eighteen months, but was helped by tips dropped into a plate on top of an upright piano. Being a singing waiter was another of those American show-business conventions, with as historic a background as the blackface minstrel. Irving Berlin had been one of the dozens of top figures in the entertainment world who had begun their careers waiting at tables and then, standing with a tea towel draped over their right arms, singing whatever was popular at the time.

That was what they wanted at the Rustic Cabin. The Depression, thanks to Franklin Delano Roosevelt's New Deal, was on the way out and the car was coming into its own in America. At the Cabin, wearing a white coat, bow tie and black trousers, Frank sang the songs of the day, some of which, like 'Night and Day', he would make into his own standards in years to come. Arden liked the Sinatra voice, which combined well with his orchestra. It was a lucky move for them both. For Arden to have a fresh new talent who came cheap – and was one that his audiences seemed to like – was a distinct bonus. For Frank it was a heaven-sent opportunity – to have a spot which he suspected customers were beginning to come to the roadhouse especially to witness and hear.

At first he was part of a trio of waiters. Before long, he was wondering if he would ever be allowed to sing on his own. The time did come – and within a few evenings.

There was only one problem: who the hell would want to listen to a man with a ridiculous name like Sinatra? If Arden allowed the thought to cross his mind that the distant cousin of Frank's father, Ray Sinatra, was doing pretty well as a band leader himself, he ignored it. His new singer, Arden decided, would be called Frankie Trent. Like Major Bowes before him, the band leader thought he knew the value of a name that fitted his establishment like the cover on a set of drums.

Frank didn't object. But Dolly did. It was not just a supreme insult; it would do her son's career no good at all. Once more, she used her influence both with her son and with the union. Two weeks later, Frankie Trent had become Frank Sinatra again.

To prove the point, he had visiting cards printed: 'Frank Sinatra, vocalist. Radio, Stage. Recording artist'. It seems incredible now that Frank Sinatra ever needed to hand out calling cards. But this one – an experience never to be repeated – carried his address as 841 Garden Street and his phone number : Hoboken 3–0985.

Frank wasn't doing spectacularly well yet, but there was the germ of evidence that something was happening. Frank Sinatra on his own was beginning to sound just like that – a singer on his own, no longer a Crosby clone, a little too similar to all the other band singers.

It didn't mean that he didn't still appreciate Crosby. He was listening to Bing, just as he listened to Russ Columbo, who sometimes sounded more like Crosby than Crosby did himself. The records that Sinatra bought now, though – and every time he played them he looked forward to the day when he would have his own discs to put on the phonograph – were of the jazz singers, and not just the men; in fact, the two vocalists who were making the most impact were Billie Holiday and Mabel Mercer. The memory of Holiday in particular was to linger for ever.

But it was his own voice that was pulling them in at the Rustic Cabin and it also seemed to be precisely what listeners to the road-houses's radio spots wanted, too. For the moment, Nancy Barbato was in the background, but she encouraged Frank whenever they were together and realised the importance of the apprenticeship on which he had embarked.

A band like Arden's was the best possible experience for the 21-year-old. Not one of the nation's top orchestras, like Goodman's or the Dorseys', not a national institution like Guy Lombardo's, but right at the top of the second division, nevertheless, providing sweet music made by highly professional artists with the discipline and authority of a symphony orchestra. Later Arden was replaced by Bill Henri and His Headliners. They exhibited similar authority and the white-coated Sinatra looked and sounded just as good standing by the small bowl-microphone in front of them. The fact that both outfits drew audiences wherever they played spoke volumes of music scores.

So did another factor, not necessarily observed at the time: the changing Sinatra style. Not just a different voice that didn't depend on copying someone else, but a new approach to singing. Nobody took much notice of this because at the time nobody took much notice of Frank Sinatra. He, however, did. The voice was developing enormously quickly. Of course, he was helped by the large and varied amount of work he was doing. Each new venue, every broadcast, was an opportunity to experiment. 'The idea,' he was to say, 'was to work consistently, to sing every night. That's what gave me a real base.'

What threw him off that base was to be watched by people he cared about. On the one evening when he had to be great, he was terrible. Cole Porter had heard about this bright young singer at the Rustic

Cabin and went along with a couple of friends. Frank spotted him – and immediately ran into the men's room to be sick. When he did go on, his was not a voice to tempt Porter to write some new 'Night and Day' for him.

But then Porter wouldn't have written for Billie Holiday either and it was she who most influenced Sinatra to change his singing style. He heard her for the first time soon after he arrived in New York, in a club on 52nd Street. She taught him, he said in an interview in the New York *Daily News*, 'matters of shading, phrasing, dark tones, light tones and bending notes'.

She and the other jazz singers were people who took notice of the words they were singing and conveyed the meaning in their phraseology and their breathing. Ever since his first voice lesson, Frank had recognised the importance of that. Holiday and Mercer may not have realised what they were doing, but, to use a phrase current in their jazz environment, they wrote the book. These were women who, Frank realised then, were not just singers but musicians – and that was, as far as he was concerned, a profession to respect.

Morton Gould once more entered Sinatra's life as the conductor of a sustaining programme – one that was used throughout the network when local stations needed a time-filler. Sinatra appeared on it, much to the delight of the outlets in New Jersey.

'From the very beginning,' Gould told me, 'he had an innate musicality. He knew how not to sing a song, but how to *say* a song. He always, even then, knew what a song was about. There were not many like that. Appearing with me in those days, with all the orchestral texture we could provide, he became aware of what he could do for the first time.' He not only became aware of it, he was in awe of it. 'He had never appeared with a symphony set-up like I had.'

They rehearsed before the live programme went on air – an important new development for Sinatra in itself. 'Look at those fucking strings,' he told the bemused conductor. 'He had never seen anything like it,' Gould recalled. 'I had fifteen violins, violas, the lot.'

Sinatra was lucky. It was a time of transition. Nobody walked around with a megaphone any more and the era was clearly over when Al Jolson could stand on the stage of a vast theatre like New York's Winter Garden and make the walls shake without amplification. What Sinatra had now was the advantage of the microphone. Already, while still in his early twenties, he had come to the conclusion that there was more to a performance than merely singing into a mike as though it were not there at all. He turned it into a musical instrument all on its own.

Sinatra was to say: 'The microphone is the singer's basic instrument, not the voice. You have to learn to play it like it was a saxophone.' It was an unorthodox thought, derided by those who thought the mike was an aide for wimps who didn't have decent voices in the first place. Until Frank came along, nobody took the microphone that seriously, but he could only learn by experience.

Morton Gould saw it. 'He knew that he had to manipulate that mike because, if handled properly, it would help perfect his style.' He also realised, that even with it, he had to perfect his breathing techniques, whereas other performers who understood little about using their diaphragms as well as their throats had failed to grasp this fact. Sinatra had learned the importance of combining correct breathing with the right amount of volume at just the correct distance from the mike itself.

In fact, he was consciously learning all the time – even if the one thing that he didn't need to learn was confidence, the sureness of youth that he would get to the top. Talking of the summer of 1939 when he was twenty-three, he was to say – using the lingo that has become as much a part of his personality as the songs he sang, a vocabulary developed by dwelling among the people he admired so much – 'I was full of zip, zap and zing and I was also full of myself. I figured, Sinatra, all you need is one lucky break and pow, lift-off, destination the Big Up There, the Top.' A rocket called Sinatra was about to get that lift-off.

He loved every chance he got to work in New York itself, still something of a distant dream for all the speed of the ferry ride from Hoboken. Yet when he could go there to sing with Morton Gould's orchestra on WOR, he was getting a flavour of what he hoped would come – and quickly. 'When I first came across that river,' he said in 1980, 'this was the greatest city in the whole goddamned world. It was like a big, beautiful lady. It's like a busted-down hooker now.'

The question was, just how ladylike would the city be to a young man in search of a career? In 1938 Frank wouldn't admit to knowing anything about hookers, although there were decidedly dangerous developments in his private life. His intense working schedule meant that he didn't see Nancy often enough to suit her. He said it didn't suit him either – although word got back to her that there had been other women in his life while he was out of town. One of those affairs got much wider circulation.

On 26 November 1938, Frank Sinatra appeared in the newspapers in an item that was calculated to do his career no good at all. It didn't criticise his performance – at least, not the one the public heard or saw. He was arrested and charged with breach of promise. 'A single female of good repute', as the charge said, alleged that he had had sexual relations with her on the promise of marriage. It cost him $1,500 bail – posted by Dolly – to get out of the police cell.

The case was dismissed when it was revealed that the 'single female of good repute' was in fact married. But the woman wouldn't leave it there. She charged him with committing adultery: ridiculous though it might now seem, a single man having relations with a married woman in New Jersey at the time could be branded an adulterer. The case was heard before a judge and jury and was thrown out. The one person not happy to leave things as they were was Nancy. She asked Frank if there had been other women like that. He said yes, but there wouldn't be any more.

Almost as if to guarantee the fact, he and Nancy were engaged and then married on 4 February 1939 at the church of Our Lady of Sorrows in Jersey City. The name would eventually prove to be perfectly apposite for Nancy's own state of mind, but for the moment she was ready to forgive and tried to be happy. She looked more beautiful on their wedding day than she had ever appeared to Frank before. Even Dolly had to say that she looked nice. Frank himself wore a tailcoat, wing-collar and a cravat. The service was conducted by a Monsignor Monteleon.

Later, everybody danced to Italian music and ate Italian food at the home of the Barbatos. The Chianti flowed like champagne (who has ever heard of champagne at an Italian wedding?). There were presents from some of the song-pluggers whose work Frank had performed on his radio programmes, a gratifying sign of appreciation. Both families gave furniture as presents, all of which was fitted into the apartment the Sinatras now made their home at Garfield Avenue, Jersey City. Frank Sinatra had finally moved out of Hoboken.

He knew he had not been behaving himself. 'I'm one of those people who attracts little troubles,' he was to say a few years later when people thought it important to know what Sinatra felt about anything. 'My life is full of petty tragedy. I leave umbrellas in buses, my plants all die. Every time I have a party my neighbours call the cops. The only difference between me and the others similarly afflicted is I never learn. I always expect everything to turn out great.'

It may have been a perfect example of the way press agents become other people's mouths, but this was a convenient way of saying he was sure the marriage was going to be great, too. Their honeymoon was spent driving through North Carolina.

Frank was lucky in that Nancy, even if she didn't come from next door, was not a show-business type. She worked as a secretary at the plant of the American Type Founders company in the New Jersey town of Elizabeth. The Rustic Cabin worried about the new responsibilities of Sinatra, their singing waiter, and wondered how long it would be before he took a full-time radio job. They decided to try to keep him and offered him $50 a week. He took it, and Nancy thought about giving up her job to run the home on Garfield Avenue. The rent cost Frank $42 a month.

Nancy continued to be on a collision course with Dolly. Had they lived closer to each other, this would have been perfect proof of the law of physics later to be laid down in song by Fred Astaire – the one about an irresistible force meeting an immovable object. Judiciously, they kept out of each other's way, but what Dolly said about Nancy to Frank when she was not around is not for family reading.

Mr Francis A. Sinatra, as he had been identified on the invitations Michael Barbato had had printed for his daughter's wedding, seemed happier than he had ever been before – when he was offstage, that is. On stage, that was never in doubt. Nancy would say that he was handy putting up towel rails and hanging curtains. Dolly was pleased with the way his career was going, even if she had doubts about his marriage.

One man, just a little younger than Frank and almost as thin and angular, heard Frank at work and thought they could be good for each other. The next day, he telephoned. 'My name is Harry James,' he said, 'and I'm starting a new band. I could do with a new singer. Are you interested?'

NICE WORK IF YOU CAN GET IT

This was really the start of it all.

Harry James was beginning to make a name for himself. He was not yet best known as the husband of Betty Grable, although that was soon to follow. He was not even one of those names on the tips of the tongues of the swing aficionados who were now the biggest customers for popular music, but that was to follow soon, too.

James was, however, a master of the trumpet, making one of the sweetest sounds to come out of the instrument known to man or woman. Benny Goodman had thought so, which was why James was his star horn player. Why, in a moment of untypical kindness and generosity, he allowed James to leave with his blessing and set up his own big band in direct competition to his own is not easy to work out. But he did – and the James band looked all set to take its own place in the musical world, at first as a 'hot' ensemble, later, with the addition of strings, to play some of the best dance music to come out of America.

Harry James was three months younger than Sinatra but when he went looking for a vocalist, there was no doubt who was the more successful. James, son of a circus bandmaster, was clearly destined for the top. What he needed was a vocalist who could help take him there.

It was to make a change from Frank's routine. The Rustic Cabin apart, he had been singing in some places that were not exactly savoury, owned by people about whom much the same could be said. Here were the first suggestions of Frank meeting members of 'the Mob'. As he was to say: 'I was a saloon singer and these joints were owned by those people. You didn't meet too many Nobel Prize-winners in those places.'

To understand the significance of what Harry James was offering is to go back in time nearly sixty years, when the bands were the real stars and the vocalists 'additional' musicians who played the larynx rather than the drums. Nobody took much notice of them, but a band leader needed to have someone singing the chorus of a song as much as he needed a trombone.

How he came across Frank Sinatra as his choice is now lost in a fog of legend and confused stories. Did he hear him on the radio? Or did he come to the Rustic Cabin? Frank himself on various occasions has told both stories – possibly because both things did happen. A 1930s band leader in search of new talent goes out to find it. He listens to the radio because that is where things happen. He travels to New Jersey because that is where, or so his informants tell him, there is a young fellow singing with a small-time band in a roadhouse who could be what he is looking for.

The indisputable result of all this is that Frank went to sing with Harry James and one of the most important stories in American show business was ushered in with all the drama of a band of court heralds blowing a fanfare. How loud that fanfare would be, and how strong the result it was promising, could not have been imagined that day in February 1939 when Harry met Frankie, soon after his wedding – and agreed to pay him $75 a week to sing with his outfit.

It seemed a perfect match, a new band led by a tall, skinny, angular musician featuring a new, not-so-tall, skinny, angular singer. With the aid of the strings that James was going to bring in to separate him from Goodman and the other swing bands, Sinatra would add lustre to the impression of quality James had already created with his version of numbers such as the revamped 1898 standard 'Chiribiribin', which, quite suddenly, was being played not just on the radio but in the palm courts of hotels and the swankier kind of restaurants.

Later on, Harry James may have considered the possibility that in addition to being gifted with a talent to play the sort of music he loved, he also had a certain degree of second sight. For while he was thinking that Frank would be an asset to his band, Sinatra was thinking the same thing. The young singer knew about James, had heard that lyrical trumpet when he had played with Ben Pollack five years earlier and launched his number 'Peckin', to which kids all over the United States were dancing. He listened to him with Benny Goodman, which was riding about as high as a swing band could go. Goodman impressed him.

Sinatra received a salutary piece of advice from him. 'If I'm not great, I'm good,' Benny told him, and it came from practice. 'I never forgot that,' Frank was to say. 'Every day I practise my vocal cords for ten to fifteen minutes to keep my voice in shape.' He was already practising, even though the youngster now felt he was the best singer in the land and only needed a few more people to listen. When he heard that James was going it alone and wanted him along, he was thrilled.

The offer came at just the time that Frank was about to sign up with a new outfit, Bob Chester, who was also playing at the Rustic Cabin. In truth, Sinatra wasn't totally sure he wanted to remain that rustic for long. So when he heard about Harry James, he persuaded Nancy to ask for a $15 advance on her salary – she was still working as a secretary – so that he could invest the money in some publicity photographs which he was going to send to the new band leader.

He didn't have to go to the trouble. At the precise moment that he was planning his campaign, James was listening to Sinatra and deciding that the 24-year-old could be what he was looking for.

However, certain details had to be ironed out first. The first one was that name. Sinatra? Like Arden before him, James thought it was so ... so ... what? He wasn't really sure. It was Italian, certainly. It was also highly uncommercial. Could he possibly put the name 'Frank Sinatra' on a billboard without making fans wonder whether this wasn't some kind of pasta he was giving away with every performance? No. In the bright, modern world of 1939 – it wasn't the end of decade for nothing – all was changing and America was bright and modern with it. Nobody would accept Sinatra as a name. 'Change it to Frankie Satin,' said James.

'No,' said Frank, no doubt more worried about the effect this might have on Dolly and Marty than what Nancy would say when he got home.

On reflection, James had to accept the Sinatra voice was more important than the Sinatra name. So they shook hands, while the lawyers got busy. It is worth a moment's speculation as to whether changing his name to Frankie Satin would have made any difference to his career. Or whether that strange name didn't have the opposite effect to the one Harry James imagined – and made audiences and newspaper men take additional notice of him.

What Frank and Nancy took notice of was that $75 a week. It may not have been what show business liked to call the big time, but in

1939, when a very good wage was in the region of $20 a week, it was riches. Frank could be forgiven for thinking, the moment he held his first salary cheque, that he had arrived.

Everything seemed to work for him. He was touring ballrooms and theatres all over America without having to sell himself in advance. But this is another point where legend and truth collide in the Sinatra story. If you believe those legends you would think that quite suddenly, and if not overnight then in the course of a few short weeks, Sinatra was now a star. He wasn't. The venues at which the James band played at the beginning of their tour were not quite the top and neither was Frank top of the bill. That place was, understandably, reserved for Harry James himself, or rather for Harry James and His Orchestra – which showed that already he was moving away from the big-band image. Frank wasn't even second on the bill. When they played at the College Inn in Chicago, the 1.15 a.m. floor show was to feature, underneath James's name, that of Frank Payne – 'Chicago's Own Mimic'. Frank Sinatra's name was beneath his in smaller type alongside those of Jack Palmer and 'The Boogie Woogies'.

The first destination of that initial tour had been the Hippodrome Theatre in Baltimore, where Frank had sung two numbers that suited his style and his personality perfectly, 'Wishing' and 'My Love for You'. By the time the party reached the Roseland Ballroom in New York City in June 1939, the most important dance spot in the nation, both the band and their male vocalist were firmly in their stride.

The music magazine *Metronome*, about as important a place for a singer to be noticed as *Variety* would be for most other performers, took note of the Harvest Moon Ball at the dancehall and paid tribute to 'the very pleasing vocals of Frank Sinatra'. Once more the arrival of the singer was confirmed, along with the 'welcome' mat that was being laid out for him.

Unexpectedly, Harry James was experiencing a new phenomenon, a root that would take, grow and flower in the months and years to come. When Frank went before the microphone to sing whatever current hit James wanted him to vocalise, some of the dancers stopped moving around the floor and stood on the sidelines just to listen. Couples who were smooching so closely they were oblivious to *practically* everything around them, found the velvety Sinatra tones a positive aid to the public love-making which that kind of dancing represented. It was a kind of aphrodisiac.

The band and its leader were the stars, however. When the singer was the principal performer, the band was merely the accompaniment. More often, Sinatra was accompanying the band. Instead of a brief introduction by the orchestra leading up to the singer's performance, the vocalist had to wait one and sometimes two minutes before being allowed to perform a chorus. Frequently he was with a group – perhaps three men in bow ties and short haircuts and one girl wearing a long dress and a smile – whose 'woo-woo-woo' on the sidelines, as they bent towards another mike, was considered a vital ingredient to this kind of show.

Whichever way Frank did it, the dancers seemed to approve.

The critics, however, were not so sure. *Billboard* thought he sang with 'too much pash'. Not convincing, said their man who saw Frank at the Hotel Sherman in Chicago, although he thought he sang 'torchy' numbers pleasantly enough. But most people seemed to like him. And if proof were needed of how much they approved, it came in a contract with Brunswick Records. For the first time, the voice of Frank Sinatra was heard on a record. 'From the Bottom of My Heart' was backed by 'Melancholy Mood'. For the first time, too, the name Frank Sinatra appeared on a record label – although you needed an eagle eye to spot it. 'Harry James and His Orchestra' was the billing under the title. In the top left-hand corner of the black-and-gold Brunswick label with the gothic script, were the words, 'Foxtrot'; in the opposite corner, 'Vocal Chorus, Frank Sinatra'.

Perhaps the lack of adequate billing had something to do with the lack of success of the disc. It came and it went, and if the Frank Sinatra story had not become the great success that it did, hardly anybody would have been aware that the record ever existed.

There were, it has to be said, also moments when Harry James himself wondered whether Frank's existence was such a blessing after all. He 'looks like a wet rag', he declared on one celebrated occasion – but a wet rag who knew his value. The band leader complained that Sinatra was thinking a little too much of himself – so much so that if there were an undue amount of praise, he would be asking for a raise.

But when James heard Frank sing numbers like 'All Alone', he melted. Sinatra has said that he was still trying to get as far as possible from Bing Crosby's style – an ideal that was to haunt him for years and verged on the obsessional. He liked to think that what he was producing was his own version of Italian bel-canto singing. It was a reasonable enough aspiration. There was soul in his work that hadn't been heard from pop singers before.

It was partly an uphill task. Bookings were not as strong as the band had hoped in the first flush of success on their launch. When things weren't going so well, Harry James had to think of reasons why. He looked for negative points about his singer's work, although he was too much of a gentleman, too nice a human being, to take that line for long. When matters improved, everybody loved everybody else. There was somewhat more luck with the next recording, this time for the Columbia label. 'All or Nothing at All' would be Frank's first hit.

But it all looked a short-term success. At the end of 1939, things were going badly again. The band were out west, in Beverly Hills. Just weeks after the incredible triumph at Roseland, the group were virtually stranded at the Victor Hugo Inn, appropriately named after the creator of *Les Misérables*. There were few who felt more like *misérables* than the James outfit when the proprietor mounted the platform in the midst of 'All or Nothing at All' and told them to stop playing. He wanted nothing at all from them – besides which he said the band were too noisy and he couldn't stand them a minute longer. From the moment the band had booked in, almost nobody came to hear them and, to make matters worse, the James records were sinking virtually without trace in the music stores.

So low had the group fallen that the Victor Hugo management even refused to pay the fee it had previously agreed with James. They were down – and out, to the point that they had a whip-round to buy enough spaghetti to feed the entire company, which Nancy then cooked.

This is the point when the Sinatra career came into conflict with what Frank always liked to claim was his sense of loyalty. Harry James was determined to brave it through. His musicians swore total allegiance and, if necessary, would wait for their salaries. Frank was not prepared to stay with a sinking ship. He was determined to make his way elsewhere.

The question was: how to move on? Every ambitious young man on the threshold of what he believed was an exciting career has his next move mapped out – particularly the name of the organisation or firm best placed to take him there. Frank knew where he was headed. Every band concert he heard, every record played on the radio, told him. He was going to join Tommy Dorsey. Even if Dorsey himself didn't know it yet.

It was, as things turned out, going to be one of those events that

signal the future. In Frank Sinatra's case, from now on all the
signals were going to be green. Just as Harry James had been on the
lookout for a vocalist, so Dorsey was now searching for a new male
singer. His vocalist Jack Leonard was about to leave him – to go
into the Army. That, at least, was the official reason. Another
was that Dorsey objected to members of the band bringing beer to
the bandstand and fired five of them. Leonard protested on
their behalf and announced his departure. If that were the reason he
quit, Frank Sinatra owed his entire career to the integrity of a fellow
artist.

Once more, it was the Rustic Cabin that came to his aid. Bob
Chester had invited Dorsey down to the roadhouse for an evening.
The band leader had put out the word via his manager, Bobby Burns,
that he needed a new male vocalist – and fast. Frank heard about it
and went along too. More than that, he inveigled an invitation to sing.
Both later agreed it had been Frank's best audition ever – although
neither of them called it that at the time.

Years later, Dorsey was to recall that he visited Chester, a friend
since boyhood, at the Rustic Cabin that night in 1939 to 'see how
things were going. What he ended up seeing was Frank Sinatra, 'a
young skinny kid with a lot of dark hair'. He was singing – although
not all that impressively. 'Right in the middle of the song, he forgot
the lyrics. I later found out that he'd always been a fan of ours and
when he saw us, he got a little flustered.'

Possibly with good reason because Dorsey, as he put it, 'had an
interest in the song'. The kind of interest, that is, which brings in
regular cash. The song, 'This Is No Dream', was appropriate to the
occasion, since Frank's dream of joining the Dorsey band was on the
way to coming true.

It took another year before they met again. Dorsey had heard a
Harry James record and was particularly struck by the male vocalist.
He made inquiries and learned that the voice belonged to Sinatra. He
was to say: 'I remembered that I liked the voice, but I didn't remember
that Sinatra was the kid I had heard in Chester's Band.'

A summons was issued and Sinatra came round to see Dorsey at the
Palmer House, one of the smartest hotels in Chicago. 'The moment I
saw him, I remembered him so well and I remember I said to him,
"You're the kid who blew the lyrics."' Both men laughed. But the
conversation got more serious. Frank said he wanted a job and Dorsey
said he wanted to give him one. It would be worth $125 a week,

although when Frank told Nancy about it, he told her he had no idea how much it would pay.

He was later to say that telling Harry James about the offer was about as easy as opening a vein. But James didn't try to keep him. He sent for the contract which still had seventeen months to run and, in front of Frank, consigned it to the wastepaper bin. It was agreed that Frank would leave as soon as a replacement for his spot with the band could be found. When Harry James announced that he had appointed a bright tubby-looking young man with a pleasing voice, he packed his tuxedo and left. His successor – not for the first time – was Dick Haymes.

What Frank's new job paid, in fact, was a lot more than money. Dorsey's was, along with those of Goodman and Glenn Miller, one of the three most important bands in the country. He was also going to be one of the great influences on the Sinatra career. For Frank had found someone he wanted to copy – not Crosby, not Billie Holiday – a trombone player.

He watched the way Dorsey performed, not out of idle curiosity or because he provided his paycheque. Rather, Frank was mesmerised by him. What was more, he knew there was an example in the way he performed. He studied Dorsey from the front, from the side, and, above all, from the back, noting the way his shoulders moved. That was the clue, the shoulders. As one superb note followed another, the shoulders danced; but what was really fascinating was the way they moved in the course of a single, long note so sweet it could have preceded by a spoonful of molasses. The shoulders expanded as Dorsey held his breath.

Of course, the band leader–trombone player had been doing it for a long time – since the days when he and his brother Jimmy had had their own joint band. They were sons of a coal miner from Shenandoah, Pennsylvania, who became a music teacher. Ever since he had set up his band just over four years earlier, in 1935, Tommy had had two things going for him: his individual style and an ability to discover talent and then to snap it up. The roster of people working for him reads like the list of alumni from some Ivy League college – names like Buddy Berrigan, Charlie Spivack, Buddy Rich, Ziggy Elman, Paul Weston, Sy Oliver and a man who will have vital importance to our story, Axel Stordahl. To that list was now being added the name of Frank Sinatra.

Frank knew how significant it was to be added to the Dorsey list.

That, in the first place, had been why he wanted so badly to join him – as badly as a budding conductor wanted to be accepted by the New York Philharmonic or a journalist by one of the world's great newspapers. Once part of the outfit – as with Harry James, singing little more than long choruses after the band had performed without him for the greater part of a song – Frank began studying his leader and watching those shoulders.

That was the big secret, Frank decided. That was how he was going to be different. That was his future. If he could hold a note so that one phrase ran into another with the ease of syrup dripping on to a pudding, the way Dorsey did with his trombone, he could establish a trademark for himself, something that would make him different from every other singer of his generation. And that, he reasoned, was what really counted: originality.

Paul Weston remembered the day Frank joined the outfit. It was not the most auspicious event. For one thing, they didn't even know his name. 'I said "what's his name?" and Dorsey replied, "Frank Sinatra". I said, "Well, the first thing we ought to do Tom is change his name because Frank Sinatra will never really mean much".'

Jo Stafford was already in the Dorsey outfit as lead singer in the Pied Pipers by the time that Frank joined. 'We knew we were going to have a new boy singer, but we didn't know anything about him. As a matter of fact, we didn't even meet him before the first show. Tommy announced this new boy singer and out came this rather frail looking young man with a whole bunch of hair, who was not terribly impressive to look at. But he sang no more than about eight bars of 'Star Dust' and a great hush fell over the theatre and you knew you were listening to something completely new, completely unique and completely wonderful.'

'Star Dust', of course, was a perfect introduction for the band and their audience to Sinatra and for him to the band. To misquote Hoagy Carmichael's lyric, each note was an inspiration.

It was in January 1940 that Sinatra and the Dorsey band were officially declared to be one. His first gig was at the Shea Theatre in Buffalo. It was a significant night. On the bill with him was a young comedian called Red Skelton. There was also an acrobat, by the name of Burt Lancaster, who was destined for other things. Within a month Frank was recording with Dorsey, including one song with a title that seemed to have resonance for some of the critics who were watching him work, 'Too Romantic'. It was not meant to be taken too seriously. An advertisement inserted by the band described Sinatra as a 'Romantic Virtuoso' and there weren't many around who were going to disagree.

But that was only after the first of a series of heated discussions between the leader and his vocalist. The first Dorsey–Sinatra records only bore the words 'with vocal chorus'. This was all right at first, but it was a state of affairs not calculated to win Sinatra's friendship. The RCA Victor organisation didn't like it either. It was one thing pandering to their top-selling band leader, but quite another when it came to deceiving the public, who were beginning to deluge the firm with requests to identify the mystery singer – a ploy quite possibly engineered by Frank himself.

Ultimately Dorsey succumbed and agreed to have Frank's name printed in small letters. Before long, the band leader was to complain that 'the type just got bigger and bigger'. But then, so did Frank and his career.

They played at all the standard centres for their kind of music, some of which demonstrated how even top outfits like their sometimes had to play the less fashionable 'joints'. They performed in universities as well as in nightclubs and theatres. In New York, the band played the Paramount and word got round that this sexy but skinny young singer was singing with Dorsey. The girls flooded in, not sure what to do – to run on to the stage or just to sit in their bobbysox and imagine he was making love to them. It wasn't yet the most important venue for the Dorsey outfit or the one that was making the biggest impression on the public, but there was something about the place that made it feel different. There was a kind of electricity in the air, and not just the sort which fed the lighting and sound systems. Frank could feel it every time he went up to the microphone. Sometimes he would hear the sighs of the girls, but they would get louder. Before very long, the theatre would be playing a very important part indeed in the Frank Sinatra story.

None of that seemed to bode well for Mr Dorsey himself. Indeed, it didn't take long for the band leader to realise that his find, Mr Sinatra, was a threat to his own popularity – because Frank seemed to be close to holding the dominant position in the outfit. Not only was Frank now being noticed, he was the one getting the colourful phrases said about him – like 'a voice like being stroked by a hand covered with cold cream'.

Frank was showing all the outward manifestations of success. Suits that cost $100, a new open car and dinner at the Stork Club were all on his agenda. Back in Hoboken they knew he had really made it – because they never saw him in the town any more. The story was that he was afraid to go back – in case he would be beaten up by representatives of the remaining Hoboken Four. The three survivors weren't totally happy to be seen as the home-town patsies – boys who were good enough to give Sinatra a leg-up when he needed it, but not worth remembering now things were going well for him.

He wasn't the most tactful guy either. Leo Deilizzi remembers him coming into the Grandezvous one last time for a plate of spaghetti. 'Leo,' he said, 'I've signed with Tommy Dorsey, so I'm not going to see you any more.'

The success may have seemed total. The idea of being in the band wasn't yet just a way station in his career pattern. After all, not only was he working alongside musicians like Dorsey himself and instrumentalists who were superstars in their own fields, but the sort of singers he wanted to emulate, too – like Dorsey's soloist Jack Leonard, who hadn't yet left the outfit. He probably already knew in his guts that he could sing the band's signature tune 'Marie' better than Leonard did, but Dorsey wasn't about to allow him to do so. Jack was number three in the *Billboard* Choice of Male Vocalists, Frank was twenty-second. For the moment, he was happy enough just to be in the charts at all but that contentment wouldn't last long.

The audiences for the Dorsey band concerts or dances weren't yet calling for Frank and sometimes he even stood in with the Dorsey close-harmony group, the Pied Pipers, which was almost an indignity for someone with ambitions like his. But he still had plenty to learn.

The same issue of *Billboard* which recorded his place on the charts said he was 'nil on showmanship', which was pretty damning. But it was not difficult to see what they meant. Singers thought to be fading from the public view like Al Jolson complained about how 'easy' the contemporary crop of crooners took their work; today they would be described as being too 'laid back'. When Jolson said: 'All they have to do now to succeed is show up,' he had performers like Sinatra in mind. In those days, all he did was stand before a microphone – which you might be forgiven for sometimes thinking was heavier and wider than he was himself. Jo Stafford, later to be a huge success as a star vocalist, was a member of the Pied Pipers. She told writer Earl Wilson that Sinatra didn't look very much, but 'Wow, what a voice!'

For the moment, that was Frank's trouble. He concentrated on the voice and ignored the presentation. He didn't yet realise that was why the girls weren't squealing when he went on each night. Dorsey did, and was unhappy with the way his new find was returning the compliment to him. He was happy with the music his total operation made; what he wanted from his singer was more showmanship.

What Dorsey did not know was how soon it would be coming, or the reason why a swift change was on its way. Unknown to almost anyone but Nancy, Frank was working on his singing as hard as if he were studying for an exam – or facing an audition for the Metropolitan Opera. Every lyric was being worked over as though it were a Shakespeare sonnet. Every performance was an audition before the kind of audience who would make or break him. He went through words, rolled them on his tongue and searched for the link that not only meant he was phrasing them correctly but that he was establishing a style that was his alone.

He said he was going to write a book on counterpoint, which few took literally. To Frank, though, it was no joke. It would show people how seriously he was taking his musical education. The fact that he couldn't read a note of music or wasn't exactly an English-language scholar was not intended to interfere with his plans. This was no publicity stunt. But it was not going to happen immediately. There was more phrasing to learn first.

It was hard work that brought no obvious results. But there were results of a different kind in both Frank's life and Nancy's. On 8 June 1940, their first child was born. He heard about it from his mother. She phoned when he was in bed in a hotel room – with a young girl.

Nancy did not find out about his infidelity this time and he was not going to tell her, either. He was only interested in the baby. He liked to tell people that as far as he was concerned, she was the image of her mother. Only one name, therefore, could be hers. Nancy. Frank didn't yet have a song about her, but from the moment he heard the news he understood that he had plenty to sing about. Nothing could ever go wrong again. He would never be unhappy. Millions of other fathers have felt the same thing and millions would later wish they always felt that way. As far as he was concerned, stars shone from the eyes of the baby he now called 'Miss Moonbeams'.

Because everything was going so well, there were thanks due. In Frank's view, there was no better way of offering them than by making Tommy Dorsey her godfather. The birth also made Frank feel much closer to his wife, a fact not calculated to make Dolly Sinatra feel any more generous towards her daughter-in-law. What was more, the younger Mrs Sinatra was guilty of the immense sin of keeping her son away from his mother. At least, that was how Dolly saw it. The truth was that Frank was travelling so much, he hardly saw anyone who wasn't part of the band. When they did manage to get together, Dolly's choice words – as reported by one of the Dorsey personnel – were: 'Where ya been, yer bastard?' He may have taken himself out of Hoboken, but he couldn't take Hoboken out of himself – or his family.

Meanwhile, the new father was continuing the learning process. In his business, there were two points on the graph to show the kind of progress which was essential: records and films. In his first year with Dorsey, he made both, although you had to look carefully for his name. The record made more of an impression than the film, although the name on the label was that of Dorsey. In 'I'll Never Smile Again' Frank sang along with the Pied Pipers, and girls who had lined up at the neighbourhood Woolworth store for their copies wept for weeks.

To Sinatra it was like being given a new Cadillac for Christmas. Here was a kind of recognition and, for the moment, it was enough. As he was to say on a radio show: 'The loot was fabulous. Every single week, 120 clams. But even more fabulous, I was rubbing elbows with Axel Stordahl, Sy Oliver, Paul Weston, Den Kinkaid – Tommy Dorsey's arrangers. With talent like that, plus the Pied Pipers, why, a myna bird could come up with a hit platter.' It was generous, modest praise, the kind that – to his credit – Sinatra would always pay in public, if with rather more restraint in private.

Undoubtedly 'I'll Never Smile Again' meant that something very big was happening in the Sinatra career. It may have been Dorsey's record, but Frank's vocal took up so much of the wax disc that it could have been his own. Rarely had a band record featured so much vocal material. People suggested that was uncommonly generous of Dorsey, but it was simply good business. Frank was on a salary, but the royalties for the disc went to the band leader and if Sinatra made him more money, what else was there to worry about?

He had the same effect with 'Those Little White Lies'. When girls heard that, they worried – could it be that Frank was *not* being totally sincere when he said he loved them? That was his appeal, they always believed what Frank said when he sang. That was why, when he sang about the white lies, the girls who didn't actually swoon, sighed and breathed heavily. The female population of America couldn't get enough of it. It was Sinatra's concentration on the lyrics that caused this flood of female tears. Other singers might have gone through the words without anyone really noticing them, but Sinatra expressed appreciation of all that the writer Ruth Lowe had written after her own husband's death. Not since Irving Berlin's 'When I Lost You', the poignant 1912 valediction to the wife who caught typhoid on their honeymoon, had a tune so captured the attention of record buyers or made so much money for its writer.

What the record confirmed for Dorsey was that Sinatra was the man to have at his side, even if he didn't look so good or bring him too much publicity. He patted him on the back, promised him great things. In the coming twelve months, the band leader would put his money where his mouth was. Forty more Dorsey titles went on sale, with Sinatra providing the 'vocal'. When the Dorsey organisation published a book called *Tips on Pop Singing*, Frank was listed as a co-author, although the volume had actually been penned by John Quinlan, Sinatra's former vocal coach.

The Sinatra touch was quietly and, at the time, imperceptibly, coming into its own. A few months afterwards, when Frank recorded 'Night and Day', he added a single word to Cole Porter's lyrics. Other singers crooned the words, 'down inside of me'. Frank made it '*way* down inside of me'.

He would hone and develop the style in the years to come. Dorsey encouraged the new touch. It meant that people were talking about Sinatra and when they talked about Sinatra, they talked about Dorsey, too. Sometimes he encouraged the band to play very softly so that when Frank's ideas on phrasing dictated it, he could sing at barely more than a whisper. When he sang the band's theme song, Irving Berlin's 'Marie', the band sang with him – staccato fashion ... 'Oh Marie ... it's true'.

All over America, young people were listening to Sinatra records and seeing him either in concert with the band or when the outfit was playing for dancing. The woman who would become Mrs Barbara Sinatra was to say that she first heard him in Wichita, Kansas, when all the kids of her generation were gathering around the jukeboxes in her neighbourhood. 'He was believable,' she said, 'and everybody could identify with him. He sang a lot of wonderful love songs, lonely songs.'

When the band featured in Paramount's *Las Vegas Nights* in 1941, long before the town in the film title was to mean more to Sinatra than Hoboken ever did, Frank was there fronting the outfit, singing 'I'll Never Smile Again'. He got $15 a day for his trouble.

The song and the picture were now both virtually his property. So much so that if he had never had another hit, it became *his* tune. He could have had no idea how small it would all seem in comparison with what was to come, but the RCA disc became a collectors' item and was to be re-released a dozen times all the way from LP through cassette to CD. He may not have known it at the time, but he had a standard. He also had more fame than he imagined possible – or than Dorsey intended. When Ruth Lowe's song appeared on the shelves – and in those days sheet music was even more important than records: charts were drawn up on the basis of how many copies were sold to people who would take them home to play on their own pianos – it was Sinatra's photograph on the front cover surrounded by the Pied Pipers. Their name was in upper and lower case; Frank's was in capital letters. The Sun Music Corporation knew what they were doing. Dorsey was convinced they had got it all totally wrong.

Sinatra always looked, said one friend from those years, 'like a terrified boy of fifteen in the presence of his first major opportunity'. Now theatre crowds would call out for the band to play 'I'll Never Smile Again' and couples smooching on the dance floor got so close to each other, listening to the high Sinatra voice cooing in their ears, that it was practically illegal.

It was the number they wanted to hear on the radio, too: Dorsey – and Sinatra along with him. There was now a weekly show for the band on NBC. The Lewis Home Company sponsored the programme and awarded a $100 prize to amateur songwriters thought good enough to have the band play their work and to have Frank sing it.

The following year, fresh from the shock of Pearl Harbor, Sinatra and the band repeated the experience of *Las Vegas Nights* with one of the first of the light, fluffy war movies that had crowds lining up for miles around movie theatres every Saturday night. *Ship Ahoy* was a mishmash of band music, spy caper – if you could believe it, a case carrying a mine was swapped for the one bearing a script supposedly written by the comedian Red Skelton – and the dancing of Eleanor Powell. Frank was the principal singer, augmented by Connie Haines, the Pied Pipers and Buddy Rich and Ziggy Elman.

The war involved a number of changes to the original script. One song written by Burton Lane and Yip Harburg was to have been called 'I'll Take Manilla'. 'But,' said Lane, 'by the time we started shooting, it was the Japanese who had taken Manilla. So we had to think of something different.' Two days later, Yip came up with a new title, 'I'll Take Tallulah' – Tallulah was Eleanor Powell's name in the film.

What was apparent now was the respect Frank's musicality was enjoying with his fellow professionals. Burton Lane – later to write such Sinatra standards as 'That Old Devil Moon' and 'How About You' – tailored a song specially for Frank in this movie, itself a sign of how things were moving on for him. The song was called 'Poor You'. 'I can't adequately convey what that felt like,' Lane told me, with the benefit of fifty-four years' hindsight. 'We went on the set and the band was giving a concert for executives, songwriters, God knows who – and there was Sinatra, who was the main singer with the Dorsey band. "Poor You" had adorable lyrics by Yip – "Poor you – I'm sorry you're not me. For you will never know what loving you can be" and Sinatra did wonderful things with it. And he got better.'

It was one of the first occasions on which Lane had experienced something that every writer for Sinatra was to know – the difference between the song they had sung in their heads and the way it came out when he performed it. Scriptwriters have known that, too. Somehow the words sound different when read by someone else. But with Sinatra, even in 1942, the difference was much more profound. 'It was better than I had imagined it,' Lane told me. But, as he said: 'I knew then what I was to learn subsequently – writing for Frank is just magic. His phrasing was always perfect. So to hear someone like Sinatra do a song, even in those days, was just phenomenal, particularly with a great orchestration. That's a wonderful combination.'

The really wonderful combination was, indeed, that 'great orchestration'. Dorsey's arranger Axel Stordahl was the man in charge, put there by Arthur Freed, head of the musical films unit at MGM and the man who – along with Gene Kelly – would within the decade almost reinvent the medium. It was just one of his amazingly prescient judgments.

All this was finally bearing the kind of fruit Frank dreamed of. No longer was Jack Leonard the main star of the outfit. *Billboard* announced that Frank was now the number-one male singer for college students in America. In six years he had become that overnight sensation.

It meant that, whichever way you looked at it, he was no longer a mere attachment to the Dorsey band. Now he was being courted by the songwriters. Among them was Saul Chaplin, before long to become a leading figure in Hollywood musicals – with Oscars for, among movies, *High Society* and *An American in Paris*. Chaplin was at the time writing songs with Sammy Cahn, himself about to play a vital role in the Sinatra story. They had first met up with Frank in California at one of the times that the Dorsey band was playing in the film town. The pair were working on a series of shorts for Vitaphone, the company which had produced the first sound system, the one used in *The Jazz Singer*, the introduction to the talkies.

As Chaplin told me: 'We gave Sinatra a lot of the material we had written for the shorts and he would use them on his personal appearance with the band.' Soon, though, it was to be a lot less casual. By the time the band came back, to perform at the Hollywood Palladium dancehall, Cahn and Chaplin were writing original numbers for Sinatra himself, which the band would then perform, almost – though not quite – in accompaniment to him. The Cahn–Chaplin office was at Columbia Pictures. 'It was a good place to hang out. People didn't have to go through the rest of the studio to get there and we used to make musical jokes and things – the kind of jokes guys tell each other which you wouldn't tell to a girl. We saw him a lot at the Palladium, where we hung out, too.'

More seriously, they would play over a number for Dorsey's attention, Chaplin would sing it, and if the boss liked what they produced, he'd say: 'Hey, write this up for Frank' or 'Write it up for the Pied Pipers.' Then he would tell Sinatra: 'Frank, this is the song you're singing.'

'I was knocked out by what he did,' Chaplin says now. 'His voice was wonderful. Just to hear him sing was an experience to talk about for a long time afterward. But nobody was surprised. Dorsey always had great vocalists. Jack Leonard had been wonderful, too.' But it sounded better with Sinatra singing tunes of his like 'Please Be Kind' and 'If It's the Last Thing You Do' – and, as he agrees, a lot of numbers that weren't nearly as successful.

He was, Chaplin told me, 'a takeover guy right from the very beginning'. The practice in the industry was for rehearsals to begin only when the band leader himself was ready. But sometimes Dorsey came later than the other members of the orchestra. Sinatra was always early – a situation that would later be reversed, as everyone involved with his professional life could testify. 'Frank would then convince the arranger to run through his number so that he could sing it before Dorsey got there. He didn't want to wait. Dorsey was only his boss. But he wouldn't wait.'

It was a significant stand. Dorsey didn't like it, just as he was not to like certain other Sinatra traits. Members of the band felt much the same way. In fact, Frank was gaining a reputation for suffering rivals with something like the kind of consideration employed in some of the less attractive parts of Chicago. Buddy Rich was to witness that effect.

It happened, he was to say, as a result of some dressing-room prank. They were pals, Rich maintained, although if that were true, it was a kind of friendship that makes you tot up your favourite enemies. The two men had been sharing a dressing room for some time. But, according to Rich, for no apparent reason at all, Sinatra threw a jug of iced water at him. In fact, he literally threw the jug, not just the water inside it. If it hadn't been for a shout from Ziggy Elman, making less of a sweet sound than the trumpet which created 'And the Angels Sing', the angels could have sung for Rich at that very moment.

What it was all about, Rich was to say to his dying day, he had no idea. Some witnesses to the event say it was because Buddy called Jo Stafford a less than attractive name and Sinatra went to the aid of her honour. There had to be some explanation, although Rich was to admit he had 'always been a temperamental man', a man others testify to losing his temper at the speed of light.

Singer Mel Tormé has his own explanation for the dust-up. Sinatra was singing 'This Love of Mine', which had the girls in the audience going out of their minds. Rich, who enjoyed a little audience reaction himself, was not too happy that he wasn't sharing in the spoils. So he interrupted the song. Frank didn't enjoy that. Next time he sang the number, Buddy Rich interrupted again and, speaking well above a whisper, called out to Ziggy Elman: 'Hey Ziggy, why don't we go over and see Ellington tonight at the Panther Room?' As Tormé recalled, 'Ziggy shrunk in his seat and Sinatra looked as though he would have liked to have murdered Rich.'

But if Rich himself didn't recall the reason for the altercation, he had profound memories of what was to follow. Two weeks later he had what he described as 'a little difficulty in a street fight'. As he told it: 'I was stopped in the street and I was hit and worked over pretty good and found out later it was someone from Hoboken, New Jersey, who was a very good friend of Frank's.'

The only weakness of that story is that, as we shall see, Sinatra now had very few friends in Hoboken. Nevertheless, long afterwards Rich asked Frank if 'any of your friends had taken the opportunity to visit me on the street'. The answer was surprising. 'He said they had. So we shook hands and became friends.'

Sometimes, Rich's friends became Sinatra's. One of them was a gawky black youngster who danced a lot and sang a bit as part of a trio that included his father and his adopted uncle, Will Maslin. His name was Sammy Davis, Jr. Years later, Sammy told me: 'I thought he was a nice guy, but we didn't have a lot to do with him because I wanted to be a drummer. So I hung out with Buddy.' One memory he did have was that Sinatra needed money – so much so that when the collar of a jacket became worn, he had the lapels taken off so that he could wear it as a cardigan.

The jacket story becomes part of the great Sinatra legend. Before very long, girls would regard that Sinatra jacket as no more than fair game. A piece of cloth, a bow tie – made floppy by Nancy so it could be easily torn off – was soon to become the perfect souvenir of an evening in which Frank was suddenly a Greek god who had come down to earth on the East Coast of the United States.

A fellow Hoboken citizen named Eddie Larkin remembers those days. He was in Philadelphia with a boy-drummer friend when the band were playing at the Earl Theatre. Frank was not the principal target of their devotions. To them, like Davis, Buddy Rich was their idol. They went backstage to see him. Rich wasn't there, but Frank was. 'He was standing by the elevator, wearing a kind of blue blazer, a yacht jacket with brass buttons,' Larkin told me. They told him they wanted to see Rich, a fact which, contrary to all the stories of Sinatra grudges, didn't immediately turn him against them. 'You wanna go up?' Frank asked them. Eddie said yes. 'OK, get in,' said Frank. 'I might as well run the elevator, too – for my $125 a week.' He took the pair to the second floor and then arranged for them to watch the show. 'When Frank went out, the girls mobbed him. They tore his Robert Hall suit.'

Later, Buddy Rich and his two fans went to a nearby record store, where a snare drummer was performing. Frank was there, too. He told them there was nothing he could do with his torn suit and gave the jacket to the young drummer. He wasn't at all sure that the tearing of clothes was necessarily a good sign of popularity. 'Along with living on onion sandwiches and sending money home, I get this, too,' he complained, looking at the rips in his coat. It was gilding the lily somewhat. Frank by now was certainly earning enough not to depend on onion sandwiches in order to send cash home.

The Davis trio thought the young man with the gaunt features had got about as far as anyone could wish to get. They themselves would have been delighted by such status. As it was, they were with the Dorsey band in Detroit because another trio, which should have played as a supporting act with the orchestra, were stranded by bad weather in Canada. Frank, on the other hand, was more than a rung or two above all that by now. He was also making the kind of impact with young girl fans that had been almost totally unknown up to then.

He wasn't yet a star, but older women saw in him someone they could mother and much younger ones thought this fellow with a slim, fragile frame needed cuddling. Already, there were females ready to take him to their beds at the merest encouragement, but for the moment, with the responsibilities of fatherhood weighing heavily on him, Frank was behaving himself.

This did not last. Quite suddenly, Dolly Sinatra was taking on the role of protector of Nancy. When she heard stories of Frank making good on some of the sexual offers he had been made, she suddenly became not just Nancy's champion, but that of Italian-American womanhood in general. Her own son was showing no respect to the woman to whom he was married. 'What ya doin' with them broads?' she asked so loudly one evening when the band was playing New York that the whole wind section heard her. Frank laughingly denied all knowledge of the reason for the charge and went on dating just the same. As Dolly could have noted, persistence was one of her son's strongest qualities.

It didn't mean that he was entirely satisfied with his lot. In fact, there was still the enormous problem of not getting the kind of status he believed was his by right. But he was, after all, being noticed – even if Mr Dorsey pretended that he was no more than a piece of musical wallpaper. Indeed, when it seemed good publicity, there would be a more buddy-buddy approach from the orchestra leader. They posed for pictures together, on tennis courts, by swimming pools. In one, Frank wears a pair of shorts and a sailor's cap while all Dorsey has between himself and the indecency laws is a towel. He let it be known that he liked the fact that Sinatra called him 'the old man'.

What couldn't be hidden from the public was their ever-increasing and amazingly strong output. The radio programmes were providing the core of future collections of Sinatra material that would be re-recorded, perfected and synthesised by a hundred computers sixty or more years later. For the first time, American audiences heard him sing numbers like 'The Night We Called It a Day', 'You're Lonely and I'm Lonely' and 'The Lamplighter's Serenade'. Not all made the kind of impression he wished, but enough did – songs like 'Violets for Your Furs' which Sinatra would resurrect in his comeback years, a tune that went with a tumbler of whisky at his side and a cigarette dangling from his lips. But the songs that really had people talking were tunes like 'The Song Is You' and, above all others, 'Night and Day'. For the first time, records of these numbers appeared in stores with 'Frank Sinatra' emblazoned in the spot usually occupied by Dorsey – whose own name was nowhere to be found.

By having his name printed on the records, Sinatra himself was being shown as a singer to reckon with. Yet it wasn't quite as simple as that. He was still taking part in the battle of the egos – his and Dorsey's. No matter how much the band leader wanted to try to exploit the Sinatra name, he constantly looked for ways to ensure that Frank's star would never rise higher than his own. As far as he was concerned, Sinatra was now a vocalist getting a little too big for his microphone.

So, some sophistry had to be devised that would have done credit to a Jesuit or a Talmudist. The Sinatra discs were being marketed by RCA, but not on their usual label. They appeared under the Bluebird banner, which meant they sold for 35 cents each, as against 75 cents for the regular RCA Victor records, the ones with the 'His Master's Voice' dog and gramophone. This was not only a means for the company to pay a lower royalty to Frank than they were paying to Dorsey; it also enabled them to get out of the complicated contractual arrangements involved. There was no doubt that Sinatra was tied to the RCA company via his band agreements, but ways also had to be found for him to record on his own – legally. Relegating Frank to a lesser label than the one on which the band appeared allowed a few fictions to be observed, the principal one being that, since this was basically a bargain basement (and by implication an inferior) product, Mr Dorsey's own pride would be unhurt. Indeed, it did pacify Dorsey – until he heard that Frank was appearing more regularly on the radio. That was too much. Somehow, then, the design of the label didn't matter nearly so much. This was the voice, after all, which one critic said sounded as if he had musk glands where his tonsils ought to be.

It was the beginning of a trawl through pieces of paper that would not always be as flattering and would, from time to time, involve numerous trips to lawyers' offices. For the moment, however, all the public knew was that there was a bright young singer who was beginning to make a name for himself. Those a little closer to the affair got to know about rows afoot – because the name Frank Sinatra wasn't now always linked with that of Tommy Dorsey.

Yet the music press didn't really think of him in any other way. In January 1942, *Metronome* magazine commented on the band's recording of 'It Started All Over Again' and 'Mandy Make Up Your Mind': The tunes were 'right there in the ... groove ... Sinatra's singing is immense and Tommy plays sympathetic trombone.' The same reviewer, Vic, wasn't as happy about another 'A' recording, 'Winter Weather', and its reverse, 'How About You'. (It's fascinating to realise that some songs which later became standards were, at this stage, no more than fillers: a second side needed simply because there were two sides to every disc. Somehow, the record companies treated them as though they were never going to be played, let alone reviewed.) Vic wrote: 'Great beat, brass and Pied Pipers in "Winter", all done with expert enthusiasm, typical of the T. Dorsey aggregation. Its reverse is all right, with okay Sinatra singing but nothing sensational.'

Of another standard, 'What Is This Thing Called Love?', the reviewer wrote that it 'would have been a tremendous side if it hadn't been for some woeful, unnecessary singing'. Now, what did that mean? Was Sinatra's voice and breath-control 'unnecessary'? We shall never know. 'This Love of Mine', which Frank partly wrote with the help of Hank Sanicola and Sol Parker, was another huge hit, also without the benefit of any *Metronome* praise.

On the whole, Dorsey and Sinatra looked like a partnership that had a lot going for it, if you didn't think it had already gone as far as it could go. You also had to accept that Dorsey was the senior partner, the one with all the money. Certainly, Frank was always ready to say just what an influence the man with the trombone had been in his life. You couldn't operate a career like Sinatra's without someone asking who was *really* behind it all.

In more pompous moods, Frank would say he was strongly influenced by the violin-playing of Jascha Heifetz. If he really spent time in those years listening to Heifetz's kind of music, it would be very surprising, although his enthusiasm could have come later. He was to recall in a radio broadcast: 'Heifetz could play a phrase that was an imperceptible feeling that the bow, as it went across the strings, never broke – it just went from one note to the other. You could visualise it, the bow going back and forth over the strings – there was the feeling of that bow never stopping. That technically was what I learned. It was my objective to keep it flowing, so that the audience was always aware of what you were trying to say.'

What all that amounted to was that Sinatra was able to take breaths in the middle of notes without anyone noticing, making it look as though he could connect one phrase with another – something practically unknown hitherto to any singers who were not American Indians. It was a technique the tribes had perfected, but Sinatra probably didn't know that. He could also handle grace-notes the way American black artists were able to do, but which white singers had found virtually impossible. Jolson had always managed to do so, but few others who had never sung in the New Orleans jazz clubs could even attempt it.

That Sinatra did manage it was merely apart of his legacy of studying Billie Holiday – who on her own very last album would say she wished more than anything else that she could sound like a female Frank Sinatra – and Mabel Mercer. Jack Teagarden and Johnny Mercer were to be strong influences, too. Frank also listed Fred Astaire as another idol, although he stressed that he never tried to copy him.

Above all, though, there was Dorsey. 'What did I learn from T-Bone Dorsey?' he asks on his 1965 LP, *A Man and His Music*. 'Just about everything I know about phrasing and breath control. In fact, I may be the only singer who ever took vocal lessons from a trombone. Old Tommy Dorsey could blow that thing a whole week on one tank of air. I latched on to the secret.'

But there was a world of difference between knowing there *was* a secret and discovering what that secret was. He may have thought he found it when he first watched the Dorsey shoulders. But the sheer extent of the man's breathing-power was only just hitting home.

Even now, when he was undoubtedly the biggest asset Dorsey had, Frank was trying to perfect the techniques that had finally been revealed to him. He took up underwater swimming – to help even more to learn to control those breaths. 'He would sneak in breaths where they were least expected,' Sammy Cahn was to say – like in the sixteenth bar of 'Not So Long Ago'. It was breathing not between phrases, the way other singers did it, but between syllables. That was not just singing, it was good showmanship. Frank Sinatra, in his twenties, was developing a new style. It wasn't just that he didn't want to sound like Bing Crosby; he didn't want to sound like Sinatra either, at least not like the Sinatra who had first stepped in front of the Dorsey microphone. He was now much too sophisticated for all that.

Dorsey's publicity people started giving Frank a title. That didn't please the old man too much, because he wanted all the titles around his bandstand for himself, but he accepted it. From then on, they suggested he should be advertised as 'The Voice that is Thrilling Millions'. Soon it was shortened – to simply 'The Voice'.

It did Sinatra's ego an enormous amount of good, to the detriment of his modesty. When one of the band's advisers talked about the danger of competition from another singer, he retorted: 'I can sing that bum off the stage any day of the week.' It was not good publicity, but the word got around that you trifled with Sinatra at your peril – and, most of all, you didn't play around with his own views of his talents.

He thought by now that he knew it all. And once having learned from Dorsey, he hoped to demonstrate the fact that he could put that learning into practice without him. The time was coming when he would be ready to say goodbye to the band. For the moment, he did little more than think about it, weigh up the options in his mind the way he studied a song lyric. But one night, the die was cast. He saw Artie Shaw sitting at a table at the club where he was playing. The man who was to the clarinet everything that Dorsey was to the trombone, was about to be posed a question. 'Could I have a job?' Sinatra asked. The answer was equally direct. Shaw said he had no vacancies. He already had Tony Pastor and there was no room for anyone else.

But it was the spur to make him move. That was the moment when Frank Sinatra decided not only that he wouldn't stay with Dorsey, but that he wouldn't get another band job either. He was going to start up on his own. Various record companies were promising deals, with enough money on offer to make him rich, to say nothing of the additional prospect of shows, films, concerts, broadcasts and all the other things that the top singers like Crosby could manage. As he said at this time: 'I decided somebody should challenge Crosby because he had had the throne for so many years.' It was that kind of self-confidence that breeds success, an asset he had by the bucketful. 'I thought maybe they're ready for a different kind of singer.'

There was, however, the matter of the contract he had with Dorsey. Everyone knew it not only promised him that initial $125 a week – a figure that had now gone up to $150, which was not anything like the figure Sinatra thought was justified by his status in the charts – but it also tied him to the band for years to come.

Saul Chaplin recalled Frank telling him of an incident that was ultimately to result in the ending of the Dorsey–Sinatra connection. 'At one rehearsal,' Chaplin told me, 'another trombone player was late and Tommy Dorsey went mad. He said: "Where is that Jew bastard?" Frank punched him.'

Later, Sinatra would say that he reacted to any manifestation of anti-Semitism because of his Hoboken background – one of the few times he ever said anything nice about Hoboken. That his experiences in the place taught him to be racially tolerant, there is no doubt. The memory of the kind Jewish lady neighbour would remain for ever and the influence of that time would reappear countless times in future years.

Neither Sinatra nor Dorsey ever spoke about the incident in public, although the old man did once say: 'Frank never backed down from a fight.' The band leader would add: 'But he wasn't very difficult. All the boys in the band got along with him. He was very ambitious, always wanting to better himself, to be a big success, to learn everything he could. He wasn't lazy, I can tell you that.'

But by that time, long after Frank had left the Dorsey band, it was politic to say nice things about him. In any poll on who was the bigger name in show business, Sinatra was fifty points ahead. You didn't argue with figures like that – unless you wanted to be a hundred points below. Nevertheless, you do have to put things into perspective: that encounter wasn't something calculated to draw the two men, boss and employee, any closer to each other. There were more rows – ostensibly for musical reasons, although plainly they were rubbing each other up the wrong way, personally, too.

At first, Frank seemed to be playing the gentleman. Soon after telling Saul Chaplin about the physical bust-up, he talked about those musical considerations – all of which centred on what was best for his career. By then, he had had another hit, 'South of the Border', and he thought there were gentle ways of saying that he wanted out of the Dorsey connection. Friends like Saul Chaplin couldn't understand it. 'I told him I thought it was a mistake,' Saul said., 'I didn't yet think he was popular enough.' Frank didn't take issue with that, although he did think his time was coming, if he could take Stordahl and Dorsey's other principal arranger, Paul Weston, with him.

That wasn't easy either. They had contracts with Dorsey, too. But not the kind Sinatra had. And they wanted to go. As Stordahl said: 'I understand that there was a certain amount of talk around New York that I had lost what little mind I had when I asked for my release from Dorsey. The people in the music business who, of course, know *everything*, were sure that Frank was just a flash in the pan; that we would be starving within a year.'

If he had relied entirely on Sinatra, that could have been a correct judgment. This was the time when it became evident that the young man with the voice did not have a business brain to match. He hadn't told anyone, but by agreeing his contract with Dorsey in the first place, he had practically signed away his life. The old man had extracted out of him a clause which stipulated that of every dollar he would ever earn in the years to come, 43 cents would belong to Tommy.

True, it was being said that the contract was 'merely' for ten years and applied only to fees over $100 – a kind of face-saver both for Sinatra and for Dorsey – but more recently the true brutality of the agreement has become evident. It was the closest thing to legal white-slave trading since Jack L. Warner sued Bette Davis in the London High Court over her breach of contract with his studio.

The significance of the Sinatra–Dorsey agreement of 1940 didn't strike home for years. Here was a young man getting the best opportunity he could ever imagine – to be the leading singer with the leading band in the country. Why would he ever want anything more? He did not know then that it meant not for just ten years – but forever afterwards – that Tommy Dorsey would get 43-per-cent of Frank Sinatra: 43 per cent of everything he would later earn at Las Vegas, 43 per cent of 'Strangers in the Night', 43 per cent of 'New York, New York', 43 per cent of *From Here to Eternity*.

Columbia Records now wanted to offer him a contract. It would give him his chance to bring those arrangers like Stordahl and Weston in on his own terms. The value of the opportunity to make real progress in his career – on his own – seemed beyond imagination. He knew that it couldn't happen for the moment, because while he was tied to Dorsey, he was also tied to RCA. But it wouldn't be beyond the wit of a decent lawyer to get him out of that particular agreement. Getting out of the 'parent' contract with Dorsey was another matter entirely.

Just how difficult this would be became obvious when Frank filled a couple of gigs on his own. He knew Dorsey wouldn't like it very much but, in its way, this was a toe being dipped in the water. He was right – Dorsey didn't like it and turned on the hot tap. His lawyers complained. They didn't so much deny his right to do the concerts – which he was not entitled to do – but demanded their 43 per cent cut.

This was when the big guns were brought in. Frank's lawyers said the contract was contrary to common justice. Dorsey's men merely suggested that they look again at their piece of paper. There it was, plain for everyone to see: Frank had sold his birthright for a mess of dancehall pottage.

When Nancy heard about it, she was dumbstruck – mainly about how dumb her husband had been. She kept asking him why he hadn't looked closely at his contract. No doubt – for the second time in recent months – Dolly was on the same side, saying the same things. She absolutely would never have allowed herself to get into that sort of situation.

Meanwhile, Frank had to consider his options. Getting out of a contract like that was akin to trying to escape from some kind of showbiz Alcatraz. He could always run out of Dorseyland and swim to new gigs, providing he wasn't swept on to the legal rocks. He might even get ashore and reach his new engagements. There could even be friendly natives who would pay him in local produce – like cheques which he would pocket and then refuse to give up.

But Dorsey and his men had no intention of allowing any of that to happen, as press reports emanating from both camps made clear. The fight attracted as much attention as any more conventional entertainment divorce and almost as much as the war in North Africa, which was to be the scene of the turnaround in the Allies' fortunes.

The media were all with Frank – something that would prove to be very unusual in the years to come, particularly where legal matters were concerned. Now they were portraying an overanxious young ingénue in the hard world of big business, who was being taken advantage of by a wicked uncle. Certainly that was how Sinatra himself saw it, especially when *Metronome* magazine described the whole affair as 'black-market meat slicing', a 1942 term referring to rations extended by unscrupulous traders who offered favours 'under the counter' for extra cash.

Frank was so overheated by the whole business that he took to discussing his situation – and himself – in the third person. 'You can quote Sinatra as saying that it is wrong for anybody to own a piece of him and collect on it when that owner is doing nothing for Sinatra. Sinatra will fight this foreclosure or whatever it is to the last ditch.' The quote, given to the *New York Herald Tribune*, showed that Frank was beginning to talk in a way that was to become familiar in years to come – a time when legal expertise would be more readily available and when he wouldn't make mistakes about words like 'foreclosure'.

It was also said that Sinatra brought in some heavy artillery, in the form of big strong men who knew how to handle situations like this. So the rumours started: gangsters (that's what the Mob were still called in those days) were being paid to do the Sinatra dirty work for him. It would be merely the beginning of a story that would run and run for the next five decades.

He did have some heavies on his side, but he insisted they were just of the legal kind. Stories that Willie Moretti, scion of a Mafia family, paid Mr Dorsey a visit and suggested ever so politely that he ought to think again about the Sinatra contract – one of them said that Dorsey had a pistol shoved in his mouth – he dismissed out of hand.

Something, however, needed to be done if Sinatra were ever to be more than a band singer. Columbia still wanted Frank to record for them as much as he wanted to be on their label. This was, after all, his first real opportunity to branch out on his own and face Crosby on his own terms. Bing had Decca Records, the biggest operation of the day, and would before very long be recording a pair of sides for them every week for the next ten years. Frank was now being given the chance to become as big a record star with the label's closest rival.

The Columbia boss, Manie Sacks, suggested the next move. He put Frank in touch with Henry Jaffe, a kind of Perry Mason among show-business lawyers – a man with whom you didn't trifle and still live to tell the tale in court. Not, it has to be said, that there was any violence either threatened or administered under Jaffe's care. It was never needed. Jaffe almost always won his cases – usually by knowing the right people and the right words to use.

The words Jaffe used on this occasion cannot now be sworn to. The younger Nancy Sinatra says in her own work that they were: 'Do you like broadcasting on NBC?' and Dorsey's reply was something like: 'I like it a lot.' Whatever the words were, the meaning was clear. Jaffe, acting for Sinatra in the way he had already represented a score of other entertainers whose names would fill volumes of theatrical Who's

Whos, was putting on the pressure. He happened to mention that he represented the American Federation of Radio Artists. That was writing on the wall – in luminous paint: If you don't release the slave named Sinatra, I have means of getting you banned from the airwaves. Jaffe didn't have to spell out any suggestion of strikes by Federation members, but the impression he left was that NBC would drop Dorsey's contract like a hot record rather than risk such an eventuality.

The band leader's lawyers weren't exactly babes in the wood either – after all, they had drawn up the infamous contract in the first place, a document that was now worth more than they could ever have imagined when Frank and Tommy appended their names to it. (They had possibly originally used the Hollywood moguls' tack of pointing out the huge risk their man was taking: Sinatra was guaranteed an income whether he was a success or not, and the money for that income came from Dorsey's pocket. They didn't say anything about finding ways of paying him off if he had not lived up to even their limited hopes, which they unquestionably would have done.)

But Jaffe didn't think his opponents would capitulate quickly. Legal problems are never sorted out that easily. So there was another card up his sleeve: he would get Frank to leave his present small-time agency and sign on with MCA, one of the giants of the agenting business. That was what happened. MCA fixed a deal – the agency would obtain $75,000 for Dorsey from radio and recording dates and. he would then release Sinatra in exchange.

In the end it turned out to be simpler than that. MCA so wanted to boast Frank Sinatra on their books that they paid two-thirds of the money themselves out of petty cash. Frank also paid for his inexperience: he had to find $25,000 of his own money to give to Dorsey. That, in turn, prompts a question: Where would he get it from? His payrises since joining the organisation meant that the $150 a week he now picked up from Dorsey was a veritable fortune for a young man, even one with a wife and child to support, but it didn't mean that he could easily lay his hands on that many 'clams'.

The answer was that the Dorsey lawyers would agree to wait. They had to admit his prospects were good enough to guarantee the sum within a reasonably short time. What was more, Frank now had his contract with Columbia and Axel Stordahl *was* there along with him. 'There was a lush, Tchaikovsky-type sound from Stordahl,' said one writer and that did no more than give some idea of the contrast he was going to provide to most of the pap that had gone before.

'Stordahl was a wonderfully kind, pleasant man,' Walter Scharf, who was later to become musical director on a Sinatra movie, told me. 'His help for Frank was tremendous. I don't think he could have achieved all his early success without him.' That was a widely shared opinion in the music business. The bald, egg-shaped head of Stordahl peeking over the top of a music stand was a kind of insurance policy for a recording or film company. He represented not just good music but also a steadying hand and that was important in an industry too used to ups-and-downs. He was there when Frank Sinatra needed him most – at the start.

All this meant the end of the overture and the beginning of the first act in the tale of Frank Sinatra, star. (Superstar and megastar were to come in the acts to follow.) All that the general public knew of these developments was the announcement that Frank was leaving Dorsey, and that everyone wished him well. You couldn't say goodbye to someone who had already made such an impact on nationally-networked radio without audiences knowing about it. So in his last outing with the Dorsey orchestra, broadcast on 3 September 1942, America heard all the goodbyes and the wishes of success that they had no reason to doubt.

The announcer was in Western mood and introduced him as 'Side Saddle Sinatra, the Hoboken Bronco Buster'. He was asked, 'How's tricks, FS?' Frank, fully in the spirit of things, spoke of his sadness at leaving the Dorsey show and, with it, the Dorsey outfit. 'Oh, I'm a sad hombre tonight. I've got moss in my chaps and even my spurs won't jingle jangle' – an allusion to the hot pop number of the day ('Spurs that Jingle Jangle').

After announcing that, after that night, Sinatra was going to be 'strictly on his own', the presenter declared: 'Frank, I want to tell you that everyone in the band wishes you the best of luck.' Frank said he was going to 'miss all you guys' and then introduced 'the guy who's going to take my place, a fine guy and a wonderful singer'. Once more, Dick Haymes was stepping into the Sinatra shoes. He had a right to hope it was but the second of many trips into the exalted footwear, but he stopped halfway – and became a successful and pleasing ballad singer who made an occasional film, but without any of the Sinatra mystique about him.

Dick Haymes liked to think that taking over from Frank was no more than poetic justice. He said once: 'Sinatra and I were always neck and neck. It happened to us approximately at the same time. It happened to me when I was with Harry James at the same time it was happening to Frank with Tommy. In time we both outstripped our leaders. Frank became more important than Tommy and I became more important than Harry.'

In a way, he was probably right, except that when he took over from Sinatra with Dorsey, it was perceived as a downward move on the bandleader's part. But he never let on that he knew it. As Haymes added: 'Harry didn't particularly like being outstripped by his singer, but Tommy adopted the philosophy of Jack Benny – he was always the star, but allowed them to do all the work, get all the laughs so that he was the brunt of their jokes, but he always emerges smelling like a rose. That was Tommy's philosophy, too. He was a star maker, employing people like Frank and me and names like Buddy Rich, Ziggy Elman, Joe Bushkin, Connie Haynes, Jo Stafford and the travelling arrangers, on the road with us, were Axel Stordahl, Paul Weston and Sy Oliver. It was a showcase, like you didn't believe.'

The singers could always take advantage of the way they were showcased. 'They were just one of the musicians until the public started to sit up and take notice. One of the perks for a vocalist was not to be forced to sit on the bandstand and snap your fingers when you weren't working. When one became big enough not to just sit on the stand, it became a step up.'

Haymes said that he was concerned about joining the 'Tiffanies of Bandom', and on that 1942 broadcast for *The Raleigh Cool Show*, told Frank: 'I don't know if anyone can really take your place . . . and you'll be knocking 'em dead on your own hook.'

Frank sang for the last time with the Dorsey band – 'The Song Is You'. Later, he recalled the night of his last performance with them: 'The bus pulled out with the rest of the boys at about half past midnight. I'd said goodbye to them all and it was snowing, I remember. There was nobody around and I stood alone with my suitcase in the snow and watched the tail lights disappear. Then the tears started and I tried to run.'

But there was a more profound memory. Just before that bus left, the old man held out a hand and said, 'I hope you fall on your ass.'

— 4 —

I'VE GOT THE WORLD
ON A STRING

The Paramount was one of Manhattan's biggest movie theatres. But it wasn't the movies themselves that drew the crowds; it was the additional features. People went to the Paramount because they were getting incredible value for their money – a stage show in between the films. Radio City Music Hall had shown the way, the biggest theatre in the world offering not so much stars in between the pictures but the most famous chorus line in the nation, the Rockettes, making the RKO films almost superfluous. The Paramount was the answer from the studios of the same name. More than that, it was the New York shop window for whatever Paramount was currently exhibiting. If Radio City specialised in girls, the Paramount specialised in bands – although, as we shall see, girls came to play an important part in this story, too.

Sinatra knew he was booked into the Paramount the moment he announced he was going it alone. He had worked there three times before, but as part of the Dorsey set-up. This time was going to be different. He was almost going to be the star. Not quite – but not just a singing accompaniment either.

So far, everything had gone better than he could have imagined possible. In the three months between leaving Dorsey and his opening at the theatre, he had been on the radio twice a week in a fifteen-minute CBS show called *Reflections*. The Paramount management liked it enough to think he could transplant the show to their stage. They could not possibly have known just how successfully he would manage that transplant.

In years to come, top entertainers from every field of American show business would recall Sinatra's debut at the Paramount in the way those of a previous generation remembered Jolson opening at the

Winter Garden in 1911. Both were seminal experiences. Jack Benny, who had experienced Jolson at work live, was there for Frank's opening. In a 1971 BBC radio broadcast he recalled that night at the Paramount: 'It was the biggest thing I knew since Jolson. When you get an entertainer who can hold an audience in the palm of your hand, I say entertainer . . . rubbish! This, like Jolson, was sensational.'

Benny had been asked by the manager of the Paramount, Bob Weitman, to introduce Frank from the stage. He didn't know what he had let himself in for. In truth, Weitman himself had not known either. He had gone down to the Mosque Theatre to scout out potential new talent and had been told to take a look at the 'skinny kid'. He heard then of the way the teenage girls in the audience reacted when Sinatra performed. He hadn't heard it himself, or if he had, he didn't necessarily believe it.

He saw Sinatra perform and was overwhelmed. 'He was not much older than the kids in the seats,' Arnold Shaw, an earlier Sinatra biographer, recalls Weitman saying. 'He looked like he still had milk on his chin. As soon as they saw him, the kids went crazy. And when he started to sing, they stood up and yelled and moaned and carried on until I thought, you should excuse the expression, his pants had fallen down.'

Jack Benny didn't know whether he wanted to get involved with a performer who looked as though his pants had fallen down. He was used to an altogether more sophisticated approach and a more sophisticated type of audience. And yet the risk had to be taken. He trusted Weitman, an old friend. More important, as he told me: 'Let's face it, when you're in my business and invited to go on stage in one of the biggest theatres in New York to introduce an act, you don't turn it down. You know that by virtue of being asked, you're the big star. The publicity value and prestige is big, I can tell you.'

But being asked to introduce Sinatra, accompanying the Benny Goodman Orchestra – yes, still *accompanying* an orchestra, still in smaller type on the posters than the band itself – did give him a moment or two of pause. Were the people there for Goodman or had they come principally to see the main feature, *Star Spangled Rhythm*, starring Betty Hutton? If Jack Benny was unsure, Goodman was not. Until that night, he was convinced that the crowds had come to hear his band – whom he conceded needed a good singer to keep the joint jumping. He regarded Sinatra as a supporting feature, someone supposedly appearing to 'accompany' him. And he didn't like what happened one bit.

Frank, on the other hand, had no idea what was about to happen. He was the lead singer and, like Goodman, was hopeful of another successful gig. He had made the choice and left Dorsey. If he won now, he could be made for the rest of his working life. 'I was scared stiff, I couldn't move a muscle,' he said.

What Jack Benny witnessed when he made the announcement was the roof falling in. 'What the hell is that?' he asked. Screams the like of which hadn't been heard outside of a Dracula movie rocked the theatre. When the house lights went up, it was clear that the Paramount was packed with hundreds of girls, some of them so young they wore their school tunics over white blouses with puffed sleeves.

This was a brand-new phenomenon, echoed twenty years later when the Beatles arrived in New York. Screaming was an understatement. The girls shouted and they wept, and like ladies in Victorian melodramas whose corsets were too tight, they swooned. Without anyone realising the extent of what had been happening, they had been listening to Frank's singing in their own homes and couldn't wait to see him in the flesh. When they did see him – indeed, when they heard him – it was as though they were experiencing some mystical happening. For them, the Second Coming would have had nothing on this.

When he heard the reaction, Frank felt more comfortable. 'I burst out laughing and gave out with "For Me and My Gal",' he was to recall. What he may not have realised was that the 'gal' in the song was sitting in the audience. Every female there that day thought he was singing just for her. It would happen again and again, for the best part of the next fifty years.

The story has got around since then that it was all the idea of George Evans, Frank's new press agent. The terrible businessman who was Frank Sinatra was advised by his agents to get his new career under way totally professionally. And that meant putting his publicity act into motion right from the beginning. Evans, so the story goes, had hired some girls to swoon and faint and so be helped out of the Paramount and into the street by first-aid men. It might have been a good idea – but it was wholly unnecessary. The women did it of their own accord, without help from anyone. The truth of the matter is that the girls had come to the centre of Manhattan from all over New York, most of them playing truant from school. Plainly, this was the worst outbreak of plague that the New York school system had ever experienced.

Older girls took days off from their offices or their beauty salons to wait in line for hours for this new phenomenon in their lives – not just a show-business phenomenon but one for the whole of America at a time when there was all too little colour around. As one girl said: 'My parents loved Caruso and now this young man with the big voice, he was our Caruso.'

The kids had found a kind of holy grail. Some of them queued up to kiss his picture on the advertising billboards. More than one took out a lipstick to write, 'Frankie I love you' beneath his printed name. They had not just listened to his radio programmes but – a nice twist, this, to the business machinations of Dorsey and RCA – had been able to afford the low-price Bluebird records, whereas they might never have had the money to buy the main labels. They knew those Sinatra titles as well as anything on the hit parade. They went mad when they heard their Frankie sing the songs he had started rehearsing at seven o'clock that morning. Calling him 'Frankie' was just right for the way they regarded this man only a little older than some of them were themselves. It was friendly and helped the older ones to accept their roles, vicariously mothering him.

It may have been imitative, but after the first few performances, no one would need any stunts to swoon and faint. The audience stood up in the aisles and fell to their knees. They sat in their seats for six or seven performances a day – eleven on Saturdays – going in for the first show and staying till the end of the day, just in time to get last trains and buses home. The ushers tried to get rid of them, but there was little they could do. The kids had bought tickets which said nothing about single performances only. Mothers went mad worrying about their daughters while girls stood at the stage door, screaming and crying once more, with one or two of the braver ones rushing towards their idol, opening coats revealing unbuttoned blouses, so that he could sign his name on their brassieres.

It was not just a pubescent thing, it had distinct sexual overtones. The story over the years has got around that when the girls did leave for the night, the seats where they had been sitting were frequently damp. In New York in 1995, one matron laughed over her memories of 1943. 'I wasn't one of them,' she told me, 'but I know precisely what happened. Girls were scared of getting up to go to the toilet in case they would lose their seats for the next performance, so nature took its course. Others were so overcome by seeing Frankie, as they swooned, they had orgasms there and then.'

You couldn't admit to either phenomenon in the newspapers of 1943, although the Paramount hysteria did provide both headlines and pictures of girls jumping up and down.

Life magazine described it as the 'proclamation of a new era'. As Betty Grable, the symbol of the morale women offered their menfolk in the Second World War (pilots about to fly out on missions would pat her bottom for luck – on the pictures they had stuck to the insides of their lockers), said: 'Sinatra sings the way Clark Gable makes love.'

The theatre blacked out the windows of his dressing room – on police advice. The young women fans had got to know where it was and when they saw him at the window, the traffic blocked for yards, sometimes for miles. Cars piled into each other when he was suddenly spotted by a driver outside the Paramount.

The newspapers loved it. 'FIVE THOUSAND GIRLS FIGHT TO GET A VIEW OF FRANK SINATRA' reported one headline. And the audience reacted to the papers in a predictable way. When there were reports of a bombing raid on Sumatra, girls all over America fainted.

All this fame, though, brought a new dimension to the story: it made Frank aware that there were bitter jealousies in the air – particularly across the Hudson in Hoboken. Not only did the citizenry avoid singing the praises of the local boy made good; no one in the old home town seemed to wish him anything approaching success.

Hoboken was a naval town. The boys he had been to school with were in sailor suits or khaki. Frank wasn't. Why wasn't he? They asked the question and didn't want to hear the answers supplied by Dolly and a few friends who stayed loyal. The truth was that the punctured eardrum and various other ailments attributed to his traumatic birth meant he was given a grade of 4-F – guaranteed to keep him out of uniform for the duration of the war that started when Pearl Harbor was attacked in December 1941.

George Evans put it about that Frank used every means at his disposal to get into one of the services. But it would have been understandable had he simply welcomed the chance to continue his career and earn all that lettuce, as they would say round about the Paramount building, and this was good ammunition for the three remaining members of the Hoboken Four who were either in the Forces or on essential war-work at the docks. They were consumed with jealousy at the success of their former colleague, the skinny youngster they had thought good enough only to drive them from one date to another. It was perhaps the way you feel when the only work you get is very part-time and, like 'Skelly', you become a bartender, or like Prince a not-too-successful comedian or, like Freddie Tamby, a piano player.

The trio fired the resentment shown by the other men who were in uniform. On one celebrated evening, just as Frank had got into 'The Song Is You', men in the audience started throwing stinking vegetables on to the stage. They were identified as coming from Hoboken. As much as anything, they were resentful that Frank had proved wrong all the doubters, those who maintained that Sinatra would never amount to anything. What was more, and rubbing more salt in the wounds, their own girls were the ones who were buying the tickets and virtually offering services to the stranger that were denied to themselves.

It was as Frank sang the final bars of 'I Don't Know Why I Love You Like I Do', on another night, that he was showered not with love and affection or even vegetables but with eggs. He left the stage, but eighteen year-old Alexander J. Dorogokupetz, who had been throwing the missiles, wasn't allowed to get away so easily. Hundreds of girls made a mad dash towards the young man. He was protected by twelve uniformed policemen who then hauled him away to the nearest precinct house. Dorogokupetz had been one of a group of sailors who had thrown tomatoes at pictures of the singer outside the theatre early that morning, but, unlike the others, didn't think it was enough. He wanted to get the real man – and did.

Not everyone's feelings in Hoboken were negative. Dolly and Marty came to the show day after day and brought Marty's father, known as Punch, along too. He confessed he was totally mystified by all the screaming, but then so was almost everyone else. In fact, Marty said: 'I couldn't hear. Who could hear? How could you hear?'

Others from the home town went to the show, too. Frank may have said he wasn't going to Leo Deilizzi's restaurant any more, but Leo wasn't too insulted to avoid seeing him perform. 'I went practically every day,' Leo says. 'He was wonderful – and, yes, I felt proud.' Youngsters like the teenage Joe Spaccavento were also among those who had skipped school to go to the Paramount.

But the question of war service worried Frank more and more – not, as his publicity declared, because he wanted to do his duty, but because he was concerned that the whole thing could rebound on him like a pile of discarded '78 records. George Evans worked even harder to get across the message that it wasn't his fault at all.

'I'm dying,' Frank declared to the Associated Press, not entirely on Evans' instructions, 'it's the uncertainty. I don't care whether I'm in the Army or not, but I'd like to know one way or another. It's embarrassing and it's annoying.'

Evans was telling everyone that Frank was frustrated and wanted to do his duty. For the moment, however, his main task was to keep the Sinatra career in business without too many embarrassing questions being asked. The show broke all records, with Paramount studios benefiting as much through the success of *Star Spangled Rhythm* as through the show on stage. The Goodman orchestra with Frank were contracted for a fortnight. This they turned into a month, but the band couldn't stay any longer. Sinatra, though, could and did.

It wasn't good news for the man who revelled in the title 'King of Swing'. Once more, there was the old unhappy, sensitive, jealous relationship between Sinatra the lead singer and the man who was currently his band leader. It all came to a head when *Down Beat* magazine revealed the results of its 1942 hit parade of top artists. Goodman had found himself sharing the honours with Sinatra on what he regarded as 'his' bill. He liked even less the fact that Sinatra had so outshone him at the Paramount that few even realised his band was the one playing there. Now the *Down Beat* poll confirmed what the theatre audiences had told him. The honours had to be shared.

The Small Combo winner was Goodman and his sextet. Sinatra was the winner of the best male vocalist section. Bob Weitman was in his element. His *two* stars were the winners of the national poll. It had never happened before. Nor had Benny Goodman ever had to share a bill with a performer who was now judged his equal. To him, nobody was his equal.

Weitman knew the publicity value of the whole affair. *Down Beat* was a very important influence in the music world. He persuaded the magazine to nominate who would present its awards and to do so from the stage of the Paramount. The choice fell on one of the most popular stars of the time, Madeleine Carroll. The problem was that Goodman refused to be part of a double bill in this instance. He would accept his plaque – but at a separate ceremony. Plainly, Sinatra came out the winner in this contest. He said he was proud to be considered on the same level as the great Benny Goodman. The 'King' went away and sulked.

When Goodman's time at the Paramount was over, Frank sang with the Johnny Long band. Needless to say, by now it was Frank's name on the marquee. And on the cheques, too. He had originally been paid $750 a week. By the time his stay finally ended – smashing into little pieces a record that Crosby, of all people, had set fifteen years earlier – he was on $25,000 a week.

Just to prove how far he had come, he was no longer being spoken of simply as Frank or even Frankie or as Sinatra. The Voice had arrived with a vengeance. Now, 'The Voice's' public may have wondered how long it was all going to last, but what did that matter? 'The Voice' was young, successful – and very, very rich.

Columbia signed their contract with him and he began a career with the label on 7 June 1943, singing 'People Will Say We're in Love', from the new stage hit, *Oklahoma!* which was doing for the theatre precisely what Sinatra was doing for popular music. Listening to that and subsequent records more than half a century later, it is not difficult to see the impact they made. Quite suddenly, popular music *was* sounding different. They weren't just sweet tunes to fit whatever mood you happened to be in; they had words you could listen to. But it was a combination of the singing and the music that made the discs so outstanding. The Voice did the selling, but the music was in the hands of Axel Stordahl, whose career forever after would be linked with the Sinatra name.

'Axel was the grand daddy of them all,' Frank was to say. 'There was no doubt about that ... He read my mind.' Through him, there had been strings in the Dorsey band. Now the strings were vitally important in the orchestras he conducted for the Sinatra Columbia recordings.

More than 280 sides would be recorded for Columbia over the next decade. In some ways, the early ones were the best. There was virtual perfection with 'I'm a Fool to Want You', and an early version of 'One for My Baby' made a huge impact. Sinatra the saloon singer had made his debut. For the first time, people could picture him sitting on a bar stool, in an alcoholic haze, bemoaning the departure of the one love of his life.

The Dorsey influence was obvious. The phrasing, the breathing, the kind of songs that went well with 'T-Bone', all betrayed the image of a graduate paying tribute, perhaps subconsciously, to his mentor.

Musicologists praised his legato and even his fans, who didn't know the meaning of the word or had never heard it before (it meant that he sang in a smooth, connected way), had to agree.

This was a singer who was conducting the orchestra with his voice – quite an achievement, quite a novelty. And most of the time, Axel Stordahl was in front of Frank, waiting for ideas as well as instructions. Columbia was happy to keep things in his hands – and why not? They were the safest hands in the business.

Frank had only just firmly got his legs under the Columbia table in the summer of 1943 when the Musicians' Union called a strike. It was wartime and the amount of shellac available for records was strictly rationed. Companies like Columbia had to decide who they were going to record and which investments they had to protect. There was never any doubt that Sinatra was one of these. With the instrumentalists on strike, strong vocalists like him were given priority. Numbers like 'Close to You', 'Oh What a Beautiful Morning' and 'I Couldn't Sleep a Wink Last Night' were recorded solely with vocal accompaniment, instead of instrumentalists. He sang with up to seventeen singers helping him out. But there could never be any doubt that it was Sinatra's record.

The polish was always there, a refinement not noticeable with any other singer of the day. Crosby, who never pretended to be anything more than a crooner – a very rich crooner, but a crooner just the same – used the nice-an'-easy approach of hearing a melody, picking up a sheet of lyrics and going through them virtually in one go. They always sounded that way, too – particularly on his radio programmes when he would fluff to his heart's content, but joke his way out of any problem that might arise. That was his appeal. Perry Como, who also liked to give the impression that he sang in between those dozes he took while sitting on a stool, did take more trouble. But neither they nor any band singer of the age worked at the sheer musicianship required to sell a song the way Sinatra did. Critics were beginning to notice that he worked his voice the way a violinist played his fiddle. Maybe, then, there was something in the Heifetz connection.

The lines along the streets of every town and city in America when a new record was announced showed how strong his appeal now was. And so was his role as a figure of controversy. The question of his draft-dodging came up with increasing frequency – in direct proportion to all the other stories about him. There was always the recurring disparaging statement querying Sinatra's absence from any army boot camps. Again and again, his press agent was forced into issuing what was virtually the same statement: Mr Sinatra would dearly love to be able to serve his country, but as a 4-F, how could he?

Danny Kaye, at about this time, performed a number called 'Melody in 4-F' (his own classification, too) about a young man being called to an army medical and then pronounced unfit to wear a uniform – until the guns started firing and then, conveniently for Washington, having his grade changed to 1-A. There was never any suggestion of Sinatra being made 1-A (or Danny Kaye either, for that matter).

It wasn't just his absence from actual service that worried people now. Other, older entertainers – Jolson was twice his age and he had led the band here as in so many other things – had gone overseas to entertain the troops. Without offering much in the way of explanation, Frank wasn't able to follow suit. He said he thought he had duties at home. The girls might have been grateful – their husbands and boyfriends were not.

Some people were saying that he was boosting morale every time he opened his mouth. There was a sustainable argument here, except when it came to wives of serving soldiers, sailors, marines and airmen writing to him, begging to be taken to his bed and offering any other favours he so desired. Those letters came to him by the sackful.

Dolly, meanwhile, rushed to her son's aid. 'He wanted to get in so badly,' she declared. 'We wanted to have our pictures taken together in uniform.' *Together* in uniform? Here Mrs Sinatra senior was per-petuating the myth that she had been an army nurse in the First World War – two years after Frank was born.

But Frank certainly was worried about the war and its effect on the people he cared about. So he took to wearing a medallion – the one given him by his Hoboken neighbour, a Star of David on one side, a St Christopher on the other. Covering all options, you might say.

The real proof of his appeal was that everything he did was now observed by the nation's media. The papers went crazy over Sinatra's reaction to a twelve year-old girl catching her fingers in a door as she left the studio where she had been watching one of his radio programmes. He took her into the Hotel Astor and bought her an ice-cream. Newspapers pictured more mature women staring in wonderment from a balcony when he entertained defence workers at Frank Daly's Terrace Room at Newark, New Jersey.

When he attended bond rallies, singing Irving Berlin's 'God Bless America', the audience cheered till the roof rattled. It was the same when he sang on the radio in his *Lucky Strike Your Hit Parade* programme, which had been set up by George Washington Hill. Time after time when he filled the Paramount, the newsreels and the newspapers covered the event in the way they reported the latest doings of President Roosevelt.

And if the White House was seemingly Roosevelt's own for life, the Paramount was now Sinatra's. There was a sustainable argument that he knew the theatre, where he was now advertised in bigger lettering than the studio's top movies of the day, better than he did his own house, newly purchased at New Jersey's Hasbrouck Heights.

When he appeared at the Paramount later in 1943, it was for a month, and for that month all New York knew about it. The traffic jams seemed to affect the whole of Manhattan, as if it were an infection – and in a way it was; every other entertainer now tried to have an element of a Sinatra performance whenever he or she appeared, if only to knock him.

But Frank was now looking for wider fields to conquer. Indeed, the soundest advice he received at this time was that it wasn't enough just to wow the kids at the Paramount. He had to widen his appeal to take in their well-heeled parents, too. When he sang at the Riobamba Club, he amazed both the clientele and the gossip writers like Walter Winchell who sat at the tables penning their columns. Jimmy Durante at New York's Copacabana had been known as the king of the nightclub circuit. By all reports, Sinatra at the Riobamba and in the Waldorf Astoria's Wedgwood Room had now taken his place. These were clubs where the footsteps of bobbysoxers never trod – and although the customers didn't scream or ask him to sign their underwear, they were as enchanted and under his spell as any who paid the few cents to see him at the Paramount.

The wags liked to make fun of him. 'Skinatra', one of them called the pathetically slim singer, and for a time it was a nickname that stuck. But it helped to get him mentioned. *Life* magazine featured him on its cover – the first of hundreds of top-magazine stories in the next half-century or more. He was talked about in the scripts of films in which he didn't take part. When those movies crossed the Atlantic to Britain, people in the audience wondered what it all meant. Few Britons had ever heard of him. But they soon would. His records were marketed in the country and beginning to sell there as well as at home in the States.

In America, the bookings were so successful that Sinatra was now a natural for the more prestigious radio shows, the ones that the top stars fought to get on. Occasionally, he allowed himself to go back to what he considered to be his roots – or at least what he considered to be his *kind* of roots. Near the Hasbrouck Heights house was a lunch wagon, the kind of place that sold hamburgers before anyone had ever heard of Macdonald's. There, Frank would grab a stool if it wasn't already taken and enjoy a burger with plenty of onions. The owner considered it his absolute duty to make Frank feel at home – by deluging him with as wide an assortment as possible of Crosby records. He also usually managed to persuade a female customer to swoon. 'Gee, that Bing is out of this world.' To which Sinatra would smile and say: 'Aint it the truth?' They knew what to say in New Jersey.

When he entertained a live audience of servicemen on the most successful radio show of them all, the *Stage-Door Canteen* programme, he teamed up once again with Harry James, who welcomed his old band singer as a performer who had now soared well ahead of him. It was the kind of gesture that always endeared 'Mr Trumpet' to his fellow entertainers.

But it was another development which really broadened the Sinatra appeal and helped to confirm his commitment to musicianship. Remarkably for the time, he started appearing with classical orchestras – with the Philadelphia Philharmonic at the Lewisohn Stadium in West Harlem, New York and then, most notably, in Los Angeles on 14 August 1943, singing to ten thousand people who crowded into the open-air Hollywood Bowl, accompanied by the Los Angeles Philharmonic. From the outset, the mere idea of an orchestra of the LA Phil's quality appearing with Frank Sinatra had had the press salivating and the local worthies tut-tutting into their cocktails. A concert at the Hollywood Bowl was a society fixture, not just something that was attended by people who enjoyed the long-hair music usually on offer there. Particularly now, when wartime restrictions put a limit on what could legitimately be enjoyed, it was one of those functions to which the rich and the influential in the movie business and commercial life of the city would gravitate – as much to be seen there as to listen to the music.

But those normal habitués of the Bowl weren't at all sure that they wanted to be seen at a Frank Sinatra concert. Everybody had heard of the Paramount crowds and that was not the kind of image they wanted for themselves. Disaster seemed to be inevitable. From the moment when it was announced that the man called 'Frankie' by

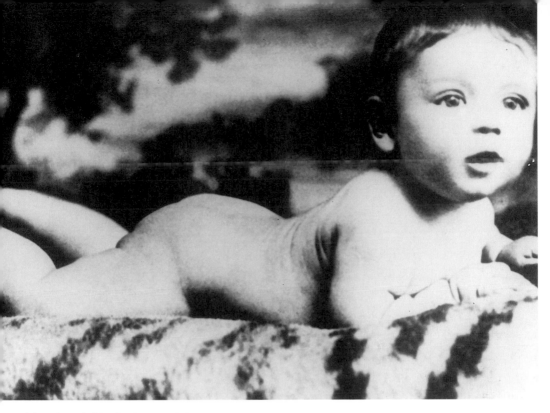

(above) Probably the first of all the Sinatra pictures –
he wouldn't have wanted to be seen like that again.

(left) He wouldn't look quite so angelic again, either.

(right) At home in Hoboken, the cradle of baseball.

(above) Dolly and Marty – on their golden wedding anniversary. He inherited from them both: the idea of power from his mother, the look of his father.

(opposite) Newly-weds – Nancy and Frank in 1939.

(above) Facing the fans. He needs a step ladder to be seen by them all in December 1943.

(below) The family is complete and it all looks so warm and nice. A 1948 group with Frank and Nancy and their children, Nancy Jnr., Tina and Frank Jnr.

(above) At home, the loving dad with the two Nancys in 1944.

(below) The arrival of Frank Jnr. in 1944. Nancy made sure that he was quickly introduced to his father.

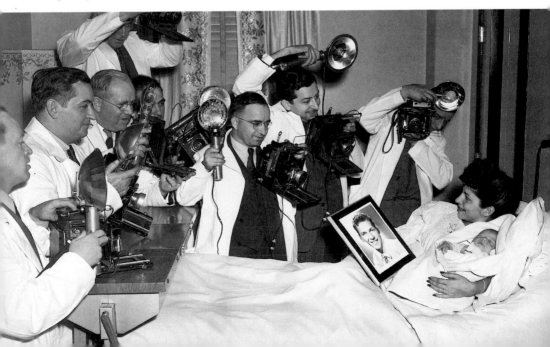

Even on radio he had to show he could do everything.
Rehearsing for a Lucky Strike programme.

That's my boy. Trying on Marty's fire captain's cap when he made his official visit to Hoboken in 1947. The coat would soon be pelted with fruit.

The Sinatra the fans didn't see – the only known picture of him wearing glasses, rehearsing in 1944.

screaming kids in New York was going to come to their favourite rendezvous, the controversy started. People wrote angry letters to the Bowl itself and to the *Los Angeles Times*, saying that the integrity of the prize music centre was being compromised.

There was, however, one consideration that the Bowl administrators could not resist – they were broke. Agreeing to a Frank Sinatra concert – the very words were difficult for some of them to spit out – *could* just help. As it turned out, every one of those ten thousands seats offered for sale at the arena in the Hollywood Hills, with the kind of acoustics which would drown out the sounds made by mountain dogs and jackals, was taken and the Bowl never looked back. The red disappeared from the Bowl's books as quickly as it rushed to the cheeks of young girls who managed to grab a ticket and see for the first time what all the fuss made by their East-Coast sisters had been about.

The orchestra that night played the first half alone, concentrating on light classics like 'The Flight of the Bumble Bee' and 'Night on Bald Mountain'. But the second half was reserved for the young man who seemed all but lost in his long white tuxedo. Actually, he was anything but lost. He was in complete command. He stood, looking out at the vast auditorium – the spotlights didn't allow him to see much, but he could *feel* the people were there – and declared: 'There has been quite a controversy out here as to whether or not I should appear here – it seems as though those few people who thought I shouldn't, kinda lost out in a very big way tonight.' You could have heard the cheers that resounded at that all the way to Beverly Hills.

When they let him, he went on: 'I have a comment to make about that. I don't see why there shouldn't be a mixture of all kinds of music at any bowl or any kind of auditorium. Music is universal, whether you hear a concert singer with a philharmonic orchestra or a jazz band. It doesn't make any difference.'

That night, he declared he was appearing with the 'finest orchestra in the United States today'. At that, even the members of the Los Angeles Philharmonic who might have thought they were demeaning themselves by playing with a kid pop idol, smiled to one another and would have clapped, had it been seemly to do so. The audience, of course, continued to go wild. They only had to hear Frank singing 'The Song Is You' for half the people out front to think he was referring to them alone, just as they had in New York.

Morris Stoloff, head of music at Columbia Pictures, conducted the orchestra for the Sinatra section. He was currently music director of the movie Frank was making at the studios, *Reveille with Beverly*, which starred Ann Miller and Larry Parks and in which he was merely a band singer crooning 'Night and Day'. When we discussed that night, years later, Stoloff again made the old comparison: 'Only Jolson had had that sort of impact. Hollywood had never seen anything like it.' The comparison was apposite. Stoloff was later to become musical director of *The Jolson Story*.

Johnny Green, later head of music at MGM and a regular conductor at the Bowl, told me: 'I was there that night and I found myself riveted to my seat. It wasn't enough just to sing. You had to be able to take charge. He did that – and at the same time opened the Bowl for the first time to a wholly different kind of music for a wholly different audience. It was to be the first of many.' Green's own annual concerts of Rodgers and Hammerstein music probably had their roots in that Sinatra evening.

Sinatra himself liked the idea of being allowed to perform in such hallowed surroundings. Next time, he wanted to have a more classical repertoire himself. As he said, he liked that kind of music. 'It's no gag I have a passion [for it] . . . I own albums and attend concerts whenever I can.' He probably did own the albums. Record companies thrust their wares at him all the time, although nobody ever reported hearing him play them. It also has to be said that he was never seen at an orchestral concert that didn't require his attendance as part of his newly-gained position in society – the benefit performances at which he wanted to be seen.

He went on: 'It's pretty disheartening and disappointing to me that people like those opposing my appearance at the Hollywood Bowl think in these channels. I'm only doing it to help finance a field of music that I really love.'

There was, however, a point to all that. Sinatra knew that it was good form to be quoted in those terms. He was intelligent enough to realise that there had to be some kind of life after the bobbysoxers – although, to be truthful, not much of it was seen that night at the Bowl.

Daily Variety, the West-Coast edition of the show-business bible, headed their report: 'Mr Swoon Bowl Debut Super; What Kids Want'. The writer George Phair noted: 'It all depends on your age and gender. To femmes of fifteen or thereabouts, Frank Sinatra was the darlingest songbird ever heard in the Hollywood Bowl, but to males of voting age he was just another crooner, crooning in the wrong neighbourhood. Most of the 10,000 customers who filled the Bowl to its wartime capacity were adolescent Sinatriacs, ready to shriek, squeal, gurgle or giggle on the slightest provocation while their masculine escorts registered ennui and asked: "How does the guy get away with it?"'

However, Mr Phair saw the problem for the orchestra and how it affected the evening's star. 'There was no swooning in the aisles, probably because the swooners had cooled off while Vladimir Bakaleinikoff and his symphonists struggled bravely but hopelessly to enamour a meadowful of jive addicts with square music under a harvest moon.'

He said that it was when Sinatra sang 'Night and Day' that he 'opened his bag of tricks and great was the gurgling and cooing among his idolaters, each of whom knew that he was singing directly at HER. He sang intimately, personally, like a guy parked with his girl in Lovers Lane, and the Man in the Moon seemed to wear a big round smile as he ogled over the trees in left field.'

His final number that night had them screaming and shouting for more. 'She's Funny That Way', he sang, and five thousand girls wondered whether they were funny that way, too. As the writer noted: 'As he was whisked away by a flock of traffic cops, there was a final chorus of gurgles, mingled with masculine sounds redolent of night-blooming raspberry.'

Not quite true. Sinatra had a fair quotient of male fans, too. They just reacted differently.

When Frank played what the critics called a long-haired venue in Manhattan that year, the reaction was, amazingly, not quite the same. He sang with the New York Philharmonic – but only five thousand fans turned up to hear him, compared with the twelve thousand who, shortly before, had streamed in to hear the coloratura Lily Pons.

Life magazine was less than impressed by the man who usually drew the 'Sinatraffic'. He was, they said, 'plenty upstage and obnoxious at rehearsal. But Sinatra got under the skin of the orchestra even more at the concert.' Not surprisingly. Frank, always ready to show his appreciation, thanked his fans for coming. He was speaking, he said, 'on behalf of myself and the boys in the band'. That was not what you spent years at a music conservatoire for – to be called the boys in the band.

So what was all the fuss about?

One writer described Sinatra as 'the first great bedroom singer of modern times. The first singer to reach the – er – great body of American women.' Frank denied it was sex – just good singing. But there had to be more to it than that, especially when a woman could walk into his dressing room and take off her mink coat – which apart from a blush and a dab of perfume was the only thing she had on that day.

One psychologist dubbed it: 'mammary hyperesthesia', although the owners of the bosoms being thrust out for Frank to sign had no idea there was a name for what they were doing. 'Musical drug,' said another psychologist, joining in the national sport of trying to analyse the Sinatra appeal. 'It's an opium of emotionalism.'

Sometimes, even the girls kept their emotionalism under wraps. In November 1943, he entertained 1,600 girl sailors, the Waves, training at what they called a 'boot-training school' (their version of the men's boot camps) in the Bronx. After the Waves' own band had performed with two uniformed girl singers, Sinatra was announced with the words, 'No announcement – Frank Sinatra'. It was the first time on record that a totally female audience failed to erupt. Frank sang nine songs, all but wooing his audience with 'Where or When', and was sent off with polite applause from 3,200 hands in crisp white gloves. The poor girls had been told to control their emotions – and they didn't think that even Frankie was a good enough reason to be taken to the brig.

It all contributed to the amazing Sinatra story, and there had never been a year in that story like 1943. Truth to tell, there hadn't been many like it in the story of show-business either. Sinatra fever was a new disease, with symptoms ranging from fans signing their letters, 'Yours frankly' and adding a 'FS' instead of a 'PS', to the receiving of huge cheques and a seven-year contract with RKO. It also marked the real start of the Sinatra film career. The otherwise forgettable *Higher and Higher* (the *New York Times* said it should have been called 'Lower and Lower') in which Frank played himself and starring Michele Morgan, the sexy French star, was the first of sixty films which would cover the best part of half a century.

If it was the first film part in which Sinatra got billing, it was to result in what was not his first brush with the law. He was sued for $100,000 in a plagiarism suit which named RKO, the Robbins Music company and the singer Jimmy McHugh. McHugh charged that the film's song, 'The Music Stopped' was a crib of his number, 'You're Mine to Love'. The matter was settled without any publicity.

Radio was still the biggest entertainment medium of the lot. Not content with the *Lucky Strike* programme, Frank had another fifteen minutes to himself in a show that was without a sponsor – plugging anyone else's product would have been in breach of his 'Luckies' contract and he didn't want to get into that one again. The programme, *Songs by Sinatra*, was ready to break all the listening records.

Higher and Higher was followed by another RKO epic, *Step Lively*, which was notable for two principal factors: it was the first movie in which Sinatra played a character other than himself (his part as Glen was of a country bumpkin – as far away from typecasting as you could get for the kid from Hoboken); it was also the movie in which he had his first screen kiss – from Gloria De Haven – a fact duly recorded in the fan magazines, one of which took a double-page spread for a countdown to the big event.

People of a more serious bent were trying to decide what the Sinatra mystique was all about. Again and again the psychologists were wheeled in. Dr Donald A. Laird came to the rescue of those who dearly wanted to know how Sinatra ticked. 'It isn't just his voice, his myriad admirers – mostly feminine – admit,' he told readers of a syndicated column. 'It's his appearance, too, they say, using such expressions as "When he looks at me, I simply swoon", or "His smile sends me right out of this world".'

Dr Laird had his own explanation for it all, particularly why it was the women who loved him and why the men couldn't understand it. 'It is Mr Sinatra's extraordinary good fortune that he looks underfed to a degree that would deceive nearly any doctor into casually diagnosing him as a victim of malnutrition. Actually, this is not true. He is above standard weight for his height, perfectly healthy and something of an athlete.' Well, that was a relief. But the doctor understood all the concern. 'He looks like a starving man, nevertheless – hollow cheeks, feverish eyes, pallid complexion, sunken shoulders and all . . .

'Far, far back in the infancy of the human race, there was implanted in every normal female the instinct to feed and nurture. This a biological urge, as fundamental as reproduction and, under more primitive conditions, equally necessary to the perpetuation of the species.' So that was the reason for it all. But there was another factor, too: 'He is probably equally ignorant of the fact that the yearning, beseeching quality of his voice, almost like the plaintive cry of a hungry child, is an authentic auditory echo of his peculiarly famished appearance.

Frank didn't really need to know any of that. What was more

important was that the girls would continue to swoon and the demands for his services increased with every day. Rarely had an entertainer been so much in demand and without having to sell himself.

Of course, Sinatra PR machine was busy, too, but it didn't have to work terribly hard either. It revealed strange things about him, such as that when he laughed there were five 'ha's' per ten seconds. Nobody took such nonsense seriously – any more than they believed suggestions that he was about to get Lloyd's of London to insure The Voice for $10 million. It was never done.

In fact, Sinatra was as much news as was anything happening in the South Pacific – and a welcome relief to it at that. You couldn't deny that pop stars sold papers – in the 1940s no less than they do now – and Sinatra wasn't any ordinary pop star. When fans rioted because they couldn't get tickets, it was news. If they were egged on a little by the press agent George Evans, well, so be it. Nobody argued, simply because it served both Sinatra and the newspapers' purposes – to say nothing of those of the wire services and the broadcasting organisations.

But squealing was still the thing that got the reporters going. George Evans knew that. After all, it brought Frank a gross income of $1,250,000 in 1944. Wherever the Sinatra operation went, he had girls on hand ready to play the game. Evans wasn't above writing the letters that turned on journalists as much as they would have aroused Frank himself – if he had ever bothered to show them to his client. 'When you hold that microphone, I imagine you are holding me; when your hand slides up and down I think it is my whole body you are caressing,' was one. Others alluded to the possible effect of *their* hands doing the moving.

Girls were no longer satisfied with offering brassieres for signature while they were still wearing them. Now they took their bras off in his presence before saying, 'Sign this for me, Frankie.' Others removed their panties and threw them on the stage. When he sang 'The Song Is You', a dozen teenagers cried out in unison, '*ME?*' Evans had paid them five dollars a piece to do so. It seemed totally unnecessary now, when everybody knew who Sinatra was, but Evans believed that the pot had to be kept boiling.

Nobody doubted that little Nancy was the apple of her daddy's eye. The pictures in the publicity shots and newsreels said it all. There are some things that can't be faked and the sheer adoration of a father for his child is one of them. His relationship with the child's mother was another thing entirely. Those publicity shots seemed to show a man with his mind elsewhere – as it frequently was. Dolly continued to offer her kind of advice about marital honesty but Nancy herself was spotted more than once with tears in her eyes. Frank's answer to it all was to spend less and less time at home, even though touring meant that the days and nights spent in New Jersey were few enough anyway.

Nancy asked George Evans for help. He responded by suggesting that if it were only the most beautiful girls that interested her errant husband, then perhaps it might not be a bad idea for Nancy to take a leaf out of their books and make herself more glamorous. As he reasoned, she could afford it. So he had the best designers come and rework her wardrobe and the costliest beauticians to do the same with her face. No doubt, too, with the aid of some equally expensive corsetry, she posed for Sinatra-at-home pictures and agreed to interviews as the supportive wife. She was transformed. The papers liked it. Frank liked it. But the stories of his extramarital activities continued to circulate, although a much more restrained press than the one in business today kept its distance.

The fans, however, didn't. They thronged round the Lawrence Avenue bungalow in Hasbrouck Heights, like, wrote one observer at the time, 'a marine attack on Okinawa'. It was all much to the annoyance of the neighbours, who might well have been the same people lining up outside the Paramount yet didn't want any dramas on their own doorsteps. The police provided a twenty-four-hour guard outside the seven-room home to keep things under control. That hadn't happened for a pop singer before either.

All that didn't stop two girls breaking into the house in the hope of catching Frank and Nancy in their bedroom. They were out for the night, so the bobbysoxers contented themselves with removing a stack of their idol's fan mail. But what really worried the Sinatras was that someone would try to make them the centre of a Lindbergh-type kidnap. What happened instead was that the fans got close enough to the house to scrawl their own kind of graffiti all over the white-painted woodwork. It was quite decent stuff, compared with what might have appeared in the 1990s. One girl scribbled in indelible pencil around the front-door latch: 'This is the lock to my heart.' Others were less poetic. On the walls they wrote: 'Frankie, we love you.' But verse was the most popular means of expression. One young lady of obviously tender years scrawled: 'Oh Frankie, How You can

Sing. Oh Frankie, Oh Frankie, You're Better than Bing.' The *pièce de resistance* was probably this: 'Give Us Frankie, Is Our Plea; For Frankie, Frankie Brings Us Glee!' It wasn't long before the white-painted walls of the house were covered in lipstick.

People worried about Frank's ever more skinny frame. Yet he ate huge meals – big steaks, sometimes more than once a day. It wasn't because of wartime restrictions that he still looked like a skeleton who forgot it shouldn't still be breathing. 'You gotta eat to belt those numbers out,' he said. And that was another of the Sinatra achievements that wasn't always given its true recognition: it never looked as though he were belting anything out. You didn't know how hard he was working to make things seem easy.

The Sinatra family was increasing. Nancy gave birth to a second baby and, as if it were made to order, the way everything else in Sinatra's life now was, it was a boy. A publicist's dream had come to life – especially when the couple called the child Frank, Jr., and Nancy was seen in newspapers throughout the world holding the little one in his white shawl next to a photograph of his father.

Frank himself was in California at the time. Nancy was less than happy about that, although this time there were no stories about his being in bed with a starlet when he heard the news of the birth. Instead he had a new film about to go into production and even the arrival of Frank, Jr., couldn't be allowed to interrupt schedules. Of course the company could have done without him so early on in the production and he could have flown home, but he chose not to ask them to do so.

Did that mean that he and Nancy were finished? Dolly and her Catholic beliefs wouldn't allow any such talk. Even so, the word was that the new baby had been conceived as a means of keeping the Sinatras together, and the strains were palpable to people who knew the couple. Yet the publicity machine cranked on and when Frank returned home, the cameras were there to record the event. The fan magazines published the usual stories of the Sinatras at rest and all looked well with their world.

He did come home for Frankie's christening (forever after, in the family, the child would always be *the* Frankie) but it ended in a huge row. Frank stormed out of the church when the priest wouldn't allow his friend Manie Sachs to be the godfather because he was a Jew. Once again, the Sinatra phobia about racial prejudice came to the fore and wouldn't be thwarted, even on an intensely happy family day.

It was all smoothed out. Sachs said he understood. But Nancy was unhappy and angry about the way things were going with their marriage, although she managed to keep her counsel. It was the year of D-Day and a virtual blackout of information on the number of troops being shipped overseas only heightened the anxieties of those left at home. The invasion of France was on everybody's lips – yet Sinatra continued to make his fortune attracting ever larger crowds to ever more expensive and fashionable venues. 'I think Frank Sinatra was the most hated man of World War II,' said the eminent writer William Manchester. He was kind enough to exclude Adolf Hitler from his list, but said that men who hadn't seen a comely female for years tended to resent all those pictures of Frank and the girls. It was probably an understatement.

One writer asked, bitingly: 'Is crooning essential?' It was a rhetorical question because everyone knew the answer – although George Evans might have tried to prove that Frank was an indispensable part of the campaign aimed at raising the country's morale. That would have nicely ignored, of course, the morale of the troops who, in the hell and mud of war zones, were not in the least comforted by the news that their loved ones were making unspeakable offers to the young Mr Sinatra.

'Go and sing to the boys,' people suggested. Frank said he would – and still did nothing. The truth was, he was afraid of the reaction he would get. Newspaper headlines continued to refer to the trouble. One report, emphasising the unchanging situation, was headed: 'Sinatra, 1-A With US Girls, Rated 4-F by Army Doctors.'

On the bobbysoxers, it was having no effect whatsoever. The girls of 1944 weren't much interested in what was happening overseas, once they knew that their fathers or their sweethearts were safe. Sinatra didn't let it worry him either. But Mr Lee Mortimer, a columnist on the New York *Mirror*, had begun a vendetta against him which was deadly in its intensity. If it hadn't been so serious, the row could have been the subject of jokes. But this wasn't Hope–Crosby, Benny–Allen stuff. The venom in the attacks on Sinatra for cowardice – a charge first levelled in the army newspaper, *Stars and Strips* – made The Voice's blood boil. The feud would get worse and more violent as the years went by.

In fact, it was the beginning of a relationship between Sinatra and journalists which at its best resembled that between a German shepherd dog and a mountain cat. Humphrey Bogart was to put the situation like this: 'Sinatra's idea of paradise is a place where there are plenty of women and no newspapermen. He doesn't know it, but he'd be better off if it were the other way round.'

The declared war between Frank and the fourth estate increased in intensity with another suggestion from the Republican press – that Frank was a Communist. That, said George Evans, was why Frank wasn't going abroad to entertain the troops. The Government wouldn't let him go. It was, of course, nonsense, but it let him off one hook while impaling him on another. Then came yet another source of controversy: the President and Frank started appearing in the same news stories.

It turned out that Roosevelt was a Sinatra fan – or so he said. So would the singer like to come up to Washington for a cup of tea? At a stroke, Frank was seen both by the vast majority as America's most patriotic entertainer and by the reactionaries in the Hearst press as precisely the left-wing troublemaker they had always said he was. And that went for the President, too.

More relevant was the fact that Robert E. Hannegan, the Democratic National Chairman, was a Sinatra fan. Or perhaps it was because, within sight of the next presidential election, he knew the value of FDR being able to show that he had Sinatra's support. Whether Frank realised it or not, this not only made sound political sense, it was the biggest accolade he could possibly receive – the President *needed* him. If Roosevelt, the commander-in-chief, gave him his seal of approval, there couldn't be much doubt about his patriotism and his contribution to the war effort, could there? Even if the bobby-soxers didn't have votes, their parents did, and it all helped to create an image of a decent guy, fighting not just a war but also the wicked tyrants of Wall Street represented by governor Thomas E. Dewey who was going to be the President's Republican opponent.

It was probably the speediest 'engagement' ever arranged for Frank. He and the comedian 'Rags' Ragland were having dinner with Toots Shor at Shor's famous nightclub in New York, when Hannegan stopped by their table and invited all three to have tea with the President at the White House the next day. It was not an invitation to be spurned.

Afterwards, the biggest crowd of the Washington press corps to gather in years was on hand to fire questions. No, said Frank, the President hadn't asked him to sing, although he did want a few tips on dealing with audiences. 'He kidded me about the art of how to make girls faint,' he said. Then he revealed that the President, always anxious to be familiar with the important new currents in world affairs, asked him what was top of the hit parade. The fact that he knew there was such a thing was meant to convey the impression that, despite his crippled legs and the pressures of the war, he was still pretty hep. Sinatra told him it was 'Amapola'. 'He thought I was talking Italian,' Frank explained.

But the political overtones of it all were obvious. Was Sinatra going to support Roosevelt's bid for a record-breaking fourth term? Frank, who had started breaking enough records himself, said he was. Why? He thought about that one. 'Well,' he opined profoundly, 'you might say I'm in favour of it.'

It was an opportunity to take swipes at both Frank and the President, who despite his landslide win in 1940 and the predictions that he would do even better in November 1944, was never popular with certain sections of the Republican Party, notably the arch-Conservatives and the isolationists. He was even less popular with the reactionary strain, who were able to blame Frank Sinatra for the underhand way in which Roosevelt was running the country – to say nothing of the election campaign. Their charges were even more severe after the night Frank seemed to sabotage an election meeting. He casually walked in front of the crowd while Governor Dewey was speaking outside Manhattan's Waldorf Astoria Hotel. Within seconds the singer was spotted and the candidate was left with just a handful of hard-core supporters. The Republicans didn't like that at all, so they used Sinatra as a weapon against the man in the White House whenever they could. In Congress, they attacked the President for wasting valuable wartime in talking to a singer of no great consequence. In the Republican press, Sinatra was dubbed the 'New Deal crooner' – in their eyes, there was little that could be more insulting.

Frank thought it was the greatest compliment of them all. The President, he said, was 'the greatest guy alive today and here's this little guy from Hoboken shaking his hand'. He made a hefty donation to Democratic Party funds and in return the President signed on to join the Frank Sinatra fan club. It was as though Franklin Delano Roosevelt had run a one-man Sinatra PR campaign. What he did for his own image seemed highly irrelevant – particularly to those kids who wouldn't have known if he were a Democrat or a Republican and didn't understand the difference, anyway.

When the Democratic Party organised a huge rally at Madison

Square Garden – and in those pre-television days, the Madison Square Garden rallies were attended by as many people as usually attended the world-title fights there – Frank was on the platform, singing the President's praises, but in a speech as well as a song. Roosevelt, said Sinatra, was good for him as he was for all the kids of America. There were no hecklers. Nobody asked him why he wasn't in uniform and he left feeling every bit as excited as when he sang at one of his more usual gigs. He didn't mind not being the star of the evening, he said – although that was precisely what he was. Secretly he probably enjoyed being away from the bobbysoxers for a night and not having any bras and panties thrown his way. There would be plenty more occasions for that to happen.

Sinatra now used all the PR tricks known to man. There were constantly people on hand to help him. Some who knew the way he worked called them his stooges. Frank called them the 'Varsity'. They were ever ready to deny the less flattering stories which newspapermen wanted to print, they hustled him out of restaurants when he had too much to drink, and when the fans got too enthusiastic, they held them back. They weren't an early version of what was to become 'the Clan', or the Rat Pack. These were gatherings of equals although there was no question who was Chairman of the Board, even if they didn't call him that. It was his jokes they laughed at – and they always did.

Nancy didn't think much of them. Like many another wife in her position, she regarded them all as rivals, almost as the 'other women' – except that there always were other women, not least of them the ones sitting in the stalls screaming to hear their idol sing 'How About You?' She began divorce proceedings and was told not to have intercourse with her husband again. She even said she would change the locks on her doors to make sure it didn't happen – a 1940s version of the chastity belt. She did change the locks – but then didn't use them. The trouble was she loved her Frank still. She backed down and dismissed the notion of separation, let alone divorce.

— 5 —

MELODY OF LOVE

Wherever Sinatra went now, he was mobbed not just by crowds, but by managements trying to lure him into their nets.

His appearance at the Paramount in October 1944 was even more unruly than his previous seasons there. This time, Bob Weitman wanted to clear the house between performances, but the publicity and the huge picture of The Voice outside the theatre announcing his appearance 'In Person' with the movie *Our Hearts Were Young and Gay* had brought all the crowds he might have expected. The five thousand girls inside refused to leave and in the end the police were called. New York historians have recorded the event as the Columbus Day Riots.

Even the Board of Education got involved. They instituted an inquiry into how 25,000 shrieking schoolgirls turned out at 4 a.m. to queue for the opening of the show at the Times Square Theatre. They were all in breach of the curfew for juveniles and, said George H. Chatfield, a member of the board, 'We don't want this thing to go on. We can't tolerate young people making a public display of losing control of their emotions.'

There was talk of Sinatra being arraigned before the nearest judge. The demos led to truancy, Chatfield said, 'and if we can find anyone encouraging truancy we can prosecute them directly. If there is evidence of that, we will do so.' Altogether, a hundred policemen, twenty policewomen and a group of plainclothesmen from the Juvenile Aid Bureau were involved in the investigations. Meanwhile, Columbia University's professor of psychology, Henry E. Garrett, exonerated Sinatra himself. The girls were victims of 'mass hysteria', he said.

Frank's appearances in New York were fewer now. The new status of Sinatra required status symbols – which was why he and the family had moved to the West Coast. There, he immediately set about joining Lakeside, one of the swankiest clubs in Los Angeles. The place which had a roster of some of the most successful stars in Hollywood – it was the club where Errol Flynn would go to get drunk and laid (in that order) between the unfortunate necessity of working at nearby Warner Bros. But Lakeside didn't like Jews and banned them from its membership.

It was a well-known fact that clubs were very snooty in the film capital – the Los Angeles country club refused to allow anybody with show-business connections to join, although they did make an exception over Fred Astaire. When Frank found out about Lakeside, he handed in his resignation and joined a Jewish club, Hillcrest. He was only the second gentile member of the club, which had some of the world's greatest entertainers sitting at their 'round table' for lunch every day – Al Jolson, Eddie Cantor, George Burns, Milton Berle – along with producers and directors who went there to play golf and eat matzo ball soup. Hillcrest had been set up simply because Jews couldn't get in anywhere else. But they had their revenge. Soon after establishing the luxury club on some of the lushest greens in California – the members could only get in if they pledged a certain annual sum to charity – they struck oil close to the fairway.

Sinatra was at home in a place where he was as warmly welcomed for his stand against anti-Semitism as had been the only other non-Jewish member, Darryl F. Zanuck, earlier on. He was more at home, some said, than at the house where he supposedly lived with Nancy and their children at Valley Spring Lane in the San Fernando Valley – a homestead once owned by Mary Astor, which could boast the Bob Hopes as neighbours.

There was a less happy experience in store for the man who bought the Sinatras' old house in New Jersey, a Mr Paul Ragona. On the day he moved in, the New York jeweller opened the door to a young lady who flung her arms around his neck, kissed him wildly and murmured softly, 'I love you darling. Sing to me, my sweet.'

The Sinatra publicity machine was in full flow now. Magazines featured pages of pictures of the Sinatra career, like the strips in a comic book. Except that there was nothing comic about this rise. Frank was going up and up and the scenes demonstrated it, giving boxer Tami Mauriello a piggyback one moment, entertaining the two Nancys in his life at the Stork Club the next. (Nancy, Jr., may not have had a happy home as far as relations between her parents were concerned, but she certainly was shown the high life). Three-year-old Nancy was seen being introduced to the slightly older Margaret

O'Brien, hailed as the new Shirley Temple, and pictures of Nancy, Sr., were captioned 'His best girl'.

Sinatra now broadcast his radio programme *Your Hit Parade* from the West Coast. He paid out of his own pocket the weekly studio rental payment to the orchestra and the necessary landline, which came to a total of $4,800. He could afford it, even if the sum was $2,000 a week more than he was being paid to do the show.

The reporter Walter Winchell announced that Frank was now the richest entertainer in the world, which was quite a change for the fellow who, not so long before, had thought $125 per week a fortune (which for most people it was). What made Frank so fabulously wealthy was a contract with MGM worth $1.5 million. That meant Sinatra was now in the exalted company of stars like Joan Crawford, Greer Garson, Judy Garland and, most significantly, Gene Kelly.

Once more, it was a case of meeting the right person at the right time. This time it was a meeting with Louis B. Mayer that did the trick. Mayer, who wept when he heard he had won a horse race, cried his eyes out at a Jewish Home for the Aged benefit. Nancy, Jr., says it was because he was so moved to hear her father's version of 'Ol' Man River' in which for the first time a performer had refused to use the word 'niggers'. Mayer vowed to bring him over to his studio. It was a promise kept and one that benefited them both enormously. Sinatra and MGM, the studio whose initials could have stood for Makers of Great Musicals, seemed to be the ideal combination.

Like almost everyone else connected with him, Sinatra was able to ignore the peccadilloes of Louis B. and appreciate his artistic integrity. He also appreciated the fact that the respect he and the other stars had for Mayer was by way of being a mutual admiration society. The mogul himself was essentially a very good businessman. But he ran the business like a benevolent chainstore proprietor who thought it necessary to cater for the welfare of the men and women behind the counter. His stars were earning salaries a thousand and more times higher than the average shop assistant, but the principle was the same. As Frank was to say about the studio: 'It was like a womb.' Mayer himself was nothing less than a genius.

Being part of the MGM circus certainly confirmed Sinatra's position in show business. After *Reveille with Beverly*, *Higher and Higher* and *Step Lively*, it couldn't have happened at a better time. Suddenly, he was in a different class of film altogether. MGM didn't just have the best stars but also the best directors, the best sets (with a predominance of white to match LB's office furnishings) and, above all, the best music. The Metro orchestra could match the finest philharmonic ensemble in the land and, indeed, was often called the MGM Symphony. And now this most prestigious studio of them all was going to feature him in one of the most notable musicals of the war years, *Anchors Aweigh*.

This film was everything MGM wanted it to be – not least an introduction to a decent story and the courage to co-star Frank against a young man who had already proved his worth to the studio, the star of *Cover Girl*, Gene Kelly. From the moment the two young men in white sailor suits got together, everything looked wonderful – until, that is, Frank decided he had to show who was boss.

He was becoming fed up with the regimen of a film star, getting up early in the morning, taking direction and being part of a double act. He didn't quite say, 'Who do they think I am? Don't they know I'm the most important star in the world?' But he thought it. His trouble was that he thought it out loud – and to pressmen.

To most everyone's amazement – including that of George Evans, the ever loyal press agent – Sinatra said he was through with movies. 'Pictures stink. Most of the people in them do, too. I don't want to do any more movie-acting. Hollywood won't believe I'm through, but they'll find out I mean it.' He was biting the hand that was feeding him a veritable fortune, to say nothing of keeping his name before a public who might not otherwise have been too concerned about a singer who wowed the girls in bobbysox.

Frank was forced to issue a retraction. He wasn't denying he had said it, but he was ready to apologise. 'It's easy for a guy to get hot under the collar, literally and figuratively, when he's dressed in a hot suit of navy blues and the temperature is one hundred and four degrees and he's getting over a cold to boot.'

For reasons best explained by the need to wrap up an expensive movie, Hollywood forgave him and got ready to weigh their own anchor on production. Two young women from the MGM stable, Kathryn Grayson and Pamela Britton, had important roles in the film, but the stars were the two men. It was to be the first of two movies Sinatra and Kelly made together, playing sailors on leave. Kelly was the bright, sophisticated one, Sinatra the unsure, bashful young man let loose in the big city – with the improbable but no doubt appropriate-sounding name of Clarence Doolittle.

By producing the picture, Joe Pasternak paid both men two

compliments – the first that he knew they could withstand the risk of comparison, the second that each one complemented the other. Kelly was the superb dancer, for the first time being compared with Astaire, with a light lyrical voice that could hold a tune with charming ease; Sinatra was the man who attracted more people around him than virtually anyone since the Nuremberg rallies, singing his heart out – and for the first time dancing a time step.

Early on Frank asked his co-star what he thought of his stepping out. Kelly told him: 'You may have set dancing back twenty years.' But that didn't matter to the man Jimmy Durante called 'Moonlight Sinatra'. In any case, Kelly didn't really mean it. 'I have to say I didn't know he could do it,' Kelly told me twenty years ago, at a time when both men talked about retirement and then decided they were going to do no such thing. 'I showed him the steps and he copied me. I taught him when to join in and he joined in. It was the same technique he used to sing. It was his timing.'

Kelly was perhaps even more right than he realised. But he wouldn't have suggested that Frank do any dancing at all if he had not been assured by other people that he could do it. He asked Sammy Cahn if he thought Frank could manage the steps. Cahn replied: 'Of course, he can do anything.' 'Frank was born bright,' Kelly concluded.

Really, it was all merely a recognition of each other's talents. 'I didn't get him to do anything that was beyond his capacity,' Gene later said. 'I couldn't sing like him, control my breathing that way.' In that, Gene was doing himself a disservice. Dancing requires breath-control every bit as much as singing does. Here Frank was phrasing with his feet. No small achievement for one who had never done anything like it before – let alone doing it on screen.

They got on well together on screen and off, with Frank getting most of the vocal honours. When they sang 'She Finally Got Her Kiss' they made a fine double act. Gene sang: 'She threatened ...' Frank came back with: 'And he's got muscles, too.'

The songs by Jule Styne and Sammy Cahn played a huge part in the film's success. The fact that they did was entirely Sinatra's own doing. MGM had wanted to use one of the 'tried' composers who were as important in those days as the stars who sang their work: Irving Berlin, Jerome Kern or that stunning new partnership of Rodgers and Hammerstein, whose *Oklahoma!* had been a bigger hit than any of them could have imagined.

Sinatra said he wanted Cahn and Styne. Sammy Cahn told me the story: 'It was one of the truly, truly memorable moments in my life and my first welcome to the decision that Frank Sinatra was one of the great people of this world. He told MGM that he wanted me and they said they didn't. Frank refused to budge, so filming was about to be put off. They even came to *me* to persuade him *not* to use me. And, believe it or not, I agreed. I said I'm sure we can work together some other time, let's give it a miss. Frank said, "Be there Monday." '

On Monday, Sammy Cahn and Jule Styne turned up at the MGM lot in Culver City and Frank and Gene were ready to start work. Pasternak never said another word, and neither did Louis B. Mayer. It was the first time that audiences heard what before long became a Frank standard, 'I Fall in Love Too Easily' – which a lot of Sinatra's friends thought he did.

Gene Kelly had a greater achievement to his credit. An even better dancing partner for him in the movie was a mouse. Jerry, the rodent in the Tom and Jerry cartoons, was made to dance with him in a scene that has become one of the most memorable in the history of the musical film.

An event close to the set of *Anchors Aweigh* turned into something equally memorable in movie history: the first-recorded serious Sinatra bust-up with a producer. Frank decided he wanted to see what his work had been like, so he said he was coming along the next day to see the rushes – or the 'dailies' as they are called now, the rough, unedited work shot twenty-four hours previously. Pasternak said there were studio rules about such things and the answer would have to be no – except ... except he would make an exception in Sinatra's case because he knew how much he was trying to make a brand new Hollywood career for himself and he would undoubtedly benefit from any lessons that the rushes provided. There was one condition: he would have to come alone. This was a privilege Pasternak didn't want to see abused or publicised too much.

The next day Frank turned up in the viewing theatre with six people. Pasternak told him they had to go. 'They go – and I go,' said Frank in so many words. 'I'll walk off the picture.'

The producer told him that could be a good idea – knowing full well how much the studio had invested in Sinatra's part and the phenomenal cost involved in reshooting his scenes with another actor. But there were rules that had to be obeyed and it was at least worth trying to call the star's bluff. It worked. Sinatra walked – and came back the next day. He needed the picture for his career's sake as much as MGM needed to have him in tow.

It was not the only backstage story circulating at the time. Another had it – and there have been witnesses testifying to the fact – that Sinatra stuck a list on his dressing-room wall containing the names of the available Hollywood actresses with whom he might deign to have an affair. At the top of the list was the name of Lana Turner, working on a picture of her own at MGM at the time, and recently divorced.

Yet another story could well have been manoeuvred by his publicity office. This, too concerned a list – but one that was pinned to the outside of his dressing-room door. This one was signed by Gene Kelly and the entire cast of the movie. It said solemnly: 'We the undersigned and those who know him well know that Frank's head-size is normal and that his hat will continue to fit.'

What was even more significant about *Anchors Aweigh* was that this was the first Sinatra vehicle that was given as much exploitation overseas as in the United States. RKO had never really bothered with sales in Britain, for instance – with the result that Frank was still a relatively unknown quantity to British audiences. They were beginning to hear about him now on the various American radio shows aired by the BBC for the benefit of GIs stationed in England before sailing for the invasion of Europe, but his own show was never broadcast in Britain and almost nobody had seen him.

The new picture meant that all this was to change. Writing in *Picturegoer* magazine, W. H. Mooring took up that point, but showed little enthusiasm for the newcomer: '... MGM decided that the boy had something besides a mediocre singing voice, and ... I'm saying quite openly that that is about all he has as a vocalist.'

Mr Mooring had met Sinatra. He said he found him 'an inoffensive but entirely uninspiring fellow with an extremely frail sense of humour'. Moreover, 'I once heard him sing "Ol' Man River" much better than I'd ever heard him croon anything before, but I resented him all the more because he fell so far short of Paul Robeson, yet received so much more applause from an American audience.' Neither did he think much of the Sinatra reputation. 'During his first days as a screen celebrity over at RKO he was so altogether touchy everybody said his fame had gone to his head. He seemed to have a chip on his shoulder all the time and took himself so seriously it gave one a pain.'

It was an amazingly prescient judgment, although at that time things looked as if they were changing for the better on that front. As Mooring said, *Anchors Aweigh* was turning Frank Sinatra into a happier, nicer individual. 'They have developed his ability as an actor – and he has some, as you will agree when you see *Anchors Aweigh* – until he is something much more important to the screen than a mere crooner.'

There was a totally happy working relationship between the two male stars. Frank sat in a deck-chair with the words 'The Voice' on the back. Gene Kelly sat in one that declared, 'The Feet'. The MGM publicity machine, the smartest in Hollywood, liked that a lot. But what they liked most of all was the image they had created for this waif of a singer – of Frank as the little man who needed to be mothered.

Yet this was a man who already made hardbitten guys around the Los Angeles nightspots quake. He had his own bodyguard – a man who had previously trained heavyweight boxers. One night after tussling with a group of fans, he told Frank: 'The heavyweights fight cleaner.' The bodyguard was known to become the heavy himself when he believed it necessary to do so and lawyers didn't get into fights with him without thinking over the proposition very carefully. In case anyone decided to become a little too friendly, there was a ten-foot-high wall around Sinatra's California home now.

The function of that wall was to keep out the various people with whom Frank had been associated during his career but it did not do a perfect job. One of Frank's visitors was his old sparring partner Buddy Rich, who had just come out of the forces and now had ambitions to start his own band. With all the *chutzpah* that he had displayed in the past, he told Frank that the only thing stopping him was the start-up cash. 'How much do you need?' Sinatra asked him. 'Forty thousand,' said Rich as casually as he might have called for the title of Frank's next number. Sinatra wrote him a cheque for the precise amount he said he needed there and then.

Now that might have been a good deed, or else one of those strange cases of the Jekyll and Hyde syndrome which associates of Sinatra knew so well – the heavy with the heart of gold. The trouble was that Buddy and Frank were not alone when the no-strings cheque was signed. Fred Tamby, from the Hoboken Four days, was there as well. Tamby had had a bust-up with Frank shortly before and recovered to tell the tale. And a strange tale it was. That, too, stemmed from what Sinatra undoubtedly thought was a good deed.

He knew that Tamby was experiencing hard times and asked him to come and talk about the possibility of a job. Naturally, Tamby jumped. Despite the fraught relationship they had experienced in the Hoboken Four days, Sinatra was showing that he could be big enough to forget their differences. When Tamby met The Voice – a man he believed had no more talent than any of the other members of their group – Sinatra told him about the job he had in mind. Frank needed a valet. 'Me, shining your shoes and getting your shirts?' Tamby asked, crestfallen and insulted. 'Me?'

Tamby stormed out, as hurt as if he had been called an Irishman. But he had to put his pride in his pocket and on the day Rich called to see Frank he came, too. Now his sights were somewhat lower. He was giving up show business and had decided to open a saloon. All the finance had been organised – or so he thought – until his bank decided that he wasn't a sound enough risk and pulled out. Could Frank help? All he needed was $5,000 – a drop in the Atlantic Ocean, he was sure, to the millionaire entertainer who, when the chips were down, wouldn't forget an old 'friend'. Sinatra was less encouraging than Tamby imagined he would be. 'Sorry,' he said. 'Not in my line.' Or words to that effect.

The putative tavern-owner might have reluctantly taken no for an answer had Rich not knocked on the Sinatra dressing-room door at the precise moment when the wound was at its most raw. When Tamby heard Frank say yes to a request for eight times the amount he had asked for he saw red. He got the near-skeletal fellow townsman up against the wall and looked ready to knock his expensively capped teeth out of his head.

Frank managed to get loose and called the police. Then he thought better of it and told them not to come after all. Remembering that time – how could he forget it? – Tamby later said: 'He knew how it would look if his old partner was arrested for beating on him.' And he added: 'I can't understand why this man never helped me. I'm not the best singer in the world, but I'm not the worst. I asked him to let me use his name for a year – to travel up and down the country and bill myself as Sinatra's original partner.'

It was a surprising thought – that Frank would ever agree to such a thing – but Tamby said he *was* surprised when Sinatra told him: 'No dice. No way.' To Tamby it was all symptomatic of Sinatra's uneasy relationship with Hoboken. People never saw him in his old town any more, and as Tamby commented: 'A lot of people in this town hate him because he made it big.'

Johnny Marotta says today that Sinatra did go home quite frequently. 'But it was always just to see his father when he was in the hospital or to his mother's house at 909 Hudson Street. But no one ever knew he was there. I knew he came because my brother lived in the same building. But when Frank came it was always in a black car after dark when nobody knew he was coming. How he got away with it, I don't know, but somehow he did.'

He got away with it to the extent that no one ever saw the bobbysoxers outside the house. If word had got out once, the place would have been mobbed night and day. The fact that it wasn't was once more due to the success of George Evans's publicity operation. He decided when the fans would know their idol was about – even, on a couple of occasions, arranging for ambulances to be on hand to scoop up the fainting mob, and telling the newspapers about it at the same time, of course.

It wouldn't have looked at all good for those ambulances to have been stationed in what certain sections of the media might have decided was one of the less salubrious corners of New Jersey. The fans wanted their idol to be seen as the great American success, living the plush life either in Los Angeles or, when he was in the east, at the Waldorf Astoria. It didn't fit his image to be associated with Hoboken, the kind of place even the fans wanted to get away from.

New York was different. Around this time, Frank was spreading the word – whenever his opinion was asked – that it was his favourite city, possibly because of all the protection that was offered him by the local police when they thought he needed it. They were there in force after a small boy spotted him going into a tiny Italian restaurant in Brooklyn, just for a plate of spaghetti. By the time the Sinatra party – Frank and a couple of pals -had left, a thousand people were gathering outside.

It was a frequently repeated story. Once in Little Italy, outside another restaurant, a crowd estimated at three thousand got into a tangle with fifty policemen sent along to keep things quiet. 'Don't leave,' the police told him. 'We couldn't be sure of getting you out safely.' Eventually, they broke a basement window and hoisted him into the alley outside, where a taxi was waiting to spirit him away. On another occasion, about twenty even keener Sinatra enthusiasts jumped all over the car as it sped away towards Grand Central Station, while one of them ran to the nearest Western Union office to send a telegram to a friend in California to say that Frankie was on his way to the West Coast.

To a lot of people he was taking it all for granted. But when pressed, he would try to analyse his phenomenal success. 'It was the war years and there was a great loneliness. And I was the boy in every corner drugstore.' That was always too easy an answer. The girls who mobbed him wouldn't have swooned over the boy from the corner drugstore. He had that amazing combination working for him – the kid who liked to be mothered with a voice that seemed to shout: 'I want to take YOU to bed.'

It was an extraordinarily potent sexual formula. As Paul Bowles wrote in the *New York Herald Tribune*: 'He sings harmless Tin Pan Alley tunes to a chorus of hysterical feminine voices synchronising their screams as he closes his eyes and moves his body sideways.'

The boy-next-door theory took a drubbing from Sinatra's own further justification for what he did. He was, he said, the boy 'who'd gone off, drafted to the war'. It was a terribly tactless thing to say about himself when he had so blatantly not been drafted to the war. Troops away on active service might have been grateful if he *had* simply been the fellow in the drugstore: then they need not have worried about the kind of active service in which he was engaged while they ran the risk of getting their heads blown off. Most of his audiences seemed not in the least concerned, however.

When it came to polls of fans, Bing Crosby was usually the winner. In 1945 Sinatra was tops – winning 571,978 votes in one poll to Crosby's 533,211. It was all meaningless, but contributed to keeping the Sinatra name in front of the public.

Yet, despite the success and despite what those more intimately connected with Sinatra knew about him, to most of the public he was still the skinny little guy who was not just remaining a civilian, but one who was extraordinarily vulnerable. When he made a movie he portrayed that corn-chewing boy from the farm country, the one totally dazzled by the bright lights of the big city. He decided that he wanted to change that image every bit as much as he wanted to sing those soulful ballads. But he wasn't complaining about the bobby-soxers' behaviour, even if what he said made him seem as innocent as the scripts of those early movies. 'I don't know how that happened,' he said at the time. 'They must have written from one town to another. We just can't account for the spread in any other way.'

If you believed that, you could believe that he had never enjoyed a pizza in his life. He was the most publicised star in the history of entertainment – so much so that *Billboard* awarded George Evans their prize for the Most Effective Promotion of a Single Personality.

Sometimes, Evans saw it as his duty simply to regale the media with stories of Frank's purely professional activities – like the time he persuaded Manie Sacks to allow him to conduct an orchestra. Old hands still talk of the day he made the album *Frank Sinatra Conducts Alec Wilder* – with both the singer and the composer getting equal billing at Frank's insistence. Sacks was to say: 'Here were all these symphony cats sitting around with their Stradivarius fiddles and goatees when Frank walks in, mounts the platform just like Stokowski and raps for attention with the little stick. The musicians didn't know what to make of it.'

There was a professional conductor standing by, but he wasn't needed. Sinatra did, however, say that he needed assistance and wanted to help the music. Sacks prepared a series of indications for him – where the violins came in, when the soloists were to perform. When it was over, all those serious symphony cats applauded. Goddard Lieberson, the most respected name on the Columbia roster – he was the head of the Masterworks Division and the inspiration of some of the greatest classical conductors – wrote the sleeve notes to go with the album.

There were other people who simply knew Frank as a good friend. When he liked people, he did everything he could for them – like ensuring that Sammy Cahn and Jule Styne got the songwriting work in *Anchors Aweigh*. Others he just appreciated because he thought they were nice people and didn't want any work from them in return. He took to distributing gold cigarette lighters worth $150 each to those 'nice guys'. Every one was inscribed either 'Frankie' – to a close friend, if he thought that was appropriate – or just 'Frank' if the gift was a more mundane thank-you. Today, these would be collectors' items worth thousands of dollars.

But another kind of Sinatra collection was becoming noteworthy – the press clippings full of allegations about Frank's connections with the Communist Party and alluding to the possible link with what was claimed to be his draft-dodging. One of those constantly finding reasons to make the association was the right-wing Hearst journalist, Westbrook Pegler.

Mention Pegler's name and Sinatra would burn up as though he had suddenly been infected with a pernicious new strain of malaria. When he heard that the writer was at the Waldorf Astoria Hotel in New York when he himself was appearing there in cabaret, the temperature raced off the scale. He threatened the management with an ultimatum: 'Either get Pegler out or I won't sing.' They said they couldn't do that. So Frank had to think of new tactics. He resolved to find a means of annoying him – and discovered the ideal way. He knew that Pegler would be in the audience when he performed. He also knew that the hotel had a rule which said nobody could be seated once the entertainment had started.

Just as Frank was due to go on, he arranged for Pegler to be called away to a supposedly important telephone call. Naturally, there was no one there – but Pegler was away long enough for Frank to start singing and was not allowed to take his seat until the show was over. Pegler responded by dragging up the old story of Frank's arrest for seducing a young woman back in 1938, without mentioning that he had been cleared of the charge.

The journalist was asked to point out that the 'romance' resulted in the Sinatra name being untarnished: he did – and added that most decent young Americans would never have got involved with that kind of 'dame' in the first place. The fire of antagonism was burning and the only way to douse it was to keep the two men apart. Thanks to the work of George Evans, Frank kept out of the journalist's way even when Pegler tried to contrive means of their getting together.

The charges of links between Sinatra and Communism went on and on. Before long, Frank was challenging the whole process of rooting out reds from under Hollywood beds. Of Joseph McCarthy's House Committee on Un-American Activities, he was unequivocal. 'Once they get the movies throttled, how long will it be before the committee gets to work on freedom of the air?' he asked. 'If you make a pitch on a nationwide radio network for a square deal for the underdog, will they call you a Commie?' When he used the word 'Commie' he probably thought that it served to distance himself from those suggestions by Pegler and Mortimer that he was a party member or, at least, a party supporter. 'I'm as Communistic as Winston Churchill,' he said in April 1947, 'and how long can you stand picking up a newspaper and reading that you're a Commie, without getting sore?'

The feud with Pegler was real. One with Bing Crosby was invented. Spike Jones, he of the crazy City Slickers, thought it would be a good idea to concoct another of those show-business rivalry rows between them. When Crosby was in hospital, Jones sent him a bedpan – with Frankie's picture inside. Bing thought it distasteful and guessed it was simply a Jones publicity stunt – so there were no takers for his idea. In truth, both singers had a remarkable respect for each other's talents.

But Crosby's talent was dangerous – dangerously successful. In 1945 he beat Frank to the top spot in a second chart, to the extent that *Variety* said he was 'the hottest guy in showbiz today'. So The Voice tried to expand his output. He wanted to see results for his efforts. 'I'm no damn freak,' he said once. 'I've worked. Nobody's worked harder.'

He worked hard, too, at dealing with those fans. One followed him to Brooklyn Armory, where he went to register again for the draft, carrying a heart-shaped box of chocolates. When he left the building in driving rain, she rushed towards him – and was held back by military policemen who managed to push Sinatra into an army car (he had certain privileges). When the car drove off, the girl was still holding on to the sodden box, all the chocolates inside as crushed as she felt herself.

The Army, it was clear, were not going to call him yet. The news hardly broke his heart, but it did mean that he had to look again to his professional work and the material he was using. He wanted more ballads to sing, to get into the soul of what a composer intended. 'I don't click with the slick chicks or the hep cats, if the truth be told,' he declared, in what could have been seen as a sign that he was getting too big for his extra-narrow boots. 'They're not interested in ballads such as I sing. They want swing and jive.'

His radio show didn't exactly allow him to broaden his output either – *Your Hit Parade* was precisely that. It was not *his* hit parade, but simply the songs that were selling from the sheet-music counters – which accounted for his having to sing, week after week, such notable contributions to the art of the songwriter as 'The Woody Woodpecker Song'.

He clearly wasn't happy with the *Hit Parade* programme, but there was a piece of paper that committed him to it, and an ever-burgeoning bank account which seemed to prove that it brought him results. However, this 'marriage' would end in divorce, with the opera singer Lawrence Tibbert taking over and making a much greater mess of songs plainly never written with him in mind. But until that divorce could be made legal, Frank battled on, worrying his lawyers with what he was going to come up with next. On one occasion he took against what was probably among the least objectionable numbers in the hit parade, 'Don't Fence Me In' by Cole Porter. Listeners to the show could have heard him mutter, 'This song has too many words.'

It was before the time of auto-cues, so words could be a problem. Eventually, he found a solution – notes which he carried in his jacket pocket. He was occasionally ready to admit that he couldn't possibly remember the lyrics of every one of the hundreds of tunes that had to be in his repertoire – especially those on the hit parade for which he cared not a crotchet or a quaver. When that happened, and he couldn't find the appropriate piece of paper, he asked his audience to help out and supply the missing links.

But he found words to allow him to go swinging, too. His 'Saturday Night is the Loneliest Night of the Week' had them jumping all over. It was the first record to be made after the year-long musicians' strike, banning their members from making new discs, and Frank had agreed not to cross any picket lines. The strike settled, he cut seventeen sides in six weeks. Axel Stordahl was as much at his side as on the podium for most of this Columbia output.

And he did have a chance to sing the kind of ballads with which he was most comfortable at the time, and see them invade the hit parade. 'They Say It's Wonderful', the big number from *Annie Get Your Gun*, followed the example of 'Saturday Night' and got in at number two. Another number, 'I Dream Of You', stayed in the top ten for fourteen weeks.

It suited Columbia just fine to let Sinatra record the sort of stuff with which he was happiest. His contract with the label, negotiated by Manie Sacks, was said to be worth an advance of $360,000 – and they were making it all back.

But his attempts at giving his own interpretations to songs weren't always appreciated. At this time, when he was still establishing the Sinatra style, he sometimes thought he knew how to sing songs better than the fellow who wrote them – even when that fellow was Cole Porter.

After having criticised 'Don't Fence Me In' on the air, he went on to annoy the composer at a gathering of his peers. It was in the offices of the huge William Morris agency that the two men came to metaphorical blows. The occasion was a birthday party for the president of Paramount, Henry Ginsberg, at which both Sinatra and Porter – in a wheelchair – were guests. So was Larry Adler.

'Sinatra seemed to be excited that Cole Porter was there and called over to Jimmy Van Heusen to play while he sang 'I Get a Kick Out of You' in honour of Porter,' Adler told me. The composer only had to hear the song-by-Sinatra once to say to his minder: 'Get me out of here.' Frank's sin was to change 'I get a kick' to 'I get a boot out of you'. He would do so for the rest of his career, and Porter never forgave him. After the Ginsberg party, he sent Sinatra a wire asking: 'If you don't like my songs, why do you sing them?'

Lorenz Hart was no more delighted when Frank started changing the words of his 'Lady Is a Tramp' and singing about the chick who was the tramp who wouldn't 'dish the dirt with the rest of those broads'. As Larry Adler put it: 'Sinatra had great gifts but really sells himself short with those things.'

But he wasn't selling his records short. Now that the musicians' strike was over, they lined up all over America to buy Frank singing 'Stormy Weather', 'Embraceable You' and even his version of the Crosby–Irving Berlin standard, 'White Christmas', which would soon become the best-selling song in the history of popular music.

This was the time of a phenomenon in the film-music business. The composer David Raksin had just written the theme music for a Gene Tierney–Dana Andrews film-noir movie called *Laura*. Thanks to Sinatra, it went down in history as the only movie whose theme tune became better known than the film itself.

'Laura' was a very strange apple,' Raksin told me. 'Everyone thought in 1944 that it would be a good tune for Sinatra to record, but I actually didn't think he would. A lot of people thought it was unsing-able. Crosby, for instance, never recorded it and other people had no confidence in it at all. Dick Haymes had recorded it before. Sinatra and Decca did it much against their better judgment – they thought they were wasting precious shellac on what was sure to be a flop.'

The result is that Sinatra did record it – four times over the years – and it became one of the half-dozen most recorded ballads in history. Says Raksin now: 'There's a wonderful pleasure in knowing a singer of his calibre sings my songs. What he did was pay attention to the melody and not louse up the lyrics either. That's respect. Frank never told me he liked it, although I've since read he thought of it as his favourite ballad.' The accounting details alone would surely justify that statement.

There was one other song that did phenomenally well. It was called 'Nancy (with the Laughing Face)'.

— 6 —

DON'T WORRY ABOUT ME

'Nancy (with the Laughing Face)' seemed to say it all – a man crazily in love with the girl whose name meant so much to him. It went to the top of the hit parade and stayed for weeks on end. It turned into a standard which, even fifty odd years later, has to be coupled with the name Frank Sinatra in any look into the things that were important for him.

The music was by Jimmy Van Heusen, already more than established as Frank's favourite tunesmith. The lyrics were by Phil Silvers, a second-banana funny man with hair in movies like *Cover Girl*, who was yet to hit world stardom in his own right – and without hair – in the immensely successful *Bilko* TV series. He penned the lyrics for Sinatra in a wonderfully ambiguous way. Everyone now knows the song was written for Nancy, Jr. But it did Frank's image no harm at all when people thought that he was singing directly to his wife. That was her name, after all. And, okay, so he did sing that she was a tomboy in satin and lace. Did that matter? The title registered with more people than the details of the lyric.

This was, after all, family-time in the United States. The Rockwell *Saturday Evening Post* covers demonstrated each week the values of a life in which Dad worked in the tool-shed, while Mom – with her immaculate coiffeur and just enough lipstick to make her pretty and wholesome – looked out of the kitchen window as Junior was setting off on his bicycle. All of it was necessary when so many men were away from home, fighting for just those values. And when a guy was not in the service, he had at least to display some patriotic virtues. Had Sinatra's shaky marriage become public property, it would have been a strike against him. So the night on his radio show when he stopped to talk to Nancy Sr., he was seen as initiating a blow for fatherhood as well as for himself. 'Pull up a chair, Nancy, and bring the baby with you,' he declared and mothers and grandmothers from coast to coast 'oo-ed' and 'ah-ed', while babies everywhere gurgled.

It came during a time of increasing unhappiness for Nancy. Frank's name was linked with some of the most beautiful females in Hollywood. Lana Turner was alleged to have removed the famous sweater to accommodate his advances and Marilyn Maxwell, as sultry as they came, was on most people's lists as a Sinatra 'dame'. It would be a little time before Lauren Bacall would reach that status, but they were already friends. (So was her husband Humphrey Bogart, which meant that Frank was instantly a member of the famous Rat Pack.)

Then, in 1945, he met Ava Gardner, a woman who not only looked just about the sexiest creature on high heels, but who seemed to specialise in that very 'mothering' quality which went so well with the Sinatra appearance. More important, she had been divorced from Mickey Rooney and was married now to Artie Shaw. Frank would later reveal that this meeting was a kind of love at first sight – for both of them. She was to say he told her: 'Why didn't I meet you before Mickey?' Had he done so, he said, he would have married her.

Despite it all, Nancy stayed firm – but humiliated. Their time together was increasingly fraught. The tension could also have had something to do with the fact that in June 1945, a month after the end of the war, Frank left America for the first time – to go overseas to entertain the troops. It was an opportunity for the cynics to have a heyday. Not only were there the stage whispers about the sheer convenience of getting away from Nancy at a time when their marriage had hit bottom, but it reopened all the old charges against Frank and his war effort – or, as many writers saw it, the lack of it.

This has to be one of the miracles of show business – how a performer managed to survive so much flak of so virulent a nature at a time when patriotism had never been so high on most people's agendas. Frank's position certainly didn't look good, visiting Europe now it was safe from shells and bombs. The troops were waiting to go home with nothing to do – and therefore in the best possible frame of mind to welcome some high-class entertainment from home. But Sinatra was not the one they wanted to see.

'They hated him when the tour began,' Saul Chaplin, who was in charge of the music department, told me: 'Hated him! No other word for it.'

The party was originally to consist of Sinatra, Phil Silvers, two girls – Fay McKenzie, who had sung in musical comedy and Betty Yeaton, who revelled in the title of a 'musical contortionist' – and a piano player. There was a long schedule – covering Newfoundland, the Azores, North Africa and Italy. None of it, they were sure, was going to be an easy ride. And they were not wrong.

Rehearsals began just before the party left the United States. Frank told the pianist what he wanted him to play. 'You got the music for this?' the pianist asked. 'That was all that Sinatra needed to hear. 'Oh, brother!' he said – and the man was out. The only thought running through Sinatra's head was that this was going to happen throughout the trip. Every time Frank picked a tune, the pianist would have to go through all the music. Besides which, he didn't like the man very much. 'He seems like a Nazi to me,' he said.

That was when Saul Chaplin was called in. At the time, he was under contract to Columbia, whose head, Harry Cohn, was not a man to be trifled with. He believed anyone trying to get out of the least important clause in a contract was insulting him personally. But Frank Sinatra was not the kind to be put off by such trifles. Besides, he knew his own importance in the world of American show business in 1945. 'Don't worry,' he said. 'I'll square it with Harry.' And square it with Harry he did. Cohn got his pound of flesh. In return, he got Sinatra to sing a song in his upcoming movie *A Thousand and One Nights*. But that was by way of being in the family. In the film, Phil Silvers played Aladdin's right-hand man. As a present for him, he was allowed to snap his fingers and ask the genie for a wish. He said he wished he could sing like Sinatra. The fingers were snapped, Silvers opened his mouth – and Sinatra's voice came out. It was a decent exchange for a few weeks of a piano player's time.

As far as Sinatra was concerned, despite all the reservations, the tour was going to be a wonderful means of self-publicity – providing it was handled properly. When he flew in a shiny silver Dakota aircraft with the words 'The Voice' painted in huge script on the nose, it could hardly have been anything but a gift from heaven.

Yet everyone else involved in the tour was prepared for trouble. They knew what had been said about Sinatra's draft-dodging and they knew, too, that the young fighting men didn't exactly share the enthusiasm of their girls for Frankie.

Officers had warned them in advance that things weren't going to be easy – some of the men had arms full of rotten vegetables ready to throw at the end of a show. 'But every place we went,' Chaplin told me, 'and there were endless examples of this, soldiers came up to us with these vegetables and said: "We came to throw these at you, but we think you're just great" – and then gave him all sorts of gifts.'

It wasn't just Sinatra's own talent that achieved the breakthrough. A lot of it had to do with Phil Silvers who, when he introduced the skeletal Frank to the assembled troops, quipped, 'I know the food here is lousy, but *this* is ridiculous.'

That was part of an opening based entirely on what Silvers thought would be the audience's response to the main star. He had a monologue prepared – which would then be interrupted by Frank. Phil supposedly did not take this interruption too kindly – not at all the usual entertainer's banter of, 'Why, if it isn't ...' which would be followed by uproarious applause. The entire group, let alone Frank and Silvers, knew that there wasn't going to be a lot of applause – of any kind. In fact, they anticipated boos and groans. So Phil said: 'What the hell is this?' And for the next two hours, Sinatra showed him. He was the butt of Silvers's jokes, which not only psychologically made the men feel that the comedian was on their side, but drew them gradually into the Sinatra net. By the time he sang 'Nancy', they were eating out of his hands.

What also helped Frank's reputation was the fact that he was so obviously moved by the plight of the men to whom he was playing – in particular, the wounded. This really came home to most of the group when they were in the Azores. Saul Chaplin explained: 'We never mixed with the officers, except when we wanted to use them for something. But on this night, we went to a lieutenant's house for a drink about midnight. There, we heard a whole lot of planes overhead. Frank asked what they were and was told, "It's wounded soldiers coming over after being evacuated from Italy. They stop here to clean the plane and refuel." That was all that Sinatra needed to hear. 'Can I go and see them?' he asked the officer. 'Sure,' he was told.

So Sinatra, Silvers and Chaplin went round to where the newly-landed wounded were lying. 'And there was every kind of wounded man you ever saw in your life,' Chaplin remembered. 'There wasn't a whole body among them. They were missing arms and legs. It was a ghastly sight.'

Suddenly a shout went up from one of the beds: 'Sing!' It was followed by the same chant from other beds, too: 'Sing! Sing!' Soon everyone was shouting out the same instruction: 'Sing! Sing!'

'I can't,' Sinatra answered, flustered and embarrassed. 'I haven't a piano.'

'Well, sing anyway,' said one. 'Unaccompanied,' said another, as if there could be any other way for him to do it that night. And sing he did – for hours. Unaccompanied.

Then came the moment when an officer announced that it was time to move on. The troops were going home. They started turning the lights out as they loaded the men on to stretchers. Instinctively, Frank knew what to say next: 'Maybe this will help you guys to get some shuteye.' And he sang the Brahms Lullaby while the boys were leaving.

Even now, Chaplin's eyes glaze and there's a lump in his throat as he tells the story. 'It was so beautiful, with the light dimming and the guys being carried out. Phil Silvers and I had tears in our eyes as those guys were leaving on their stretchers. It was a great scene.'

In Italy, there was another incident. They were sent to Foggia, on the coast, and they relished the idea of a day on the beach. Afterwards, totally refreshed, they would move on to Bari, the next stage in the tour, the town with all the Hoboken connections. First, they booked, exhausted, into their small hotel in Foggia. The opportunity of a good night's sleep was the most tempting thing that had happened for days.

The next morning, in shorts and light shirts, they were ready for their day at the beach. A group of soldiers was waiting for them. 'Where are you going?' an officer asked.

'To the beach,' Frank replied, sounding no doubt like a child asking for his bucket and spade.

'You can't do that,' the officer said. That was not good news for battle-weary entertainers planning a day of rest in the sunshine. But the reason was overpowering. 'There are mines out there which haven't been cleared yet.'

They were asked where they were heading next. 'Bari,' they said. That, too, was on the coast. 'You can go to the beach there,' they were told. It almost placated them.

'First of all,' Chaplin remembered, 'we had to find the two dames who were with us. When we found them, we got on the plane and were ready to go swimming the moment we arrived.'

But these plans were also to be thwarted. As they landed in Bari, an officer was waiting impatiently. 'Where the hell have you been?' he asked – a question that might have been considered reasonable enough for an underling or even for other entertainers. Not, though, for Frank Sinatra.

'Look,' said Frank. 'We're not supposed to be here till this evening, so we're going swimming. See you tonight.'

'What yer talkin' about?' the officer asked, not at all impressed with either Mr Sinatra or the answer he had just given him. 'There are five thousand guys out there, sitting in the hot sun, sweating it out and waiting for you to start singing. So you better start singing.'

It was not the sort of talk Frank Sinatra was used to hearing and he didn't like it, either the message or the tone.

'We're not gonna do it,' said Frank.

Even Chaplin couldn't understand his boss's attitude.

'We're not doing it until tonight,' Sinatra repeated, almost spelling out each word, emphasising every syllable. 'I'm going swimming.'

They walked to their car, Sinatra sulking and Chaplin, at first laughing quietly and then so that he could be heard in the auditorium where the soldiers, half of them apparently carrying rotting vegetables, were waiting.

'I can just see *Stars and Stripes* tomorrow,' said the piano player. 'Imagine the headlines: "The Voice Refuses to Sing for GIs".'

Even Sinatra, the man you upset at your peril, balked at that.

Chaplin went on: 'Those papers are certainly not going to say that the Army fucked up here.'

'Well, they did fuck up,' Sinatra, responded, his gaunt face flushed.

'I know,' said Chaplin. 'But they're not going to say so.'

The wisdom of the argument was too strong to refute. Frank went in the Bari stadium and sang his heart out to the boys, who put away their rotten vegetables and cheered their heads off. And nothing was ever said again about the mess made of the proceedings and who had caused it in the first place.

In Rome, there was another kind of mix-up. The Army were again out of step with the Sinatra troupe – although this time there was reason enough to believe that it wasn't entirely accidental. The problem was over hotel accommodation, with Frank and party booked into the kind of hotel that usually rents out its rooms by the afternoon, if not by the hour. 'We're not checking into this fleabag place,' he said. 'This is Rome. There's got to be a better hotel.' At which point he commandeered a Jeep and told the army driver to find a better hotel. They alighted at the Hassler, a brand-new building that had only that week gone into business.

Sinatra booked in – and faced the increasing wrath of the US Army, who plainly saw no reason why a man who hadn't fought during the war should expect accommodation so superior to that which the serving soldiers had had to endure. 'I have no authority to put you here,' the senior officer in charge of their arrangements declared officiously. He plainly didn't know that that was precisely the way to make sure that his argument was lost.

'Listen,' said Frank. 'When we had to sleep with the GIs, we slept with the GIs, but this is Rome and there's no reason why we can't be made comfortable.' So they stayed the night at the Hassler.

That was when the commanding officer came into the picture. 'I understand that the Sinatra unit is staying at the Hassler,' he said.

'Yes, they are, sir,' said his underling.

'Well, get them back to the other hotel.'

'I can't, sir,' said the other officer.

'Why not?'

'Because they say they will leave Rome if we do.'

'But they haven't got a plane,' the CO answered, triumphantly, he thought.

'Yes, they have,' the other man responded. 'I'm afraid the pilot has been told to report to Frank Sinatra and obey his orders. So he can take the plane in a second and leave here.'

It was too powerful an answer to fight – again. Later, the party heard that Frank Sinatra was not the first USO entertainer to be booked into inferior accommodation. Another party had complained about something and been moved officially to the 'fleabag'. From then on, the officer decided that he was going to stand no nonsense – from Frank Sinatra or anyone else.

'That's why they put us in that toilet,' said Saul Chaplin. But the officer didn't know who he was dealing with.

What nobody in the party had reckoned with was Sinatra's real reason for wanting to be in Rome: not just to entertain the troops; not merely to see the ancient Roman memorials and the other sights; not even because he had a dame stashed away somewhere – which he probably did. No, it was more important than all that: he was going to see the Pope.

'We said, "Oh sure you are. Of course!" And we laughed,' recalled Chaplin.

He said: 'I'm going to arrange it.'

The rest of the party continued to laugh. But the next thing they knew was that Myron Taylor, the US Ambassador to the Vatican, had been contacted and was going to make those very arrangements. Perhaps Frank didn't know it at the time but it wasn't so much the influence of Sinatra, but that of the US Government, which had swung the deal. The war was just over, the Vatican was anxious to look good in the eyes of the Americans, and if the price was being nice to some crooner called Frank Sinatra, even the Pope – whose own role in the war had been suspect in the eyes of the Allies – wasn't going to argue.

A private audience was arranged. The pontiff spoke to each member of the party in turn. When he came to Sinatra, he said: 'I understand you are very popular in your country.'

'Yes,' said Frank. 'I've been very lucky.'

'Ah,' Pius responded. 'And what do you sing?'

The Pope, used to the stars of La Scala and similar institutions, wanted to know if he was a baritone or a tenor. Sinatra didn't get his drift. 'Oh, I sing, "Oh Candy", "Ol' Man River", "The Song Is You", Cole Porter's "I've Got You Under My Skin", you know the sort of thing.'

'The Pope looked at him,' Chaplin recalled. 'And didn't know what the hell he was talking about. Frank thought it was quite reasonable to just list the kind of songs he was singing at that time.'

Hearing Frank sing his radio signature tune, 'Put Your Dreams Away', was not a shared experience for the Allies who had fought Germany together. What the British troops managed to pick up in the way of radio programmes in the Far East, where the war with Japan was still continuing, was not available to those in Europe or to their families. But the Japanese knew how important Sinatra was to the Americans in the jungles of the South Pacific. Their propaganda 'voice', nicknamed Tokyo Rose, played Frank's records in between the vitriol. And there were frequent references to what he did at home – with veiled hints about what he was actually doing to their wives and sweethearts – while they were sweating it out in all the heat and humidity.

Back in the US, he turned out new '78s, which now crossed the Atlantic as a matter of form. The Columbia label had its British offshoot, marketed in Britain by the His Master's Voice company – but sales were still not dramatic. Even hits like 'Begin the Beguine' and 'That Old Black Magic' didn't have anything like their American success. His 'Soliloquy' from *Carousel*, later to become a foundation stone of every Sinatra concert, was never even heard in Britain. A music convention of the time had it that no songs from a show could be released in the country until the play opened. In the case of *Carousel*, that wouldn't happen for another six years. They weren't even much interested in his tunes from *Oklahoma!* when that production came to Drury Lane in 1946. Who wanted Sinatra singing 'Oh What a Beautiful Morning' and the other hits if Bing Crosby sang them, too? Besides, a youngster called Harold Keel (before long to change that first name to Howard) was a sensation in London and the people who saw him on stage there wanted *his* version of the songs to play on their wind-up gramophones.

However, the American media continued to follow his progress with avidity. There were cartoons in the newspapers and magazines – perhaps the best was of the girl telling the fellow standing on the ladder they were about to use for their elopement: 'Do you mind waiting for a minute, Henry? I'm listening to Frank Sinatra'.

Frank now needed to consolidate that appeal at home and to extend it. If, until the triumph in Italy, his war image had been suspect, he now took advantage of the new spirit of goodwill to mount his own morality campaign. Not sexual morality, that is, but preaching the gospel of racial equality, which became a personal crusade. Again, it prompted criticisms from the right-wing in American politics, but there was no doubting the sincerity of his aim proving 'We are all Americans', very much the catch phrase of the immediate postwar period when the horrors of the Holocaust and the results of Nazi Germany's racial policies first became apparent.

This was clear in his next movie project, *The House I Live In* – which made no impact whatsoever outside the United States. Any showings it received were for curiosity value. But it did the heart good to hear the young Sinatra in this ten-minute short, proclaiming tolerance to a gang of kids of all races.

'Look, fellers,' he told them, 'religion makes no difference except to a Nazi or somebody as stupid. Why, people all over the world worship God in different ways. This wonderful country is made up of a hundred different ways of talking and a hundred different ways of going to church. But they're all American ways.' He then sang 'What Is an American?' A question to which he knew the answer very well, as he then added: 'My dad came from Italy, but I'm an American. Should I hate your father because he came from Ireland or France or Russia? Wouldn't I be a first-class fathead?'

The House I Live In was a triumph. The idea came from the time Frank met Mervyn LeRoy on a train. 'I'm firmly convinced that the cause of the war has been this hatred, this refusal to respect other men's religions and beliefs,' the publicity machine reported Sinatra having told the director/producer. LeRoy was sympathetic. 'Why don't you put your ideas on the screen?' he asked. The result was that LeRoy directed the piece and Frank Ross produced it for RKO. This was the last vestige of Frank's agreement with that studio and he went out with all flags flying.

The picture was a non-profit-making venture, with all proceeds going to fight juvenile delinquency. This was an opportunity no self-respecting publicist was going to ignore. In the climate of postwar America, it was a demonstration by an all-round good guy. So the thesis of the film was copied a hundred times in radio talks quoting Sinatra, and in newspaper articles supposedly penned by him. It showed a good actor and an intelligent, thinking man – not merely the idol of the bobbysoxers.

For years afterwards, the showing of the film was featured as part of the syllabuses of forward-looking Sunday schools all over America, although the political climate would change drastically and then it was no longer relevant. That anyone could be against such sentiments in 'respectable' circles was at first beyond most people's imaginings.

On 21 March 1945, Sinatra spoke at the World Youth Rally in New York City, held under the auspices of American Youth for a Free World – precisely the sort of organisation that would have Senator Joe McCarthy salivating ten years later. Frank believed he had a receptive audience. 'I've noticed,' he said, 'that kids today are smarter than they used to be. Anyway, they're smarter than *I* used to be.' It was, he agreed, a 'pretty big admission'. But it put him in a good frame of mind to exploit the confidence he was showing those kids. There was, for instance, the old saying about sticks and stones not breaking any bones. 'Want to know something?' he said. 'That's not only corny, it's wrong. Names *can* hurt you. They can hurt you even more than sticks and stones.'

In a wonderfully prescient statement, he rallied against people who called 'Negroes' – a totally acceptable word in 1945 – 'dirty niggers'. Using the word 'dirty' only compounded the offence of the 'n' word. It was as bad as calling Jews 'kikes' and 'sheenies' and had led to what the Nazis had done in what was still not yet called the Holocaust. As Frank said: 'The Jews are a cultural and wonderful people, peace-loving, home-loving and industrious. But the Nazis hate culture; they hate peace; they hate love.'

Plainly, Sinatra didn't write the speech himself, but the fact that it was delivered by him, with his imprimatur upon it, was good for his image. Neither is there any doubt that these represented sentiments with which he agreed.

There was, though, a backlash. At Gary, Indiana, he found himself on the receiving end of a racist campaign. It was a remarkable event for two reasons – not only was he being attacked for his own fight against racism; it was the first time on record that a group of teenagers made a concerted decision not to squeal and shout for Frank Sinatra, hero, but to squeal and shout against Frank Sinatra, villain.

In November 1945, he was booked to speak to the student body at the Froebel High School in the city. His subject was indeed going to be intolerance. And the white youngsters at the school decided to boycott the event – no matter how badly the girls in the white bobbysox wanted to see and hear him. What Frank didn't know when he accepted the invitation was that the school was in the forefront of an equality move which, for its time and its location, was nothing less than remarkable. Fifty years later, the very idea of the source of the trouble being considered a reasonable cause of dissent would be almost laughable if it weren't in many ways a landmark.

A new principal had been appointed at Froebel who, with one move, had advanced the case for race relations by a quarter of a century. The school had as many black pupils – 270 – as whites and the head decided it was about time they had a square deal. He said the blacks should be allowed to sit on student councils and admitted them to the school orchestra. Worst of all, they were allowed to use the school swimming pool. Segregated, of course – and for just one day a week.

To the citizenry of Gary, that was the thin end of a very dangerous wedge. The white children's parents said it would lead to them losing jobs in the local steel mills to 'Negroes'. When Frank turned up to talk to the Gary kids, his audience was entirely black. The white kids had called a strike.

Sinatra called for the strike to end. To him it was all beyond the pale. As he said at the time: 'In show business you get all kinds of people. I've got all kinds of friends, good friends, Negroes, Catholics, Jews. They're nice fellows. We get along great. When some tramp keeps bringing up a person's colour or his religion, it gets me sore. It gets me sore and then I'm through with him.'

He sang songs and made a speech about the American way of life and the hot dogs kids of all colours liked to eat. From the platform he asked some of the black youngsters to join with him in singing 'The Star-spangled Banner'.

It was as good an exercise in race relations as any he knew. A later statement, intended to appease the red-baiters, went down less well. Frank declared that he didn't like Communists – which didn't do a lot of good for his standing as a defender of free speech – and the only organisation to which he belonged was the Knights of Columbus. It may have been what the UnAmerican Activities Committee wanted to hear; on the other hand, it might not – they liked targets to attack and, as events proved, were not going to be so easily put off what they considered to be their crusade. Neither did it offer any comfort to those left-leaning figures in show business who were grabbing at any kind of support they could get from within their own community.

Still, rabid right-wingers (and crypto-fascists) like Gerald L. K. Smith gave the Committee precisely what a lot of its members wanted to hear. In 1946 Smith pronounced – to much nodding and super-cilious smiles – that Sinatra 'has been doing some pretty clever stuff for the Reds'.

Nancy was worried for him, but at the same time might have appreciated more concern for herself and her family. It was a time when the rumours began to spread of Frank's affair with Marlene Dietrich.

'Oh I know they had a thing going,' Sammy Cahn told me. 'And frankly she would have been difficult to resist. She had powers as a lover that were spoken of behind people's hands – not least because she was supposedly the champion in the oral sex department.'

As for Frank himself he went along with every publicity campaign that stressed his belief in family values and everything else to which an honest-to-goodness member of the Knights of Columbus would pay tribute. He was trying to show that he believed in the good Lord and that there was no way other than that of the righteous. To prove his point, he was still wearing his double medallion – the one with a St Christopher on one side and the Star of David on the other. Now he was having duplicates made for friends – and, after the stunning success of his visits to the troops, was sending them to soldiers and sailors, too, as they awaited their final demobilisation.

He told the gossip columnist Louella Parsons that he was equally concerned about labelling too many young people as juvenile delin-quents. 'No child is born bad. All they need is proper training at home. If parents were less selfish and would take time to teach their boys and girls the golden rule – the milk of human kindness and that there is something else in the world besides greed and hate – we would have a much better world.' Part of his change of attitude came from his experiences as what was now known as 'the King of Swoon'. In an amazingly po-faced statement he told Ms Parsons that a lot of the youngsters who squealed at his performances were nice kids, 'but at different times I have been appalled at their language'. This was the most amazing piece of hypocrisy from Sinatra – if he ever did say it. The young man who was so much his mother's son was the last person to complain about swearing.

He was only thirty years old, but he somehow felt he should sound like an old man. And it only served to enhance his standing with other artists in America. 'People are pretty much the same all over the world,' he repeated. 'The Negro loves his children with the same sort of devotion that the white man does; the Chinese likes laughter and friendship and good times just as much as you and me. All people are human beings and no matter what their race, religion or nationality is, they are alike in their loves and their fears, their needs and their hopes.' It didn't do his image in the film community any harm at all. It won him a special award for *The House I Live In* from the Academy of Motion Picture Arts and Sciences – his first Oscar.

The official history of the Oscar describes this award as the 'most significant of the evening'. Indeed, on the evening of the presentations for 1945, the assembled gathering of film producers, directors and fellow actors gave Frank a standing ovation worth every bit as much as the award itself.

Certainly, the black population of America – even if he did call them Negroes – gave him one large metaphorical ovation. When they heard that he had punched a man at a lunch counter in the Deep South for refusing to serve a black member of his entourage, they cheered even more. It happened when he was touring an army camp and he admitted, 'I lost my temper. But don't think I'm sorry. I'm not.'

The man dishing out the food made it obvious that he wasn't going to serve a black musician who, contrary to army practice at the time, happened to be standing in line with the white troops and players awaiting meals.

'How come?' Frank asked the man behind the counter. 'We don't serve niggers,' came the reply.

That's when the Sinatra temper was lost. 'I reached over that counter and smashed him one on the nose. He got up and started after me. I gave it to him again. Then the other fellows got up and we all walked out.'

The stories about Sinatra multiplied, stories about the music he was having pumped into his mobile dressing room – he liked Tchaikovsky and Debussy – about the books he was reading, like *The History of Bigotry in the United States*, *The American Dilemma* and one entitled *Freedom Road*, 'a sensational book, everybody in the United States should read that one'. There were stories about his career – which, if they were engineered by George Evans, were usually true and if they were written in spite of him, certainly were not. The stories about the women in his life, unless they concentrated on the wonderful home he shared with Nancy and the kids, were usually considered dirty pool. Sometimes they were just plain ridiculous – like the one that he employed a flunkey solely to feed him two 'invigorating pills' a day. Evans was fast off the mark. Frank, he said, was '138 pounds of solid, healthy guy who eats five good meals a day'.

Columnists like Sidney Skolsky wrote the usual rubbish – about the kind of cigarettes he smoked, about his food, about his silk pyjamas, always in loud colours, and about his insomnia. 'He has the radio on and listens to the disc jockeys early in the morning. He can be soothed by Sinatra singing.'

A radio station in Detroit decided to try to get beneath the Sinatra mystique and held a competition entitled, 'Why I Like Frank Sinatra'. More than 1,500 people – mostly young girls – entered. The winner said: 'I think he is one of the greatest things that ever happened to teenage America. We were kids that never got much attention, but he's made us feel like we're something. He has given us understanding. Most adults think we don't have any consideration. We're really human and Frank realises that. He gives us sincerity in return for our faithfulness.'

Fans wrote his name over their coats and sweaters, just as they would have done on T-shirts today. When he himself appeared in public wearing the sleeves of his jacket rolled up, it instantly became a fashionable thing to do. The idea was copied everywhere, even if he himself hadn't any idea that he was creating a trend.

These youngsters continued to adore him. They took his photograph, swapped dark, unrecognisable shots of him outside theatres, and one fan even rushed to his restaurant breakfast table to scrape up his cornflakes leavings when he walked out of the door. The difficulty was to be truthful about the way he felt about his adulation. 'The kids who hang around stage doors and ask for an occasional autograph – they're fans. But the ones who follow me all over the place – they're fiends.'

There was, however, one group of women with whom Nancy could feel entirely safe: the ladies of the press. Only the year before, in November 1945, Sinatra had been awarded the Women's Press Club's Outstanding Achievement Award for 'industry relations'. They said he was the man who had done 'remarkable work in furthering racial tolerance and approaching the problem of juvenile delinquency'. No one had ever been recognised in that way before.

Twelve months later, there was another award from the same women – for the 'least co-operative star of the year'. Their reason for giving him their 'stinker' prize was his constant reluctance to appear for interviews with fan magazines. He didn't even show up to have publicity pictures taken – which wasn't just a sin for MGM, it didn't do George Evans much good either.

By setting Sinatra on the road to ignominy, as they saw it, the press women were showing solidarity with one of their brothers – Erskine Johnson of the Los Angeles *Daily News*. 'If you don't stop referring to my temperament as temper, I'll personally punch you right in your stupid mouth,' wrote Sinatra. They were the sort of words that would haunt him for the rest of his professional life.

— 7 —

HIGH HOPES

S inatra may have been too big for his handmade boots but, equally, there was no doubt that the future looked good for him. He was the superstar of pop music. At the beginning of 1946, his sales in America were higher than those of almost any other performing artist, although Crosby was always ready to produce more, and so sell more, most of the time. Perry Como was giving him a run for his money, too.

Everything that Jolson had been and the Beatles would be, Frank Sinatra still was. He was headlining another radio show for a cigarette firm, this time Old Gold. Every Wednesday, the *Songs by Sinatra* show provided reasons for people not to go to the movies – unless they went to see Sinatra films.

And there were always new pictures on the horizon. In 1946 Frank had donned that favourite white tuxedo of his and sung 'Ol' Man River' in what was supposedly a Jerome Kern biopic *Till the Clouds Roll By.* And in 1947 there was a romantic comedy in which he co-starred with Jimmy Durante, *It Happened in Brooklyn.* It was his first dramatic role – as a newly demobilised GI who loses the girl with whom he thinks he is in love (Kathryn Grayson) to Peter Lawford.

The black-and-white movie had a cheap look, despite the expense that was lavished upon it: the stars, the songs by Sammy Cahn and Jule Styne, the musical direction of Johnny Green and the solo piano-playing of a callow youth named André Previn, dubbing not just for Sinatra but for Lawford and the young boy at the centre of the drama (but who only appears in two scenes) for whom they were trying to provide a music scholarship. There was one scene on the Brooklyn Bridge, but everything else smacked of being wrapped up in the studio and on just two or three sets at that. Grayson certainly wasn't at her best and Lawford was quite appalling, never more so than when he was supposedly wowing kids in a record store, attempting to show that he could bebop with the best of them, which, of course, he couldn't. But Durante virtually played himself, which was enough for his fans, and Sinatra was extraordinarily good. His singing – from grand opera ('La Ci Darem la Mano') to 'It's the Same Old Dream' – was velvety-smooth and his acting convincing

Peter Lawford was to remember: 'He called me "Lassie", a name of which I'm not overly fond. And he spent a great deal of time making up quips to answer the things that Crosby and Bob Hope were saying about him. He was great fun at this time.'

Johnny Green, who had a reputation for pontificating about every-thing, told me: 'Working with Frank Sinatra on this picture was a great influence on what I did. He was very young then [actually he was thirty-two] but he dominated everything by the sheer weight of his personality.' That is probably true. Certainly the picture would have been nothing without him. As it is, it is a simple movie that is worth watching when the mood is right.

There are two interesting things about this film – a unique day's shoot and the kind of behaviour that the studio had long been com-plaining about suddenly reaching crisis proportions. The location scene on the Brooklyn Bridge beat, by three years, *On the Town* which has the reputation for being the first film of its kind shot outside of a studio. There were cheers from the film technicians for the way Sinatra sang on the bridge, avoiding the traffic and fighting for the odd break in the fog. There were none at all for some of his other antics – like refusing to turn up for rehearsals, or not appearing before the cameras because Jimmy Durante was not present either. Then, when he was asked to appear on a Burns and Allen radio show – one that would plug the film unmercifully – he stayed away from the set, forcing all the shooting to be shut down. He had previously asked for time off – or at least for the production to be completed by that date – but when it was refused, he went anyway.

As a result Louis B. Mayer was in despair, amazed that there could be such disloyalty from one of his 'family'. A telegram went to Sinatra's home, stating in no uncertain tones that his appearing with Burns and Allen was 'in violation' of his MGM contract. 'These incidents are the culmination of a long series of violations of your contractual obligations to us.'

Of course, the story went all round the world and the columnists were delighted. One who enjoyed the Sinatra discomfiture more than most was the top bitch of gossip columns, Louella Parsons. To her credit, when Frank sent her a telegram, she printed it in her column. 'I'll begin by saying,' Frank wrote, 'that if you care to make a bet, I'll be glad to take your money that MGM and Frank Sinatra do not part company, permanently or otherwise. Secondly, Frank has not been a very difficult boy on the lot. Frankie has only been heard from when it concerns the improvement of the picture, which you will find happens in most pictures where you use human beings. Your article claims my pout was caused by something about a song. Regardless of where you get this information, from some gossipmonger or otherwise, you can rest assured that if I pouted at all, it would have been for a much bigger reason than a broken-down song. As an added thought, I have always been one of the most stalwart defenders of the phrase, "Nobody is indispensable", so apparently your line about my being irreplaceable was all wet. Last but not least, in the future I'll appreciate your not wasting your breath on any lectures because when I feel I need one I'll seek such advice from someone who either writes or tells the truth. You have my permission to print this if you desire and clear up a great injustice. Frank Sinatra.'

But there was nothing about *It Happened in Brooklyn* to make Frank think he was going to restrict his life to making movies, the way most other MGM stars did. There was nothing about the reviews to convince him to do so either, although some were nice enough about his own performance. The noted writer James Agee wrote: 'Aside from Sinatra and Durante the show amounts to practically nothing, but there is a general kindliness about it which I enjoyed.' However, his old sparring partner Lee Mortimer was less impressed, commenting that the film 'bogs down under the miscast Frank (Lucky) Sinatra, smirking and trying to play a leading man'.

The reference to 'Lucky' was an allusion to Charles 'Lucky' Luciano, an alleged relationship with the Sicilian gang leader that would not die down. Mortimer would keep trying to build up a connection between them, a fact that would come to a head very soon afterwards.

Publicly, Frank was trying to give every impression of being exactly where he had always been. He continued to make standing-room-only personal appearances, even if the girls were now slightly more restrained. He was hard working and still doing what he believed was the right thing by his friends. When he heard that Phil Silvers had a problem, he was by his side. The difficulty was that Rags Ragland, the comedian with whom Frank had gone to the Roosevelt White

House, had died, just a matter of days before he was due to star with Silvers at the Copacabana nightclub, one of the swankiest places in Manhattan. This meant that Silvers would have difficulty in completing his act. Sinatra knew that – and, without telling his friend, flew from California to sing with him. On the first night at the club, he simply walked into Silvers's dressing room and asked what time they were due to appear. For the hour or so they were on, Sinatra was treated the way the members of the motor pool were in the *Bilko* series. Silvers had the audacity to shape the Sinatra lips with his fingers. Frank accepted it and so did the audience.

This was a fickle business, particularly in late 1946. Quite suddenly, and totally unexpectedly, something very strange happened. The music industry had found a new competitor for the title of The Voice – aged sixty. That same Al Jolson with whom Frank had been compared so often was back – bigger than ever. On 1 October 1946, Frank performed at a surprise tribute to Jolson, hosted by the former Mayor of New York, Jimmy Walker. It was a thank-you from show business to the man who had been its biggest name. Had Frank realised Al was about to regain that title, he and the others performing that night might have thought twice about being there. Except, there was still something in being part of any celebrity list, like the one on parade this evening, a list from which no one wanted to be excluded.

The new biopic, *The Jolson Story*, was the biggest hit since *Gone With the Wind* and there was a sudden demand for Jolson records. At everyone else's expense. Frank was turning out new standards like 'Body and Soul' by Johnny Green and 'Always' by Irving Berlin and 'The Nearness of You'. They couldn't have been more different from the sort of thing Jolson was singing – 'Swanee' and 'Mammy' and Jolson's new hit 'The Anniversary Song'. But now the public couldn't get enough of these.

There was also discord on the domestic front when Nancy found a diamond bracelet in a new convertible car in which Frank was teaching her to drive. New Year's Eve was around the corner. There was a party planned and she knew the bracelet was going to be a present to be worn for the first time on that night. The problem was that the woman who wore it was not Nancy but the singer Marilyn Maxwell. In the presence of her guests, Nancy told her husband to go to hell. She also ordered a distraught Ms Maxwell out of her house.

Not for the first time, they separated – and to make Nancy even less happy than she had been for months, she received daily reports of Frank's activities – accompanied by newspaper clippings and fan-magazine photographs of him dancing with Lana Turner or sitting at restaurant tables with Ava Gardner.

Somehow, he hoped to persuade her that these women were just good friends, but Nancy was no fool. The stories were circulating all over about their antics together. One was revealed in 1986 by Kitty Kelley in her book *My Way* about how Frank and Ava ended up in jail in Indio, California, after driving round the town shooting up shop windows and streetlights – and grazing one of the town's citizens. The affair didn't get into the newspapers because George Evans's California representative Jack Keller, armed with $30,000, paid off all the people concerned – including the local police chiefs.

Nancy heard about it and wanted no more, but she also knew the damage that a separation would do for her children. For the moment, they agreed to bury the hatchet. But neither would forget it in a hurry. For Frank, it was an unpleasant incident that before long was the talk of Hollywood, the subject of hilarious gossip at the Brown Derby and the Polo Lounge.

He seemed to be in trouble on all fronts. It was about this same time that Frank finally declared war on his old *bête noire* Lee Mortimer. The affair came to a head in April 1947 when Los Angeles District Attorney investigators revealed that Frank had had a fight with Mortimer with the help of a music publisher, Sam Weiss – a credible scenario since, it was pointed out, Mr Weiss weighed 200 pounds, almost double Frank's own weight.

Mortimer, motion-picture editor of the New York *Daily Mirror*, was continuing what Sinatra regarded as the campaign against him which he had begun in the days when Frank supposedly was dodging the draft. Mortimer said he was hit from behind as he stood outside the Ciro's café nightspot with a singer named Kay Kino.

That fact alone was enough to get other newshounds sniffing. But the real significance was in the complaint that Sinatra had made against the newspaperman after he wrote about Frank's association with 'Lucky' Luciano, implying a relationship between Sinatra and the group of gangsters who became known as 'the Mob'. He described Frank and Charles 'Lucky' Luciano being together in Havana in 1946 – a vacation which ended up with Cuba deporting the racketeer to his native Italy.

What had happened, according to Frank, was that on his way to Mexico City he had stopped over to go to the casinos on the island –

then an outpost of the kind of gambling you couldn't easily do in America, even illegally. He refuted entirely the suggestion that he had carried two million dollars in small notes to Luciano on behalf of the Mob. 'If I had carried it in single-dollar bills,' Sinatra replied, 'the cash would have weighed 6,000 pounds. If the bills had been in twenties, the bag would still have required a couple of stevedores to carry it.'

It was a lesson that Sinatra should have learned and never did: he was a man always judged by the company that he kept. On this occasion, he had indeed been seen with two gentlemen from New Jersey with a somewhat unsavoury reputation – Rocco and Joe Fischetti, who came from his own neck of the Hoboken woods. He was photographed with them leaving an acroplane and then again with some of the Fischettis' friends, among them Luciano.

In a way it only helped to nail a case against Sinatra which he said was all part of a conspiracy. Nancy, Jr., says it was because he was very much involved in the campaign to re-elect President Harry S. Truman in 1948. The Republican press, not least of all the Hearst empire, were already gunning for the man they believed had no right to be in the White House: the Vice-President who had succeeded Franklin D. Roosevelt on his death and therefore had not been elected to the highest office in the land. But they didn't like Roosevelt either and thought he too should never have been living in the mansion on Pennsylvania Avenue.

For whatever reason, people were gunning for Sinatra. To use a word that fitted very well into those Italian circles, a vendetta was being crafted. He should have known better but, by being careless about the people he met and the way he met them, he was falling into a deep, deep trap.

Sinatra was incensed at the sort of thing Mortimer, in particular, was writing about him. Now, according to Aldo Corsinis and Chester Sharp, the District Attorney's investigators, he took the law into his own hands – with the help of Mr Weiss. Both Kay Kino and a Hollywood photographer named Nat Dallinger, who conveniently happened to be near by and supposedly went to Mortimer's rescue, swore to the fight taking place. The investigators' report stated: 'We are convinced that Sinatra, with a gang behind him and with the active assistance of one man, made an unexpected and unprovoked assault on Mortimer.' Ms Kino said that after the first blows, Sinatra struck him again, while Weiss held him down.

This was all fascinating stuff. It had been a long time since a well-known Hollywood idol had been so involved in a scandal. Not since Fatty Arbuckle was acquitted of a particularly brutal manslaughter charge, had there been one quite so juicy, with the possible exception of Errol Flynn and his forays into statutory rape. The whole film community rushed to buy newspapers. The men who still resented Frank's success – success with women, success in show business or just success generally – revelled in the notion of Sinatra being uncomfortable. The news went down with relish in Hoboken where the remaining Three Flashes hadn't been as collectively happy for years.

Frank was released on bail of $500 – which even in 1947 seemed barely more than a cab-fare to him – and charged with battery. He would be answering to the charge the following May. Meanwhile he, in his defence, said he resented hearing Mortimer saying: 'There goes that dago.'

Mortimer, Ms Kino answered, 'never said a word at any time'.

Frank was loquacious on his way to the Beverly Hills Justice Court. 'Sure I hit him,' he said. 'I just saw red. He had been needling me for a long time in his column and as he left the café, he gave me a sneering look.'

The Sinatra case was not helped by the fact that five people who were in Frank's party all refused to give any testimony. Sinatra's lawyer, Al Pearson, did come to the aid of his client. 'Maybe Frankie's no angel,' he said, 'but he's a good guy – a helluva regular fellow. Why, we've got telegrams from newspapermen all over the country congratulating him for socking this guy.' Others were not so sure. *Daily Variety* noted: 'It looks as though Frankie Boy has taken on the whole Hearst organisation.'

In fact, the press had their usual Sinatra field day. Earl Wilson wrote from New York: ' "He shouldn'ta done it ... the Kid has blown his wig ... he's acting like a cornball" was the way his pals prattled of the fisticuffing. Few around here thought Furious Frankie, who fights not with 14-ounce gloves but a 14-ounce body, should have clouted Mortimer, even if Mortimer made the crack attributed to him by Frank ... personally as your friend, I got to say, "Frankie, you shouldn'ta".'

He then took a swipe of his own at Mortimer, 'who's known in the cafés for liking all champagne (except domestic) and Chinese girls, the latter so much that he sometimes brought in practically their whole families.' Wilson went on: 'You don't belt columnists. You don't take laws in your own hands. You had guts. But Mortimer's friends are mad at you now for beating him. His enemies are mad at you for not busting him harder.' It was, he said, a hopeless battle: 'Another singer, Al Jolson, swung at Winchell once. Winchell got more famous. Won't somebody swing at me?'

When the time for the full hearing came, the matter was settled before going to court – with the considerable help and advice of Louis B. Mayer – by the payment of $9,000 to the writer (and the addition of almost another $25,000 in costs). The sum would be worth in the region of $100,000 today.

It was announced in open court, where Frank sat on the jury-box rail wearing a flying jacket, T-shirt and grey slacks, with his hands in his trouser pockets. Mortimer was in court, too, but neither spoke nor smiled at each other. Mortimer told Judge Cecil D. Holland: 'I acknowledge that I have received satisfaction for the injury done to me. Furthermore, Sinatra has publicly acknowledged that I did not call him the vile names he stated I called him.'

In many other cases, that would be the end of that. But a pound of flesh was being paid, too. Frank's lawyers Isaac Pacht and N. Joseph Ross issued a statement: 'Frank stated that the whole episode arose when acquaintances stopped at his table and claimed to have overheard Mortimer make a remark which aroused Frank's anger and resentment. On further inquiry, Sinatra has ascertained that Mortimer had made no remark and had not even known Sinatra was in the café and, therefore, no provocation really existed for the subsequent occurrences.' The statement added: 'Frank expressed his keen regret over the whole episode.'

Officially, it was over, but the matter stayed in Sinatra's mind for years. He would never forgive Mortimer – and Mortimer would never let him off the hook. In fact, soon afterwards, Sinatra was quoted by the New York *Daily News*'s David Hanna as saying: 'No, I wouldn't do it again and I'm sorry it happened in the first place. But that guy has been badgering me for years, calling me a Communist and a radical.' Neither did he see any reason not to give his own explanation for the feud. 'Mortimer wrote a song once and sent it to me. It was no good and I said so. I'm not implying that this is the reason he dislikes me, but it's a coincidence, isn't it?' If he were not implying it, he was making a very poor job of giving the opposite impression. And he added: 'From that point on, he started badgering me in the column.'

Then came time for Sinatra to defend the people who were responsible for his success. 'It wasn't that he picked on my singing or even that anaemia gag, I'm used to that stuff. He always had a personal crack to make. If he's not calling me a crackpot Communist, he picks on the bobbysoxers. Time and time again, he's referred to the kids as Sinatra's juvenile delinquents. That's no way to talk about American youngsters. They don't deserve it.'

He also had a good word – for once – to say about other people in Mortimer's business. Most journalists supported the Sinatra case, said Frank. 'I know that newspapermen feel the same way about each other as cops. They stick together, but this is one time when the boys are acting differently. I guess they understand that someone in the public eye gets pretty tired of being pushed around in the gossip columns. The trouble is, you have no defence unless you're willing to go into court every five minutes.'

Meanwhile, the man at the centre of the row, Lucky Luciano, was in court himself. No sooner was the Turkish steamer *Bakir* docking at Genoa, than he was arrested by police at the harbour and taken on to Palermo, the Sicilian capital, where he was to be the subject of further investigations. Luciano had already been deported from the United States earlier that year and the Americans wanted to know how he could have got back into the Western Hemisphere and been allowed to land in Cuba. What everyone else wanted to know was how he struck up the alleged friendship with Frank Sinatra.

Before long, Frank replied. He wrote an open letter denying any friendship with Luciano. In his note from the MGM studios in Culver City he said how grateful he was for the support people were giving him – including other columnists like Ed Sullivan and Walter Winchell. But nothing seems to have compared with the help he got at MGM. 'Finding me under fire, everyone from messengers and prop men to the biggest MGM stars took the trouble to stop me on the studio's streets, on the sound stages and in the commissary to shake my hand. They all said the same thing. "If it means anything, Frankie, count me on your side." If it means anything! It meant everything, a great comfort, a great incentive.' He ended by saying: 'The one thing I can do in return is try to live in such a way, both as a performer and a human being, as to merit your confidence, respect and affection. Please, all of you, believe me when I say you have given me an experience that I'll always remember, an inspiration few men have been fortunate enough to enjoy. Gratefully yours.'

The letter was in all probability written by George Evans who was the first to warn Frank about the risks of associating with people like the Fischettis, let alone with another Lucky Luciano.

This was the first blip in the huge Sinatra success story. And it wasn't going to be the only one in 1947. Out of the blue, as far as Frank himself and most of the industry was concerned in April that year, an advertising agency announced that Old Gold were dropping him from his radio show *Songs by Sinatra*. That was a blow nobody would have predicted.

The decision, said Ray Vir Den, vice-president of the Lennen and Mitchell Agency, was made for 'cold business' reasons. People were just not tuning into the Old Gold radio show he had been fronting for some time and, consequently, they didn't want him as their star.

Columbia Records couldn't understand the decision. They were still selling his discs – particularly numbers like the ever-beautiful 'Autumn in New York', which sounded more enchanting than any autumn Frank himself used to spend in the city in his early days. So, was a perceived unpopularity the real reason for the show being dropped? Did it have anything to do with the fight with Lee Mortimer and the Luciano affair?

All Mr Den would say was that it was due to those business decisions, 'although naturally we are not happy' about the fight and its possible cause. These were supposedly highly moral times and companies which considered themselves the height of respectability were scared that the slightest infraction of what was believed to be common decency could have effects on their products.

Why was Sinatra doing that sort of thing? The answer seems to be that he was still insecure about his position and regarded every personal insult as an assault on his public credibility. No matter what advice he received from George Evans and the rest of his helpers, he could not grasp that he was harming himself every time he acted the heavy.

On the other hand, there was plenty of reason to think that Sinatra was as big a star as ever. Hoboken certainly *said* it thought so, when it decided publicly to make up for all the problems that had existed between itself and its favourite son. In 1947 the city announced the time had come to pay an official tribute to the man who had put their town on the map – an event so important in the history of the waterfront community that pictures of the occasion still adorn City Hall and are stored in the personal archives of those who think they have a duty to preserve the vital events of their past.

It was probably Dolly who persuaded Frank himself to rethink his opposition to returning. She was at a stage when things were changing for her in the political life of Hoboken and she now regarded praise for her world-famous son to be as much a thank-you to herself as an honour for him. So when the formal invitation arrived, to many people's surprise in those parts, Frank said 'Yes'.

The invitation came from City Hall over the signature of a new mayor. Barney McFeeley was no longer the first citizen of Hoboken and – much to Dolly's delight – Fred Di Sappio was sitting at the desk the Irishman had occupied for so long. A fusion ticket between the Republicans and the Democrats had shoed the Italian Di Sappio into office and he was planning what was unofficially being called a victory parade along the length of Washington Street, where City Hall stands. He thought Frank would be an ideal star for that parade. He was. When he came, he was presented with a huge wooden key to the city, 'from the hearts of the city of Hoboken, New Jersey'. It added the date as 'Sinatra Day – October 30 1947.'

Dolly helped him carry it. Marty, in full uniform, including his fire officer's cap, stood beaming – on a lower step, which made him look eighteen inches shorter than his son. Everyone who was around at the time remembers that day. Frank, star of the show and proud to be so – if not half as proud as Marty and Dolly and Di Sappio himself – rode through the street on a fire truck which Marty drove, and looking as pleased as if he himself had just been presented with a medal by the President.

Twenty thousand people lined the streets that day and when the ceremony took place inside City Hall, council officials couldn't cope with the photographers who wanted to record the event. Then Frank went out on to the steps and spoke to the crowd. He recalled his time working on the New Jersey *Observer* – helping to reaffirm the legends about his early days in journalism. 'Gosh,' he said, 'little did I think when I worked for the Obby that I'd be greeted like this. You know, I've met people in cities all over the country but the folks here in Hoboken, well, they're just wonderful – that's all.'

He didn't mean it, of course, but the people of Hoboken were in a mood to be lied to – especially when Frank recognised some boyhood pal. 'Hi, Gus, how are you?' Nobody knew whether there was really a Gus out there, but it sounded just great. If Gus was real, he was to remember that greeting forever afterwards.

Joe Spaccavento too remembers it extremely well. 'Frank wore a camel coat. It was the most beautiful garment I had ever seen,' he told me.

That was when it happened. The Hoboken Revenge struck. A group of fellows-about-town threw garbage at him, instantly spoiling that beautiful coat – and its effect. People in the crowd laughed. Frank didn't.

Later, there was a dance organised by the Fire Department at the Hoboken Union Club. Marty asked Frank to sing. It was another of those offers he couldn't refuse. So he said yes and went on the Union Club stage to sing 'Put Your Dreams Away' for up to five hundred people. But the Revenge came to the surface again – in the shape of a group of local men who threw coins on to the stage. He didn't need the coins and saw them for what they were – one of the biggest insults that could come the way of a professional performer, as serious an adverse comment as the hook on amateur night.

'I've never seen anything like it,' John Marotta told me. 'Suddenly, Frank turned white. I could see it from where I was sitting. What he looked like to those closer to the stage I cannot imagine.'

It was the final straw and the cause for the absolute decision: a vow he made to himself and to his family that never again would he appear in public in the town where he was born. He would keep that promise for almost thirty years.

Marotta put it into perspective: 'Those guys thought they owned Sinatra and they always wanted something from him. No wonder he didn't want to come back.'

Dolly had her words for it: 'Yes,' she would say years afterwards, 'my son is like me. Cross him and he never forgets.' That was, to use later Sinatra parlance, saying a book.

Sinatra's own revenge took the form of denying that he came from Hoboken at all. Suddenly, press biographies would say that he hailed from Hasbrouck Heights, although he had only lived there briefly before moving to California. Local traders in their turn said that not only did he come from Hoboken but the last time he was in town, he owed them money. A barber put it around that Frank had a $25-bill outstanding – a totally unsubstantiated claim, but it was open season for attacking Sinatra and the neighbourhood enjoyed the sport as much as ever.

By crossing Frank Sinatra, they were crossing Dolly Sinatra, too, and she wasn't ready to forget either. It would be some time before she agreed to help the town with anything that wasn't likely to be of direct use to herself. It also provided her with ammunition. She liked to say that she was the only person who could control her son, or make him do things that he himself might not want to do. 'He can't make his mother do anything she doesn't want to do. Even today, he wears the kind of underwear I used to buy him.'

Sinatra himself continually felt now that he was being put upon. The question was, what was he going to do about it? Was he now planning to take the law into his own hands, should anyone try to hit him with anything worse that a mouldy cauliflower? That was the thought that was immediately provoked by the next series of photographs which appeared in the newspapers. He was pictured paying a visit to his neighbourhood police station in Los Angeles and then being fingerprinted. It had nothing to do with his pending appearance before the judge. He was applying for a permit to carry a gun.

The permit was granted and the press revelled in the news. Not that Frank was any more amenable to them than usual. 'It's a personal matter,' he maintained. In other words, everyone else needed to mind their own businesses. What he did say was that he thought the whole population ought to be fingerprinted as a matter of course – so that people like him would not find themselves accused of things of which they were strictly innocent.

George Evans asked Lee Mortimer at this time to 'lay off Frank because he is trying to get back with Nancy'. Not that he had officially left her, but they were spending so much time apart, it certainly felt that way – and there was virtually nothing between them now, a situation not helped by the press's constant intervention. But that interest from the newspapermen of America was spawned by two things: Sinatra's own success, which was in no small way due to those journalists, and his code of conduct, which made them watch out for any possible infringement.

He was being advised by friends to slow down, to stop stressing himself out constantly. For a brief time, he took their advice – and decided to take up painting, which gave him a certain solace and allowed him to relax. But it couldn't last. He was a singer, he was an actor, and as far as he was concerned, he was the best of the lot.

If he couldn't convince all the people in the industry that he was as big as ever, he set about assuring his various buddies, like Jimmy Van Heusen and Sammy Cahn. A psychiatrist might analyse it all as a kind of inferiority complex, expressing itself through megalomania, but at times he behaved like some latter-day Louis XIV. While staying at the plush Fairmont Hotel in San Francisco, he decided he wanted a grand piano in his suite – a brand-new one. At four o'clock in the morning. So he awoke a music-store proprietor and the piano was brought to his suite. The following morning, he had another whim – to go to Palm Springs. 'Get me a private plane,' he ordered. In this respect, he was unlucky. No planes could be found.

He was also doing all he could to shout the fact that he was still America's top star – a fact that was no longer totally true. But he was big enough not to worry about it – for the moment at least. And he still seemed to be in demand. Not least by Ava Gardner, whom he was meeting more often now, especially when Sinatra found what he thought were good reasons to spend nights at an apartment in Hollywood lent to him by a friend. Ava said she found him irresistible.

He was doing his best to keep their relationship out of the papers, to concentrate on his work. Most of Frank's radio listeners seemed to be satisfied. The ratings every time he appeared on the air were satisfactory if not sensational. With no Old Gold show any more, he was back fronting *Your Hit Parade*. He was also still guesting on other stars' radio programmes and starring in a Lux Radio Theatre of the Air production of *Anchors Aweigh*.

The records spun out of the factory as quickly as they sped round a turntable. But no longer were they the ones Frank wanted to make. Even with people like Axel Stordahl behind him, too often it seemed that he was being reduced to cover versions of what other people were doing. But he was still considered to be worth advertising. One 1948 campaign showed a picture of Frank alongside the legend: ' "Wrap me up and take me home", says Frank Sinatra'.

It was the year of the Fred Astaire–Judy Garland film, *Easter Parade*. Frank recorded two of the Irving Berlin hits from the movie, 'A Feller with an Umbrella' and 'It Only Happens When I Dance with You'. But it didn't really happen when people played the discs. Astaire's 'Dance with You' was the definitive version and although what Frank sang was pleasant enough with all the old attention to detail and to phrasing, they were also-ran tunes.

Yet there were enough records to justify at least one New York radio station playing nothing but Sinatra records for twenty-four hours, an unheard-of tribute. And there was a new film that year, Frank's first non-musical movie *The Miracle of the Bells* – in which, like all good Catholic actors, he finally played a priest. Dressed for the part, a woman, the mother of George 'Bullets' Durgom, a top Hollywood agent thought he really was a man of the cloth and knelt to kiss his ring.

'It was the funniest thing I ever saw,' George told me. 'I've seen some convincing performances from clients in my time, but I wouldn't have cast Sinatra as a real live priest in a million years'. For years the bald-headed agent – hence the nickname 'Bullets' – went around telling people about the mistake his mother had made.

It was a dreadful casting error. Audiences expected him to sing, and left cinemas in droves, disappointed and worrying about their favourite star's future. 'Sinatra plays the priest with the grace and animation of a wooden Indian,' said *Time* magazine. 'I hereby declare myself the founding father of the Society for the Prevention of Cruelty to God,' wrote James Agee.

Had Frank managed a performance strong enough to become his own version of *Going My Way* or *The Bells of St Mary's* – in which Crosby did sing – things might have gone a lot easier. But who could imagine going to confess to a priest with Sinatra's reputation? This was a man of the cloth most people would have willingly unfrocked.

A timely distraction was the birth of his third child – Christina, forever after known as Tina and yet another attempt to cement the relationship between Frank and Nancy. A radio announcer gave the news to the American public: 'Frank Sinatra got a terrific Father's Day present today – a brand-new baby girl.' Nancy, Jr., recalls shouting 'Yippee!' when she heard the news sitting with her dad in his car.

But Frank's relationship with the senior Nancy didn't stand a chance – not now that he was involved with Ava Gardner. He was smitten like he had never been hit before. The rumours did not help his career. Already there were worrying signs. His income in 1946 had been less than $1 million before tax – which was a third down on the $1,500,000 he had chalked up in 1944. It was like a schoolchild coming home with a perfectly good report, just not quite as good as the brilliant one the year before.

His publicity people maintained that there was a perfectly good reason for this. He was only working part-time – for money, that is. Much of the rest of the time was being spent making speeches and doing good work. Not really true. Many of his speeches were free, it is true, but he had his valuable MGM contract to keep him going while he was out there. His career was not being helped by the kind of material he was being offered. Not just the films, but the records were worse than ever – and even Manie Sacks, the head of Columbia Records, now agreed he wasn't cutting the kind of success that had so recently been his. He soothed Frank by saying that before long he would be on top again.

It was all too clear that things were slipping. The fact that Sacks and others tried to make him feel better with kind words didn't help. What Sinatra couldn't accept was that such words were necessary. Even having Ava around didn't help his general outlook on life much, although he knew he always felt much worse when she wasn't about. They quarrelled and bickered, but he now needed to be with her – even just to be in the same room. In bed would be better still.

How much Nancy really knew of what was going on it is difficult to be sure. What *is* clear is that Dolly did know and, more than that, she connived in the arrangements made by her son. According to John Marotta, whose brother lived in the same building, Ava was smuggled into the senior Sinatra apartment by Frank himself when he made his secret visits to Hoboken.

'I remember my brother telling me how you could hear the two women talking well into the night. They spoke the same language, both swore so readily that my brother said he was highly embarrassed.' Marotta told me that it was to Dolly in Hoboken that Ava first made her frequently quoted comment on Frank: 'He weighs a hundred pounds, most of it all cock.' Dolly is supposed to have laughed uproariously.

There were more seemly connections between Marotta and Dolly in 1948. On Frank's thirty-third birthday that year, he organised a tribute to Sinatra, a concert in Hoboken which he conducted. There was a big backdrop to the stage with a huge blow-up of Sinatra in white tie, just as he appeared when he sang 'Ol' Man River' in *Till the Clouds Roll By*. The picture was flanked by the words in big white script, 'Frankie Sinatra'. Local musicians and singers – the girls in plaid skirts and sweaters, the boys in white shirts and slipovers – came to chant Frank's praise.

Marotta wrote a song for the occasion:

> We dedicate this show to Frank Sinatra.
> He's New Jersey's pride and joy.
> He's Hoboken's son.
> He's second to none.
> Just think of the wonderful things
> That Frank's done.
> His songs are number one

Throughout the nation.
From coast to coast
He's a big sensation.
Valley started to moon,
Crosby started to croon,
But it took our Frankie boy
To make the girls swoon.

It wasn't the greatest lyric in the world, but it was all heart and the Hoboken citizenry thought he wouldn't be able to turn down such an occasion. He did but Dolly did not. Nevertheless, they had a huge birthday cake, cut it and took it over to the box where she was sitting and sang 'Happy Birthday' to her.

'We hoped,' Marotta told me, 'to get some word from Frank which we could read to the fans who were gathered there, but he just ignored us. So I said he had sent us a telegram. I just made something up and read from a blank sheet of paper – "read" it to the people who were there as though it really said something. They all thought it came from Frank.' Even today, there is a sense of resentment as Marotta recalls the time when part of Hoboken, at least, wanted to say nice things about Frank and their efforts were spurned.

MGM had started to worry about their contract with Sinatra, but kept him working. For his part, he grabbed enthusiastically everything that came his way – including the film *The Kissing Bandit*, in which he starred with Kathryn Grayson, both of them floundering through a ridiculous script as though they had fallen into the Pacific from the Santa Monica pier without life jackets.

It was supposedly a story of a young businessman in the nineteenth century who is a little too conscious of his family responsibilities: his father had a reputation both as a criminal and a great lover. It was his duty to try to emulate the old man. As the dancer Ann Miller described the film: 'It was just horrendous'. Extra music was added to try to make it work, but it only served to show the weakness of the whole package. Kathryn Grayson remembers that they all knew how bad it was while they were making the movie. 'We used to joke, "What are we going to do for the sequel"?'

It was all a hundred times worse than *The Miracle of the Bells*, which was a remarkable achievement for a film not just from the MGM studio but one produced by Joe Pasternak. There were compensations, however. It was while working on *The Kissing Bandit* that Sinatra bumped into a producer named Howard Koch. 'I'd like to work with you one day,' Frank told him. Before long, they *would* work together and Mr Koch would play a very important part indeed in the Sinatra story, when he became his 'resident' film producer.

In later years, Sinatra would be the first to joke about *The Kissing Bandit*, to mock the movie as his very own *Horn Blows at Midnight* – the terrible film Jack Benny made and would constantly refer to on his radio programmes for years afterwards. For the moment, however, Frank was not laughing. *The Kissing Bandit* was set to all but drive him out of his mind.

It wasn't the only problem. His records, which had been losing ground for sometime, were now making even less impact. To make things worse, 1948 was the year of another musicians' strike. Artists were again driven to record with vocal accompaniments only – the Mills Brothers and their guitar had never been so busy. Singers performed with choirs for the first time in their lives.

Larry Adler told me he was asked by Columbia to accompany a set of Sinatra records on his mouth organ. 'I wouldn't do it because I wasn't going to turn into a scab,' he said. In normal circumstances, Frank wouldn't have wanted to be a scab either, but now he was having to think of his own career before anything else and was taking whatever work was on offer.

Nor did his next movie improve matters. It was originally to be called *It's Only Money* but became *Double Dynamite*, made for RKO and in particular for its owner, Howard Hughes, who wanted to team Sinatra with his busty girlfriend, Jane Russell. The third co-star was Groucho Marx. The film was so terrible that Hughes decided he had to shelve it. Not even Groucho could save it.

Melville Shavelson, who wrote the script, talks of it now as the first computer movie – Sinatra got blamed for a bank robbery he didn't commit. In the end, it turned out that the real criminal was the adding machine which had gone berserk. He only had a couple of songs in the film and now the main fascination has to be the love scenes he performed with Miss Russell. He would have been a lot more convincing with Ava Gardner.

The delayed release was frustrating for Sinatra. As Shavelson told me: 'He was only doing this because he needed to make a buck. He wasn't doing well at the time – he had a lot of debts and was spending wildly. It was a semi-quickie with a very reduced shooting schedule.

But Frank was very hard-working and professional – and was paid peanuts for it.'

But Hughes was so unhappy that he paid the producer Irving Cummings not to release the movie at all – 'a lot of money,' says Shavelson. Three years later and with the benefit of the new title, he relented. It would have been better for all concerned, had it all been allowed to remain on the cutting-room floor.

But not everything in which Sinatra participated in 1948 was so disastrous for him or for the people with whom he worked. Certainly, there was a more favourable response to another kind of entreaty made to Frank earlier in the year – to help what would soon become the State of Israel. In her book, Nancy, Jr., tells of her father's contribution to smuggling money out of America for the putative Jewish state, but until now the full details of his efforts have remained secret. Teddy Kollek, who was to become a legendary Mayor of Jerusalem and is one of the last of the state's founding fathers still alive, told me exclusively what happened.

'We had a ship leaving New York which had to stop, I think, in Mexico to collect arms for Israel,' he said. 'This was at a time when the United States had made a rule not to support any country arming itself for war. All the surrounding countries had arms, but Israel didn't. We needed arms to save ourselves – to survive.'

It was that kind of necessity which resulted in the idea of turning Frank Sinatra into a money runner.

Kollek and a group of people anxious to find ways of skirting the American prohibitions were living at the time in a small New York hostelry, the Hotel 14. It was above the Copacabana nightclub. 'The FBI were watching us,' he told me. 'We were much under their magnifying glass and realised that everything we did was being thoroughly investigated. Because we lived above the Copacabana, we used to go down to the club and enjoy the acts. We used to go there to relax.'

The principal act at that time was Frank Sinatra. The group not only enjoyed his show, they became friendly with Frank himself. Night after night they went to his performances and, night after night, Frank stopped by their table for a chat. What they discovered early on was that the Catholic Italian with a lot of Jewish friends had not forgotten that Jews had been nice to him in Hoboken. He became enthusiastic and sympathetic about their cause and Kollek wondered if perhaps he could be persuaded to assist them.

Not only could Frank be persuaded, he rallied to the cause with more enthusiasm than they could have thought possible. They told him of their problem: they had something like $1 million which they needed to get to various overseas arms suppliers immediately. Could Frank help?

'Sure,' he answered. 'What do you want me to do?'

What they needed him to do was to take a satchel full of money – cash collected clandestinely from Zionist supporters in America – to a ship waiting at one of the New York piers. 'We knew that we would be arrested as soon as we tried to deliver a briefcase containing the money,' Kollek recalled for me. 'But we thought there was a chance Sinatra would not be watched. I knew of his sentiments for us and asked if he would take the satchel of money to the pier and hand it to the captain. He agreed and did a great job.'

'We could never forget that help which Sinatra gave us then,' said Kollek. As a result, the name Frank Sinatra was immediately recorded in the minds of those who were at that moment compiling the history of what was soon to become the State of Israel. But, to date, it has never formed part of any official document. These facts alone are enough to enshrine the name Sinatra in the State's golden book of honour. With the money – probably all of that $1 million – delivered to the dockside in a leather satchel, the nascent state was able to purchase the very arms which enabled Israel to survive infancy in the face of professional Arab armies. It was to be the beginning of an association between Sinatra and the State of Israel that has always remained important for him. No less so for the State itself.

Sinatra's relationship with Jewish entertainers was always equally strong – which was why he still cherished that membership of the Hillcrest Country Club, the establishment which once again regarded Al Jolson as its king.

On radio programmes, the connection between the old king now reclaiming his throne from the new one was constantly being referred to. On one show, in which Jolson was guest, Bob Hope told the old-timer still revelling in his incredible comeback: 'Say, Al, I understand that even Sinatra is imitating you.'

'Frankie's imitating *me*?' an incredulous Jolson asked Hope.

'Yes,' Hope replied. 'I hear he's getting up on one knee' – a reference both to Frank's physical stature and to Jolson's favourite stage stance of getting down on one knee to sing 'Mammy'.

There were other times when the link between Jolson and Sinatra was not as funny. Morris Stoloff, the musical director of Columbia Pictures who had supervised the award-winning soundtrack of *The Jolson Story*, told me about a party at which both singers were present.

Then, as now, Hollywood parties were more than anything occasions for stars to perform for their colleagues and contemporaries. Point them to a piano in a crowded room full of other show people and the opportunity to sing or do conjuring tricks was usually too strong to resist. Particularly for Sinatra and Jolson. At this party Jolson started singing his latest hit from *The Jolson Story*, 'The Anniversary Song', followed by 'Mammy' and 'Avalon' and all the numbers with which he had wowed the audiences to the biopic and the people at the party were enthralled.

'Then, when Jolson took a break, we asked Frankie to sing,' Stoloff recalled. '"I can't follow that," Sinatra said, and he slunk out.'

That had never been known before. To make things worse, Columbia were even expecting Frank to 'cover' Jolson records, a virtual insult if he hadn't appreciated the strong commercial reasons for doing so – and the need he now felt to keep his record company happy. So he 'covered' a sweet Jolson ballad called 'If I Only Had a Match', a number which now had to be added to an ever-growing assortment of Sinatra discs that got absolutely nowhere.

The supreme insult came with the annual Hooper ratings for 1948 the principal poll indicating listening figures for the time. For the first time for four years, Frank wasn't among the top three male singers. He was fifth. Jolson was first. Bing Crosby was second, Perry Como third, Billy Eckstine fourth. Como did his best to make Frank feel as though he were still on top. 'Since Frank and I have a feud on,' said the former barber jokingly, 'I want to give him a real haircut. In fact, I've wanted to cut his hair for years – but not his throat.'

Sinatra had reason to be grateful for that. Jolson had come from nowhere to knock him off his pedestal. The most remarkable comeback by an entertainer of the past was presaging the most remarkable fall for one from an entirely different generation. The friends who had been with Frank in the great moments were with him still. You didn't abandon anyone who had been good to you when he had problems, or so he hoped.

Nancy was outwardly loyal, which was much more than Frank was to her. 'Ida', the woman from Hoboken who told me how she had double-dated with him before Nancy came on the scene, with her

The real love of his life. The statuesque Ava Gardner making it clear that she
was the real star of the family – in 1951 at the première of her film *Show Boat*.
Frank himself was already on his uppers.

(above opposite) Friends – Frank's investment in the future. With John F. Kennedy at the Democratic Convention at which the man about to become President was nominated.

(below opposite) Escorting Jackie Kennedy at the inauguration ball. Frank battled with the weather to compere the night's entertainment – and told the President not to interrupt when he was eating.

(above) The Presidential Excuse-Me. Only Ronald Reagan would dare interrupt Frank dancing with the First Lady.

(opposite) The gratified father – knowing that his son's kidnappers have had their just deserts.

(above) He was always generous with fellow entertainers whom he respected. Here with Nat 'King' Cole.

(below) Recalling old days – an elegant older Frank in 1979 with the man who gave him his first important break as a soloist, Harry James.

(above) This studio's made for singing. A proud father recording with his daughter, Nancy Jnr.

(opposite) The title of the sheet music seemed to say it all. Serenading Grace Kelly on the set of *High Society* – before she became a princess.

He's an Indian too. Juliet Prowse was something else – in every respect.
At a charity costume ball during their torrid engagement. (It was the evening
he almost had a punch up with John Wayne).

own fiancée, was once more part of a foursome – with Frank and Ava. 'I have never seen anyone so smitten, so much in love as he was with Ava,' she told me.

The love affair was to provide a full ration of problems for the Sinatra marriage. His friends tried to tell him that it was not only doing nothing for his private life, it was threatening to play havoc with his ever more fragile career, too.

Frank was not in the business of listening to such talk. His heart was ruling his head and he wanted Ava above everything else. She was sexually alluring. He thought he had more to talk to her about than he ever had to discuss with Nancy and nothing was going to divert him from loving her. The trouble was he didn't want to lose his marriage, either.

So the publicity machine got busy once more, saying what a lovely home-loving man he was – a person who enjoyed buying garden furniture, who wanted nothing more to eat than a constant supply of banana splits. It read a lot better than the press reports of the parties he went to with Ava and what happened afterwards.

Frank didn't like it, any of it. He complained about his privacy being invaded. What he couldn't accept was that being a star meant exposing everything to public view. It was one thing to be happy that newspapers reported the appearances that brought fans out in their thousands – the kind that meant there was every reason to buy his latest record or see his newest movie – but he couldn't accept that they had any rights to his spare time. He was not the first star to fail to grasp the fact that he was public property.

In 1949 he was still a big star, but he was fading. There were still the records, still the radio programme *Your Hit Parade* sponsored by Lucky Strike, or as the announcer introduced it week after week, 'Your Hit Parade with the Lucky Strike Orchestra, Lovely Joan Edwards, the Hit Paraders, and starring Frank Sinatra. Here they are, the Big Three [the allusion was to the name they gave the three big powers in World War II, the USA, the USSR and Britain] – the trio of tunes that head your hit parade this week ...'

There were also still the concert performances. But fashions were changing and so were his fans. The girls who screamed and squealed outside the Paramount were five years older now. Many of them were married. Hundreds of thousands of them were mothers. Did they now have time to go out and scream for Frankie? Those girls who were changing from bobbysox to nylon stockings underlined the feeling that perhaps he had just been a new toy that was about to be discarded in favour of something – or someone – else.

Few outside the immediate Sinatra circle knew it, but it was getting close to crisis-time in his world. He was worrying about his future and so was his record company, even though Manie Sacks was continuing to send soothing words from the Columbia Records headquarters.

He was still waxing cover versions of contemporary song hits but there continued to be problems when well-known numbers were compared with the originals. His recording of 'Some Enchanted Evening', the big hit from what was then the most successful show ever, *South Pacific*, was dismissed by *Down Beat* magazine as being 'without intimacy'. They even spotted a few 'off-pitch notes'. They said that his 'Bali Hai', the *South Pacific* number which everyone in the country who had recorded 'Some Enchanted Evening' also sang, 'very seldom comes to life'. Worse than that, both bore all the marks of being numbers that were down in the book for him to record whether he liked it or not. He seemed to be getting tired of the things he had been doing for the past six or seven years, but went on doing them because it was expected of him – and he was still being paid pretty handsomely for doing so.

Did Sinatra not care? All the evidence, from people like Sacks who reported his unhappiness, both private and public, was that he did. His ambition was as burning hot as it had been when he first shyly spoke to Major Bowes, but a lethargy had descended upon him. He was not really prepared to do anything about it. Perhaps the answer lay entirely in Hollywood. He hoped that what he had planned to be an expanding movie career would do something more for him. And for a time it seemed that it might.

Indeed, it was MGM who came to the rescue, with a couple of little projects they thought were just right. One of them was going to be called *On the Town*.

SAME OLD SONG AND DANCE

The year was 1949 and Arthur Freed, with Gene Kelly at his elbow, was reinventing the musical. Freed's musicals unit at MGM was now in place, a laboratory for cooking up a new look to what had been a staple of the Hollywood output ever since the movies found their voice with *The Jazz Singer*.

The whimsical picture in which the little girl in pigtails mooned over the boy next door in his striped blazer was all but consigned to the scrapheap. In its stead, Kelly and Freed – Kelly had the ideas, Freed the means of putting it all together – were creating an altogether sharper, in some ways more brittle kind of film. It would be one where the most natural thing in the world would seem to be to break into a dance routine while walking down Fifth Avenue. Seeing those films was infectious. They induced an urge to dance out of a movie theatre and on the bus waiting outside, still humming the hit number from the picture.

The new musical was proving itself; a genre where the singing and dancing were the best you could see and hear anywhere in the world – but, and this was the real difference, the stories were as strong as anything coming from a Hollywood sound stage.

Dancing was being made a much less leisurely affair than Fred Astaire gave the impression of its being (it was only an impression – Mr Astaire was a perfectionist). But to go with that dancing were the finest sets, the greatest orchestras, the best lighting and photography – and the most enterprising co-stars. That was where Frank Sinatra came in. He was about to be involved in the most important movies he had made to date, as the junior partner. Not to the female love interest, but to Gene Kelly.

None of the women with whom Kelly played were likely threats, but then neither was Sinatra. The fact that he took this role without complaint says a great deal about the way his career was going. He needed the work more than ever – if he had said no, he would have been put on suspension without pay.

By signing Frank up to play opposite Kelly in the first of the two 1949 movies, *Take Me Out to the Ballgame*, Freed was doing nothing less than mounting a Sinatra rescue operation. It just about came off – within the limitations of turning Frank into a highly successful stooge to Mr Kelly. Just as they had in *Anchors Aweigh*, they both sang and danced in the film, and as in the earlier movie, audiences were ready to tolerate Kelly's light, pleasant voice because there was his dancing to go with it. Frank's dancing was another thing. It was clear he was there merely to give a new dimension to Kelly and if he could do a couple of steps, so much the better.

They played a pair of hoofers on the vaudeville circuit who, when people weren't going to the theatre, played baseball – with somewhat more success than they achieved on stage. There was a great deal of singing. The songs were written especially by Betty Comden, Adolph Green and Roger Edens, numbers which sounded as if they had been precisely what people sang on the baseball terraces forty years earlier. The pair also looked great in their vaudeville costumes of white suits (with red stripes), straw hats and canes. But nothing was allowed to detract from the fact that this was essentially Kelly's movie. Esther Williams, more used to a swimming pool as *her* partner, was no trouble to either of them.

It was a pleasant enough romp, focusing, of course, on a baseball diamond – and those Edens–Comden–Green songs. The film historian Leslie Halliwell was to describe it as 'a fast-moving, funny, tuneful delight with no pretensions'. And it did a lot for baseball – although it could be argued that Hoboken-invented baseball was about the one American activity that was never in need of any publicity.

By then Frank was baseball crazy – with his own, not-too-serious team called the Swooners. Sammy Cahn, Jule Styne and Anthony Quinn were among those who donned uniforms and turned out to play almost anyone who would agree to face them on the field.

And they had their supporters – among them four luscious young women who with a giant 'S' curving amazingly around their bosoms were there to shout encouragement – Virginia Mayo, Shelley Winters and two thoroughly dangerous signs of the times, Marilyn Maxwell and Ava Gardner.

On the Town, later that year, was a much more important picture, often described – along with *Singin' in the Rain* – as one of the two best musicals of all time. It was based on a highly successful Broadway show with an original score by Leonard Bernstein, featuring three sailors with a day's leave in New York, determined to make the most of every minute. The picture was directed and choreographed jointly by Kelly and Stanley Donen, with music supplied by a collection of writers. Betty Comden and Adolph Green who had written the original play and lyrics did the same for the movie. Only Bernstein's 'New York, New York' remained from the original production, although he did write the ballet music and that for the 'Miss Turnstiles' dance sequence.

It was in many ways a reunion of the *Ballgame* crew; not just Sinatra and Kelly but also Jules Munshin, and Betty Garrett. Ms Garrett – who had experienced the Sinatra magic in her youth: she told me she remembered being crushed by the crowds at the Paramount – has, on the whole, happy memories of working with Frank on both pictures. 'He was great fun,' she recalled. But, she added, 'you knew that Kelly was more the real artist of the two when it came to the dancing numbers – and they were the ones that held the movie together.

'There was no question that he told Frank what to do and I don't really think Sinatra was given anything very complicated, but what he did, he did well – very well.'

Nevertheless, there was trouble on the set of *On the Town* – nothing serious, but the kind of upset that casts a pall over the cast and crew, all working to make this the most important movie that ever happened.

Saul Chaplin, assisting the musical director, Lennie Hayton, and working on his first Sinatra film, told me, 'He wouldn't show up for rehearsals. There was that story all the time. But I literally didn't care. One thing I've found out about Frank. He's prepared. I don't know how he does it. He doesn't rehearse. But I've never seen him forget a line on stage. Maybe he covers it all up with footwork, I don't know.'

Chaplin agrees, though, that 'it was always annoying'. Frank made his excuses to the director, Stanley Donen, and to Kelly and they were gentlemen enough not to reveal them to anyone else.

There was one episode which got slightly beyond the 'annoying' stage. 'Gene and Stanley Donen would plan a rehearsal after shooting a previous scene. Frank wouldn't show up. He always had some cockamamie excuse. This one time there was a number being done by Ann Miller called "Prehistoric Man" [it was shot in the Natural

History Museum]. The other five people are her chorus.' Frank declared, 'I'm not going to be a chorus boy for Ann Miller.'

Finally, he was mollified. Like Chaplin and everyone else (to say nothing of Leonard Bernstein), Frank was angry that almost all of the good songs from the highly successful stage show had been omitted. So he came up with a typical Sinatra solution: if they would let him sing 'Lonely Town', a beautifully sorrowful, soul-searching ballad from the Broadway production, he would do the chorus number.

Said Chaplin: 'Freed agreed. Frank sang his song as I rehearsed it with him and it was indeed beautiful. But then Freed went back on his word, and it wasn't in the picture.'

Comden and Green were as disappointed as was Frank. 'It's a very emotional song and he did it completely differently from the way it had been done before,' Ms Comden told me. 'Frank really believed in that song. He sweated over the arrangement for a very long time. We loved the musicality of his performances, which I think were influenced by the way he had studied the work of Vaughan Williams.' That was a little known fact about Sinatra. He may not really have listened to Heifitz in those early days, but now he was becoming conscious of the need to learn more about music and its creators.

But it was in the lyrics that they believed he shone. 'Nobody is quite like him in getting the lyrics,' Adolph Green told me. 'He was born with the gift to be able to do so, but it is also a respect for words. A very bright man.'

But rehearsals were a problem. It was the old Sinatra story – and would become the new Sinatra story and the continuing Sinatra story in the decades to come. What everyone else regarded as unprofessional behaviour, Frank took as no more than expressing his own personality and the way he liked to work. Over-rehearse, he said, and he lost his spontaneity. What he didn't accept was that he was holding up everyone else's work, particularly when – as he frequently did – he came late.

'We thought it was time we taught him a lesson,' Betty Garrett remembers. 'We decided to play a joke – but one that he took all too seriously. We gave him the silent treatment. We let him know that because he was coming in late, he was seriously affecting all that we were trying to do and it was not just unprofessional, it was causing severe problems. We agreed that we would not speak to him.'

'He went mad. He was so upset, as though we were ostracising him – which I suppose we were but much more seriously than we intended. Actually, I think he was very hurt and surprised that we all took it like that. But we were all aggravated by what we took to be his very unprofessional behaviour. After all, we regarded him as part of our team. We all came in for rehearsals in our work clothes – and worked like dogs.'

But the act of shutting out Sinatra didn't last long. 'In a very short while, he got the message and we all became friends again. He really is a very nice guy and was very nice to us all.'

As Betty says: 'He was wasting a lot of time and making Gene so angry. Frank eventually apologised to Gene, then stayed for as long as he was wanted and even stood in for lighting and everything.'

Betty had got into the habit of giving Frank a gentle pat on his backside – 'for luck', she said. She had done it for weeks during the rehearsals that he had attended, but the time she did when they were ready to go before the cameras, the reaction was less than friendly. 'Don't ever do that again,' he thundered.

It wasn't that Sinatra had suddenly developed a new prim, moral outlook on life, or was offended by such 'intimate' behaviour. He had simply got to hear that people were saying things about his appearance in his white sailor suit. Someone suggested that it was as though he didn't have a bottom at all, an insult compounded by the fact that the studio thought it worth 'implanting' what they called enhancers into the seat of his pants.

Long before the era when women liked to talk about sexy small male posteriors, he regarded it as an insult. But Ms Garrett, who seems to have been everybody's friend on the set of both this film and the *Ballgame* picture, managed to soothe him.

What was so significant about *On the Town* as far as the cinema historians are concerned was that it really was the first musical shot entirely on location – as though the scene on the bridge in *It Happened in Brooklyn* had been a rehearsal for something much, much bigger. This was a celebration of New York, shot in New York – uptown and downtown, with Brooklyn thrown in for good measure. There was no back projection used at all.

The film did provide a great deal of entertainment for the people of New York who watched the shoot as though they were actually part of it.

'New York, New York' was to be the most outstanding celebration in song of America's biggest city (even though sanitised from the stage version which had declared it to be 'hell of a town'; now it was a 'wonderful town') until Sinatra's 1970s hit version of the entirely different Kander and Ebb song with the same name. But, as Leonard Bernstein's *On the Town* song made clear, the Bronx is up and the Battery is down and both were on the agenda of the three sailors, determined to see everything and find romance, too.

We see both things happen – with Kelly looking for Miss Turnstiles, the girl next door picked by the people who run the subway system to appear on posters boosting their mode of transport. Munshin winds up with a student of anthropology played by Ann Miller, whose long legs seemed to end somewhere on the second storey, and Sinatra with Betty Garrett, playing the taxi-driver who decides that this country boy (Frank's role yet again) needs educating in the ways of New York – and she didn't just mean the number of floors to the top of the Empire State Building.

Nothing could make up for so much of the original Bernstein score being discarded, but Frank did well with everything he was given. He perhaps scored best with a new song called 'You're Awful', a 1949 update on the big hit, 'De-lovely', from the thirties. Certainly, it was a happy enough romp; as *Time* magazine said of *On the Town*, 'So exuberant that it threatens at moments to bounce right off the screen.'

Sinatra danced a bit but he didn't sing alone enough, and although he proved to be a consummate actor, he left the people who paid to see the movie thinking that he was perhaps no longer strong enough to be a solo star.

If this were going to be his main career now, as it was for those actors and actresses who rejoiced in the job description of film star, then it wasn't unfolding all that successfully. There wouldn't be another Sinatra film for two years – and that was the previously rejected *Double Dynamite*. *Meet Danny Wilson*, the second Sinatra vehicle released in 1951, was to be described as a 'self-parody' of himself. As the two years between that film and *On the Town* were to prove, that could be said about Frank's own life at the time, too.

In the meantime, he was doing his best to give some new kind of image to his career. He jumped at the opportunity to appear with the Philadelphia Orchestra, normally Leopold Stokowski's ensemble – 'and the orchestra showed him all the respect one of the great singers of the 1940s deserved', Morton Gould, who conducted the concert, recalled.

It was a similar story when Gould conducted the orchestra for a benefit starring Sinatra soon afterwards. Jule Styne and Sammy Cahn provided new material. 'I remember Jule Styne saying to Frank, "Hey that's a great coat you're wearing." At which, he took it off his shoulders and said: "You want it? Take it."'

Not many people were prepared to give the coat off their backs, but Sinatra was, just as he gave of himself at all those performances. 'I remember the orchestra being a little sluggish,' said Gould. 'But he got them out of it. He was different from anyone they had ever worked with before.'

To many people, the image of the Hollywood star was of a womanising, irresponsible individual with too much money to spend. In fact, Sinatra was getting more and more involved with only one woman, Ava Gardner, who had 'Dangerous' written all over her. She was someone who might have had much to lose if the ever-inquiring press started going into details about their affair, but the difference was that she was a free woman, whose marriage to Mickey Rooney had lasted no more than a year and she had now divorced Artie Shaw.

She was the epitome of the character in the Irving Berlin song, 'A Man Chases a Girl Until She Catches Him.' In 1949, after years of an on–off relationship, she caught him as he chased her in his car. It was the day every single MGM star was due to pose for a movie scene and still photograph that would become one of the most famous in the history of Hollywood. It was the studio's 25th anniversary and to commemorate the event, the Metro publicists dreamed up the idea that all its stars would be invited to have lunch, sitting next to each other on some giant set arranged in tiers on a vast plinth. As they ate, the cameras purred. Later, the tables were removed and there were more pictures. Frank was second from the right in the second row from the top between Ginger Rogers and Red Skelton, two places from Walter Pidgeon and in the row behind Mario Lanza and Gene Kelly. Also in the picture were Katharine Hepburn, Fred Astaire, Lionel and Ethel Barrymore, Judy Garland – and Ava Gardner.

Ms Gardner was to recall how Frank overtook her in his car at speed and then slowed down so that she had to overtake him. She did it three times. After that last perambulation, he raised his hat and both drove off to the same destination – the picture session. As Ava wrote in her autobiography: 'He could even flirt in a car.'

They flirted at a party in Palm Springs soon afterwards. They didn't make love, but they had a fairly good idea of what was happening to them. The body language was strong and so was the mental torment.

'I think it must have frightened both of us,' Ava later wrote.

What neither of them was yet prepared to admit was that they had found the love of their lives or the stormy future it would entail. From time to time they would try to resist the fact, but by all accounts, it had never been the same for either of them before and never would be again. 'We became lovers eternally,' was how Ava put it.

Ava was to write that Frank told her she was much more important to him than was his life as a singer – a fact that was obvious to everyone who knew him. Was it simply that he had achieved his singing ambitions beyond most people's wildest dreams? Hardly. Sex and, with it, love had become forces too strong to resist – much, much stronger than they had ever been when he was first courting Nancy, or Marilyn Maxwell, or the host of chorus girls and hookers readily available to him whenever he wanted them. 'You're all I want,' he told her.

One thing *was* certain – despite an aberration from present form when his record of 'The Huckle Buck' got into the top ten – Ava was proving too much of a distraction. It was causing agonies for Nancy, a situation not helped when well-meaning friends told her to pull her husband into shape. 'I told her,' Sammy Cahn once revealed to me, 'to tell Frank to lay off the booze and lay off the broads. It's going to kill him.' Others have since claimed to have passed on the same advice – although, depending on their closeness to Sinatra himself, most of them seem to have drawn a line at passing on the warning directly. As it was, Nancy was the one who needed help after the messages had been passed to her. She would have had to have been made of stone not to be seriously affected. And yet the marriage continued.

Whether it was because of Nancy's strong Catholicism or simply the undoubted love she still felt for Frank, she resisted any suggestion of divorce. With the hypocritical morality of the day in full evidence – via the comments of gossip columnists like Hedda Hopper and Louella Parsons – it would have been much more dangerous, for Sinatra's career, to end his marriage than merely to carry on an affair in public – which was virtually what was happening now. No cameras actually captured him and Ava in bed together, but you no longer even had to read between the lines to know what was happening. If the gossip had been legitimised by a divorce, the Catholic League of Decency and all the other do-gooding organisations could have stepped in and put a block ban on Sinatra's movies.

If there was any doubt that the Sinatra career was on a slippery slope, listening to the 28 May 1949 transmission of *Your Hit Parade* would have removed all doubt. It was the last one. Yet, strangely, in September he was back again working on the radio – and for Lucky Strike again. But *Light Up Time* was a further indication of how much lower his standing now was. The show was broadcast five nights a week – and any radio star who agreed to work five nights a week was saying he needed the money. The show only lasted fifteen minutes – and, worst of all, he was sharing the billing with Dorothy Kirsten, star of the Metropolitan Opera who was known to like to dally with popular entertainers. (She had sung on Al Jolson's radio show and appeared to have struck a popular chord.) No superstar would have considered such a status but Sinatra went along with the idea, with the same kind of gratitude he showed to sharing billing with Gene Kelly on screen.

Everything seemed to be going wrong. The annual *Metronome* poll, which Frank had come to accept as virtually his own property, now had Billy Eckstine at the head of its male singer charts. If you looked for an explanation, you could say that Frank was simply worried about his private life. But the quality was so obviously different. And if you searched for an explanation for that changed quality, you found it in one word: inconsistency. One week he was as brilliantly good as he had ever been before. The following day, he was simply terrible.

The music critic, Barbara Hodgkins, wrote: 'He seems to feel his days as a romantic whisperer are numbered.' If he were going to be a whisperer on *Light Up Time*, Dorothy Kirsten offered too much competition from the shouting corner for him to be comfortable. It was a different Sinatra on a different sort of show – but it wasn't necessarily bad. 'Though he sings the old sweet things,' wrote Ms Hodgkins, 'he does them with a touch of humour, a spot of jazz feeling.' This wasn't quite the Swingin' Sinatra of the later fifties and sixties but he was moving there.

One of the reasons for the change of sound was that on this new radio show, Frank was without the services of Axel Stordahl. A whole industry had got to know the value of the man whose name appeared on those blue-and-gold record labels below that of Frank himself. He would be there when Frank recorded with the likes of Dinah Shore, Pearl Bailey and Rosemary Clooney, offering advice even when he wasn't standing in front of the orchestra and waving his stick. But now the man who had been Sinatra's principal aide in his recording career was stepping this one out, although no one ventured to ask why. Could it be simply out of deference to Ms Kirsten, who might have thought Stordahl would be moving things too much Frank's way? This is highly probable.

Standing now in Stordahl's familiar place was Jeff Alexander, with whom Frank had previously recorded. He was not in the job long, again for reasons no one has been able to satisfactorily explain. Replacing him was Skitch Henderson, who provided the real impetus for the jazz influences that would one day play such an important part in the Sinatra output.

It was Sinatra's own idea that Henderson should be the man with the baton. He tracked him down in Lexington, Kentucky, where Skitch was leading his band for a one-night stand. 'How'd you like to be my musical director?' he asked. Henderson was by his side virtually by the time Frank put down the receiver.

Sinatra was managing to keep his name before the public, few of whom seemed to be as concerned as he was about the way his career was going. He even managed to resist attempts made by the Un-American Activities Committee to name him as one of the people who had 'followed or appeased some of the Communist party line'. It didn't stick because there was absolutely no evidence to support it, and in fairness to Frank, had there been any he would have defended what he did as being in the cause of promoting goodwill and decency.

Decency was not a word that was very often used in connection with Frank – particularly when it came to stories connecting him with Ava. Did a chambermaid at the Hampshire House Hotel in New York spot them in a compromising situation, or an observant bystander see them in the hotel lobby? Whichever, the news that they were both there, and together, was published all over the United States.

Louis B. Mayer called Frank and Ava into his white-carpeted office and read them the Hollywood equivalent of the riot act. Another secret conversation had less positive results. Mayer told Sinatra that California's Governor Earl Warren – later to be Chief Justice of the United States and the man who headed the famous investigation into the shooting of President John F. Kennedy – had requested that he sing at the National Conference of State governors at Warren's own capital, Sacramento. Mayer was beside himself with excitement at this tribute to the studio from the Republican party to which he owed so much. Sinatra said he was excited, too. The Governor was going to fly him from Hollywood in his own private plane. Frank said, thank you, that sounded very nice. The aircraft waited at the airport at the precise time it was supposed to get there, but Frank didn't show up. To this day, he has never explained his absence from an event which would have made his boss ecstatically happy. How long he could last at MGM was now a topic for conversation at every bar, deli and restaurant in the film city.

Frank's inconsistency was also putting a strain on Sinatra's other 'marriage' – the one between him and his press agent, George Evans. After constantly warning Frank to keep his love life quiet if he could not avoid it altogether, the relationship that had existed since the first Paramount Theatre days was over.

Frank was to discover to his cost just how much he would miss Evans, his gentle hints of what he needed to do to try to recover a damaged public image, his smoothing-over of disgruntled journalists, his friendship. Seven weeks later, Frank flew to New York – for Evans's funeral. He had died of a heart attack at the age of forty-eight.

It had all sorts of repercussions for Frank. Instantly, he realised how much he needed Evans's advice and how much he would miss it now. The loss of Evans also meant that Frank lost enthusiasm for much of his work. An album had been scheduled with Lena Horne. When Evans died, he decided not to go through with it and it was never made – to both their regrets.

Had Evans lived, he might have been able to prevent the event which finally ended the Sinatra marriage. Frank and Ava were spotted together at the official opening of the Shamrock, a new hotel in Houston, Texas. Frank had been invited to the opening and Ava went because she knew he would be a guest. Later, they were photographed together at the Sorrentino restaurant by the *Houston Post*. Ava wrote that Frank 'reacted as if he'd found a live cobra in his salad'. As she said, it doomed 'for ever the "just good friends" line we'd been successful with so far'.

Nancy, of course, had never believed that her husband and Ava Gardner were just good friends and she announced that it was all over. There would be no divorce – as a good Catholic, she could not consider it but there was no doubt that they were separating. Yet suddenly they were together once more. Frank had come back, but after staying a month, he left again. This time, it would be for good. February 1 1950, was the date when it was certain that they would never live under the same roof again.

Nancy Jr., would later tell how she had got to know of the romance – she found some copies of fan magazines which had been kept from her, all of them showing her father with pretty ladies she had never met. As she said: 'He had left me, too.'

— 9 —

MY ONE AND ONLY LOVE

Ava Gardner wasn't the easiest person to deal with. As she once said, 'If I were a man, I wouldn't like me.' Knowing those faults, however, didn't make Sinatra's relationship with her any the less difficult. 'He has a temper that bursts into flames, while my temper burns inside me for hours. He never finishes an argument. He just gets up and walks away, leaving me frustrated and furious.'

She was as close to being a nymphomaniac as a Hollywood star could be in the early fifties without losing her contract. Her flings with various men were the subject of constant Hollywood gossip. She considered herself to be the most important person around. Yes, she was willing to help other people at all times, but only providing it didn't give her too much trouble.

But at a time when Frank couldn't find a new song he wanted to sing, Ava was the bright spot on the horizon – once he accepted the fact that she wasn't going to be the home-loving type that Nancy had been. He also had to accept that she would take not just as much as she gave, but probably a lot more. This was a highly volatile, highly sexed woman who wanted everything to be on her own terms.

And that was precisely what Frank saw and liked about her. As the British writer Olga Franklin said at the time: 'She was, or pretended to be, indifferent to him. To a man swamped by love, it was the final attraction.' As she also said, 'If only Ava had been easier to get, he might still be married to Nancy today.' Perhaps. Inevitably, the phone in Nancy's home rang incessantly. Would she be going back to her first – and only – love? 'There is positively no chance of a reconciliation between us,' Nancy was quoted as saying. 'All the rumours about Mr Sinatra and me are false.'

Of course, they were. He had nothing in common now with such a homebody whose only faults seemed to have been that she put first her role as a thoroughly decent wife and mother. For Frank, who had come from poor beginnings, achieved riches beyond imagination and believed he needed all the symbols that would keep him in his current status, Ava was the ultimate trophy. He had kept away from Hoboken not only because there were so many people there who didn't like him, but also because it reminded him of times and situations to which he didn't want to return. He didn't want a homely wife from New Jersey, either. He wanted the woman who once sat on the piano stool with a young André Previn and asked him to take her home. 'Don't you have your own car?' he asked. 'Go fuck yourself,' she answered.

Ava's character, too, had a lot to do with her upbringing – in Boon Hill, North Carolina, where her father, a hillbilly farmer, had kept her under a firm rein – as much to keep her away from black men, whom he refused to employ and about whom he was paranoid, as because he was frightened of her sleeping around with the local 'white trash'. A woman who begins life like that is inclined to find ways of making sure such an existence is left firmly behind her.

She was dubbed 'the most beautiful animal in the world'. When she heard what Frank had declared when they first met – 'This is the woman I am going to marry' – she decided to make him fight for her. The trouble was she loved his advances, so much so that she always found them difficult to resist. Robert Mitchum was not the only one to give her some firm advice: 'Sleep with him if you want to, but don't marry him.'

Frank, who one would think was well educated in the way of women, knew none of this. In fact, he was sure that she would be his whenever he was ready. His desertion of Nancy in the hope of Ava wasn't universally popular. Quarico 'Willie Moore' Moretti, reputed to be the Mafia godfather for the state of New Jersey, thought Sinatra was letting down the side of good Italian Catholic family life. He sent an angry telegram to the singer, demanding that he do the right thing. 'You have a decent wife and children,' it said. Frank took no notice.

If only his career was that easily achieved. The records were proving little short of disastrous, the reviews were terrible. Said one *Down Beat* summary: '"Lost in the Stars" seems pitched too low for Sinatra – he has trouble making the notes of "dim" and "him", nor is he able to make the rather complex lyric hang together.'

His recording life was beset with problems, not just those arising out of record reviews, although they influenced sales. The bobbysoxers really had really grown up now and had moved on from buying records. Their younger brothers and sisters were finding new favourites, like

Frankie Laine – who was wowing them in the record stores with 'Mule Train', 'Cry of the Wild Goose' and 'That's My Desire' – and Johnny Ray, a big name in cabaret, soon to go to the top of the pops, dabbing his eyes with a big handkerchief while he sang 'Cry' and 'The Little White Cloud That Cried'. Meanwhile, Bing Crosby continued to make a fortune with one new disc a week and Jolson was forever amazing the music industry. (His new film, *Jolson Sings Again*, was the most popular musical in 1949.)

When Frank appeared on other people's shows – and he still did – he was getting the less demanding jobs. Bud Yorkin, who a few years later would direct Sinatra in his film *Come Blow Your Horn*, met him when he was working on *The Dinah Shore Show*. 'She took all the high notes and he took only the low ones. I saw the psychological effect it had on him. He was very unhappy, going through a period that was highly emotional for him.'

But Frank's real problem was that his old pal Manie Sacks was no longer at Columbia and his successor in deciding what should or should not be recorded, Mitch Miller, was cut from another piece of cloth altogether. He was not suggesting that Frank stop recording for the label. That would have been stupid, particularly since so many of the stars were working for the rival Decca company, but he was beginning to make life uncomfortable.

Sinatra may not have been top of the pops, but there were still people out there buying his records. Miller thought he could make him more successful – by changing the songs he sang and the way he performed them. To a singer who had studied Tommy Dorsey's shoulders before working out how to breathe and how to phrase, that was close to sacrilege. It was the beginning of one of those relationships defined as 'fraught', to put it mildly.

To be fair to Miller he was planning a strategy that he considered would be good for the label. But it cannot be denied that he was also endeavouring to find ways of stamping his own impression on to every disc that was being pressed. The audacity of that plan was that it applied not only to newcomers or small-time little-hopers, but to stars like Sinatra, too.

There were, of course, limits on how Frank could say no and how many recording dates he could turn down. There was also a limit on how heavy a stick Miller could bring down on the man who had given the Columbia label no fewer than eighty hits. Miller, Sinatra's supporters declared, wasn't a music man at all, but a merchandiser.

That seems to say that they thought he sold records as though he were selling popcorn in a cinema. But it was an incontrovertible fact that he kept his job on the strength of a balance sheet. And he was determined to record only what sold.

Frank was interested in the cheques that came every quarter – the ever-present threat of future (he hoped near-future) alimony requirements made them essential – but for all his problems he thought there had to be integrity in his music. In upholding that integrity, Sinatra could also be modest. 'All of us are interpreters,' he would say. 'Without mikes and electronics, we're nowhere. We're a commodity, that's all.' Saying that seemed to be stating that he considered himself and Miller to be soulmates. They were anything but.

Miller was soon to introduce new sounds of his own – highly successful singalong numbers, always with French horns, played by the Mitch Miller Orchestra. 'Tzena Tzena Tzena' and 'My Heart Cries for You' were tremendous hits. The orchestra and chorus accompanying Guy Mitchell on songs such as 'She Wore Red Feathers' and 'My Truly, Truly Fair' had a style all their own. He seems to have thought he could turn Sinatra into a kind of Mitchell. To Frank's everlasting credit, he balked at the idea of making a career out of novelty songs. But that did not mean his career was safe or that Miller was always wrong. He sang 'Goodnight Irene' with Miller and it was a nice choice. Others were a lot less happy. 'American Beauty Rose' was a disaster; 'Kisses and Tears' with Jane Russell totally forgettable, which was indeed fortunate.

Miller said he wanted Sinatra to do 'more jumpy things', but the thought cannot be totally dismissed that what he really wanted was for Frank to jump right out of the Columbia building. The A & R man and star vocalist were not made for each other – and even when Sinatra did as he was told, the records still barely moved out of the shops.

New techniques were tried. In this pre-tape era, the musical backing was prerecorded on acetate discs before Frank was allowed near the mike. To an artist who always eschewed the isolation of a recording booth and liked to see his orchestra when he sang, it was just one more insult. But Mitch Miller was determined to do things his way. He said it was just a way of allowing Frank to re-record tracks without having to call back the band if anything went wrong, that Frank would record some phrases beautifully but then follow them with others that were terrible. Having him sing to a track allowed as much editing to be done as was possible at that time.

Occasionally Sinatra was allowed his own way. He recorded seven songs with the help of one of his radio arrangers, George Siravo, which he thought artistically satisfactory. He was not totally unhappy with the four sides he cut with Hugo Winterhalter. He liked, too, three with Morris Stoloff, who was doing so well with Jolson and was trying to live down the experience of seeing Sinatra slink away at his party.

'I never really understood this man,' Stoloff told me. 'He was unbelievably generous with anyone whom he thought appreciated his music, yet would snap at the slightest thing going wrong. Mitch Miller made him snap all the time, of course. He was so insecure at this time, it was pitiful.'

What was really pitiful was the advance Columbia now paid him for future work. The star whose royalties in 1946 alone had been over $20,000 was now going to receive a mere $150. Nobody else was making any better offers, so he accepted the cheque. At least it meant he could carry on recording.

Occasionally, he still worked with Axel Stordahl – most notably, during those dreadful times, with 'Birth of the Blues', a superb piece of artistry that showed a new Sinatra altogether – a ballad singer turned jazzman, which presaged what would follow in a couple of years.

Matters really came to a head when Frank recorded a so-called novelty number – complete with howls and barks – called 'Mama Will Bark', with a lady named Dagmar who was better known for the size of her bra than the range of her voice. History has turned it into *The Kissing Bandit* of the record world, not forgettable but at least remembered as a joke no one would mention unless things were otherwise going well.

Things were no better in Hollywood than they were in the record studios. MGM signalled that they intended to punish Frank for his past behaviour and chose the cruellest weapon of all – billing. When they released *On the Town*, they changed the way his named appeared on the poster – from 'Frank Sinatra and Gene Kelly in ...' To 'Gene Kelly and Frank Sinatra...' And there was nothing he could do about it.

Since he knew that Louis B. Mayer had plans for him – like calling his lawyers and getting his contract cancelled – he started putting out feelers with other studios, hoping they would offer him work. After all, he still needed the status of having a film to make as much as he needed the money that a new contract would bring. There were no takers.

At one time, he believed he was going to conclude a deal with Columbia Pictures and that a book called *Knock on Any Door* had all the answers for him – especially since Columbia had bought the film rights. There was a character in the story that was made to measure for him – a youngster from New Jersey about to go to the electric chair for murder. He started using the same technique he would bring to bear in contacts with the studio three years later. He inquired, he phoned, he badgered. But Columbia thought they needed someone younger.

That was a new thing for him – to be rejected because he was too old. Frank had always been everyone's young person. He believed his own propaganda. If anything, he thought he was too young for most of the interesting parts. He had told himself he was still the kid who wowed them at the Paramount. Once more, his sense of identity was being undermined.

At this time, Ava Gardner's star was rapidly rising. The girl from the Deep South who wasn't allowed to speak on screen until the elocution experts had got hold of her and trimmed her accent (and that took a year) had already been nominated by movie extras as the most beautiful woman in films. And after a number of so-so roles, she was now at the height of her own career and preparing for her starring part in *Show Boat*, her most successful film.

To Frank, she was not just a highly desirable sexual diversion but someone whom he believed was perfect for the trouble he was in. Sure, she had a vicious temper and her language could made even him blush, but she also had a wonderful way of making Frank try to forget all his troubles. Somehow, he could not understand that she was also the root of many of those troubles.

Frank thought everything would be better if Nancy gave him a divorce. She was adamant that she would never do so. Not even Dolly could persuade her. It would have been difficult for the older woman to reconcile her contacts with the Catholic Church of New Jersey by openly countenancing such a move, but she was ready to try. Her daughter-in-law was at the bottom of it all, she let it be known.

Instead, Nancy filed for maintenance and the size of the demands floored Sinatra as much as had the threats from MGM. Nancy, the comfy little wife who had never demanded enough from him, now said that if they did part permanently, she would require alimony commensurate with the close-to-a-million dollars which her husband had earned in the previous year. She also wanted half of all community property and custody of all three children.

The younger Nancy was ten years old when it happened. 'I was old enough to know what was happening and to know that he wasn't coming home and to feel my mother's pain.' The pain was increased by the fact that the Sinatra family home was under siege at the time. 'My mother says there were always faces at the window.'

Frank went into this period knowing full well what he had let himself in for. He didn't want to break up from his children, but he did want to end the marriage. As for the cost of it all, well, he thought, at least that would get him off the hook and allow him finally to stop worrying about Ava's intentions. He would marry her now. No, he would not, said Nancy. She was as determined as ever not to give him a divorce. That which the Catholic Church had ordained in New Jersey was not going to be torn asunder by a bitch of a beauty queen in Hollywood. Separation and suitable maintenance payments were another thing entirely.

Louis B. Mayer seemed to be coming to his own conclusions about the affair. In 1950 he ended Sinatra's contract with the studio. There had been just too many difficulties, too much of the star wanting his own way.

That was an entirely unusual event at MGM. As historians have noted, you usually had to be much worse than Sinatra – like Judy Garland, for instance whose behaviour made Frank seem like an angel – to merit being fired. But Mayer was adamant.

One of the reasons was something that had been noted before. Other MGM artists regarded the studio as their life, certainly their main job. With Sinatra, it was never going to be more than an optional extra. That being so, Mayer thought he had the option to fire him. But another reason was much more basic. Mayer had a mistress named Ginny Simms and Sinatra had insulted her.

It happened after LB, as everyone given access to Mayer's inner sanctum called him, had been thrown by his favourite horse. He ended up in hospital, covered in plaster. Predictably, it was the talking point all over the MGM lot. Not surprisingly, Frank and Gene Kelly were talking about it as they had lunch in the studio commissary. 'I understand that LB fell,' said Kelly. 'Yeh,' said Sinatra, 'he fell off Ginny Simms.'

Mayer heard about this and one of the first things he did on returning to work, rested and minus plaster, was to take action. Frank had meanwhile totally forgotten the off-hand remark. He had no idea why he was being called into the mogul's office, the all-white room immaculate as an MGM set. Frank was warmly welcomed, invited to sit down in one of Mayer's Louis XIV upholstered chairs. He was offered a cigarette. The secretary, who was LB's eyes and ears, brought in the coffee in exquisite near-transparent cups. She poured and then left.

They talked. The tears were welling in the chief's eyes as he told the young Frank how much he liked him, no, he loved him – like the son he never had. It was the kind of meeting stars relished. Then Mayer's expression changed. 'I hear you tell funny stories,' he said. 'One very funny story about me and Ginny Simms.'

That was when Frank knew he was in trouble. He apologised – an experience not to be dismissed lightly by anyone hearing it. But it was not enough. Sinatra was out.

Frank had for years been asking himself if things might not be better overseas. So, in June 1950, he flew to London for his first civilian performance abroad. It was a notable experience.

The London Palladium was justly known as the world's most famous variety–vaudeville theatre. It had always been so. But in 1947, it had been given an entirely new lease of life in the shape of the man born David Daniel Kaminsky. Danny Kaye was a huge sensation at the Palladium – the King and Queen came to see him and Princess Margaret had a seat reserved for her every night. As a result, one star after another came to the theatre with various degrees of success. Some were sensational, some were dreadful, some no more than all right.

Sinatra appeared on 1 July 1950 on the same bill as Max Wall, one of Britain's most popular radio comedians of the day, and the comedy act, Wilson, Keppel and Betty. The fact that he shared the bill with that sort of act gives some indication of the Sinatra status.

But the British press liked him. 'Bless me, he's good!' said the *Sunday Chronicle*. *The Times* commented: 'Here is an artist who, hailing from the most rowdy and self-confident community the world has ever known, has elected to express the timidity that can never be wholly driven out of the boastfullest heart.' The *Manchester Guardian* brought in its big guns. Philip Hope-Wallace, its eminent critic, wrote: 'An Orpheus of our time, Mr Frank Sinatra, an Italo-American crooner, made a first personal appearance in this country last night at the Palladium.'

The audience liked him, too. Mr Hope-Wallace reported: 'Not to be outdone by their American sisters, a mob of respectable young women surged and moaned outside the theatre throughout the evening.' That audience had been patiently looking forward to their idol's visit, although perhaps patience is not the most accurate description of their enthusiasm. This was the London equivalent of the Paramount experience – at just the time Frank felt he could do with it most. Londoners hadn't been told yet that worshipping Frank Sinatra was no longer the fashionable thing to do. Balloons marked 'Frankie' were carried alongside a banner proclaiming undying love, 'Sinatrally yours'. Once more Frank experienced having his bow tie torn from around his neck.

It was a new kind of Sinatra act, tailored to the Palladium and its audience. Plainly, he wanted to reprise Danny Kaye's success and proceeded to steal one feature of the Kaye act. Every night, Kaye used to have a cup of tea brought to him on stage – it established a rapport with the tea-drinking British audiences for whom coffee at the time was an undrinkable strain of dishwater. It also gave a nice impression of sobriety; all of which had combined to make Danny Kaye an even bigger hit in London than he had ever been in the United States. It didn't quite do the same for Sinatra, who had probably rarely drunk tea in his life before.

His material included 'A Foggy Day' and 'Ol' Man River' and an excerpt from *Carousel*, then at Drury Lane, demonstrating just how well American songs and singers could go down in Britain. The American voice, said Hope-Wallace, was the 'lingua franca for the tongue-tied British. This is the language of love as the cinema-educated youth of our country understand it ... Mr Sinatra is the incarnation of every lovesick GI, the new myth, the new English dream.'

It was as though Frank Sinatra were just beginning his career and doing pretty well at it, instead of being down on his luck at what many were saying was that career's very end. The Palladium was all his. Ava came to the show one night but had to leave before the evening was over, to avoid the photographers.

As he left on his last night, there were more banners. One said: 'Thanks Val Parnell [the man who ran the Palladium]. We knew he'd be swell.' The Americanism had been taken to heart along with the American.

Back in the United States, Frank was not 'swell' at all. His appearance at the Copacabana in New York was a disaster – but one that was different from anything he had faced before. A critic of the 'Copa' show had noted that the old Sinatra voice wasn't quite what it used to be. He didn't know why – or quite how much less a voice it now was. One night later on in the run at the nightspot, during his rendition of the *South Pacific* hit 'Bali Hai', he reached for a high note – and it wasn't there. He tried to coast on a middle-range note and that wasn't there either.

Psychiatrists and ear, nose and throat specialists had seen the phenomenon before – people losing their voices in the midst of intolerable stress. It was a terrible thing to happen to anyone, but for it to happen to Frank Sinatra was a tragedy of immense proportions. Somehow, he managed to finish his act that show, the second of the evening. But when he went on, as expected, for the third show, the band struck up, he opened his mouth – and nothing came out. 'Just dust,' he said later.

Sinatra was 'panic-stricken'. So, in their way, were the audience. About seventy people were in the place. They didn't shout or boo or laugh or do the things that nightclub audiences frequently do when the man they have paid good money to see doesn't come up to snuff. The face of Skitch Henderson, who was at the piano, resembled a ball of chalk. Frank managed to say 'Goodnight', mouthed what he hoped would sound like an apology and walked off.

A haemorrhage was diagnosed by Dr Irving Goldman, the specialist who was immediately called. The patient had to rest. That was a word that had never been in the Sinatra vocabulary. But now he had no choice.

In recent years, Sinatra has found an explanation for what happened, but until now it has never been published. He told the composer David Raksin about it. Raksin said he always doubted whether there had been psychosomatic reasons for the breakdown. 'I told him,' he said 'that it was one of the things in his career that didn't add up.'

"No," he told me, "it didn't add up, but what had happened was that I had been asked to do a benefit at the Hotel Pennsylvania, close to the old Pennsylvania Station. As usual things were slow and they kept me waiting and waiting. Now I had agreed to do this on condition I could get back to work at the Copa on time. I didn't want to start off any of those 'Sinatra is an impossible man' type stories. Should I leave it and go on to the Copacabana? Then they said, 'You're on', so I do my numbers, get off the stage and realise I had better catch a cab. No cabs. So I ran across town, up from where the Pennsylvania was to 59th street where the Cop was and it was cold, cold, cold. I got up on stage – and nothing happened." '

Would that voice ever come back? The doctors made reassuring noises, but Frank feared the worst.

— 10 —

THE MUSIC STOPPED

S inatra has described the first three years of the 1950s as 'the dark ages'. So dark that he spoke of himself as a character from history. It was the period 'when his career had that little stroke. When his voice ran away from home, when his records started selling like used Edsels.' Manie Sacks moved from Columbia to RCA Victor and tried to take Frank with him – but the sales force all told him they couldn't shift a Sinatra disc and didn't want to try.

But Frank was still news when it came to his marital state. In September 1950, Nancy was finally granted a legal separation on the grounds of his mental cruelty. She said: 'He humiliated me by going away for weekends alone.' Of course, he was not alone at all and he was lucky that she wasn't alleging anything more. He agreed to pay her a third of his income up to $150,000 a year and to give her the house they owned in Holmby Hills, just down Sunset Boulevard from the more plebeian Beverly Hills.

So was divorce on the horizon? Nancy's lawyer issued a statement saying it was highly unlikely. On the other hand, Ava made it very clear that she wouldn't sleep with Frank any more until he was a free man. It was not a threat likely to be taken seriously – she enjoyed the sex even more than he did and Frank knew it. One of his last records had been 'I'm a Fool to Want You', which he partly wrote. This was Sinatra's cry from the heart because he couldn't believe that Ava would ever be his. He ran from the studio after the recording, tears cascading down his cheeks.

Now, months later, it didn't look as though his life with Ava was going to be any more encouraging. In New York, they were staying as usual at the Hampshire House, a discreetly luxurious establishment opposite Central Park, less showy that the Plaza, less restrained than the Pierre. The hotel shielded them from publicity, which was always an issue when the Sinatra–Gardner team were in place. As Ava has always made clear, their relationship from the word go was stormy. They quarrelled constantly on this particular trip. So much, that she took a taxi to her ex-husband Artie Shaw's house to talk over her troubles. He soothed her and she went back to the hotel – in time to take a call from Frank in another room (an indication of how far downhill their affair had already gone) saying that if she didn't come back to him straight away he was going to kill himself.

When she said that was the last thing she wanted to do, she heard a gunshot. Ava rushed into the Sinatra room and saw what looked like a body on the bed. It was a collection of pillows into which he had shot the gun still smoking in his hand.

The miracle was that, even in New York, they were able to keep the incident quiet. Rumours about it floated around the city but, said Ava, when Frank himself answered calls his replies were so convincing they 'could have won him an Oscar'. Meanwhile, his friend Hank Sanicola took the incriminating bedding down a back staircase.

Later, from Lake Tahoe in Nevada on the West Coast, there were rumours of another suicide attempt. He and Ava had gone to the Christmas Tree restaurant with Hank Sanicola and his wife and there was a big row. Frank made 'an offhand remark' to which Ava took exception. She flew back to California and Frank took some sleeping pills – and a couple of brandies. Sanicola rang Ava in a panic and said Sinatra had attempted suicide. When Ava returned he told her, 'I thought you'd gone' – but he hadn't taken enough pills to endanger himself.

Frank maintained that he just stupidly took Seconal tablets after 'drinking a lot of brandy' and it was simply that he had forgotten how allergic he was to sleeping pills. A doctor came, gave him a glass of warm water with salt 'and I threw up and I was all right'. Others thought differently. Ava's leaving him immediately after the dinner only heightened the rumours of a 'suicide attempt'. 'I forgave him in about twenty-five seconds,' she said.

In one amazingly frank interview, he admitted his troubles in trying to get Nancy to give him a divorce. So, he said, 'this would be a hell of a time to do away with myself. I've been trying to lick this thing for two years and I've practically got it licked now.'

Usually his attitude towards interviews and columnists was more guarded. On a radio programme at this time, he said of Hollywood columnists: 'All day long they lie in the sun and after the sun goes down, they lie some more.' It was a demonstration of typical Sinatra

bitterness combined with the equally typical Sinatra gift with words –
which singled him out from all the others. A performer could never
have phrased lyrics in songs the way he did without knowing and
loving the words he used. Even when he condemned reporters, he
phrased it perfectly.

About this time, the London *Daily Herald* resorted to the old trick
of hiring a psychiatrist to work out what it was that made Sinatra
tick – even if ever so slowly at this time. 'He has built up a series of
illusions about himself and a newspaperman is capable of puncturing
them,' said the doctor. 'The problem is that Frank feels he's a fraud.
Success came too easily to him. Each time his voice comes out, it's
only a momentary reassurance. He keeps asking himself: "How will
it be the next time?" So he has a deep dread of being too closely
investigated, a fear that a reporter can bring his whole world crashing
down on him. That's because he has invented a world of illusion; he-
man Frankie, the big tough guy who likes to be seen with boxers and
gangsters.'

That last comment was hitting below the belt. Frank did not like
to be *seen* with gangsters; these people, he maintained, were in his life
simply because they owned the joints in which he performed.

Now Ava was going to Spain to make a new film, *Pandora and the
Flying Dutchman*. Sinatra flew over to join her, not so much because
he pined to be with her, but because he was suspicious of what she
would get up to if he was not around. He was a bundle of anxieties
and she was not impressed that he was willing to fly halfway round
the world to keep her under tabs.

But, he reasoned, there seemed to be no other way of keeping in
contact. Once he tried to telephone her. Attempt followed attempt
and always he was told that he could not be connected. Finally, an
operator explained the reason. There was a national emergency and
only government calls could be put through. 'I AM the fucking
government,' he responded. If he couldn't get his calls through, then
he had to go and see her for himself. He told her he had heard stories
about her relationship, not with the star James Mason, but with the
Spanish bullfighter turned actor, Mario Cabré. The *Los Angeles Times*
had reported her running into the street and blowing kisses at the
Spaniard – and worse, shouting 'Mario *mio*, Mario *mio*.' Later, in the
full glare of the public, the bullfighter took her in his arms and hugged
her tightly to his bare chest. 'Hello baby,' he said in what he assumed
to be the expected American greeting of man to woman.

Ava's answer to Sinatra's protests was typically blunt. 'We're in the same fucking picture!'

He seemed pacified and issued a statement about Ava to the press. 'She is the woman I love with all the strength of my soul. I believe this love and sympathy are both reciprocal and mutual.' But he said he knew it could never be easy. 'I am really a family man; all I ask is that my wife looks after me and I'll see she's looked after too. In some ways, though, I am a hard man to live with.' The Sinatra gift for understatement was being demonstrated. 'I want everything in its place and I don't change the place easily for a woman.'

Pandora was a film about bullfighting and so Cabré was the centre of attraction. He showed Ava where the bull's horns had brushed against his flesh. Then he said: 'I was thinking of Ava even when the bull had me up against the rail.' Such statements were not calculated to make Sinatra happy. But he had to say something. Reporters and photographers were like moths to flames.

Later, in Mexico, it was the same story. The press decided that Frank was there to get a Mexican divorce and hounded both him and Ava, just as they would never leave Elizabeth Taylor alone when she was with Richard Burton. Frank predictably took it all fairly badly. 'It wasn't the press who made me famous,' he told the newsmen. 'It was my singing, you miserable crumbs.' Not necessarily the language to win friends and influence people at a time when he needed all the help he could get. Worse, to drive the point home, he directed his car at a Los Angeles cameraman named Bill Eccles. He later apologised.

It was two months after that the seemingly impossible thing happened: against all her Catholic beliefs and contrary to what she thought would be the best interests of herself and her children, Nancy granted him a divorce. She would never marry again, she said, and she never has. But she wanted to move out of the no-woman's-land in which she now existed. The decree was awarded in Santa Monica. Frank, never the most trusting of individuals, decided that he wanted to be sure it was really true – and got a divorce of his own in Las Vegas.

Less easily ended was his perceived relationship with the underworld, which he would always protest involved nothing more than knowing the people who ran the clubs where he sang. He was likely to be investigated by a committee set up by Senator Estes Kefauver to look into organised crime. Frank was summoned to a 4-a.m. meeting in the law office of one of the committee members, Joseph

Nellis, who had in his possession a picture of Frank and Lucky Luciano in Havana. He had also heard those stories of Frank allegedly carrying money, supposedly for Mafia use.

Frank said he knew 'some of these guys' but never did business with any of them. In fact, he said, he only knew the people referred to as far as saying hello or goodbye. As for the Mafia, he knew nothing about it – except it was 'some kind of shake-down operation'. Sinatra was handed a subpoena but was not called for a public hearing. The story then faded for a time, but it did not die.

Instead, the focus switched to the question of Frank's marrying Ava. Would there be a wedding soon? Before long, he and Ava did make up their minds. In November 1951 they became engaged and, to mark the event, he gave her a six-carat diamond engagement ring.

Everything should have been wonderful. But in New York, a seemingly delightful evening ended with another of those typical Sinatra–Gardner tiffs that looked as though it were going to turn into an immediate crisis. At one point, Ava's temper was such that she opened the window of their Hampshire House hotel suite, took off the engagement ring and flung it into the street. It was never found. Despite that, they decided to go ahead with a wedding.

The big problem would be trying to keep the marriage quiet. When it seemed obvious that it would be held in Philadelphia, all steps were directed towards trying to find some way of keeping people off the scent. However, try though they may, they couldn't hide the fact that a mere twenty-four hours after being granted his Nevada divorce, Frank and Ava were applying at the Philadelphia City Hall for a licence to marry. But they still tried to keep secret the location of the nuptials, using Isaac Levy, a radio executive, as their decoy.

Later in November 1951, he and Ava were married in Philadelphia at the home of Manie Sacks' brother, Lester. Frank thought the press would never discover the venue. But that said nothing for the powers of the newsmen. 'How did you creeps know we were here?' he asked kindly. 'I'll knock the first guy who tries to get inside on his back – and I mean it.'

But he had time for his friends – Manie Sacks certainly and Axel Stordahl, too, who was best man, with his wife June Hutton as matron of honour. Manie gave Ava away at the ceremony conducted by Judge José Sloane. Just as the band was playing 'Here Comes the Bride', Ava and Manie slipped down three steps and the bride was left swamped in her wedding dress, lying at the foot of the stairs. When newsreel photographers came to film the wedding breakfast, Frank placed his hand over the lens – which was polite behaviour compared with what had gone before.

Certainly, his second marriage apart, this was a terrible time, but Frank tried to let people know that he wasn't out for the count. As he said: 'That man is an incorrigible optimist.' Optimism is not the word that immediately comes to mind when discussing Frank Sinatra, 1951 vintage.

He and Ava had gone back to London convinced that he would get a kinder reception from the gentlemen of the British press. It was also a chance to hobnob for the first time in his life with royalty. He topped the bill at the benefit for the National Playing Fields Association, a favourite charity of Prince Philip, at the London Coliseum and brought some of his American buddies with him. Orson Welles and Tony Curtis and his then wife Janet Leigh were on the bill.

The American press were not impressed by the evening. The *Daily News* in New York reported: 'The Voice falls flat at British yawn party.' But the Prince was happy. He was later pleased to note that £25,000 was raised by the evening for the National Playing Fields Association, of which he was president, a large amount for the time.

Not everyone who wanted to be close to the Sinatras was kindly disposed towards them. While at the show, their hotel suite was entered and some $17,000 worth of jewels were stolen. Journalists, too, made capital out of what they thought was an opportunity to knock the couple. Westbrook Pegler reappeared, dipping his pen in vitriol. He said he couldn't understand what all the ballyhoo for Frank and Ava had been about. 'These two are discredited so badly in the United States that the New York *Daily News* ran an editorial in which it filed him away in the who-gives-a-damn folder and the *Richmond Times-Dispatch* published one headed, "Goodbye Frankie and Ava and Don't Come Back". The *Times Dispatch* pretty well expressed American opinion on these two.'

As for Prince Philip, 'the husband of Princess Elizabeth who one day will become Queen of England', he was, Pegler told his readership, 'also known as the Duke of Edinburgh ... [and] seems to be genuinely dumb. If he isn't dumb, he is even worse off for an excuse.'

Pegler's venom against the Duke and against Lord Beaverbrook, proprietor of the *Daily Express* which was giving the visit a great deal of publicity, seemed to be justified by their liking for Sinatra. So here was an opportunity to remind everyone of all the old charges. 'Briefly, as character background, Sinatra has a police record of one arrest, later dismissed, a folder in the FBI and another in the Bureau of Narcotics, putting him into company with the Fischettis of Chicago, veterans of the old Capone mob and gambling racketeers in their own right, the Moretti mob and Lucky Luciano.'

The bit was between his teeth and he was not letting go. Frank was a 'financial backer of an underworld sheet which made a practice of accusing prominent movie people of using narcotics'. Mr Pegler seems not to have worried about having his cake and eating it, too. Was Frank a bad boy or merely spending money to name other bad boys? He even associated him with George Raft, the actor who had gone through similar experiences of being linked in the media with the Mob. Sinatra denied it all and was furious. But he wasn't the only person being attacked by that writer.

As for Lord Beaverbrook: 'He certainly had no excuse not to know what kind of people these two [Frank and Ava] were who came to appear under the royal patronage in a spectacular hassle in the smutty West End of London which is nowadays about as exclusive as the old Chicago line or the old New York tenderloin. It is crawling with streetwalkers and other scum.'

People were obviously gunning for Frank. A Las Vegas attorney named William G. Ruymann – a member of the National Conference on Uniform Law and the Nevada Marriage and Divorce Committee – questioned the legality of Frank's Las Vegas divorce and, consequently, his marriage to Ava, ignoring the fact that Nancy had had a divorce of her own, which would have been quite enough (although, it had to be admitted, hers was only an interlocutory decree which would not become final for a year).

Ruymann said there had been fraud in Frank's own decree. In his divorce application, the lawyer claimed, Frank had sworn that he was a resident of Nevada. In the marriage form, he had given his address as '177 South Robertson Boulevard, Beverly Hills'. Both couldn't be right.

But the Nevada Bar Association decided there was no reason to undo the undoing – the divorce counted, although a commission was being set up to look into 'quickie' marriage dissolves.

In 1952 Frank's depression was lifted a little when the voice began to regain something of its old glory. Some reported that it was better than ever. Perhaps it was deeper, with a sandpaper tinge, but certainly better than it had been for a long time. The only trouble was persuading people to hear it.

Then came a blow. Columbia Records announced that they would not be renewing his contract. No more would the name Frank Sinatra spin at 78 revolutions per minute. It was a mere nine years from the time when you couldn't walk down Broadway without being trampled to death by the swooning crowds outside the Paramount Theatre. But there's no loyalty in the entertainment industry or among fans.

There was no film contract either. Nobody wanted to risk putting Sinatra before the cameras – at least, not since his disastrous movie in 1951, *Meet Danny Wilson*, in which he played a hard-up crooner (sounds familiar?) who gets involved with a racketeer who controlled the place where he sang and is taken under the wing of a busty young star (where had they heard of that one?) played by Shelley Winters.

That just left *The Frank Sinatra Show* which had recently started on CBS television. This, however, was another indication of how bad things were. With the exception of 'Uncle Milty' (Milton Berle) and Bob Hope, who was successful enough to do precisely what he wanted without anyone asking any questions, no star as big as Frank had yet done television in any major way. It was very much the poor sister of radio and if he had continued to get the ratings for his radio programme with Dorothy Kirsten, he would never have embarked on it. But *Light Up Time* was cancelled, too. He did have a late-afternoon CBS radio show, *Meet Frank Sinatra*, but after a few months, it was plain this was an invitation few people wanted to accept and that show, too, was snatched off the air.

The TV show, meanwhile, was boring. Frank sang, but there were dreadfully amateurish so-called drama episodes, too. *Look* magazine did a picture feature headed 'Sinatra Celebrates an Opening Night' – but that was as much out of curiosity as anything else. Besides which, they concentrated not on the show but on the party Frank threw at Toots Shor's New York restaurant. Three hundred guests turned up – including Gypsy Rose Lee and Celeste Holm. Whether they realised it or not, their very presence was a gesture of defiance, two fingers in the air to those who were saying Frank was finished.

The ratings were so bad that Milton Berle introduced a brace of newcomers on his TV show with the words: 'These people have never been seen on television before. Last week, they were on *The Frank Sinatra Show*.'

All of this combined to demonstrate just how low Frank had now sunk. There was too much evidence of decline – not least Frank's appearance at the Chez Paree nightclub in Chicago, the kind of place which just two years earlier started turning people away the moment a Sinatra appearance was announced. Now, performing in the summer of 1952, nine out of ten of the 1,200 chairs at the club were empty.

Frank's last Columbia record had been 'Why Try to Change Me Now?'. Maybe the label realised they couldn't. Worse, his agents MCA were showing that they couldn't change him either, by taking him off their books. This was the final insult. But they had good reason to think he was a back number. Not only was there no recording contract and no film studio wanting him to make movies but his TV show now followed the radio series into oblivion. Perhaps worst of all, his return to the Paramount in New York for a personal appearance season was a complete flop. The bobbysoxers were gone and the only squeals could be heard from the usherettes when a mouse was seen running through the theatre after the show had finished.

If all that was terrible, there was still a *coup de grâce* to be administered. It came from the Frank Sinatra fan club – which decided to dissolve for lack of members. A few of the former bobbysoxers who would have willingly died for their Frankie just a handful of years before were asked to rejoin to save the organisation, but not enough bothered.

Depression was a minor ailment compared to the utter despair in which Francis Albert Sinatra now found himself. In Manie Sacks' New York apartment, he walked into the kitchen, turned on the gas taps and lay down. Sacks came just in time to revive him. If only he could do the same for the Sinatra career – or the Sinatra marriage. Ava twice became pregnant and twice went to London for abortions. She knew she couldn't devote the time to a child that she thought she needed to spend on her own career. When Frank found out, he was in tears. Was there nothing in his life any more? He adored Ava and would continue to do so, but he always felt she was an unattainable object, even when there were marriage papers to confirm their relationship. Their rows only seemed to drive more wedges between them.

They came together, however, when both decided to go into politics, throwing in their lot with Governor Adlai Stevenson who was the Democrats' candidate against Eisenhower. With an assortment of other stars, they agreed that it was their duty to tell the nation they were 'madly for Adlai'. But were they madly for each other? Frank couldn't appreciate that Ava needed wooing, even now that they were married.

So he grabbed at any chance he thought was available to him to make a comeback. Italy seemed a safe bet. There, he felt sure, he would be greeted as one of their own. A series of concerts were booked – co-starring 'the most beautiful woman in the world', Ava.

It was a disaster. Ava didn't want to appear on stage. She wasn't the kind to play the little wife. She wasn't going to purr and simper while Frank sang. So she didn't turn up. The audience made it clear they had no interest in Sinatra's singing; they had paid to see the most beautiful woman in the world, and when it became obvious she wasn't going to be there, they demanded their money back.

The trip was doomed. Frank punched a photographer, and there was a huge row with British European Airways officials who wouldn't allow them to board their plane to Milan before anyone else. 'I'll never fly BEA again,' said Frank. 'I'd rather swim the Channel,' said Ava. Then, when they left the airport, their car broke down.

In Copenhagen and Malmo, the next stops on the tour, the audience stayed away and to make things worse when there were outdoor concerts, the rain didn't. Newspaper editorials proclaimed: 'Mr Sinatra go home.'

Things were no easier when Ava went to Africa to make *Mogambo* with Clark Gable and Grace Kelly. Frank's friend, the actress Ruta Lee, revealed to me for the first time how hard that time was for him.

'Ava was up, up, up, and Frank owed money to everybody,' she said. 'Frank had a friend who ran a club in Montreal and he borrowed money from this man so that he could fly out to Africa to be with Ava for Christmas. He was broke, but he is this generous man and he flew out to Africa with packages for everybody and brought a Christmas tree with him because he knew there wouldn't be any in Africa.' He hired a plane to take him directly to the base camp being used by the film crew. Before the cast and crew returned to camp, Frank had already set up the tree and the lights. Ava finally came, saw Frank, saw the tree and said: "That's nice!" He was devastated. He died a thousand deaths because she wasn't enchanted and giggly about it and didn't say, "Oh, you've brought me Christmas!" which was what he expected.

Frank's disappointment with Ava matched the mood of the *Mogambo* shoot. For one thing, she insisted on swimming in the nude – not just in front of men, but before black men, too. Director

John Ford, who wore a black eye patch, had to turn a blind eye to that one. He could not, though, turn a deaf ear to her language. The talk that had so delighted Dolly Sinatra shocked the prim Grace Kelly, soon to become Princess Grace of Monaco. The ice-cold blonde complained and Clark Gable tried to persuade Ava to conform. She turned that into some useful practice for her four-letter-word vocabulary.

Frank was the only one who didn't complain to Ava's beautiful face. He had his own worries far removed from the *Mogambo* set. There was something going on in Hollywood that had got his juices going. Columbia Pictures had a property with a part in it that he knew was right down his alley. It was a role he craved. The film was *From Here to Eternity.*

— 11 —

FROM HERE TO ETERNITY

Sinatra had found a new obsession, as powerful as the one that made him go after Ava. He had wooed Ava and in a highly brittle, shaky way, had won her. Now he was wooing a film studio, but at the same time he was taking control of an idea and he was not going to let go.

Broke, unhappy and unsure, to him, the part represented a possible lifeline. His career had sunk to such depths that he now featured in a weekly radio series called *Rocky Fortune*. In this, he was involved in a series of incidents, all of which spelt trouble.

After a blues note, the young Sinatra was introduced as 'that foot-loose, frequently unemployed gentleman'. And Frank would say: 'Hi, I don't know about you, I'm the kind of guy who can't stay put. I get restless. Give me a nice soft job, a buck in my pocket, and a meal ticket, and one'll get you ten I'll quit the job, lose the buck on the gee-gees and exchange the meal ticket for a train ticket.'

But now he thought there was a chance of reversing his own rocky fortune and perhaps getting noticed again, if not as a singer, then as an actor.

James Jones's book, *From Here to Eternity*, set in Pearl Harbor at the time leading up to the Japanese raid, was a story about Americans of Sinatra's age in situations like those he had been involved in for as long as he had been able to walk. They were Americans who loved and fought, puny Americans who stood up to bullies, unlucky Americans who thought the world was against them. The fact that these were also Americans in uniform did nothing to spoil the original concept.

Frank's previous roles in non-singing movies had had only limiting results. He knew that. But the acting he had done in *On the Town* and *It Happened in Brooklyn* told him he could do it.

Convincing Harry Cohn, who still ran Columbia Pictures the way

Mussolini used to run Italy (he had a picture of Il Duce on his desk), was another matter entirely. Why take a risk with a has-been? Especially if, as far as straight acting was concerned, the has-been was really a never-was?

The part that Sinatra wanted as much as he had once yearned to leave Hoboken was that of the undernourished but brave Private Angelo Maggio, who rushes to the aid of the almost equally slight Robert Prewitt, the former prizefighter who refuses to box for his unit because he has already blinded a man. Prewitt, who is also the best bugler in the Army, is almost destroyed by his so-called comrades in arms because he won't box. Maggio is destroyed – for trying to rescue him.

What happened when Sinatra made his first approaches to Columbia to be allowed to play Maggio has become part of legend as well as of American movie history. We know for sure that Cohn didn't want him, that Sinatra waged a campaign as serious as that of a contender for a presidential nomination to win the part, and that finally it was his. There have been stories of the Mafia being involved. Mario Puzo's *The Godfather*, complete with tales of bloody horses' heads in-the-bed, has been suggested as being based on what happened when Sinatra tried to get the Maggio part.

Puzo denies that any references to strongmen concerned Frank. The director and writer of the film deny it, too. 'Just bullshit,' was how Dan Taradash, who wrote the screen play, put it to me. But something of the kind *did* happen at this time, although they may not have known it, something involving Harry Cohn and some of his senior executives.

It is also a story that has never been told before – could never be told before. It was never true 'that the Mob was going to stick a trombone down Harry Cohn's neck if I didn't get the part', Sinatra later protested. But what is true is that someone did make threats but not involving Sinatra and his quest for the role.

'It was the talk of the executive suite at Columbia at just that time,' Richard Quine, then one of the studio's most enterprising young executives working at the Vine Street lot, told me shortly before he died.'There was a great deal of talk of Mafia heavy boys trying make a deal on behalf of an Italian-American singer. The only thing was Cohn didn't care. He had his own mob who could deal with any such disturbance.'

The message that Columbia could benefit by employing the Italian-

American singer came at precisely the time that *From Here to Eternity* was ready to leave the story department to go to the studio floor, but the singer in question was not Frank Sinatra. 'It was Dean Martin,' Quine told me when I was writing my own Dean Martin biography. This statement could not be published at the time, but other Hollywood executives confirmed it, including various Columbia producers. Morris Stoloff said: 'I knew that Martin had a set of heavy boys who tried to get him jobs. They came knocking on my door too.'

Dean Martin was not in the same straits as Sinatra. He had been nothing like as big a star as Frank. Neither was his career at its nadir. It was just that he also wanted to be known as much as a serious actor as a singer – and he was fed up with being the straight man to Jerry Lewis. 'He came begging,' Quine remembered. 'But nobody at Columbia would take him seriously. When the Mob moved in, Cohn told them to move out again – and they did. Perhaps Dean hadn't paid all his dues!'

It took another five years before Martin was given his chance and played, ironically, in another army picture, *The Young Lions*, made for Twentieth Century-Fox. In that, he gave a brilliant performance. He didn't work for Columbia until 1960 when he made *Who Was That Lady?*, a stupid comedy involving spies and mistaken intentions, that would never have been worth involving the Mob and certainly did not.

Yet the image of Sinatra needing the Mafia to help him get the role of Maggio still lingers, despite the evidence to the contrary. The director Fred Zinnemann, one of the most respected of elder statesmen in Hollywood, told me precisely what did happen. 'Sinatra told everyone at Columbia that he wanted the role and begged to be allowed to test for it. But we already had our Maggio, Eli Wallach who was brilliant in his own test. I wanted Wallach and Cohn wanted Wallach.'

But Sinatra was so persistent, Harry Cohn agreed to allow him to do a test, too – without pay. What was more, Frank was in Africa at the time. When he heard that he would be given the chance to test at Columbia, he flew back at his own expense.

'His test was very good,' Zinnemann remembered. 'But it wasn't as good as Wallach's.' So there seemed to be no reason why the original actor should not be offered a part for which he seemed so ideally suited. Except that a play came up that Wallach wanted to do more. 'So we gave the part to Sinatra, whom we thought wouldn't be at all bad in it.'

James Jones's story had had a long gestation. So had the movie. Dan Taradash said that at one stage he didn't think the novel would ever go before the cameras. 'I knew it could make a great film, but I thought, with the restrictions of the time, we would never be able to do it. It was full of pornography, which is what they would have called it at the time. It was also very long and very complex and rambled and went on for, I think, 180 pages after the Pearl Harbor incident.'

In fact, there had been tremendous fights over whether even to buy the story in the first place. The New York office of Columbia was totally against it. When Harry Cohn overruled them and agreed to pay $85,000 for the work, they thought he had taken leave of his senses. They called it 'Cohn's Folly'. It wasn't *just* that they saw it as pornographic, which meant too much sex for the movies of the early 1950s, but it was perceived as an anti-Army film. All those years before Vietnam, when the memories of the Second World War were so strong and now with America in the midst of the Korean War, that was a sin like condemning motherhood and apple pie.

Buying the book didn't necessarily mean the movie would be made straight away. But Taradash set about making it happen. 'I went to see the studio and in particular Buddy Adler' [who was to become its producer]. It wasn't an easy sell. The studio had bought the rights quite some time earlier and it was to lie on the shelf, gathering dust. Nobody thought it could be made.

'In the book,' says Taradash, 'Maggio leaves the story halfway through when he goes to the stockade and is thrown out of the Army and sent back to Brooklyn, with an honourable discharge. He is mentally unstable, so couldn't make a soldier.' But Taradash had his own ideas about transferring it all to the screen. 'The first idea was that Maggio should not be thrown out, but die as a result of the beatings he received in the stockade. That night, we hear Prewitt playing "Taps" from the quadrangle and from that you have the perfect curtain for the second act. Everybody loved Maggio. He was a feisty little guy with great spirit, a good soldier in a crazy way and they would be devastated to see him die and that lent poignancy to a great scene.'

Taradash had told this to Harry Cohn – and emphasised that the dehumanising scenes in the stockade should be omitted, too. Then he came up with the idea that Maggio should not just die, but die in Prewitt's arms – a lot more poignant, certainly, than being dis-honourably discharged for mental instability.

Adler liked this interpretation of the story and when Cohn was back home, rang Taradash to ask him to come over to the studio boss's house to go through it with him.

The mogul was a man with his own firm ideas – on making films and on the way he ran his business. He was the master of the casting couch with as many mistresses as movies on the stocks. He also had a personality that could have been created by a computer. Cohn was the archetypal Hollywood chief, the model for a dozen movie roles about the people who controlled what went in and out of the sound stages. He was a former song plugger who established his studio with borrowed money in an area of Hollywood known as 'Poverty Row'. In a long career in the movie capital he made as many careers as he broke – stars like Gene Kelly, Gary Cooper, Claudette Colbert and Rita Hayworth owed him everything. He was big, bluff and crude – and his directors and other employees now say they loved him. But he bugged the dressing rooms of his actors, fired people at will, and when thousands attended his funeral, Red Skelton wryly joked: 'It's the old story – give the folks what they want and they'll show up for it.'

Yet because he always stood by his hunches, Cohn earned the respect of those who worked for him. He did most of his business in the bedroom of his house. That was where he and Taradash had their meeting. He was convinced Taradash had the right idea. 'Do you mind if I write some of it at home?' the writer asked Cohn. 'I don't care,' Cohn replied, 'I don't care if you write it in a whorehouse.'

Cohn was committed and once he had his teeth into an idea, he wasn't going to let it go. The molars were firmly into *From Here to Eternity*. He was even going to make the film with the co-operation of the Army. Like all the other moguls, Harry liked people to think he was a patriot who saluted the American flag every morning and evening. Besides which, using army facilities, to say nothing of soldiers as extras, would cut bills tremendously, even though union rates would have to be found. He wanted to keep the budget to under $2 million, which he eventually did.

Frank began scheming for the part of Maggio the moment he heard the talk in the trade that the picture was going to be made by Columbia. When he eventually met Harry Cohn, the mogul was typically blunt: 'Maggio is an actor's part, a stage actor's part. You're nothing but a fucking hoofer.' This wasn't true, of course. Apart from his experiences in the Kelly films, his hoofing days were practically nonexistent. But then, to Cohn, calling Sinatra a singer would have been stretching things too. He didn't sing the kind of songs the old plugger enjoyed.

According to Jonie Taps, then head of the music department at Columbia, what really swung the deal Sinatra's way was his promise to do the role without pay. Taps, who liked to feel that he was indispensable to every operation on the schedules at Columbia, told me: 'Sinatra had phoned me. He was on the balls of his ass. I then phoned Cohn and said, "It's very tough on the guy. Let him come and talk to you." Within three days, he was talking to Harry and saying, "I'll play Maggio for nothing in *From Here to Eternity*."'

Cohn was reluctant from the very start. Nothing would persuade him – not even Sinatra's earnest plea: 'Look, I know Maggio. I went to school with him in Hoboken and was beaten up with him. I might have been Maggio.' But not only did Cohn want Wallach, he actively did not want Sinatra. As he told Taps, 'I can't have him in the part. People will expect him to sing.'

That was when Ava entered the story, possibly the most decisive factor of all. She used her influence with Harry Cohn's wife Joan. 'She came in when I was sick with the flu,' Joan told me, 'took off her shoes and put her feet on Harry's desk. She said, "Frank's going to kill himself if he doesn't get the part." I said that was silly.'

But Ava was putting a lot on the line. She had the image of the gas-oven incident seared into her mind, to say nothing of the other attempts with sleeping pills which might or might not have been serious. In this case, she knew how much success – or failure – would mean.

'So what do you want me to do?' Mrs Cohn asked. 'Get Harry to give him a test,' Ava answered.

By the time Cohn finally agreed to give him the test, Frank was in Africa but there was never any doubt that he would make the trip back. Sinatra had been sending a telegram every day to Cohn reminding him of his existence. He kept adding the syrup to his demands: 'I've got to have this part – it was written for me – for me and nobody else.'

The test was going to be the scene where Maggio was bitching about how lousy his life was. Maggio is desperate and Prewitt – by now the part had gone to Montgomery Clift – is half drunk. It was a scene in the garden of the Royal Hawaiian Hotel. Maggio is stripped to the waist, pulls off his shoes and throws them at the military policemen who club him down.

Just before the test was made, Sinatra went into Taradash's room at

Columbia. 'He looked terrible and he was very nervous. He really wanted the part so badly. "Tell me," he asked, "how do I have to do it?" I said it was very easy. "All you have to do is make them laugh and cry at the same time." '

As an actor, Frank was not in the same league as Eli Wallach and he knew it. Cohn and the business department had thought Wallach would jump at the chance once they had decided that the part was his. But not at all. First of all, he wanted twice as much as he had made on his last picture – and Sinatra was still willing to do it for nothing.

Frank thought it wise to emphasise just how much of a bargain Cohn would be getting. He told him, 'I get $150,000 a picture.'

'You mean you *used* to get $150,000,' the mogul replied.

But offering to do the part virtually without pay was certainly an ice-breaker. Cohn was now infuriated by Wallach's demands. He was not in the business of doubling actors' salaries. Wallach, however, knew how good he was – a fact confirmed when the tests were shown. Joan Cohn was there with her husband. They saw them both twice, so did three or four other people in the projection room with them.

'What do you think?' Cohn asked his wife – after telling her that, despite himself, he still preferred the Wallach scenes.

'It doesn't make sense,' she said. 'Eli Wallach is brilliant. But he's a Jew.' (So, of course, were Cohn, Buddy Adler, Fred Zinnemann and most of the executives connected with the project.) For that reason alone, there was a plus in Sinatra's favour.

'All I did was give my opinion,' Mrs Cohn recalled.

Then Wallach's agent started to turn the screws. He knew that Cohn wanted his client for the part. But he emphasised there was no way he would do it for the cash on offer. Besides, he had that stage deal waiting – the starring role in Tennessee Williams's *Camino Real*. He could have had no idea how wrong his move was – or how right it would be for Frank Sinatra, who would have reason to thank him for it for the rest of his life.

Cohn sent a message to Wallach from his holiday hideout in Honolulu, according to Taradash, 'in words more profane than sacred', to tell him to forget it.

It wasn't a happy scene on the Columbia lot when they realised that Wallach would not be their man. 'Cohn, Zinnemann and Buddy Adler were quite blue about it,' Taradash told me. 'I quite liked Sinatra's test, but I didn't think he was as good as Wallach, either.'

They still hadn't made up their minds. It wouldn't be Wallach. But would it be Sinatra? Before deciding, there were other concerns to be reconciled. The role of the base captain's wife who has an affair – the steamy kissing scene on the beach with the sergeant to be played by Burt Lancaster – hadn't been cast yet. Eventually, they came up with Deborah Kerr. 'An off-the-wall choice,' Taradash now says. 'Strange but very good. We originally expected Joan Crawford to do it – but she called and said she wanted her own cameraman. That was out. Zinnemann wouldn't stand for such nonsense.'

Then they went back to the matter of Maggio. They looked at the Sinatra test again – and decided that, after all, he would be their man. "This isn't bad," we said. It wasn't bad for a physical reason. When Wallach stripped to the waist, he was a very well-built guy. Not like Stallone or anyone like that, but I'd like to have him on my side in a fight. He didn't look as though he wouldn't survive a beating. Sinatra, on the other hand, looked like a plucked chicken. He was pitiful. You immediately felt sorry for this man who was fed up with the Army, this little guy, this weak guy, taking on the US Army in battle. That was the way it went.'

In fact, even Cohn told Buddy Adler he was impressed with the Sinatra physique, or rather the lack of it. It was the point he made when he – and Mrs Cohn – saw the test yet again. 'Did you ever see that guy without a shirt on?' he asked his producer. 'This is a thin little guy with a caved-in chest but with a great heart.'

Cohn agreed he would take the risk. A contract was drawn up. Frank would get $1,000 a week for eight weeks. Cohn had to be happy with that – he had budgeted $2,000 a week for the actor taking the Maggio role, whoever he was.

There was talk of Sinatra recording the title song from the movie. Jonie Taps, ever the astute business brain behind Columbia's music department, told him: 'If you record the song for promotional purposes, I'll give you the rights to it. Your own music publishing firm can handle it.'

That was considered to be a very generous offer indeed, or at least Taps thought so. 'I remember Mel Brooks was in the room with me. He said I was a "fucking Sinatra lover". And that was a fairly rare breed at the time.'

What has to be emphasised is that Maggio was very much a subsidiary role in *From Here to Eternity*. The big part was that of Prewitt. Aldo Ray was the original choice and the man Cohn wanted.

He made a test with an unknown contract player named Donna Reed, playing the soldiers' club hostess, who was not in line for the part. After the test was shown, Reed got the role she didn't imagine she would get and Ray was rejected for the one he assumed was his. Cohn stuck out for Ray, but Zinnemann said that if he didn't get Montgomery Clift he wouldn't do the picture – and Cohn knew that Zinnemann was the only man for the job.

One of Zinnemann's most important contributions to the film was to back Sinatra all the way once the deal had been made. Taradash now says: 'To be fair, if there had been no Wallach, we wouldn't have looked anywhere else. It was also a good publicity idea to have Sinatra. If this fellow came through and really turned something in, we really would have something going for us.'

Frank Sinatra turned in the performance of a lifetime and the studio had quite a lot going for it, too. *Camino Real*, starring Eli Wallach, flopped badly. Had Wallach been Maggio, the Sinatra story would have taken a very different turn.

— 12 —

DON'T WORRY 'BOUT ME

Frank ended eight weeks of gruelling filming $8,000 the richer, which would just about cover his alimony for the period. He needed the money – Ava's salary, despite her success in *Show Boat*, only covered her dress bills and, in any case, she saw no reason to share it with her husband – but he needed the job more.

There were two reasons why he needed it so badly – for his own self-esteem, the feeling of being wanted; but also because he knew it was the talk of the town. For the first time since the days at Paramount, Sinatra wanted it to be known among his peers that an important studio was investing in his talent. Harry Cohn was unlikely to pick up stray dogs out of the goodness of his heart; he must be sufficiently impressed with Sinatra's talent, not as a pop singer but as a serious actor, to give him a pivotal part in his big production. Moreover, the fact that Maggio was a supporting role only served to boost what he took as a vote of confidence. A star part could have been seen as purchasing a name; giving Frank a subsidiary role meant it was his abilities that were essential to getting the project to work.

Sinatra knew all that and behaved accordingly. 'He was very, very good – all the time,' Fred Zinnemann told me, 'no histrionics, no bad behaviour, he always took direction.'

He even showed up on time and for all rehearsals. It was as though the cliché of a person making a new man of himself had come true. But there was a lot of the old Sinatra in Maggio. His language at times was almost Runyonesque, employed with an accent straight from the waterfront.

Yet they were wonderful lines he was given, and he spoke them wonderfully. As he lay dying after having got away from the stockade and Fatso, the prison sergeant who had given him hell, he said: 'I escaped in a truck. Only the tailgate opened . . . you should have seen me bounce!' He bounced into a new career.

As well as being a marvellous opportunity for Frank, it was a gamble, too – the film could have died and he would have been even worse off than when he started begging for the role; alternatively, the film could have been good while his own estimation of his talent was exaggerated – and the rest of the cast would have wound up supporting *him*. Also, Sinatra's name was going to be billed above the title, along with all the other stars, which was fine for his prestige if he had a hit, but if the film flopped his failure would be even more marked. Cohn, for his part, took a lot of persuasion to allow this – 'People will think it is a musical picture,' he said, but was persuaded to allow the billing in lieu of real money.

Cohn's gamble was, of course, the biggest of all. The $2 million he was investing in the movie was the biggest sum he had put into a film since *The Jolson Story*. The producer, Buddy Adler, was under strict instructions not to spend a cent more, even though it involved not just an otherwise expensive cast – Lancaster, Kerr and Clift were getting paid much more than Sinatra – but also the huge costs of the location in Hawaii and transport by chartered plane.

There were a number of discussions on the script between Cohn and Taradash before it went to Fred Zinnemann. 'There were several drafts – which really were the same draft but with some punctuation marks changed,' the writer now recalls. Cohn wanted Prewitt to play 'Taps' after Maggio's death but he also wanted him to play the bugle earlier, too, to establish his talent. 'I was totally against this, but I knew I couldn't win that argument. I had to find a way to do that without undercutting the effect of the "Taps" moment.'

So it came in one of the scenes in which Sinatra really displayed his talent as an actor. 'Fatso', the part that established Ernest Borgnine as an important performer in the fifties, makes a nasty crack about Maggio's sister when he sees a picture that the young private is showing around. Sinatra picks up a chair and hits Borgnine over the head with it.

This is not a happy moment in the film. Maggio has committed the sin of offending the least popular man on base and so guarantees that he no longer has an existence worth living. Prewitt meanwhile is irritated by another soldier playing around with a bugle mouthpiece – so much so that he shows what he himself can do with it and plays 'Chattanooga Choo Choo'.

The fight scene was the one that was going to give most problems. The industry's voluntary censors, the Breen Office – they had taken over from the Hays Office, which had laid down such things as the depth of women's necklines, the length of kisses and how many feet were allowed on a bed – were making trouble over the plan to use bottles in the fight. Burt Lancaster, the office sergeant who apart from falling in love with the captain's wife is dedicated to not making trouble, joins in the fight by breaking a beer bottle on a table and calling to Borgnine: 'Kill us! Come on.'

Taradash saw the effect of the scene but whispered to Buddy Adler: 'We told the Breen Office we wouldn't break the bottle.' 'Fuck 'em,' said Adler. 'We're going to make the picture our way.'

Some of their success in making the film 'their' way stemmed from Sinatra's undoubted acting ability. He acquired it by asking Clift for advice and daily the actor coached him in the basics of what was, in fact, 'Method' acting. He was never to forget that help. Cohn allowed Zinnemann to make the film he wanted to direct, except in one instance. This was a scene in which both Clift and Sinatra were drinking heavily. Cohn had studied his director's plans and told him to change one particular aspect of his shooting arrangements. Instead of having the two men sitting down on the bench outside the barracks as they grew more and more drunk, he said they should stand up. When they rehearsed that moment in the script, both agreed that it would look a lot more natural if they sat down. And that was how it was being shot – until Harry Cohn arrived on the set (rumour was that an informant had told him his orders were being countermanded). He didn't just arrive, he came dressed in a dinner-jacket, in a long limousine, accompanied by a general who was also in evening dress complete with decorations.

Cohn was in a rage. 'You shoot that scene the way I told you or I'm shutting down the film,' he shouted at Zinnemann, loud enough for the general to hear and plainly in no mood to suffer the embarrassment of having his instructions disobeyed. Zinnemann acquiesced – and regretted it ever after. 'I think it was a mistake to agree,' he told me, 'but for some reason or other Harry Cohn thought it looked undignified for soldiers to be sitting down outside a barracks.' How it would have been dignified for them to be drunk, standing or sitting, was not explained.

The scene was pivotal in another way and that was largely due to Frank. Dan Taradash told me about its filming – on the Columbia ranch at Burbank, soon after the crew had returned from Honolulu. 'I got to the ranch at about seven or eight o'clock in the evening when they should have been in the middle of the scene, but there was no one around, there was no traffic about. There were no lights. I thought, "What the hell is going on?"'

Sinatra was there, the director was there, the camera and lighting crew were there, but Montgomery Clift was not – at least, he was not on the set. He was in the dressing room, blind drunk. As Taradash said: 'As a Method actor, he was getting into the spirit of the part.'

So for the first hour of what should have been the night's shooting schedule, Frank sat with him in his dressing room – pouring coffee down him, talking to him, walking him up and down in an attempt to sober up the man who was now not just a fellow actor but a pal.

'I think everybody,' said Taradash, 'had good reason to be grateful to Frank. Without him, it might not have happened. Besides which, after that, Frank had his big scene to play that night – his dying scene.'

There have been stories of rows between Sinatra and Zinnemann over that scene – that the director wanted it to go according to the script but that Frank insisted otherwise. Zinnemann denied that. 'It was Harry Cohn's insistence. I had no rows with Sinatra over that,' he told me. 'In fact, ninety per cent of the time he was perfect.'

Just occasionally, though, they had an argument – and, once, when Frank thought that Clift wasn't returning the compliment and was agreeing with the director against his own views, he lost his temper, and hit him. But he later apologised and they were good friends throughout the rest of the production. Those good relations helped make the filming go better than it might otherwise have done: Clift was not just drinking heavily, he was also on drugs. Sinatra, meanwhile, had his own problems. The Internal Revenue Service had worked out that he owed $109,000 in back taxes and there were all sorts of difficulties with Ava: she had again been pregnant and decided once more on an abortion. He hated her for that.

Yet Frank behaved as if the film was the only thing in his life that mattered. It probably was. It was up to him to do well with that part or let it go the way of his MGM, Columbia Records and radio contracts.

Filming proceeded apace and the only additional problem arose when it came to cutting the movie. Zinnemann had a contract that decreed he had the right to make all the cuts that he wanted. Cohn, however, had the right to say how long the film should be and he was determined it should not last longer than two hours. Theatre operators didn't like movies to be longer than that because it cut down the number of shows they could have and, thereby, the number of tickets they could sell. Such factors were less important for the other big studios who had theatres of their own into which they could be certain of booking their products, whether the managers liked them or not. Columbia had no such advantage.

Two valuable scenes, in particular, were lost – a moving moment when Prewitt thinks that the Germans have invaded and another in which a group of soldiers improvised a blues number which Zinnemann had hoped he would be able to reprise as a kind of theme for the film, on the lines of *High Noon*, his own big hit of the previous year.

Cohn won the battle and the movie went into the theatres at 118 minutes, which could be described as cutting things fine. But then the studio boss thought the whole thing was fine – so much so that he did something he had never done before: he allowed his name to appear on the advertisement for the picture, the one single advertisement. His strategy was dangerous. He would only advertise once to start with – in the hope that the fact would get people talking about his new 'baby'. That advertisement would be in the *New York Times*, a whole page.

More than that, he headed the one announcement with a statement that declared how proud he was to invite the public to see his magnum opus. It was, he said, one of the best pictures to come out of his studio. 'That was enough to make a director feel very happy,' Zinnemann told me. It was followed by a further dangerous gamble which was also a powerful declaration of support: the film opened at the Capitol Theatre in Manhattan in the middle of August. August, when the New York climate resembles the output of an oven drenched in hot water, could be suicide in those pre-air-conditioning days. 'But Harry had confidence in what we had done,' said Zinnemann, 'and wanted it to be the biggest picture of the day. He was right. The lines of people wanting to get in went round and round.'

In fact, news of the success came very quickly. 'I wasn't in New York,' Fred Zinnemann remembered. 'But the next day I had a call from a lady I had never spoken to in my life. Marlene Dietrich was on the line. They were lining up five-deep outside the theatre, she told me. I couldn't understand it. There had been no advertising. "They can smell it," she said.'

The press smelt it, too. The New York *Post*'s Richard Watts wrote abut Sinatra's performance: 'For the first time, I find myself in the ranks of his ardent admirers. Instead of exploiting a personality, he proves he is an actor by playing the luckless Maggio with a kind of doomed gaiety that is both real and immensely touching.'

Time magazine said it all: 'He does Private Maggio like nothing he has ever done before. His face wears the calm of a man who is completely sure of what he is doing as he plays it straight from Little Italy.'

The word was out on how good this movie was long before most people had seen it. But word was good enough for Frank to be booked in for a week in Las Vegas – what could be described as his 'quickie marriage' with the town that was, unlike many Vegas nuptials, to go on for years and years. People crowded into the Sands Hotel, which from that moment on became virtual Sinatra territory. For the first time in ten years, he was on a stage on which he could do no wrong. When he sang 'They Can't Take That Away From Me', it seemed a statement of fact.

The crowds couldn't get enough of Sinatra and the hotels didn't have enough accommodation to offer them. Their new-found loyalty and enthusiasm was such that for many of them it just didn't matter. Police would report lines of parked cars along the Strip – filled with sleeping drivers and their passengers.

But the triumph at Vegas was only one aspect of Frank's return to form. The picture itself was a huge success. It grossed $80 million in its first full year, which for 1954 was phenomenal. Even more significant was the fact that it won six Oscars, including one for best picture, one for Dan Taradash, another for Fred Zinnemann, a fourth for Burnett Guffey for photography, and Best Supporting Role awards for Donna Reed – and Frank Sinatra.

He had had stiff competition, from Eddie Albert in *Roman Holiday*, Brandon de Wilde in *Shane*, and Robert Strauss in *Stalag 17*. When Mercedes McCambridge announced that Frank was the winner on the evening of 25 March 1954, the whole of the Pantages Theatre in Hollywood erupted, as though his contemporaries and peers had finally found a legitimate reason to be nice to him.

Frank jumped on to the stage and said: 'God has chosen to smile on me tonight.' He said of the evening later: 'Talk about being born again, it was one time in my life when I had such happiness I couldn't share with another human being.'

The kid from Hoboken was on top again – in a place few people have the good fortune to visit twice.

— 13 —

MAKIN' WHOOPEE

The fact that nobody expected it made it all the more surprising. Sinatra was like the boy soprano who after too long a time with a broken voice had become a tenor of immense range. Quite incredibly, he had gone through the most rigorous rite of passage. The pop singer had not merely become a fine actor, but the fine actor had become a singer again. That was what no one could have anticipated: that the triumph of *From Here to Eternity* would also revive his musical career and put him on a special pedestal for life.

Actors have always traded on the success of their movies. The spin-off possibilities of a box-office smash are virtually limitless: publicity; growth into other branches of the media; and, of course, the studio contract for ten or more times the amount paid for the previous film. Sometimes, and usually disastrously, those actors are encouraged to make records – novelties that no one will take seriously.

That was not what happened to Frank Sinatra. The man who couldn't give away his talent was now being flooded with offers from Columbia and from the other studios, too. There were radio programmes and TV shows for his choosing.

The first radio show was a fifteen-minute programme called *Perfectly Frank* – in which he mostly played his own records, sometimes singing with a group he called the Sinatra Symphonette. It began with the sound of Sinatra footsteps and a whistle – 'To be perfectly Frank, it's Sinatra,' said the announcer. 'Fifteen transcribed minutes of NBC's time for the very best guy in the business.

'Lots of music, couple of words. OK, Maggio, stop goofing off with those yardbirds and take a quick brace...'

'Yardbirds? Sir!' Frank would reply. 'You are speaking of the Sinatra Symphonette, five of Local 47s bravest and truest who face the music against fearful odds. It's rhythm to melody four to one. A fate worse than Perry Como ... Listen and learn, Daddy.' It seemed to be the right kind of image. After which he launched into something like 'This Can't Be Love.'

Any time now that he wanted to go back to the Hollywood Bowl or to any of the other posh places where he had appeared in concert, there were sponsors lining up to dust the seats, replace the sound equipment and write the kind of cheques he used to get for singing at the Paramount.

Harry Cohn telephoned Frank immediately after the Oscars ceremony. Sinatra refused to take the call. He figured that he now had the right to snub the man who wouldn't allow his senior employees to meet him.

Jonie Taps still wanted Frank to record the *From Here to Eternity* theme and, of course, he wanted him to do it free of charge. Yes, he said, he would record it – but not simply for publishing rights. He expected all the usual royalties. Most important of all, there was a brand-new recording contract ready to be signed. A new sophisticated audience, the same people who enthused over the *Eternity* film, now thronged the record stores and bought the results of the agreement he had just signed with Capitol, an old label which, like Sinatra himself, was about to have a new and totally different life.

Frank hosted a party at his small but elegant house off Wilshire Boulevard that evening and everyone connected with the movie came to pay him court. 'All I remember now,' Taradash told me, 'is that he was an absolutely superb host and so pleased about what had happened. He kept saying, "Anything I can get you? You want another drink?" A most lovable man on this occasion.' He was totally sober but 'probably all his guests were two-thirds drunk'.

Of course, he sang. But this was not at all the Sinatra of old. His voice was more mature, more thoughtful. It was not just deeper, it had rounded edges, it had a fluency that benefited from his old commitment to phrasing. Except that he was now phrasing songs that were suited to that voice.

Axel Stordahl had also changed with the passage of time. Somehow, it seems he didn't fit in with that new sound that was so manifestly now Sinatra's. No one doubted that Axel had made the early Sinatra. 'He was the loveliest man you ever met, Walter Scharf, musical director on hundreds of Hollywood films, told me. 'And he was so shy. But he was wonderfully talented. He set Sinatra's style, governing the breathing, deciding where the orchestra's important and where Frank himself was important.'

Frank's first Capitol sides, 'Lean Baby' and 'I'm Walking Behind You', were made with Stordahl, but they didn't do very much. They represented a parting of the ways in what had seemed to be an unbreakable partnership. The record could have come from the old pre-Miller Columbia stable and that was not enough, sweet and smoochy though it was. A new label, it seems, had to be a new start. Stordahl, even though it was he who had brokered the marriage between recording company and recording artist, represented a past age and memories of the latter years when nothing that Frank and Columbia had done together seemed to go right. He virtually disappeared from the scene after that – and died at the age of fifty.

By the time Frank cut his second Capitol disc, 'South of the Border', the arrangements credit were awarded to a man who would be very much part of the new Sinatra output – Billy May. When May wasn't available for the next session with the label, a new name appeared on the scene, chosen by Frank's current recording manager, Voyle Gilmore – another example of the differences that were becoming apparent and probably the real reason for Stordahl's departure. The name was Nelson Riddle.

What Riddle now produced sounded as different from anything that had come before as Sinatra himself now sounded compared with his days with Dorsey. With it was the promise of more that was better still. As Walter Scharf says: 'With Stordahl and Gordon Jenkins who worked with him later, it was Frank Sinatra and orchestra. Riddle was more of a co-star.' Sinatra himself was to echo that. 'Nelson was the best,' he said a generation later. 'He was peerless and brought a special energy and drive to our recording sessions at Capitol. I was maturing as a vocalist and Nelson built on the lower range of my voice – less crooning and more hot numbers.'

Very occasionally, Frank and Capitol allowed themselves to slip. Two weird choices followed on the early Riddle discs – 'Two Hearts, Two Kisses, One Love', and 'From the Bottom to the Top', accompanied by The Nuggets and Big Dave's Music sounded like Mitch Miller at his worst, perhaps even worse than that.

But these were aberrations. With Riddle in charge and occasionally Gordon Jenkins – his 'There's No You' was notable – the quality was consistent. The pity was that Axel Stordahl, to whom the early Sinatra had owed so much, wasn't part of this positive future.

Something new had now entered the Sinatra career. There was a confidence about him that he had never shown before. He believed that everything was going right and, most important of all, going right on his terms. That applied as much to Ava as to his career. He didn't want the current Mrs Sinatra to be another Nancy. He would never have married her in the first place – or had his various affairs – if that had been the lodestone he wanted to follow. Yet, when he remembered to do so, Ava was the person he would take his children to see.

Today Christina (Tina, to all about her) who was just two years old when her father moved out, says: 'I remember visions of her. My sister Nancy, of course, was older and just wanted to gawk at her and emulate her. Frank would dress us up and take us in the car to spend time with her and I remember she'd brush my hair and she taught me to sew.' These interesting comments are about the only documented statements about Ava's domesticity.

The children went on tour with their father, 'which was always a lot of fun.' They went to London and to New York together and even as a tot, Tina says she was sensitive enough not to tell her mother too much.

Frank phoned both Nancy and their children every day, no matter how close he was to Ava at the time. He came home for birthdays, and sometimes he would take his children for a day's outing in California or New York. One day, Tina found that she was the object of a lot of attention as they drove down Sunset Boulevard. 'Daddy, why are all those people staring at me?' she asked. 'Honey,' he told her. 'They're not staring at you. They're looking at me.' As she says: 'That was when I realised exactly who he was.'

Frank himself knew that he was on top again now and also thought he knew how to keep himself there. So a lot of the bravado he had previously needed to maintain his image was now left behind. He did a stint at the 500 Club in Atlantic City run by his friend Skinny D'Amato. It was one of those moments in the Sinatra life which demonstrated his decency, a part of him that had always seemed to go hand in hand with the more aggressive side to his nature. When three girls made the trip to the club from Brooklyn – they just wanted to see their idol; they could never have afforded to go inside – they found themselves stranded afterwards in a heavy rainstorm. They had no umbrellas, no raincoats, no decent shoes. Frank heard about it – and paid for a hire car to take them home.

He didn't boast of his kindness, any more than he went to the 500 Club for reasons other than wanting to help his old friend D'Amato who was going through hard times. It wasn't an important club and didn't bring in big money, but he knew it would help D'Amato. The trouble was, the club was partly owned by a gentleman called Sam Giancana. He was best known as a Mafia don – one the police constantly wanted but could never pin down for a specific offence.

Sinatra's visit was the most important thing that had ever happened to the club. Before his arrival, D'Amato put up a sign declaring, 'He's Coming'. Everyone knew what it meant and who 'He' was. When he left, D'Amato put up another sign. It said simply: 'He Was Here'. Missouri Avenue was blocked. When Frank heard that four hundred people were outside, after missing his performance, he told D'Amato: 'Well, let's do another show'.

He was never paid even for one show, although he was put up 'on the house' at the prestigious Claridge Hotel ('my home away from home', as he called it). Paulajane D'Amato said her father used to say: 'Atlantic City only needed three things – the sun, the sand and Frank Sinatra ... Sinatra doesn't just fill a club, he fills a town.'

Jerry Lewis told me of a similar experience.

'It was 1951,' the actor-director remembered for me. 'Dean [Martin] and I were making an extensive tour of the United States, personal appearances to sell the film we had just made. We got back to Los Angeles and I get a call from Frank. He says, "Meet me at the airport at 5 o'clock and bring the Italian with you [Dean]. And bring your work clothes."

'We got there at five o'clock and said to Frank: "Are you going to tell us where we are going?"

'He says: "When we get in the plane." He had his own private plane at the airport. And he was going to fly us half way across the country. While we're in the air, we're told what it's all about. He was made aware of a fire fighter who died in a fire the week before, leaving a wife and five children – no benefits; six people floundering.

'Frank sent his advance man to Rockford, Illinois, got the Mayor to open up the basket ball court at the high school, charged $100 a seat, got a thirty-piece orchestra from Chicago, and took them to Rockford. We got there at 10 o'clock that night, rehearsed and did a midnight show. We raised about $30,000 for that family.

'We did two hours like you can't believe, we got on the plane, he thanked us, got back to Los Angeles, drove to our respected homes and felt very satisfied. It was one of ten occasions when he asked us to do something like that. He was notorious for that kind of conduct and it was nobody's business. He paid for everything.'

The other side of Sinatra's behaviour was that it was now a matter of record that a mobster owned a club in which Sinatra appeared.

Ava was with him when the show opened and was then introduced to the gang boss. It was a meeting between Beauty and the Beast. Afterwards, Ava asked why Frank wanted to get involved with a hoodlum. 'That hoodlum,' he said, 'is responsible for giving me a job.' But that was not true. He went to the club of his own volition, to help a friend. Not because he needed the work. Now he had more work than he could cope with.

Sinatra was also subject to a whole chain of investigations. He wasn't content to be a mere entertainer. Now he wanted 'a piece of the action'. When, in 1954, he was offered a percentage of the Sands Hotel in Las Vegas – two per cent for $54,000 – he had to go before the Nevada Gaming Commission, who then looked into every aspect of the Sinatra lifestyle. So did the FBI, who later found that Frank Costello and Joe Adonis, neither of whom one would care to meet in a lonely street on a dark night, had interests in the hotel. Frank always denied he knew that they did and Jack Entratter, who ran the place like a fiefdom, claimed it was untrue – if they owned the joint, how come they never came to look at their money? No action was taken at this time, but it was an issue that would come back to haunt the singer.

He would always deny any intimate relationships with the Mob. It would not stop 'Doc' Fischetti who gloried in his reputation as one of the last survivors of the Capone gang, telling how he helped Frank out of a serious problem at the Sands Hotel: Sinatra had ordered a pastrami sandwich on an onion roll. A waiter made a mistake and it was delivered on rye bread – with predictable results. Fischetti, who had been used to doing people favours of a different kind, made the hotel kitchen aware of the delicacy of the situation – and personally delivered a fresh pastrami sandwich on an onion roll to Frank.

When Sinatra increased his stake in the hotel to 9 per cent no one took much notice. His life with Ava, however, was always going to be front-page news.

— 14 —

THE GAL THAT GOT AWAY

S inatra liked to give the impression to the outside world that he and Ava were perfectly matched, even if a little volatile. Yet Ava began to move officially out of his life at just about the same time as the new success moved in. Now she occasionally dated his friends – like Peter Lawford who received a note from Frank promising to break the legs of any 'asshole' who stepped in where he did not belong.

At the height of his success, Ava left him. As she said: 'When he was down and out, he was sweet. But now that he is successful again, he's become his old arrogant self. We were happier when he was on the skids.'

Sinatra–Gardner watchers had seen the signs for a long time. In the midst of the *From Here to Eternity* publicity campaign, the couple were asked to appear together on a TV programme. The interviewer knew of the problems they were having and liked Frank. He thought it could help to get the two together, or at least look as though they were together, to the point of making it embarrassing for them to consider separating soon afterwards. Frank was excited by the notion – another example of how things had changed; previously he would never have dreamed of wanting to share his air time with anyone else, not even his wife, but now he agreed to do so. Ava patently did not. 'This is a personal matter,' she declared in language that was more restrained than any she normally used. 'It's my marriage, my life.' Then, directing her response at her husband, said: 'It has no place on your show. I won't come.'

Strangely, the official announcement of their separation came from neither Ava nor Frank, but from MGM. Louis B. Mayer had stopped being the 'father' of his studio and had lost his job in a boardroom coup. Yet the family instinct was still there. Frank was no longer one of the children, but Ava, with the glories of *Show Boat* lingering in their memories, still was.

The statement, issued on 27 October 1953, from Culver City said: 'Ava Gardner and Frank Sinatra stated today that having reluctantly exhausted every effort to reconcile their differences, they could find no mutual basis on which to continue their marriage.'

They both expressed their regrets. One suspects that Frank's were greater than Ava's. She was ready to move on to the next man who would do her bidding – and there were always plenty of those for a woman who didn't want to be tied to a husband any more than she had wanted to be tied to a cradle.

The undoubted fact is that for all his attraction to glamorous women with careers of their own, like Ava, Lana Turner and Marilyn Maxwell, what Sinatra really wanted was another Nancy Barbato, someone who, while agreeing to make up nicely and dress perfectly, was not interested in a career of her own. It wasn't that he wanted someone to cook his dinner and be ready with a pipe and slippers, he needed a partner who would be as excited about his progress as he was himself, who would be with him when *he* went filming, not someone who was going off filming on her own account and who might or might not come to an opening night dressed in a white mink.

Ava had enjoyed the excitement of the chase and loved the sex, but marriage to Frank Sinatra was asking too much of her. Frank, despite his statement, wouldn't accept this. He was determined to follow Ava to Europe where she and Humphrey Bogart – leader of the Rat Pack of Hollywood icons who dedicated themselves to having a good time – were going to make *The Barefoot Contessa*, a singularly appropriate title for the woman known as 'The Barefoot Venus from Smithfield, North Carolina'.

In order to go, Sinatra did something that had only just been made possible by the latest 1950s technology: he taped advance editions of the radio shows in which he was appearing. But all he got for his trouble was a stay at New York's Mount Sinai Hospital suffering from exhaustion, weight loss and 'a tremendous amount of emotional strain'. That was what the papers said. What they didn't say was that he had been found on the floor of an elevator with his wrists slashed. It was at the 57th Street home of his songwriter friend Jimmy Van Heusen, who gave the doorman $50 to keep the story to himself (which, remarkably, he did for years).

Whether he had actually hoped to kill himself or not, Frank was making a statement of how desperate he really was. He had never been smitten so badly at any other time in his life and the pain of what was clearly unrequited love, even after eleven months of marriage and years of courtship, was stronger than he could have anticipated.

But Ava had a new flame – another bullfighter. This one was Luis Dominguin, whom she also met while filming. Frank heard about it and flew to Spain in a private aircraft, but she wouldn't see him. Since second thoughts about divorce were as common as weddings in Hollywood, nobody could be sure whether the separation would be for ever or not. But one day, in New York, Frank discovered that Ava had returned to husband number two, Artie Shaw.

Evelyn Keyes, who became a Mrs Artie Shaw herself, told me a story never revealed before: 'I remember Artie telling me that Ava would come running back to him once she had had enough with Frank. And she did. But Frank was not having any of it. He showed up with two gangster types with hands in their pockets on either side, shouting, "Where is she?" She was not to be found that day.'

Frank was as much in love with Ava now as he had ever been. He had not only lost her from his private life, she was missing from the public Sinatra existence, too. She wasn't around to share his success and, though he would never be short of women to squire when he wanted to do so in public or to take to his bed on more private occasions, Ava was the one he wanted.

Months after the separation announcement was first made, Frank would still phone Ava, plucking up a kind of courage he never needed when with some less pleasant people. 'Let's try again,' he would say. Once or twice she tried. They spent five or six hours together. Sometimes a whole night. Sometimes she was in the same town as Frank but didn't tell him. When she returned to America after filming, *Knights of the Round Table* in London, it took a photograph in a newspaper for Frank to know she was in New York. As he told a reporter, barely able to hide the tears that were choking him or the anger that was consuming his every thought, 'I saw a picture of Ava at the airport and that's the first inkling I had that she was in town. I don't understand it.'

Miraculously, it seemed, a reconciliation *was* perhaps now in the wind. When Frank was appearing in New York, he took time off to see the new present he had just bought his parents – a luxurious new home in Weehawken, the New Jersey town that borders Hoboken. Much to Marty's and Dolly's surprise, Ava had been in the audience at the Riviera Club that night and came with him for the dinner. She seemed as exultant over the response to the show as Frank himself had been. Earl Wilson had noticed it: 'With Ava in the audience, Frank changed one of the gestures in his act that had been getting a good laugh during the battling. Singing 'I Get a Kick Out of You', Frank had illustrated it as though he were getting booted in the derrière by love, represented by Ava.' But on this occasion, Wilson reported, he dropped it. Ava wouldn't have appreciated the gesture. It was almost like old times, but no good was to come out of it.

If Frank and the boys spent an evening together, Ava didn't enjoy it. If he went with her to the opening of *Mogambo*, he was only interested in his own career. He loved her in an all-consuming way, but only realised it when they were apart. Their reunions would always stop at the twenty-four-hour barrier. They just couldn't find a common cause. Frequently, just meeting again was enough for the fireworks to start.

Matters were now serious enough for Ava to be ordered out of Frank's plush new home in Palm Springs when she attempted a reconciliation. He was always doing that – pleading for her to come back, to make up – and then showing her the door. Finally, it became clear that Ava was not going to come back again, at least for the moment.

Artie Shaw, Ava's ex-husband, could have added his own contribution to the saga. He told me, in sentiments that Ava herself might have accepted as her own: 'He's pretty good at what he does. But what does he do? Cry into his beer. Yet he was the only one I know who could make people forget Bing Crosby. But those terrible lyrics! It's like his head was filled with snow. Just pap. Zany. Idiotic – like one of those glass balls you hold upside down and it snows. It's prolific. But poetic? It's just plain stupid.'

Time magazine didn't think Sinatra stupid. He was a phenomenon that excited them quite as much as it thrilled the new generation of fans. In August 1955, they made him the subject of a cover story, one of the highest accolades in the fame business, for both heroes and villains.

On the whole, Frank Sinatra's cover put him in the hero columns, although it did recall a situation when the kid Frankie, all dressed up in his Little Lord Fauntleroy suit, was chased by a pair of Hoboken roughnecks who provided him with generous helpings of rotten fruit only to be answered 'by Little Lord Fauntleroy himself who was spouting profanity in a highly experienced manner and carving the breeze with a jagged chunk of broken bottle.'

As the magazine's feature made clear: 'Francis Albert Sinatra, long grown out of his Little Lord Fauntleroy suit, is one of the most charming children in everyman's neighbourhood; yet it is well to remember the jagged weapon.' It added: 'The one he carries nowadays is of the mind, and called ambition, but it takes an ever more exciting edge.'

For eight pages, the profile dwelt on the man they called 'The Kid From Hoboken'. The first page was headed by a photograph of a soulful-looking Sinatra, in his hat, band even wider than usual, a check waistcoat and a black tie protruding from his open-collar pink shirt. It revealed that he was likely to face an income-tax bill for the current year in the region of $1 million – with payments from five movies in twelve months likely to raise some $800,000 towards his bank account fund. It may sound like chickenfeed compared to the salaries of the 1990s, but to Sinatra, then exactly halfway through his first eighty years, it was a fortune.

After all, as the article said, this was a man with $30,000 worth of cuff-links and with polo grounds for a closet.

It quoted another friend as saying: 'He bleeds for the underdog because he feels like one. Don't ask me why.'

Robert Mitchum was strictly in the praise department. 'Frank is a tiger – afraid of nothing, ready for anything. He'll fight anything. Here's a frail, under-sized fellow with a scarred-up face who isn't afraid of the whole world.'

It went on to regale readers with details of the hundred suits and fifty pairs of shoes he owned – to say nothing of his fifty hats. And it also said that he hated cops and reporters and knew people like Joe Fischetti, 'who is prominent in what is left of the Capone mob', and mentioned the alleged meeting with Lucky Luciano in Havana.

If Ava didn't want Frank any more, it seemed that nearly everybody else did. He had his pick of new film scripts the way an art collector is offered paintings to buy. Everything about the projects was weighed up carefully – how much money was likely to come in, how much good (or bad) it would do his career prospects. What he could not afford to do now was to 'coast' and take an inferior script. If it appeared that *Eternity* was a flash in the pan, it could take another eternity before anything good happened again.

There was one film he desperately wanted to do now – even if it meant going back to Hoboken. Columbia was about to make Budd Schulberg's *On the Waterfront*, about union corruption on the docks in his old home town. The part of the young stevedore was, he decided, right up his gangplank. There was the same spunk that Maggio had, the same defiance against all the odds. And, as with Maggio, he had gone to school and played hookey with young men exactly like him. He wanted that part, yearned for it and, as when he wanted Maggio, felt it in his bloodstream. What was more, he was telling everyone that the producer, Sam Spiegel, and the director, Elia Kazan, had promised the part to him. But now they said they wanted Marlon Brando and nothing was going to make them switch.

Frank's response was to sue for $500,000 in damages. He said he had been promised $50,000 to make the picture, as well as 10 per cent of the profits. The matter was settled out of court.

Afterwards, he had to face up to his disappointment and move on to other things – this time with the help of a new agent named George Wood of the William Morris organisation. Wood – very much involved in making Las Vegas the prime spot it would become in show-business history – was geared to watch over the Sinatra career like a mother hen who knew that one of her chicks was about to be a load of trouble. The Morris connection had been established when Milt Ebbins, who managed Count Basie, had seen Sinatra, pre-*Eternity*, on the pavement outside the Morris building with his head in his hands. He told him how bad things were and Ebbins responded by saying, 'You'll do better.' Nobody then could have imagined how much better.

Soon after his Oscar success, Frank performed at the Beachcomber in Miami Beach, Florida. The audience packed into the place and, remarkably for a nightclub when Frank Sinatra came on stage, all was quiet. You couldn't hear a glass being clinked or a knife and fork being moved. The company was his from the moment he took the microphone in his hand. And that was another of the changes since he had last been on top: the mike was no longer static, something to be hugged; instead it was an extension to his hand and he instantly learned to use it as though it were an identifiable part of his body.

This seemed to be a kinder Sinatra, who now appreciated just how much he owed to the people who had remade him in his new image. One night during that Miami Beach tour, he spotted Dan and Madeleine Taradash sitting out front. He interrupted his act to introduce them and said: 'You can be a good actor but with a lousy script you can't do anything, and I just want to thank Dan Taradash for *From Here to Eternity.*' Says Taradash now: 'Well, that's a moment you don't forget.'

There was another movie that he thought he would be doing now that he was again a big star, but that went the way of *On the Waterfront.* There was talk of his making a film with Marilyn Monroe, which he considered was the ideal set-up. No one was linking their names romantically – yet. But Frank felt that they would look good together on the big screen. *Pink Tights* in the glories of Cinemascope was going to be the perfect antidote to *From Here to Eternity.* What was more, the well-tried and trusted team of Jule Styne and Sammy Cahn were on hand with an imaginative new score, including – in the scene when he was trying to make it with Marilyn – a pretty number called 'The Best Shoulder to Cry On'. Unfortunately Marilyn cried off and decided to marry Joe DiMaggio instead.

As a consolation, the composer and lyricist were invited by Twentieth Century-Fox to write the title song for a non-musical film – which they wanted Frank to sing. The two would go over to Frank's house on Sunday evenings and work out their plans for new numbers. 'Three Coins in the Fountain' was one of their better ideas. It was also to feature in one of those movies in which the music becomes better known – and better remembered – than the film itself, although it was a huge hit at the time. The song became an even bigger triumph for Sinatra himself. He took it to the top of the hit parade. Best of all, though, it cemented his relationship with two music men who could write a hit for him as easily as he put his name on a cheque. Until then, Cahn and Styne had never had a bigger success. It won the pair an Emmy award and the title is inscribed under a bust of Cahn at the Songwriters' Hall of Fame – along with the words: 'To Sammy Cahn and all men of words who make the music sing.'

But Jule Styne upset Sinatra by not giving the song to Frank's own music publishing company, Barton. As a result, he refused to speak to the composer for five years. Not only that: Frank, who had been his landlord, sent him packing from his apartment. That much was well known. What has not been revealed before was that Styne was living there rent-free. Hearing that the songwriter had been devastated by a broken romance, Frank had done the usual Sinatra thing and come to his aid. Now he thought there was no more reason to be nice.

'Three Coins' was soon followed by another Sinatra hit. In 1954,

Frank Sinatra could do anything he wanted to on stage – even drinking a cup of tea in 1975.

Little girl found. Mia Farrow plainly enjoying the limelight on the voyage when she agreed to become the third Mrs Sinatra.

(right) The Clan in their natural habitat. Frank with Dean Martin, Sammy Davis Jnr., Peter Lawford and Joey Bishop. At Las Vegas, of course.

(below) He only made a fleeting appearance, but in 1962 'spacemen' Frank Sinatra and Dean Martin could be guaranteed to cause a jam on *The Road to Hong Kong*. In London in 1962.

(above) The first screen role that really meant anything – even if Gene Kelly did get top billing. In *Anchors Aweigh*, also with Kathryn Grayson and Pamela Britton.

(below) *Lady in Cement* in 1968. By then the film roles had got stuck in cement too.

(above left) About the only thing you could say about the movie *Assault On A Queen* was that Frank looked fetching in a diver's helmet. The film itself didn't fetch in the customers.

(above right) From the film that turned a has-been into a super star. He won an Oscar for his role as Maggio in *From Here to Eternity*, and the plaudits of critics and public alike.

(below) His second powerful dramatic performance. Playing a junkie as well as a card–sharp in *Man With The Golden Arm*.

(opposite) A kind of immortality. Sinatra offering homage to his first idol Al Jolson as his hands and feet are preserved for posterity in the cement at Grauman's Chinese Theatre in Hollywood.

(above) The new family: Nancy Jnr., Frank Jnr., Barbara Sinatra, Dolly and Tina soon after the last of Frank's four weddings, this time to the former Mrs Zeppo Marx.

(right) Giving Nancy away on her wedding day. They would always remain close.

The elder statesman.

Frank did equally well with 'Young at Heart'. The new Sinatra voice was earning dividends, boasted by the marketing techniques of Capitol Records who knew what a commodity they had to sell in Frank Sinatra and proceeded to peddle him the way vendors on the Lower East Side of New York sold neckties. But the extra sparkle was contributed by Nelson Riddle, who was now established as Frank's new Axel Stordahl. Riddle would work with other people, too, like Nat King Cole (notably with 'Mona Lisa'), Judy Garland and Dean Martin, and somehow each vicariously brought something new to the other.

Riddle had been a trombonist and arranger with Charlie Spivak, Jerry Wald and, most significantly, Tommy Dorsey. But it was coming together with Frank Sinatra that made everything gel for him. He not only knew what Sinatra needed, he knew how to implement it – by paying as much attention to the musicians he was conducting as to his own arrangements and stick-waving. The use of a sidesman like Harry Edison proved invaluable, but so did the unique way in which he moved bass clarinet or trombone alongside his phrasing. Where Stordahl played music that sounded the way Sinatra sang it, now Sinatra sang with a new style that Riddle had framed. It was a 'Swingin' Sinatra', although the albums didn't yet say so.

'Young at Heart' was played on jukeboxes all over America and in Britain too. More important, radio stations played it for as long as listeners could take the style that Riddle was creating, inventing the alternative sound of the 1950s – the sound that would before long have to compete with Elvis Presley and Bill Haley. It was at the head of the hit parade for twenty-two weeks.

He was back. As a result, NBC gave him a radio show on Tuesdays and Fridays. Once again, it seemed that people couldn't get enough of Sinatra in all his incarnations.

That included Jack Warner, head of the Warner Bros. studio and the man who decided what should or should not be put on film. He still had a decade or so to run in his job and liked to think he was as much in touch with things as he had been when he made *The Jazz Singer* in 1927. Warner heard 'Young at Heart' and immediately decided it would be great as the title of a film. Furthermore, he wanted Frank to sing the title song. Then he thought he should star in it, too. The only thing he hadn't thought out was what the story would be.

It is at moments like this that Hollywood can be relied upon to be inventive in the extreme. This one was to be no exception. Warner thought about the title and came up with the idea of remaking an old movie, the John Garfield weepie, *Four Daughters*. There was a script by Julius Epstein, the kind of Hollywood genius who made writing screenplays seem as easy as scribbling a grocery list. 'Well, we weren't making *War and Peace*, you know,' he told me in mitigation for the way his industry operated. He had written the original movie as well as a little thing called *Casablanca*.

He says he didn't have a lot to do with Sinatra while writing *Young at Heart*. 'He wanted a script conference and that was what had to happen. He sent a telegram with his demands. I think he just wanted his lines explained. I think he had some respect for my script in those days. But as the years went on, I know he got more and more of a pain in the ass.'

With the benefit of the Sinatra title song, written by Caroline Leigh and Johnny Richards, the film did even better than the 1938 original, this time with Frank playing the penniless composer who falls for Doris Day. It was not a difficult thing to do. Doris played one of the four daughters of a small-town music teacher, all of whom have romantic problems of one kind or another. The movie represented a perfect mix for Sinatra. It was a chance to sing with that 'new' voice. But it was also a wonderful opportunity for his acting, playing a man with a chip on his shoulders as large as a music stand. In its way, it was as powerful a performance as that of the soldier in Honolulu.

Perhaps even more importantly, the movie gave him a chance to sing songs that would forever after be identified with him. He had the advantage, of course, that practically any Sinatra mood was right for a song. With Ava having gone, there was no reason not to cash in on the morose Frank, the one who was lost and lonely, as well as the one who could swing. 'One for My Baby' was one of those perfect lachrymose numbers that sounded so right simply because the singer knew how to hold a glass and a half-smoked cigarette as well as he knew how to hold a tune. He had done it before, but never with such intensity. The other song that made its mark in the picture was perhaps the most beautiful number Sinatra ever performed: Gershwin's 'Someone to Watch Over Me'. It was not just a superb song magnificently rendered, it was and has to remain the prime example of Sinatra's phrasing. Every word, every syllable, counts.

> I may not be the man-some
> Girls think of as hand-some

was made to sound as though he himself had dreamed up the stanza as he sat in a hammock pensively thinking of the girl who had got away ... who may or may not have been Ava. Only he and Ella Fitzgerald have performed those lyrics the way Gershwin intended. It is a difficult conjunction of words which you have to understand to perform. As Burton Lane has noted, Sinatra found meanings in lyrics that even the writers sometimes didn't know were there.

Also in 1954 came *Suddenly*, the film in which Frank gave a strong performance playing an unsympathetic role. It was the first time he had played a heavy – if a man weighing under 120 pounds whom girls still wanted to mother could be described as that. In this movie, he was a prospective assassin who accepts $500,000 to kill the President of the United States as his train steams into a small town. It was a prescient enactment of what would happen nine years later – the murder would be performed with a rifle from the window of a building. The difference was that the Sinatra character was caught before a shot could be fired. He also worked with henchmen, not alone as the Warren Commission would claim Lee Harvey Oswald did.

Frank's enemies were not, however, residents of the White House but more likely to be newspapermen. In August 1954 he was once more accused of hitting a man whom he claimed to dislike. James Byron, a publicity agent, said that Sinatra came at him with a left hook and knocked him to the ground. Byron alleged: 'He screamed at me, "You're a newspaperman. You're nothing but a leech".'

Sinatra defended himself. It was Byron who struck the first blows, he maintained. 'Two guys held my arms and Byron dented my shin-bone. It ended when I broke loose and gave him a left hook.'

Frank, when he wasn't fighting, was on a movie kick now. One picture after the other would come off the assembly line and if it weren't for those records with Nelson Riddle you might be forgiven for thinking that Frank Sinatra had finally decided to settle down to the life others found very profitable, as a film star.

But there were those records and there was the fun – and the money – he seemed to be getting from playing other people's discs, too. In *Perfectly Frank*, he was playing the DJ, spinning other people's discs as well as his own. His farewell at the end of each show was always identical. 'Ladies and gentlemen, I wish you everything you want in life for yourselves and your families, lots of hugging and kissing and sweet dreams. And God bless.'

He was back at the top of the tree now, so confident, sitting on those branches, that he took the problems of life nice and easily – or at least he liked to give the impression that he did. *Swing Easy* was the title of his first important LP because it set the mould of the Sinatra who was now taking over. It was a ten-inch disc (that's how popular albums were at the time) with a mauve sleeve, but it was the word 'Swing' that gave him his new image.

The album established a new trend altogether. The big bands were virtually all gone. Sinatra was the only survivor of the genre left. But instead of swing making him appear a relic of a past age, it established the new Sinatra for a new, highly sophisticated, record-purchasing public. Young men in their twenties gave the disc to their fiancées; young women no longer swooned at Sinatra, they listened to him. The record spun at 33 revolutions per minute in homes all over the world and almost every one of the people listening became a confirmed fan, the kind who read articles about Sinatra in the chic magazines, who wanted to read interviews in music papers. It was not the old fan stuff about the kind of pyjamas he wore and the breakfasts he ate or even the girls he was dating, but this time serious writers noting the way he performed his lyrics, writing about the time he took extending a note, about how different 'Just One of Those Things' sounded on this record from the way he had sung it before in concert or from the way other entertainers performed it. The voice was deeper, more vibrant.

He not only brought back his own kind of swing, the sort that socked-it-to-'em but never lost the rhythm, he introduced the songs of the thirties and forties to audiences who had either never known them or who thought of them as the kind of thing their parents had thrown into the loft. The Sinatra–Riddle team was a winner. Frank would always recognise the debt he owed his conductor–arranger. He said Riddle had a 'fresh approach to orchestration and I made myself fit into what he was doing.' Riddle himself was to say: 'There's no one like him. Frank not only encourages you to adventure, but he has such a keen appreciation for achievement that you are impelled to knock yourself out for him. It's not only that his intuitions as to tempi, phrasing and even figuration are amazingly right, but that his taste is so impeccable. This is because his interest in music has never been hemmed in.'

Riddle had another superb characteristic. He managed to catch not just the mood of the music but, above all, the mood of the singer. There was no point, he believed, in trying to get Frank to perform a number for which he felt temperamentally unsuited. He had the same advantage, of course, that had proved so useful in *Young at Heart*. Practically any Sinatra mood was right for a song. 'A Foggy Day' was as reflective and powerful under Riddle as under any other music man. 'One for My Baby', the national anthem of the saloon junkie, sounded as good coming from a record player as it had in the movie theatre. But with Ava leaving his life there had to be something to reflect his feelings as he sat, wearing his new, trademark, narrow-brimmed hat with its wide band firmly over his brow, smoking his cigarette, perched on the edge of the stool, a microphone dangling between himself and the bandstand. It was 'There Will Never Be Another You'. He might be ready to take a glamorous woman to his bed after the recording session, but the sheet music was metaphorically rolled into a torch and he was carrying it for Ava.

He thought of her too, when he recorded 'In the Wee Small Hours', the retrospective Sinatra on disc. 'When Your Lover Has Gone' could have been perceived as advice from a man who needed a little information on the subject himself. 'I Get Along Without You Very Well' was the kind of lie he would tell himself every time he tried to forget her.

Nothing would make him accept what had happened to them. Anything he could do to bring her back, he would try. The people he had condemned for their interference in his life he now called on for aid. Louella Parsons, who had done her share of castigating Sinatra, was one of the vehicles for his appeals. 'Ava doesn't love me any more,' he told her at the Sands Hotel's Copa Room – 'my room', as he liked to call it after another triumphant opening which should have been reason enough for his face to be covered in smiles. 'If she did, she'd be here where she belongs – with me. Instead, she's in Palm Springs having a wonderful time.' He couldn't grasp the fact that he was never again going to be the centre of her universe.

He found what solace there was in his songs. The astounding thing about Sinatra was his interest in music way beyond his own field. He may or may not have been influenced by Fritz Kreisler, but he told Riddle, of his love for the music of Vaughan Williams and got the conductor 'all excited' about the British composer, too.

Riddle always knew what kind of garment it was that he had to cut for his singer. Like a Victorian poet, Frank was pouring out his emotions, getting things off his chest, but as far as the people buying his records were concerned, they were just another interesting part of his output and they wanted everything he could produce. Some of it came on single seven-inch discs revolving at 45 revolutions a minute, but mostly now he produced for the LP album market which was proving to be so much more commercial than anyone thought possible when the discs were tentatively introduced in 1948. He was giving all the answers to the questions posed at that time. Would people want to play records that went on for twenty minutes or so per side? Would they spend their money on records that suddenly cost up to $5? And the machinery needed to play it? Frank Sinatra was helping to prove that this was now the accepted way to play music. For his much more sophisticated clientele, it was the only way.

The industry certainly agreed that was so. The popular music world was no longer the fiefdom of Crosby, Como, or that bright young man Nat 'King' Cole. With Jolson now dead for over five years, it was all Frank Sinatra's. This wasn't a mere comeback. It was as though he had reinvented himself and the old Sinatra was a distant relative to whom he owed nothing. His *Songs for Young Lovers* album featuring numbers like 'My Funny Valentine' and, once again, 'I Get a Kick Out of You' sold better than anything on LP had ever done before.

Had Sinatra decided that he was going to do nothing but make recordings – as a number of the best of his contemporaries did – he would already have become a multimillionaire. But then came *The Tender Trap* – another chicken-and-egg situation; which came first – the film or the song title? The story of the movie was slightly retrospective – Sinatra, the womaniser, falling for the beautiful ingénue, played this time by Debbie Reynolds who was still glorying in the success of *Singin' in the Rain*.

The song came about as a result of a bet with Sammy Cahn. 'Can you imagine this man challenging me?' Cahn remembered. 'He said: "I bet you can't write a song with that title, 'The Tender Trap'" Well, when anyone gives me that sort of challenge, particularly when Frank Sinatra gives me that sort of challenge, am I expected to resist? Of course, I didn't resist.'

Sinatra has taken up that story. 'There were two studios,' he told a radio interviewer. 'One was empty. I kept a piano and I ran through some songs there. The boys [Cahn and Jimmy Van Heusen] came over and we told them what we were doing. They went into the studio next door and after forty minutes they came out with it and I was knocked out.'

Everything he did now knocked out his audience. His was an enviable career, in which he was being hailed by those very people who had happily watched him slipping back down the road when they were travelling so far forward and so fast. He did, however, mix with those entertainers as well as with others who were going through rough periods. This was the time Sammy Davis, Jr., was involved in the car crash that robbed him of an eye. Frank was among the first people to go and see him. He told jokes and brought him an eye chart – with the words attached, 'Practice, Practice.'

As for Frank himself, he had done all the practising he thought he ever needed to do. He was on top – for everyone to see.

— 15 —

WHY SHOULD I CRY
OVER YOU?

With Ava now out of his life, Frank bought a new home for himself, a magnificent bachelor pad on Coldwater Canyon, one of the most select streets of Beverly Hills. There were only a couple of houses in the vicinity, which he could see, although they could not see him, and he was high enough to be able to look down on the rest of Hollywood – which was precisely what he did every time he thought of the indignities to which the film community had subjected him over the years.

It was smart and fashionable – and secluded. Only a mailbox indicated there was a house at all. The home was high on the hill, and hidden by a mass of foliage. James Cagney lived near by, so did a clutch of lesser actors who believed that their fame was in inverse proportion to their availability. Frank went one better with his home on the very summit of the hill: he had a 200-yard stretch of unpaved private road leading to the house on which he decided he wanted to build a helicopter pad. It became one of those moments when Frank once again played the immovable object fighting an irresistible force.

The story has never been told before. Beverly Hills Council said no to the plan. Frank Sinatra replied, using the kind of language Ava would have delighted in sporting herself. He was furious – but even more so when they built a fire station near by, which *was* given permission for a helipad. It annoyed him so much that he had to find ways of getting his own back. He closed the private road, which had been used as a kind of bypass. There was nothing anyone could do about it – or about his decision to charge for the use of a key that would open a gate and allow access.

It upset the fire service more than anyone else. It was a useful route for their engines. But not even nostalgia for the Hoboken brigade and

Captain Martin Sinatra would soften his heart and give them access. As Mrs Madeleine Taradash, who lived near by, told me: 'It was just another example of the way Mr Sinatra always considered himself above the law.'

He didn't feel himself above old love, however At the very time that he was moving towards the official divorce, he put up a sculpture in the garden of the luxury house – a statue of Ava by Assen Peikov, who had made it for *The Barefoot Contessa*. Frank explained: 'If it took another seventy-five years to get a divorce, there still wouldn't be another woman for me.' It was the truth. Even when Ava took up temporary residence in Nevada, the first step towards being allowed to qualify for a divorce in Reno or anywhere else in the state, he still secretly hoped he could bring back the past.

But in July 1956, when Ava was filming at Elstree Studios north of London, Mrs Sinatra became Ms Gardner again. Sinatra was morose, inconsolable. But this was the only glitch in his seemingly unstoppable career.

To go along with the new success, there was also a new abrasiveness. The fact that he didn't have to worry any more about whether audiences (as distinct from Ava) still loved him didn't sweeten his manners. David Raksin was at a party at the Democratic Party convention in 1956 at which both Sinatra and Sam Rayburn, Speaker of the House, of Representatives were guests. Rayburn patted Sinatra on the shoulder and began, 'Mr Sinatra, I'd like ...' To which Frank responded, 'Hands off the threads, Bud.' Said Raksin: 'Sam Rayburn was a very senior man, an elegant old gentleman with a bald head, and that was quite shocking. It sounds like one of those things that people in one of Francis Ford Coppola's movies might say.'

Sinatra's political activities were on a much lower scale than had previously been the case. Of course he revelled in being invited to the convention that would nominate Adlai Stevenson for a second time, knowing full well that he would go down with the ship once more against Eisenhower. But he didn't want the same treatment for himself. It was safer just to enjoy his mammoth success without complications.

McCarthyism was still to the fore and too much support for the Democrats could be seen by the hunt-the-reds mobs as the thin end of the wedge. To the extreme right wing, the Democratic Party at its worst and most excessive was a form of communism. The fact that Sinatra had once had tea with President Roosevelt was as great a sin as his support of the Hollywood Ten at the time that the House

Committee on UnAmerican Affairs Committee was asking perfectly innocent people, 'Are you now or have you ever been a member of the Communist Party'.

He decided there was no future in the old medium of radio and he now gave it up. Films were taking so much of his time and there were always the records to keep happy the people who just wanted to hear his voice. He could do television whenever he wanted to. His most interesting film venture at this time was *Not as a Stranger*, based on the Morton Thompson novel, in which he and Robert Mitchum play young doctors involved with a too-old Olivia de Havilland and with two senior medical men played by the ageing Broderick Crawford and Charles Bickford. It's a worthy piece in which Mitchum has gone on record saying that he had to fight Sinatra for every scene. 'Earnest filming of a best seller with all the actors too old for their parts,' commented Leslie Halliwell.

He was equally miscast in Sam Goldwyn's film version of *Guys and Dolls*. In this he played Nathan Detroit, the man in constant search of the 'oldest established permanent floating crap game in New York'. It was altogether a momentously badly-cast movie that somehow turned out much better in its total sum than in its parts. Jean Simmons in her finest pristine English rose guise played Sister Sarah Brown of the Save-a-Soul Mission and just didn't fit. Marlon Brando was totally wrong as Sky Masterson, the sharp-suited gangster who would bet his mother's life away if he thought the dice were loaded in his favour. He played Sky as if he were a footballer who somehow forgot what he was supposed to be chasing. Frank wanted to play Masterson, but Goldwyn wouldn't hear of it.

His was a role that had been brilliantly performed on stage – both on Broadway and in London – by Sam Levine, who was as tailor-made for the part as his suits had been for his body. Sinatra looked as if he had got his clothes off-the-peg from a charity shop. Nathan was Jewish, Frank manifestly was not. Sam Levine was great in wide-shouldered chalk-stripes, Sinatra looked as though he still had a hanger in his jacket. Levine saying, 'So noo, so sue . . . call a policeman and sue me,' was right up his Brooklyn street. Sinatra seemed as though he had got lost on the journey from Hoboken and was with a crowd of people he didn't know very well.

His voice was good but it wasn't enough. Things might have been helped had he and Brando got on well together. They didn't. And the reason was simple: for the second time in months, he had lost out to

Brando. Sinatra showed his disdain for Brando by demonstrating his hatred for the Method school of acting. He dubbed his co-star 'Mumbles'. But there was a revenge of sorts on the way. Sinatra's version of Sky's principal song 'Luck Be a Lady' was by far the best recording of the number ever made. To the usual phrasing was added a wonderful cynical note – something no other singer could manage.

Years later, Sinatra would describe his role in *Guys and Dolls* as 'the only part I was ever very disappointed with'. That was in 1959, a time when he couldn't imagine that there would be so many more in the decades to come. 'I was pressured into doing it,' he said in an interview with *Newsweek*. 'I wanted to play Masterson. I mean nothing disparaging about Marlon Brando, but Masterson didn't fit him and he knew it.'

There were still the frequently told stories of Frank taking what he considered to be the law into his own hands – like the time he grabbed a 66-year-old hotel desk clerk by the collar. It was almost a re-enactment of the Great Pastrami Story two years earlier, the sandwich on rye or the onion roll. It happened when Sinatra and his party ordered hamburgers. 'They called back and wanted two with mustard and one without,' the clerk reported. 'They said they wanted four. Then five. I got a little flustered. A couple of minutes later, in walked Sinatra and Killer Gray. Gray called me an old bastard. Sinatra grabbed me by my shirt collar and started ragging me around.'

Photographers and reporters upset him so much that the best-known columnist in the country, Walter Winchell (who, as we have seen, in the 1930s was involved in a punch-up himself – with Al Jolson at a boxing match) made a public appeal: 'Frank, I wish you would stop hitting people. It makes it bad for guys like me on your team to fight for you.' Frank's reply was insouciant. 'When a guy bothers me, I belt him.'

Winchell countered that by saying: 'This was and always will be Frank Sinatra'. So there were no surprises if more 'beltings' followed. One such occurred when he was in a nightclub and walked straight up to a man – and hit him squarely in the face. As he walked away, he explained: 'The man called me a dirty Jew. I don't mind "Jew", but nobody calls me dirty'.

Stories like this would be retold in one form or another for years. In November 1958, a row developed when Frank and friends left another club and a reporter asked him: 'Hey, Frank, what are your plans?' He didn't like the familiarity. 'I'm MISTER Sinatra,' he replied.

When the photographer Mel Finkelstein thought this was a good moment for a snap, Sinatra, not schooled to walk past a phalanx of lensmen as though they were shadows on the wall, retorted: 'You want to try it buddy? No pictures.' Then he got into his car, accompanied by David Niven and Joe E. Lewis, and told the driver to run the picture man down. The hapless photographer was brushed by the car's bumper (the driver knew better than to ignore an instruction from his boss).

Finkelstein was taken to hospital for X-rays, and when he was released, went to the nearest police station to register a complaint. 'On the basis of this investigation,' declared the police's Deputy Commissioner Walter Arm, 'it will be determined what police action, if any, will be taken.'

The story was splashed over the newspapers. Frank was sufficiently concerned to issue a statement: 'What I read in the papers must have happened to three other guys. Certainly nothing like this happened with me. Isn't it ridiculous?

'New York has been home base for me for many years. I love this town. I come from here and grew up here. The only words said to a photographer were simply, "Don't take any pictures of me and I won't take any pictures of you." Our party then got in the car and drove off. It was that simple.

'This is a tempest in a teapot and none of it my making. I sure would like to know what that guy was drinking. I would like to buy some of it for myself and for Joe E. Lewis.'

Luckily for everyone concerned, he lived down this sort of row as he did his performance in *Guys and Dolls*, which was a box-office hit despite all the miscasting.

Songs For Swingin' Lovers, his 1956 album, was more than just a hit, however. Not only has it become the archetypal Frank Sinatra LP of his 'comeback years', it was more than anything else the defining image of Sinatra's place in American popular song. It was the first Sinatra 12-inch LP, which from then onwards would become the norm. The fawn cover with a smiling, enigmatic Sinatra in the background, like some benevolent ghost, and a couple of hip youngsters of the mid-fifties in the foreground, has become an icon of the age. But the most important feature of the album were the songs – fifteen of them, more than on any previous Sinatra record. It was value for money. Every one of the numbers became a standard, but more than that they became *the* way to perform them. Songs like 'You Make Me Feel So Young', 'Old Devil Moon', 'It Happened in Monterey' and 'Swingin' Down the Lane' sound, forty years later, as though they had just been pressed. He would never do better.

What was most important about the *Swingin' Lovers* album was its sheer longevity. Rarely has it been out of the catalogues – whether sold at the regular price or on a bargain label – and it is now available as a CD.

Not included in the album was Frank's hit song 'Love and Marriage', which won another Emmy in 1955 for Sammy Cahn and Jimmy Van Heusen and also the Christopher Award (a giant-sized St Christopher's Medal). However, it did feature in one of his best TV performances – a live production of *Our Town* by Thornton Wilder, in which he shared credits with Paul Newman and Eva Marie Saint. Once more rehearsals were a problem, with NBC going out of their minds when Frank failed to turn up for the two principal dress rehearsals. But he did show up for the transmission. As a result of his being there, the *New York Times* was able to say that he was 'effectively unobtrusive and his songs were an important contribution to the success of the presentation'.

One could not say the same about his next movie, *The Man With the Golden Arm*, which also starred Eleanor Parker and Kim Novak, although it featured drum-playing and jazz that was so good the music press showered the director Otto Preminger with praise for choosing Shorty Rodgers to lead the band. In this film, undoubtedly one of the very best in the Sinatra canon, Frank played a drug addict – and with such force, such terror, he had audiences crouching in their seats. It wasn't just a virtuoso performance, it was a demonstration to be used in drama schools forever after of how an actor can make a picture so much his own that nothing else about it seemed to matter. Eleanor Parker and Kim Novak were extraordinarily good, too, but the film could have been a Sinatra soliloquy – with actions – as far as his audiences were concerned. Ironically, the part might have gone to Marlon Brando. Otto Preminger sent forty pages of script to both men. Frank said 'yes' the next day – before Brando's agent had even opened the envelope. It was to be the only time that Sinatra scored a point over his rival.

Frank and Preminger got on so well together that they adopted nicknames for each other. Preminger was 'Ludwig' (his middle name) or 'Herr Doktor'. Sinatra was 'Anatole', supposedly because Preminger thought he resembled a character in a play he had enjoyed.

The only trouble between them arose when Frank decided he didn't like the cameraman and asked Preminger to replace him. 'Anatole,' he replied gently, 'on your pictures, when you are producer, you can do the hiring and firing. On my pictures, I will do it.' The matter was never referred to again.

The Johnstone Office, which had taken over from Breen and Hayes as the guardian of American morals, was up in arms about the picture, which broke all the codes then in force. The Office was even more concerned about the dangers of the drug business than the sweaters which shaped Kim Novak's breasts in such a provocative way. 'The illegal drug traffic and drug addiction must never be presented,' their code declared, and not since the days of the silent screen's attempts at showing the opium trade had it been so graphically portrayed. There were denunciations galore from the Johnstone Office – until it finally realised that such complaints usually had the one effect they didn't want: the box office would roar like MGM's lion. Their calculation was totally right. People flocked to cinemas to see the quite incredible performance of Frank Sinatra holding his arms in agony, his face wreathed in horror as he undergoes cold turkey.

As *Time* said of *The Man With the Golden Arm*: 'On the screen ... the picture provides much more than the cheap thrill it promises. The hero is a man who gets lost on the West side of Chicago and does not bother to go looking for himself.' The Academy of Motion Picture Arts and Sciences were obviously of the same opinion. They nominated Frank for an Oscar for Best Actor. He didn't win but there had to be some satisfaction in the mere nomination.

The film made, released and praised, it was time to get back to the Capitol studios, this time to conduct an orchestra. It was Sinatra's first LP as a conductor – *Poems in Color*, based on verses by Norman Sickel and with tunes composed by Victor Young, Billy May, Gordon Jenkins and André Previn among others. It was an experience he liked very much.

Next, he decided to produce a film, *Johnny Concho*, a western featuring Hank Sanicola and Nelson Riddle, who composed his first film score for the picture. It was not a great movie, and gave advance warning of what could happen when Frank decided that a film set was a place to have fun.

His other film of 1956 was far better. *High Society* was a brilliantly cast movie with little dramatic value, but one that can be watched again and again without a viewer ever feeling he has seen enough. It also just happened to make Cole Porter a quarter of a million dollars richer in exchange for the nine songs he wrote specially.

This remake of the famous Katharine Hepburn–James Stewart classic *The Philadelphia Story* had Frank co-starring with Bing Crosby, Grace Kelly and Celeste Holm. Grace Kelly was the ice-cold beauty due to marry for the second time while her first husband (Crosby) was still on hand.

What really attracted Sinatra to the movie was the opportunity to work with his idol, Crosby. Saul Chaplin, who with Johnny Green was the musical director and shared an Oscar nomination for the movie, told me: 'Sol Siegel, the producer, already had Crosby and Kelly and it happened at a moment when Frank was free. He wanted to do the picture and we all wanted him too.'

Once more, there were the difficulties over rehearsals. As Chaplin told me: 'Bing would always come on time and do his rehearsing and Frank would every now and again show up late.' But a formula was devised. 'I'd continue with the rehearsal with Bing,' said Chaplin, 'and when it came to Frank's turn, he'd say, "Come into the next room and show me what my part is."' Frank either did not know his lines or was showing a kind of humility in the face of his idol.

The truth of the matter was that Crosby was a conscience point for him. 'It was the first time he felt self-conscious. He was embarrassed about not doing things right – in front of Bing.' It seemed to be a recipe for lost illusions, if not disaster, but it didn't work out that way. 'They adored each other,' said Chaplin.

Grace Kelly's putative husband, played by John Lund, was only involved when it was absolutely necessary, but Sinatra and Celeste Holm as the journalist and photographer who come to record the festivities became part of movie history. Remarkably, they really convinced audiences that when they surveyed the displayed wedding presents, they were looking at a world that could never be their own. That took fine acting. It also posed the need to establish a mutual admiration society. Miss Holm was to say: 'A woman doesn't have to be in love with Sinatra to enjoy his company. I wasn't and I did. He's a stimulating talker on any subject: books, music, cooking, his children, whom he quotes oftener than most fathers, and sports.' Frank sang 'Who Wants to Be a Millionaire?' with Celeste Holm and the result was another memorable moment on celluloid.

Better still was the duet with Crosby, 'Well Did Ya Evah?' Chaplin was looking for a number for a duet and found this song, which the studio already owned, in the MGM archives. The lyrics were largely changed by Chaplin himself, a brave thing to do with lines written by Cole Porter, but then those originally topical lyrics were written for the 1938 show *Dubarry Was a Lady* and were hardly suitable for the postwar world of the 1950s.

Its best (new) line is the one in which Sinatra sings in an aside to Bing, 'Don't dig that kinda croonin' chum' to which the older man replies, 'You must be one of the newer fellers'. Crosby came up with that line in rehearsal. They liked it so much that it was written down and then recorded. So was another response: 'Sauced again!'

The one person involved in the shooting of *High Society* who wasn't so impressed with Frank's performance was Johnny Green, a veteran and a somewhat pompous musician who liked to talk about the great and the good as his best friends. In his case, all the stories were absolutely true. Jerome Kern was a mentor but also a dear colleague. Leonard Bernstein used to go to Green for advice on film music. He talked Danny Kaye out of a nervous breakdown – a service that was returned very soon afterwards.

Sinatra and Green were not the closest of friends, but Green admired the singer's talent. 'His work was good, exceptionally good, most of the time. But in one song he really wasn't – as you British say – up to snuff. In fact, I thought his work on that was quite poor. It didn't have the usual Sinatra polish and worst of all I thought his phrasing was bad.'

Now, as we have seen, these were not easy words to put to Frank Sinatra face to face. But Green did more than that. He asked Frank to re-record the number – which he refused to do. The song was 'You're Sensational' – which Green patently did not think Sinatra's rendition was. Again, Sinatra refused. The man who would do one take in a movie and think he had done enough work for the day was not about to re-record a song he thought was perfect, even though when he made discs for commercial distribution he would do so willingly. 'In which case,' said Green, 'you'd better see Sol [Siegel]. I will not allow a film that I have anything to do with to include inferior material.' Eventually, Sinatra agreed to sing again and Green pronounced the result to be acceptable. As he told me: 'It was just a small matter of professional disagreement. We sorted things out quite happily.'

Sinatra had a happier relationship with his old idol, Crosby. When he posed with Bing's son Gary for photographs, he said it was all to 'dispel those rumours that I don't like photographers'.

He continued to give expression to that sort of view. Per J. Oppenheimer, writing in *Family Weekly*, said he went to an interview with Frank determined that he would 'swing back' if Frank hit him. But he was prepared. 'I'll call him mister when I do.'

It was easier than that. 'If you play it Frankie's way an interview goes smoothly if dully. Never lower your guard, though. The Voice has so many hot spots, you might ignite him without realising it. Sinatra considers questions about his career, if respectfully asked, fair game.' Sinatra, said Oppenheimer, 'sat before me tensely, not like a conqueror on top of the world but like a little guy who finds himself on a smouldering volcano'.

The singer said to another writer in London: 'You misquote me, kid, and you're dead with me. In fact, I'll sock you on the jaw.' An aide then told the young journalist, 'Nothing personal was intended by Mr Sinatra.'

One man did manage to get into his bad books. Donald Zec, one of the most respected names in British journalism, wrote something in the London *Daily Mirror* to which he took exception. Sinatra was quick to the telegraph office: 'I THOUGHT WE WERE FRIENDS STOP BUT AS OF THIS MORNING YOU BLEW IT.' Zec said that the message, compared with most of the things Sinatra said to reporters, was 'almost a greetings telegram'.

Sometimes his reaction was unexpectedly mild – like the time he caught an intruder at his California home. He floored him with a wonderful football flying tackle, held the man till the police arrived – and then refused to press charges. That didn't do his reputation any good at all.

The rumours of a Mob connection continued. An anonymous letter was distributed alleging links with racketeers. 'It's full of poisonous lies,' Frank declared. Nevertheless, he liked to give the impression that he was too busy to worry about those 'poisonous lies'. But was being so busy all that good for the Sinatra career? Billy Wilder once told the writer Richard Gehman: 'If he didn't involve himself in all those enterprises, nineteen television shows and records by the ton and four movies all at once and producing things and political things and all those broads – this talent on film would be stupendous. That would be the only word. Stupendous. He could make us all, all the actors, that is, look like faggots.' But, Wilder added, 'I don't believe I'd work with him. I'm afraid he would run after the first take – "Bye-bye, kid, that's it. I'm going. I've got to see a chick". That would drive me crazy.'

But the mounting pressure of work told Frank Sinatra what he most wanted to know. He was wanted. After the time in the wilderness, he had found the promised land.

— 16 —

THEY CAN'T TAKE THAT
AWAY FROM ME

It wasn't that Frank Sinatra in 1957 could do no wrong – it was simply that none of those wrong things seemed to matter. He had established himself as *the* megastar of the year and nothing was going to knock him from his perch. Not even the California state senate investigation into the Wrong Door Raid in February that year.

This was the closest Frank Sinatra ever came to starring in a French farce. It was a story with an all-star cast, about a distraught husband trying to see what his wife was up to. There was also a case of mistaken identity, a scandal magazine and the flashing of cameras in the face of a lady in a nightdress who was innocently sitting up in bed, just minding her own business. It ended up with a California state senate hearing, allegations of perjury against Frank Sinatra and threats of action by the District Attorney, culminating in a Grand Jury hearing. And – yes – Marilyn Monroe was in the middle of it all.

The 'Wrong Door Raid' had people laughing over their beer throughout America. Even Marilyn Monroe thought it was hilarious. The only people who weren't laughing were Frank Sinatra, who said he had no idea of what had happened, Joe DiMaggio who had instigated the whole thing, and a certain Ms Florence Klotz whose room was broken into as she sat up in bed, trying hard to scream but unable to find the energy to do so.

DiMaggio, Sinatra, and a team of private detectives whom Frank had helped the baseball star to hire, had mistaken the room of the poor Ms Klotz for one in which they believed Marilyn was having a good time with a friend. She *was* with a friend in the Los Angeles building at 8122 Waring Avenue. But in a different flat. The friend was a certain Mrs Sheila Renour.

Marilyn heard the disturbance and wondered if it was a car backfiring: 'My first thought,' said Mrs Renour, 'was, "Is Florence having a party?" She was – with Frank Sinatra as the principal guest, but didn't know it until the private detective, Barney Ruditzky, kicked in a door panel. He had already failed to break the door open with his shoulder. It was like a scene from a thousand Hollywood films.

Frank protested his innocence throughout. He had taken DiMaggio to the apartment building in his Cadillac, nothing more. 'It was none of my business,' he kept repeating. DiMaggio 'was too wrapped up in his own thoughts about his marital problems' to discuss them with him. He didn't know what had gone on inside the building. The world's most prestigious chauffeur was to stick to his story, although the landlady, the homely Mrs Virginia E. Blasgen, said she saw both Sinatra and DiMaggio hanging around outside just before the raid. 'One was tall, the other was short. The tall one was mad and was walking up and down. The little one was jumping up and down and looking at me, smiling. They seemed so familiar and so well dressed. They looked out of place in the neighbourhood.'

There was one important witness to the whole event, another private detective, working for Ruditzky. Philip Wayne Irwin alleged Sinatra was there in the thick of it. He himself had been told to take a photograph of what he saw – to be used in the divorce action DiMaggio was bringing against Monroe. What he took was a shot of the petrified Ms Klotz sitting up in her nightdress, mouth open, with, we are assured, nothing coming out.

The picture later appeared in the scandal magazine *Confidential*, under the headline, 'The Reel Reason for Marilyn Monroe's Divorce'. Afterwards, Irwin was beaten up by six thugs who waylaid him in the Los Angeles Highland Park district. He said he was warned to keep his mouth shut – and to deny that he had any knowledge of the affair.

All this now became public property because California Senator Fred Kraft of San Diego had begun investigations into the role of scandal magazines. Sinatra maintained that he knew nothing about the 'Wrong Door' events. Irwin countered: 'Almost all of Mr Sinatra's statements were false.' to which State Senator Edwin J. Regan commented: 'There is perjury here' – and said he would take the matter to the Attorney General of the state. Irwin said in evidence that he was 'still very much afraid of being beaten up again'. And that was not all. 'I have other fears,' he said – without specifying what they were.

Now there would be a Grand Jury hearing into the whole affair – with Frank Sinatra subpoenaed to appear. But when it met, the case fizzled out. The jury members came to the conclusion that Frank had not been guilty of perjury, so no further action would be taken. As Frank told them. 'Who are you going to believe, me or a guy who makes his living kicking down bedroom doors?'

Three months later, Ms Klotz sued Sinatra, DiMaggio and the other men involved in the Wrong Door Raid for $200,000 and the matter was settled out of court for an undisclosed sum. As for Frank himself, he was making enough to cover such incidental expenses.

When, in 1956, Mike Todd went into his huge venture in his own wide-screen process, Todd-AO, *Around the World in Eighty Days*, starring David Niven, his idea of an insurance policy was to stack it with the biggest stars he knew and give them all cameo parts. Being asked to take part was like an invitation to a benefit. If you were on the way up, you would be honoured to appear; if you were big, you wouldn't want to be left out in case anyone thought you were slipping. Frank, like everyone else, jumped at the invitation that came to his agent's office at the William Morris building. He played a honky-tonk pianist whose face was only seen when he turned round for the camera.

There was rather more of him in his next movie, called *The Pride and the Passion*. It was a production in which nobody had much pride and which involved very little passion – even, remarkably, between Frank and the luscious Sophia Loren at what was close to being the beginning of her film career. They became good friends – which was one of the reasons why Ava saw the picture as the final straw in her marriage to the man she now called 'Mr Sinada' – a corruption of the Spanish word for 'nothing'.

The movie also resulted in Frank establishing a lasting friendship with one of the charismatic names of the era, Cary Grant, but there is little else to commend it.

This was *Kissing Bandit* territory – without the benefit of songs. As a peasant who takes it upon himself to march 2,000 miles across Spain accompanied by no fewer than 6,000 extras and a cannon weighing as many pounds, Frank was not just woefully miscast, he was ridiculous. Instead of being the hero of the post-Peninsular War era, fighting against all odds to regain Spain's honour, he looked more like the proprietor of a tequila bar in Tiawana.

When the director Stanley Kramer said at the time: 'This may not be a great film, but it will certainly be memorable,' he had apparently not learned the lesson of *Not as a Stranger*: working with Sinatra inevitably brought its strains. 'No, not one of my great moments,' was how he put it to me twenty-eight years later, looking back over a career that had a lot to commend it, not least his introduction of Marlon Brando to movies with the classic story of war-torn young soldiers, *The Men* – to say nothing of his *The Wild One* and Humphrey Bogart's classic, *The Caine Mutiny*.

He took a risk with Sinatra and would regret it for years afterwards. Frank was not in the best of moods while making the movie. He was also unwilling to do any publicity. If a journalist did get close enough to request an interview, the answer invariably was: 'Take this guy away before I punch him on the nose and roll him down the mountain.'

With Sophia Loren, however, his mood changed. 'Before he came to Spain, I hear all sorts of things,' she told a reporter. 'He is moody, they say. He is difficult, he is a tiger, he fights. Here he is kindly, friendly. He has even helped me with my English, and has *teached* me how people really speak in Hollywood.' But then, as Otto Preminger had observed with Kim Novak, Sinatra was remarkably patient when there were pretty women around. When they were beautiful in a statuesque way, he was monumentally ready to be helpful.

But apart from his devotion to the duty of being nice to Sophia, there was nothing counterbalanced about Frank Sinatra's behaviour – even though Stanley Kramer gave him a Mercedes coupé and provided the best quality hi-fi in his super-luxury Madrid hotel suite. Frank ran up a $600 phone bill – which included calls to his bookmaker in Chicago – and put it all on the company tab. His sheer rudeness to Kramer became legion. For years, people would tell of the ultimatum he handed his director: 'Either get me out of this village by 11.30 tonight or I'll piss on you.'

It was soon after that episode that Sinatra read a series of articles in *Look* magazine that upset him even more than having to work in Spain with a gun as co-star. They were invasions of his privacy, he decided, not least because they referred to such things as Dolly's abortionist background. He didn't like being described as a 'neurotic' either: the writer Bill Davidson said he was a 'libertine' with suicidal tendencies. He also referred to Sinatra's alleged comments to Sam Rayburn about getting his hands 'off the threads', which Frank still strenuously denied. Then there was a piece about the women in Frank's life, including one called 'Ezzard Charles' – the name of a famous boxer. One newspaper described Ezzard 'as an eyeful in a shocking-pink gown, shoes, coat and lipstick'.

Sinatra sued – at first mentioning a figure of more than $2 million, but later demanding a sum 'in excess of $3,000'. The magazine replied that it had a duty to inform its readers about public figures. Frank, for his part, said he was making a stand on behalf of everyone who had their privacy exposed. 'I have always maintained that any writer or publication has a right to discuss or criticise my professional activities as a singer or actor, but I feel that an entertainer has a right to his privacy that is as inviolate as any other person's. Otherwise, it means that a "public figure" is a second-class citizen in that he is denied rights which others enjoy.'

It would be the first of several attempts by Sinatra to keep his activities out of the press. His case had hardly been helped, however, when the conductor Serge Koussevitsky failed to stop articles about himself. The courts then ruled that no public figure could ever claim that his privacy had been invaded.

Somehow, though, Sinatra's fight over the *Look* articles established something else: that he was becoming attracted to the legal process as the answer to all his problems. If he couldn't punch his adversaries with impunity, he would sue them – always looking for some kind of case that would stick.

So was this a new kind of bullying Sinatra? A different man from the one who used his, or other people's, fists and was now seeking to rely on his and other people's brains and voices? He could still be ready to show respect where it was due. In Monte Carlo, in September 1957, Frank approached Sir Winston Churchill with great deference. 'Sir,' he said to the 84-year-old former Prime Minister, 'I've always wanted to shake you by the hand.' Churchill obliged – and then introduced him to his wife.

The records he was producing at this time were an unbroken sequence of success. The classic 'Come Fly With Me', showing a smiling, behatted Sinatra standing in the foreground of a wide-blue-yonder scene, had Billy May's Orchestra accompanying him. More jazzy than the Riddle recordings, it was yet another winner – except with an English lady named Bainbridge. Mrs Bainbridge was the daughter of Rudyard Kipling and she was not amused by Frank's recording of her father's paean to Empire, 'The Road to Mandalay'. The Kipling estate were as furious about Sinatra's changes to the author's verse as Cole

Porter had been about the mangling of *his* words. Frank had the temerity to sing about a 'Burma broad' instead of a 'Burma girl'. (Martha Hyer, the high-class girl in a forthcoming film, *Some Came Running*, maintained that he used the term as a compliment: 'He only calls his best friends "old broads",' she said.)

Kipling's daughter backed her lawyers. Her agent wrote: 'Mrs Bainbridge feels that her father knew best how to express the ideas embodied in his poems and that what he created should not be tampered with.' The result of this contretemps was that 'The Road to Mandalay' was replaced on the British edition of the record with another travel song, 'French Foreign Legion'.

In spite of this, the record sold more than half a million copies. So did *This is Sinatra, Vol. 2* and the much less effective, *Come Dance With Me*, which showed on its sleeve a Sinatra who, in soft tweed hat, looked as though he were about to audition for the role of Henry Higgins in *My Fair Lady*. This last wasn't up to the standard of the other albums, even if it did contain 'Cheek to Cheek' and 'Something's Gotta Give'. But devoted fans continued to buy everything he put on to vinyl.

In 1959, *Come Dance* was voted Album of the Year and Sinatra was awarded a Grammy Award for the best male vocal performance – possibly intended as a consolation prize for the superior 'Come Fly With Me' and 'Only the Lonely' both losing out to 'Music from Peter Gun' by Henry Mancini. The recording sessions – all of them late at night because he said that was the only way he could work – were a kind of triumphant ritual, with Sinatra holding court and giving his commands via the songs he was singing. The orchestra always knew the tempo he wanted and he always knew they would follow whatever beat he chose – which, as usual, varied with his moods.

The recording venue was not the most comfortable place in which to work. There were no harsh lights as in a TV or film studio, but there were few comfortable chairs either. The walls were bare and you could hear the constant sound of music racks rattling before the light went on. The routine was usually the same – the same hat, the same tie and open shirt, the same cigarette dangling from his mouth, the same hunch of the shoulders.

The performer who wouldn't do more than one take on film, was perfection incarnate when it came to making his records. Five, six, eight takes were not unusual. When he recorded 'Learnin' the Blues' in March 1955, it took thirty-one goes before he was satisfied. The classic 'I've Got the World on a String', pressed in April 1953, had taken ten takes. The archetypal 'Witchcraft', in May 1957, succeeded only on the fourteenth attempt.

He himself would interrupt the orchestra. Making '(How Little It Matters) How Little We Know' in May 1956, he stopped them in mid flow – but blamed himself. 'Once more . . . I was trying to cheat with the notes, you can't cheat with notes, you've got to sing 'em.' And he did it again after a lot of finger-snapping and a few bars of 'bah-bah-bahs'. Before starting again, he knocked his fingers on the music stand. 'Bartender! It's not too late, is it?' Mr Riddle didn't see the joke. All he said was: '315 – Take 12.'

But there was a sour note to 1957, too. On 14 June his marriage to Ava ended in Mexico City. Ostensibly, he just carried on. There were other events in his life to distract him – notably centred around women.

— 17 —

TIME AFTER TIME

Sinatra was forty-two years old and, if they used such expressions in those days, it could be said that he had had his share of mid-life crises. One recent sadness had been the death of Humphrey Bogart of throat cancer in 1956. There had always been a strong link between them, not least of all, Lauren Bacall, or Betty as everyone knew her.

The idea of Sinatra running the Rat Pack after Bogart's death was singularly appropriate. By the following year, Frank had taken his place at the top of a group which before long would change its name to the Clan and call him Chairman of the Board.

Bacall was the group's 'den mother', which, as far as she was concerned, was an office to be cherished. There was the need, she would say, for an organisation like theirs which had 'dignity'. As she explained: 'We had principles. You had to stay up late and get drunk and all our members were against the PTA.' More important – and this had to appeal to Sinatra – 'Woe betide anyone who attacked one of our members. We *got* them.'

In a way it was a select kind of trade union in undeclared war against the moguls. Sammy Davis was to tell me: 'It's very important that these people know they are facing up to a gang of actors who are not prepared to be thrown around with a lot of garbage – and who insist on having a good time.'

But that was altogether too serious a reason for the gathering of this clan. Essentially, it had to remain the hedonistic grouping that Bogie had envisaged – a kind of boys' club that always had a couple of women around to lend glamour and a steadying hand to most of their excesses.

Such groups were a fairly well-known Hollywood phenomenon, although usually centred on stars who didn't have very much to occupy their minds. Errol Flynn had his group of drinking buddies with

240

questionable racist and political ideas. Before him, there was the one run by John Barrymore, the Warner Bros. star who sometimes had to be held up by a man in a black glove as he stood before the cameras. Both these sets required, as a principal means of entry, that members have as great a familiarity with alcohol as the other fluid flowing through their veins.

Sinatra's pack certainly didn't eschew alcohol – with Dean Martin a member, that was impossible. But Frank wasn't particularly interested in benders any more. He was busier bringing in new members. Before long, the group had settled down to Dean Martin, the comedian–actor Joey Bishop and the ever-faithful Sammy Davis, Jr. Peter Lawford was on hand, too, although he wasn't yet a fully recognised member, and Lauren Bacall remained as the principal link with her late husband's past. Before very long, Shirley MacLaine became a kind of cuckoo mascot, and when Marilyn Monroe entered Sinatra's life not long after the setting up of the group, she became an honorary member.

To become a member of the Clan was to be invited to a hundred benefit concerts, to star in a thousand cameo roles. But it was to be taken seriously indeed. All that was said about freemasonry applied to them. They vowed not just to drink and travel in private planes together, but if one of their number fell on hard times, to club together to make sure those times could be made easier.

When they appeared on a nightclub platform together – which they frequently did – etiquette dictated that they had to go through certain routines. It was like an old-fashioned vaudeville turn which never changed its act from year to year. Dean Martin would turn to the Jewish Joey Bishop and ask: 'Did you ever see a Jew jitsu?' Bishop, for his part, would turn to both him and Sinatra and reply: 'Watch out. I've got my own group – the Matzia.' 'Metzia' is Yiddish for bargain.

Shirley MacLaine was never so sure about broadcasting the existence of the organisation. She insisted it had all been dreamed up by a writer for *Life* magazine, Dave Zeitlin. Besides which, there was something about the Clan that made her a little uncomfortable. As she joked: 'Here I am, surrounded by the most attractive men in the world, and they make me feel like a boy.'

Frank wouldn't admit its existence either, but everyone knew it operated. There were articles written about it. At least one book was entitled *Sinatra and His Rat Pack*. And the sort of frolicking around that they did, on each other's shows and going to each other's parties, would have made people look for a name, even if they didn't publicise one. There had to be a name for a group that included Martin and Sinatra, the two whom Joey Bishop described as 'The Italian bookends'.

Frank would eventually persuade Warren Cowan, his PR man and one of the most experienced press agents in the business, to issue a statement. 'As far as I know,' it declared, 'the various guilds that are part of my professional life are the only organised groups to which I belong. "The Clan" is the figment of someone's imagination. Naturally, people in Hollywood socialise with friends, as they do in any community, but we do not gather together in childish fraternities as some people would like to think. There is no such entity as "The Clan" and there never has been. I am fortunate to have many friends and many circles of friends, but there are no membership cards.'

You could say it was simply a way of getting people together for one of those celebrated Hollywood parties without issuing formal invitations. The members would sit around, tell dirty stories (as many about Jack Warner as possible) and Frank and Dean would be asked to sing – while honorary members like Sammy Cahn played the piano. If Judy Garland were there, she would join in. If someone upset Judy, Frank would respond as though she had paid all her dues as a member herself. When she was in a rest home, recovering from one of her bouts of depression, and worse, there was no question but that she was a Clan member. Frank sent her flowers, not just once or twice but every day for a year. Then, when he thought she was getting lonely, he chartered a plane to take a crowd of her friends from Hollywood to Boston, just so that they could catch up with each other after such a long period of absence.

That, he would have said, was what Clan membership was all about. Even if you doubted it, you had to accept as proof the titles its members gave each other: before he became Chairman of the board, Frank was known alternately as 'the Leader', 'the General', 'the Dago' and even 'the Pope', which was understating his status somewhat. Some people were beginning to say now that Elvis Presley was king, but Sinatra's followers never thought so.

It was the Clan who formalised Dean Martin's title of 'Dino' and left him to choose the booze. Similarly, Joe E. Lewis was known as 'In Ebriation'. The one missing name from the roster of Sinatra friends who were admitted to membership was Manie Sacks. Sacks had died of leukaemia at the age of fifty-six – and Frank, fifteen years his junior, walked ahead of the coffin at the funeral in Philadelphia.

The writer Gay Talese reported a moment when Dean interrupted a series of Jewish stories from Don Rickles and asked him why he never talked about the Italians. Rickles replied: 'What do we need the Italians for – all they do is keep the flies off our fish.'

Sinatra laughed and then said he had to go.

'Shaddap and sit down,' Rickles countered. 'I've had to listen to you sing.'

Sinatra wanted to know who the comedian thought he was talking to (after all, you didn't speak like that to the Chairman of the Board, far less to the Pope).

Rickles came back with: 'Dick Haymes'. Sinatra laughed.

Not that Frank performed all his good deeds via the Clan. Lee J. Cobb was an actor whom he greatly admired – a big, burly performer who put anger into his work that was so real it could be frightening for anyone fortunate or unfortunate enough to share a scene with him. When Sinatra heard that Cobb had had a heart attack and needed instant medical treatment which he couldn't afford, he made sure that nothing would be denied to someone whose work he cherished so much. He paid the bill. Then he lent Cobb his Palm Springs house to recover – and when the weather got too hot, paid for a Los Angeles apartment in which he could complete his convalescence. 'He took over my life,' said Cobb.

It was an oft-reported story. Ruta Lee, the young actress who says she owed her professional start in films to Sinatra, told me: 'I'd hear Frank on occasion say to his secretary, "Dorothy, I hear So-and-So is not doing too well in hospital. Check to see if there is something we can do." And he'd pay the bill.'

As his old Hoboken admirer, Joe Spaccavento, said: 'You've no idea how many people he helped when their businesses went belly-up. He always did what he could. If Frankie liked you, he'd give you the shirt off his back. He's got a lot of shirts.'

The writer Don Maguire said: 'You can call him any hour of the night and tell him you've got flu and he will bring you some minestrone.'

When Charles Morrison, host at the famous Mocambo nightclub, died, Frank offered his widow, Mary, the full armoury of Sinatra support. He knew she faced financial disaster. His solution was a comforting phone call. 'I thought I could come over and sing for a couple of nights,' he told her. Then he added: 'I'll bring the band, too.'

The club was bursting at the seams – not only with Mocambo patrons, but with a full celebrity list from Hollywood's Who's Who. It was said they paid $100 bribes to head waiters to get tables.

Another time, a comedian named Jack E. Leonard – 'Fat Jack' because he weighed in at 350 pounds – was ill and Frank thought he had the cure to what ailed this near total stranger – a blank cheque to cover all his business losses and expenditure. Leonard returned the cheque, but accepted Frank's daily telephone calls. Later, Leonard went on a diet and lost so much weight, he started billing himself as 'Thin Jack'. Frank phoned him: 'I understand you've lost weight.' 'I've lost more weight than you ever had,' said the comedian, who by now regarded Frank Sinatra as his best friend.

In many ways, that was what set Frank Sinatra apart from other big stars. It was true that he could drop you just as easily the moment he felt he had been slighted – but his loyalty had no parallel when friends were in trouble.

There were others for whom the Sinatra gift routine was a two-way street. The comedian Jack Benny had a rapport with Sinatra – mainly because Frank took easily to his act as the stingiest man in Hollywood. But it turned into a friendship that surprised many people.

'Frank knows I have a lot of gold watches,' Benny told me just before he died in 1972. 'He also knows that I can't be bothered to wind them. So he sent me a Timex watch with a note saying, "This will run a year". He's a very peculiar guy, but a wonderful guy. I can send Sinatra a beautiful gift and not get a thank-you note, but then four months later, get the most gorgeous gift you've ever seen in your life.'

When Benny had a TV special to mark his twentieth anniversary on the small screen, he asked Frank to appear. He did – without fee. 'How can you pay Sinatra?' the comedian put it to me. 'It would be a fortune, so we agreed to alternate on each other's shows for nothing. He said, "Just forget about it. I'll be there" – and he turned up. You could depend on it. He even got his secretary to ring up and ask what we wanted him to wear.'

That sort of Sinatra response had less pleasant echoes, however. There was, for instance, the time he told a friend, supposedly in a gesture of supreme comradeship: 'I wish that someone would hurt your family so that I could find that person and hurt them back'.

The connection with the other members of the Clan was based on the fact that they liked each other, liked doing the same things and had a kind of admiration for what each did in show business. When Frank was really settled into his regime at the Sands Hotel in Las Vegas, he made perfectly clear that he wanted the others to be featured, too. Dean was there frequently.

Sammy Davis, Jr., had problems of his own which Sinatra would sort out before long. 'Frank won't see anyone, I know,' he told me once. 'So you're never going to hear from him about the things he did. But I wouldn't be alive, let alone a success in show business, without him.' He could never forget the psychological help Frank had been after his accident.

The Clan cheered Frank's new album , *A Swingin' Affair*, a sequel to *Songs for Swingin' Lovers* that could have been the second disc in a two-record set. It was every bit as good as the first with, this time, standards like 'Night and Day' and 'I Wish I Were in Love Again'. Now the cover had him full-face, smiling, while a whole room jumped and jived in the background. It was vintage material and once more was currency for every serious Sinatra collector.

The Clan, who took it upon themselves unofficially to swear allegiance to whoever was leading the Democratic Party, were just as ready to bad-mouth the people with whom Sinatra quarrelled, particularly, those behind the records that were put on the market to rival this superb new Sinatra output. Mention the name of Columbia and there was a collective grip on their noses. Columbia Records now earned Frank's opprobrium – to say nothing of Capitol – by re-releasing some of his less dreadful recordings in order to cash in on the 'New Sinatra' era. There was nothing he could do – even when the worst stuff he had recorded with Mitch Miller suddenly appeared in albums, too. 'Before Mr Miller's advent on the scene, I had a successful recording career which quickly went into decline,' Frank said in a statement – from which it was fair to gather that he still didn't like the man very much.

It was the start of another one of those feuds that were as regular a part of Frank Sinatra's life as a bowl of cornflakes for breakfast. Mitch Miller retorted: '[Sinatra's] career went down the drain because of his emotional turmoil over Ava Gardner. I had nothing to do with him losing his movie contract, losing his television show, losing his radio show. I had nothing to do with him losing his voice. He should look to himself as the cause of his own failure and stop trying to blame others.'

Whatever they said to each other, it was clear that Sinatra and Miller were not going to get along and it was also plain the material Miller had given Frank to record was downright bad – insultingly bad. Frank's mistake had been to record it in the first place – and now the new Columbia releases were coming home to roost – with, it has to be said, Frank's bank account being the principal beneficiary.

It was the same old story. Just as he would succeed at some ventures and no one was surprised, so, when he failed at others, everyone knew that he wouldn't be down for long.

— 18 —

COME RAIN OR SHINE

Frank Sinatra's cinematic career now consisted of turning down as many parts as he accepted. It surprised nobody that he rejected a plan to shave his head and play Gandhi in a film. Turning down the part of the fairground barker in *Carousel* was another thing altogether. It has to be classified as one of the poorest judgements he made – especially since he had actually recorded 'Soliloquy' and 'If I Loved You'. Then again, taking the title role in *Pal Joey* was clearly one of the cleverest – even though it did seem to be the cause of another row with Harry Cohn, who wanted to boost the two women stars, Kim Novak and Rita Hayworth, a particular favourite. Much to everyone's amazement – and Cohn's relief – Frank said he had no objection to being 'in a sandwich' – billed between Hayworth on the left and Novak on the right.

But that was because Sinatra wanted to do the film as much as Columbia Pictures wanted him to do it. Yet this wasn't always such a foregone conclusion. The property had been on the shelf at Columbia for a long time. There was talk about making it a black musical, a kind of *Cabin in the Sky* set, presumably, at the Cotton Club or some other Harlem nighterie. Fred Kalmar, the producer, had another idea. He fancied Kirk Douglas for the role of Joey, the nightclub entertainer who believed that while he had other people around, he didn't need a doormat. Harry Cohn, who was in the middle of one of his regular spats with Sinatra, wanted Douglas, too.

It would have been a strange choice for what was essentially a musical role (Douglas's only experience with a musical before had been *Young Man With a Horn*, in which he played a tormented trumpet player). They even talked of making it a non-musical film. Jerry Wald, the producer, who always had the ear of Harry Cohn and was for a time going to have this as one of his movies, thought of Van Johnson, who surely wouldn't have been right either.

Jonie Taps, then still head of the Columbia music department, vetoed both ideas. Lillian Burns, Cohn's aide-de-camp, was another who rejected the idea of Kirk Douglas. Ms Burns, whose previous connections with Sinatra had been limited to the fact that she had given Ava elocution lessons, told me: 'I always thought that Frank was born to play Joey.' So her solution was to invite Cohn and Sinatra to her home to dinner. Abe Lastfogel, the boss of the William Morris agency, was invited, too.

Lastfogel returned the next day to pick up the *Joey* treatment. As Lillian Burns remembers: 'A buzz came several days later that Mr Lastfogel was on the phone. Remember that Harry Cohn had the big desk. There were Oscars behind and the machine in front of him on which he could get anyone in the studio. He put the call on the speaker. We had a bet – a box of cigars against a bottle of perfume – that Frank wouldn't do it'.

'Abe said, "Frank loves it." I could see Harry's face – it meant he would have to give me a bottle of perfume.'

Jonie Taps claims that he was the one who finalised the deal. 'It took two years for it to be done,' he told me: 'I was in Las Vegas and met some of the men from the Morris agency. I asked them for Sinatra. They said yes and I then made sure that he got the score of the picture. Harry Cohn wasn't happy. "Schmuck!" he told me, "that's as good as a contract." I said, "Yes, Sinatra's word is as good as anyone else's contract." Which, of course, is not what everyone else says.'

In this movie, Frank played a louse who two-times, but one who is able to sing 'The Lady Is a Tramp' and 'My Funny Valentine' better than anyone else in the world. Columbia also had the rights to inter-polate whatever Rodgers and Hart song they wished, which must have gladdened the heart of Harry Cohn, the former song plugger.

Director, George Sidney particularly wanted 'The Lady Is a Tramp'. '"But that's a woman's song," insisted Cohn. I said that anyone could sing it. Harry wrinkled his nose and said "OK".'

The film was based on a story by John O'Hara, who was asked what he thought of the Sinatra portrayal. He replied that he hadn't seen Sinatra in the role, but then he didn't need to. 'I invented him.'

Both *Pal Joey* and *Carousel* had been highly successful on the stage. Both had music by Richard Rodgers. *Pal Joey* was the last show of Rodger's partnership with Lorenz Hart and the screen version was to become a portmanteau of the finest numbers they wrote together, many of which, as planned, did not come from the original production.

If some of the acerbic nature of the original stage show – which starred Gene Kelly – was tamed down, then that was easily compensated for by a whole slew of songs that Sinatra knew how to sing best.

Carousel, with music by Rodgers and his last and even more successful partner, Oscar Hammerstein II, would also have been perfect Sinatra territory. It was a moving story of a poor circus barker doing everything – including going to his death – to keep his wife happy at the very moment they were expecting their first child. The show combined some of the finest numbers in the Rodgers and Hammerstein music book, including 'Soliloquy' which was to remain in the Sinatra repertoire right up to his last concert.

But what should have been Sinatra's role in the film fell foul of the way Twentieth Century-Fox decided to deal with new technology. This was the age of CinemaScope, Fox's own patent wide-screen system that was both an answer to TV and more manageable than 3-D. It was already serving to rescue much of the depressed film industry, giving a whole new shape to motion pictures. The trouble was that not every theatre in the world was equipped to show it yet – it needed not only wide screens, but also special wide-angle lenses that broadened out the original frame.

The studio came up with a solution just in time for *Carousel*. They would make it in two systems – CinemaScope and conventional 35 mm. All they needed to do was shoot every scene twice. Twice! Imagine saying that to any actor who didn't like rehearsing! Then imagine saying it to Frank Sinatra, who wouldn't do two *takes* if he could help it, quickly getting himself the nickname of One-Take Charlie. 'You're not getting two Sinatras for the price of one,' he declared and walked off the set at Boothbay Harbour, Maine, the New England fishing community that Rodgers and Hammerstein could have had in mind when they first planned their show.

Hollywood at the time was in a panic. Television had got bigger than anyone had ever imagined. Warner Bros., for one, refused to allow a TV set appear in a set, which gives some idea of the worry the little box caused – so wide-screen was seen as the panacea: let the public pay to see something they couldn't possibly have in their own living rooms. The problem for the Twentieth Century-Fox bosses was that now they had Frank Sinatra involved in their desperate scenario and he wasn't playing.

Even if the studio had paid him twice the price, he still wouldn't have done it. Filming the same scene twice was, in his book, doing two takes and he always believed he got it good only once, usually the first time. The studio responded by suing him for a million dollars – later mitigated when he agreed to do another movie in its place. As for *Carousel*, even with the great settings, the lovely music, the stirring performance of Shirley Jones as the wife, it didn't quite take off with Gordon MacCrea, Frank's substitute, in the lead part.

But Sinatra was going through a changeable phase. At the same time as he walked out of *Carousel*, he also broke off negotiations for a long-term TV contract. He left behind him, NBC executives stated, 'a great deal of bitterness'. When had he made his television version of *Our Town* in September 1957, the NBC lawyers said that he would have walked out of that deal, too, if he could – but changed his mind under threat of legal action'.

The eminent director George Sidney pondered Sinatra's unpredictability. 'I always liken him to a rubber ball. At the lowest point, you throw him against the wall and he will come back at its highest trajectory. And it was *always* a struggle to get him to rehearse.'

Saul Chaplin gave me a similar explanation: 'Because what comes out when he *does* work it is so sensational, it's worth it.'

Frank was currently starring in *The Frank Sinatra Show*, a weekly TV programme in which he both acted and sang. The public and the critics didn't like it much, even though he had guests like Bing Crosby and Peggy Lee. It was the only series of its kind from him. Now, he decided, it was his duty to come to the aid of the sort of respectable music he had made his own. He declared open war on rock'n'roll as if it were some sacred commission he had been given.

'My only deep sorrow is the unrelented insistence of recording and motion picture companies upon purveying the most brutal, ugly, degenerate, vicious form of expression it has been my displeasure to hear, and naturally, I'm referring to the bulk of rock'n'roll,' he wrote in an article in the magazine *Western World*. Plainly, he was no longer 'one of the younger fellows'. The music of Presley, Haley and the others, he said (without naming anyone), 'smells phoney and false. It is sung, played and written for the most part by cretinous goons and by means of its almost imbecilic reiterations and sly, lewd – in fact, dirty – lyrics, it manages to be the martial music of every sideburned delinquent on the face of the earth.'

There were delinquents galore in *The Joker Is Wild*, the film he made at the end of 1957, his only biographical role – playing Joe E.

Lewis, the cynical nightclub comedian and singer who had his throat cut by gangsters. Mitzi Gaynor co-starred in this black-and-white picture, but it was all Sinatra from beginning to end, a superb performance both as an actor and as a singer. For this picture, Sammy Cahn wrote 'All the Way' for Frank, which became one of the Sinatra theme songs, at least until it was overtaken by 'My Way'. 'Somehow,' Sammy told me, 'that word "way" has a lot of meaning for Frank. His way in everything he does is nobody else's way and if I captured that in the song, then I am the one to be grateful.' Grateful, in particular, because Frank said he loved the number and also because of the Oscar it won him.

Also grateful was Walter Scharf, the film's musical director. 'It was thanks to Frank that I got a very big chance with this film,' he told me. Victor Young, who had just done the music for *Around the World in Eighty Days*, had died and Scharf – with credits like *Hans Christian Andersen*, *The French Line* and *Holiday Inn* – was available. It was Sinatra who smoothed him through the contract process with the veteran producer Charles Vidor.

'This joker was never wild,' was how he put his relationship with Sinatra. 'He did everything he could to make me happy.' On the other hand, everyone did everything they could to make Frank happy, too. 'We did things the French way – which sounds a lot more sexy than it really is. It meant that we started work at noon and worked through to about seven in the evening.' There were objections aplenty to that notion, but, as Scharf reminded me, 'that was before there were rules about that sort of thing. Frank liked to sleep late, but other people needed to get home for dinner.' But Frank wasn't going to bend. As he explained at this time: 'My theory is, actors are creators. Anyone else who creates something is allowed to do it when he wants to. What we have to do – playing a love scene, for example – is difficult to do at nine a.m. I work better, sing better, later in the day. That's why I only record at night.'

The technicians were in awe of him, Scharf now remembers. 'And would you believe it, during that time I never heard any of them say whether they liked or disliked him. They were afraid to make a statement. I wouldn't say he frightened people, but when he made an appearance, you knew he was there. His whole demeanour was one of drawing attention to himself.'

In *Joker* all the nightclub scenes were performed in a real nightclub – to keep the spontaneity right. There was no lip-synching of music –

when an actor sings to a pre-recorded track – although some performances had to be re-recorded later in the studio. 'If he could have done the whole thing without pre-recording, I think he would have been the happiest man around. He was trying to establish a style and didn't want to keep repeating what he was doing,' said Scharf.

Sinatra told him: 'When I do a concert and someone coughs, I like that. I like the scraping of chairs. You get the feeling that it's really happening. I've always thought Lewis was one of only about four or five great artists in this century – one of them was Jolson – and I remember him screaming like the devil when he made a soundtrack.'

It was a superb Sinatra performance. 'He was consciously studying Joe E. Lewis,' Scharf remembered. 'He finished sentences with a question mark. He would take an adverb and use it as something he would say afterwards.'

The movie was previewed in San Francisco, rather than in one of the customary Los Angeles suburbs like Santa Barbara or Santa Monica. Frank phoned Scharf at home that night. 'Walter,' he said, 'I think we have an Academy Award in this picture.' He was right, and could also take some of the credit. He had asked Scharf to find ways of fitting 'All the Way' into more parts of the score. Sammy Cahn's Oscar was seen by Frank as a vindication of his own faith in the number. 'See,' he told Scharf, 'I know about these things.' The music man answered: 'You sure do.'

He also knew the wisdom of singing 'Chicago' in the film, breathing new life into an old standard, but with Scharf's help making it sound like a brand-new Sinatra original.

The relationship between Sinatra and the real Joe E. Lewis was equally good. They were old pals and Lewis had actually asked Sinatra to play the part in any movie made of his life, a story that was written so brilliantly by Cohn. Only one event spoiled that relationship – the night when Lewis, performing at a club with Frank in the audience, asked him to come up on stage and sing. Lewis himself was too much the worse for wear after drinking all day. He knew that the people out front would appreciate the chance of hearing the superstar and, anyway, a singer with a voice would make a change from a comedian who, because of his injuries, still croaked.

Frank refused to help the man who regarded himself as a friend. He was there to enjoy himself, not work – and, rather than do so, walked out. Later, he apologised.

There were other problems between Frank and his *Joker Is Wild* musical director. Sinatra and Scharf enjoyed working together so much that Sinatra immediately arranged for the musician to be on his next picture, *A Pocket Full of Miracles*. Scharf did make the film but Frank didn't. He said he was going to be committed elsewhere and the part went to Glenn Ford.

But it wasn't simply a matter of Frank having other commitments. The fact that Scharf made the picture himself was simply because Frank did not. True, Sinatra had suggested that he work with him on the movie – but he then actually withdrew the invitation. He now wanted Nelson Riddle to be in charge of the music work, but at the last minute the conductor to whom he owed so much had to bow out – his daughter had just drowned. Without Riddle there, Sinatra didn't want to be in the picture either. Scharf was the first in line for Riddle's job and Ford for Sinatra's.

The next item on Frank's agenda was a tour of Australia. He insisted on taking Hank Sanicola and Jimmy Van Heusen with him. The only problem was that the Qantas airline couldn't guarantee berths of a suitably high standard for the party. Sinatra not only cancelled their bookings, he paid the promoter more than $75,000, enough money to keep the group who were going to play with him happy. When he had other things on his mind, such trifles as money – or the disappointment of audiences – really didn't matter to him.

As far as he was concerned, once more everything was going right, including his love life. Early in 1958 Lauren Bacall accepted his proposal of marriage – she says it took her fully thirty seconds to make up her mind. She even went so far as to sell her house – because she thought Bogey's ghost would be too much for Frank to handle.

The Los Angeles *Mirror* reported: 'Frank Sinatra and glamorous Lauren Bacall will be married in the near future, climaxing a fast and furious romance which has been Hollywood's number-one gossip topic for several months, the actress revealed today.' There was the usual speculation about wedding dates. March 26, the paper suggested. Why else had both stars cancelled plans to be at the Oscar ceremonies that night?

The *Mirror* readers were thrilled – all of them except Mr Frank Sinatra who hadn't been told that the news was going to be made public. He not only said he was angry, he called the marriage off and refused to see Bacall again. They didn't talk for another six years.

Was a leak to the press a good enough reason to call off a marriage? It was when you were Frank Sinatra. When he and his ex-fiancée did meet up again after those six years, Bacall was to tell Nancy, Jr., for her book, it was as if they were complete strangers.

There was probably no better indication of the way Ms Bacall felt about Sinatra than the statement she issued about the Clan. 'The Rat Pack automatically dissolved in 1956' [the year of Bogie's death]. 'I don't recognise the present group at all.' She said they were 'small minded' and added: 'Any colour they might have escapes me because I think it's pretty manufactured stuff.'

But why really did they break it all off? Was it just because of the press reaction or did Frank get cold feet? Undoubtedly, the latter. As far as the jilted prospective bride was concerned, she had even gone as far as writing the name 'Betty Sinatra' on table napkins. But although Frank was smarter than she was – so she says – he was also 'a complete shit – because he couldn't face the fact that he couldn't handle it'. The likely truth was that she was a threat to his individuality, another powerful woman, and when it seemed she was demonstrating that power, he took fright.

Soon after the break-up, a reporter asked Bacall about their relationship. She was more polite than Frank would have been in the circumstances. 'Do me a favour,' she said to the newsman (which was almost using the word 'please'), 'never mention me in the same breath as Frank Sinatra.' Now she is glad the marriage never happened – because she knows it would never have lasted.

Frank's relationships with other women continued much the same as before. After all, it was Dean Martin who quipped, 'When Frank dies they're going to give his zipper to the Smithsonian.' Equally according to form, he was churlish to those who upset him and courteous to the ones whose approval he wanted without any romantic attachments.

In June 1958, he went to Monaco to sing at a charity function for Princess Grace – in aid of UNICEF. Then he went on to London where he was seen with another aristocrat, Lady Beatty – the former Adele O'Connor. He had not been seen with anyone else on a regular basis since Bacall. When he was invited by Danny Kaye to join him at the royal premiere of his brilliant new film, *Me and the Colonel*, Lady Beatty was with him.

Romance wasn't enough for the London papers or the American journals, which avidly reprinted the stories that the two were going to marry. Once more, Sinatra was furious. 'The so-called announcement,' he proclaimed, 'has embarrassed the lady and my children. I love London more than any city in Europe, but they are going to drive me out of it.'

He went on the stage of the Odeon Leicester Square to introduce the people taking part in the show in aid of the Imperial Cancer Fund. In the presence of the Queen, he said he had to make an announcement: 'I did not come here to get married. Some of your papers would have me marry as often as King Farouk, and I'm not even as fat as he is.'

Before long, Lady Beatty married Stanley Donen, Gene Kelly's director partner in an assortment of musicals, including, of course, *Singin' in the Rain*.

The one gap in Sinatra's professional life now was a long-term television commitment. He told ABC that he didn't want any more regular series. He said he couldn't stand 'that rating stuff' and would just do one or two specials a year when the fancy took him. And that was what happened. He was in control there, too.

Control was the Sinatra watchword. He was a success in Hollywood simply because he knew the market and fitted his work around what he knew would sell – providing he wanted to do it. The box office was the sole arbiter and he knew there was a strong enough core audience for what he did to make it worth his while.

There was a pattern to his film-making now. He often played the underdog who believes he really ought to be the overdog but knows he never will be. In *Kings Go Forth* in 1958, he partnered Natalie Wood, who plays the Frenchwoman with whom he falls in love while he is an army 'sparks' – radio operator – in the Second World War. Natalie tells him she is the daughter of a white woman and a black man. He said the film was important to him because 'the message is that love can conquer anything, including racial and religious differences'.

Frank's sensitivity to race issues was why he helped Sammy Davis, Jr., find work at a time when it was difficult for him. Frank told a newspaperman: 'Sammy to me represents the finest traditions in our business. His talents are so staggering that each time I see him I experience a greater thrill.' So good was he, Sinatra believed, that he wouldn't follow him on to any show or nightclub spot. It was the old 'I can't follow that' syndrome, but he made it sound like a compliment now.

He would champion any minority whom he thought was getting a rough deal. It still wasn't a good time to be black in America when, in 1958, he declared: 'I have always believed that the love-thy-neigh-bour idea should be universal and be practised by all men everywhere. It is not always practised in our own country and this makes me terribly sad at times. I have a lot of optimism, though, and I believe that the future is full of promise.' He also said: 'The fact is that I don't like Negroes any more than I "like" Jews or Moslems or Italians or any other group. I don't *like* according to the colour of a man's skin or place of worship.'

It was about this time that Nat 'King' Cole was assaulted on a stage in Birmingham, Alabama. To its eternal credit, practically the whole of show business rallied to his support, condemning the thugs' violence. Frank heard about the incident at the same time as everyone else and spent the whole evening trying to phone Cole to offer sympathy. 'I finally reached him in a motel on the road at 3 a.m. the following morning and conveyed my concern and sympathy and I simply said I was shocked, sorry and angry over that outrage. I am proud to count him as a friend.'

Frank was finally getting his life sorted out now, including working out who his real friends were. More important, he wanted to organise his working life. 'I think I have matured,' he said. 'For the first time in my life, I'm organising it. I know that I can do only one thing at a time. I wasted ten years trying to do everything at once and getting nothing really done well.'

For that reason, he had gone into psychoanalysis for a time. 'I had some specific problems to work out,' he confessed – without announcing what they were. 'I got them off my chest and that was that. It's the same thing you could do with a close friend. The trouble is, in show business, it's hard to have close friends and I don't feel that I should burden them with my problems.'

His next film was *Some Came Running*, as effective as anything he had done in recent years although very different for its director. Vincente Minnelli was taking a break from his usual musical repertoire to tackle something heavier and a lot less melodic. Another novelty for him was what he considered to be an arch lack of self-discipline on his star's part. Other people might tolerate a 'One-Take Charlie', Minnelli would not. Yet at times it turned out to be a good partnership.

Sinatra plays a writer who won't accept he has talent and who at the end of his military service goes back to the small Midwest town where his brother, played by Arthur Kennedy, is a bigwig and his sister-in-law the prize snob. Shirley MacLaine is the girl he meets on the bus into town, a hooker with a heart of gold who falls in love with him and doesn't believe that he can't return the favour.

The film helped him to establish a firm relationship with Shirley that was bigger than her sideline membership of the Clan. It also gave Frank an even stronger blood brother feeling for Dean Martin, who plays the hat-wearing, card-playing, dying man the audience is supposed to sympathise with despite themselves. *Some Came Running* was the cement for much of what would happen to the Clan in years to come.

Plainly, Sinatra was a perpetual-motion machine. He now directed some of his occasional TV appearances as well as being seen in nightclubs, recording studios and film lots. *Only the Lonely* was the album that gave a new, deep look to the Capitol Sinatra. Sammy Cahn, who wrote the title song with Jimmy Van Heusen, told me: 'One of the things I could never understand about Frank was the way he could make you feel like swinging when he was doing it. When he sang "Only the Lonely", he made a lot of lonely people feel they were understood.'

What was really exciting for him at this time was another film. *A Hole in the Head* introduced him to Edward G. Robinson, one of the really important actors from Hollywood's first glory years, an idol virtually since the time Frank first went to see movies at one of those old theatres in Hoboken. Robinson had played in countless gangster films for Warner Bros. His most fascinating role of all was as the insurance investigator in *Double Indemnity*. But it was always *Little Caesar*, the archetypal Mob picture for which he was going to be remembered. In his audience's eyes, he was the hood who couldn't possibly ever be considered a decent human being. Yet that was what he was in *A Hole in the Head*, one who was constantly despairing of his younger brother, played by Frank.

Frank loved Robinson in this new film. The Jewish and Romanian-born Robinson (né Emanuel Goldenberg) specialised in playing Italians but this was very much a Jewish story into which Sinatra didn't fit any more comfortably than he had in *Guys and Dolls*. Here he played a hotel owner, a widower looking after his eleven-year-old son. But no matter how much he admired Edward G., it didn't change his methods. 'I don't believe in exhausting myself before the take,' Frank explained to him. 'On the other hand, I read the script fifty times before I ever go to work. So you can't say I'm unprepared.' Robinson, who had been in the business since Frank was in his Little Lord

Fauntleroy suits, had to bow to the requirements of the younger but more powerful man.

By all accounts they got on well. Female co-star Carolyn Jones was also particularly impressed with the courtesy Sinatra displayed. As she said: 'I attended a dinner with Frank. There were a lot of good-looking young girls, yet he was most attentive to an old lady who could have been his grandmother. How she beamed!'

It was also an opportunity for him to work with the director Frank Capra, who specialised in comedies with a particularly light touch. And another strong point was the song from the film which won Cahn and Van Heusen yet another Oscar, 'High Hopes'. John F. Kennedy made it the campaign song for his 1960 presidential election bid.

There were hopes for Sinatra in the business world, too. The actor who sang was now an executive. His company, the Essex Corporation, spent $2 million on three radio stations in Portland, Oregon, and two in Washington State, in Seattle and Spokane (he must have particularly enjoyed the latter; Spokane was Crosby's home town).

He made an album with the Hollywood String Quartet called *Close to You*. It was not as popular as some other recordings, but it stands as classic soulful Sinatra, in the vein of 'Violets for Your Furs' in *In the Wee Small Hours* a few years before.

'I've been recording my brains out,' Frank said at the time. 'Right now I wouldn't care if I never saw another disc.' And when he recorded two albums and eight single discs in four weeks he was likely to please his fans more than he thrilled himself. They all stand as perfect archives of the Sinatra of the time – good songs to listen to; a perfect demonstration of what was, musically, a wonderful age.

It all contributed to the new Sinatra success story – a more mature Sinatra, some people said, certainly a much more secure Sinatra, although there were still bust-ups. That was what happened with Sammy Davis, Jr. The Clan's sole black member offended Frank and found himself excluded from the Sinatra set. Suddenly, a member of the central Sinatra–Martin–Davis trio was out – out of the Clan, out of the picture, literally. A part made to measure for him in Frank's new movie, *Never So Few*, was changed so that Steve McQueen could play it instead.

Why? Hollywood has been debating it for years. Hilly Elkins, now a top Hollywood agent, who knew them both at that time – and was to have his own experience of the Sinatra cold-shoulder act – told me:

'I think you can say it was simply *cherchez la femme*, a woman had to be involved there somewhere.' Others think it was due to an interview Davis gave to the writer Jack Egan, in which he said: 'I love Frank and he was the kindest man in the world to me when I lost my eye in an auto accident and wanted to kill myself. But there are many things he does that there are no excuses for.' He alleged that Frank had no manners – and talent, he said, was 'no excuse' for that.

Also what Frank did more than occasionally was to lose his temper. Totally out of character – as we have seen, racism was the one thing that did not normally figure in his vocabulary – he was supposed to have told Peter Lawford that Sammy was 'a dirty nigger bastard'. Kitty Kelley reported that as fact, although it seems so unlike him.

There was no doubt he was ruling the roost in *Never So Few*, which also featured Charles Bronson and Richard Johnson, who immediately became a Sinatra fan. 'People seem to want to be rude to him for kicks,' he declared.

It was another World War II story, this time about the anti-Japanese war in Burma and involving allegations about corruption, with the Chinese Government selling arms to the Japanese. It also had the overwhelming presence of Gina Lollobrigida as the mistress of a corrupt businessman (played by Paul Henreid). Steve McQueen played an army driver.

On set there were Clan-type antics to which Steve McQueen was rudely introduced. Sinatra, aided like a dutiful member of a school gang by Peter Lawford, put a lighted firecracker among the rounds of ammunition in his gun belt. McQueen answered back by firing a prop light-machine-gun directly at his two assailants. Later, he lobbed a firecracker into Sinatra's dressing room and blew out his dresser's hearing aid. It was the one time during the filming, the director John Sturges informed McQueen's biographer Penina Spiegel, that Frank got sore. McQueen told reporters: 'Frank and I are on the same wavelength. We both grew up the hard way.' Sinatra seemed to think so, too. He ordered Sturges: 'Give the kid close-ups.'

Never So Few was a competent enough picture, but not one of the greats. Certainly it did more for Steve McQueen's career than it did for Sinatra's – although McQueen earned $20,000 for his role, about a twentieth of Frank's earnings.

Louella Parsons, in another one of those pieces which did not endear her to Sinatra, wrote: 'Steve McQueen stole the show right out from under Frank Sinatra.' He did even better going straight from *Never So Few* into *The Magnificent Seven*.

Everyone by now knew of Sinatra's quirks. His behaviour was common currency both inside and outside the film industry. Al Capp, creator of the Li'l Abner cartoon series, included an actor called Danny Tempest in his comic strip and you didn't have to be terribly knowledgeable to realise that he was modelling the man on Frank. When you lived like Sinatra – taking the top floor of the Hotel George V in Paris or having his own penthouse suite at the Fontainebleau in Miami Beach – you had to expect that sort of treatment.

He was also allowed the privileges of his position – including a degree of conceit. Evelyn Keyes told me of the party to which she was invited at Sinatra's house in Palm Springs. 'What we did after dinner was to sit around, listening to his records.'

In fact, Jule Styne asked Evelyn to star in a musical about a singer who sent his ex-wife for her birthday a jukebox filled with his own records. 'That was based on those evenings when we went to Frank's house and played his records,' she said. The show, however, no doubt to Frank's relief, never happened.

Hollywood parties were never the easy thing they were with other people, a mere chance to meet old friends, drink good wine and listen to amusing stories. Hollywood guests as well as Hollywood hosts were always 'on'. It was always something of a contest with one entertainer hoping to top another. Sinatra had experienced this himself at the party with Jolson all those years before. Now, he was conscious that people were feeling precisely that way about him – and, like Jolson before him, gave no quarter.

At this stage in his life, Sinatra no longer complained about gentle parodying, so long as he was in the mood. *Time* magazine quoted him as saying: 'I'm going to do as I please, I don't need anybody in the world. I did it all myself.' He did not add: 'My Way'. But the magazine later admitted that their writer had invented the quote.

— 19 —

CAN I STEAL A LITTLE
LOVE?

His success affected everything he did. As he told Joe Hyams, the celebrated Hollywood writer: 'The career is going ahead wonderfully. People are wonderful to me and I'm a happy, happy man.' And there was so much of which he was at the very peak – as a singer, of course, and not least as an actor. In 1960, he had another opportunity to put his two principal talents together – in a screen musical that had none of the miscasting problems of *Guys and Dolls*. He sang and he acted and audiences everywhere left cinemas happy.

Casting Sinatra in the movie version of *Can-Can* was based on the premise that there would always be a market for his kind of music and the way he performed it, no matter what Elvis Presley and others were trying to prove. As David Raksin told me, 'He is not really a consummate musician. He's a man of great musical instinct. His talent is very great. It has always been a talent to be able to sing in a wonderful way of being sassy over a song, the ability to develop material, the ability to look into a score, develop it, find out what it's about. There are not a lot of people who are not musicians who are able to do it. He knows what to do with his music.'

Saul Chaplin was once more working with Frank on a Cole Porter musical, this time as associate producer. Frank said he wanted new lyrics for 'Let's Do It', which didn't please Porter at all. But rather than allow Frank to insert more 'broads' and 'boots' into one of the best-known standards in the popular music catalogue, he agreed that new lyrics could be written. The trouble was that he didn't want to do them himself. The man who had had dozens of operations after his legs were crushed in a riding accident, told Chaplin: '*You* do them.'

'I didn't feel I *could* do them,' said Chaplin. 'I had written the few lines for *High Society*, but this was different.' 'Let's Do It' was almost a sacred text, even though Noël Coward was going to have his own way with it about the same time. 'I thought, I'm not writing any Cole Porter lyrics!' It was plainly tiger territory in songwriting terms.

So who were they going to get? Chaplin suggested Ira Gershwin. Porter had to agree that Gershwin couldn't possibly be bettered. Gershwin wrote the lyrics.

'Then Frank came in, read the lyrics – and decided he wanted Sammy Cahn to write them.'

That was an example both of Sinatra's clout and his bloody-mindedness but also of the changing tastes of a generation that had not been brought up with classics like 'Summertime', 'A Foggy Day' and 'Love Walked In'. As Chaplin recalled: 'I was left in the position of having to buy Ira Gershwin an expensive gift for lyrics which we never used.'

At least this was one problem solved. Another was never sorted out. Chaplin and Sinatra needed to decide who was going to sing another song. 'I went out to see him when he was living at Toluka Lake. A group of us went. We were all on shore and Frank is on a raft in the middle of the lake, sunning himself or reading. When he wanted something he would grab a megaphone and someone in a boat would row out and give it to him, like some kind of regal sultan from the Far East or something.' So it was impossible to talk business under those circumstances. But then, like many other top stars, Sinatra was spoilt. 'Yes, he was. He had to have his way all the time. But I had gone through so much with Judy Garland that it didn't bother me at all.'

And Sinatra had his way with that, too. He didn't like the song and it was removed. Those stories inevitably made the movie significant for people like Chaplin. But it was important in the Sinatra story for two other reasons. It marked his involvement in international politics for the first time and introduced him to a new woman in his life.

The film also saw a reunion with Shirley MacLaine as the owner of the café where the illegal can-can dance is featured. Sinatra was the lawyer who was defending her against the charges of indecency and – the most important part of the casting, this – Juliet Prowse played one of the dancers. Other co-stars were Louis Jourdan as the prosecutor and, above all, Maurice Chevalier playing the judge who was using his influence to get the charges against his favourite Paris institution dropped.

Chevalier was impressed with Frank. This was the smooth Sinatra of the *Songs for Swingin' Lovers* era, more relaxed than in the *Swing Easy* and *Come Swing With Me* albums he had recently recorded with the Billy May Orchestra. Working with Chevalier was one of those occasions that Sinatra would treasure too, a chance to pay tribute to one of the elder statesmen of his business. Certainly, Chevalier was the doyen of the entertainers born two generations before Sinatra. Like Eddie Cantor and Sophie Tucker, he came straight from the period dominated by Al Jolson. That was enough to endear him to Frank.

Chevalier gave me his very last interview – for a BBC radio programme – and we talked about *Can-Can* and about Sinatra. 'I found him as an entertainer *incredible*. He had the punch of the old music-hall performers, the kind who gives everything. I always admired that – and he had a very sweet voice.' Whether he was so impressed with all the usual Sinatra prima-donna behaviour is another matter. There was never a better example of this than in the matter of Frank and his television set, the one he had had installed in his dressing room – a very unusual thing at the time.

'The Dodgers were playing in the World Series,' Saul Chaplin recalled. 'That was exciting because it had never happened before. Now Frank had a deal with the studio. He didn't have to show up until eleven o'clock. We knew that when he said eleven, he meant one. We're sitting there at one o'clock and he's still not there. Everyone's looking at the TV set. Then we hear the announcer say, "Everyone from Hollywood is here today. There's Gene Tierney ... And there's Frank Sinatra." Frank Sinatra at the ballgame when he should have been working.' The 'wow!' that went up in the studio that day could be heard rocking the sound stage from one end of the Twentieth Century-Fox lot to the other.

The repercussions of all this showed Sinatra at his unrepentant, self-justifying best. He came in next day with his agent, who decided that the best form of defence in this case was attack. 'Mr Sinatra didn't like the scene you thought he was going to shoot yesterday,' he announced – and that was the end of the story.

Nor was that the only time Sinatra quarrelled with the script. One day the producer Jack Cummings was out of town, so it was Chaplin who got the standard telephone call from the Morris agency. Sinatra wanted changes.

Sinatra himself came on the line. 'I'm not going to do this scene as written.'

'Why not?' Chaplin asked him.

'Because the speeches are too goddamn long. Change them.'

Chaplin told him he had no right to change the speeches. 'I'll get the writer,' Sinatra said.

Charles Lederer was called. 'The writer came with his pyjamas on – it was early in the morning. We worked for about two and a half hours. Then when we shot the film, he didn't do the new lines either. He made up his own lines – and they worked just as well. But then, the originals weren't prose carved in stone, either.'

A rare visitor on the set of this movie was Nikita Khrushchev, First Secretary of the Communist Party of the Soviet Union, who on his September 1959 visit to the United States indicated that he wanted to see Hollywood. Frank Sinatra, Spyros P. Skouras, the head of Twentieth Century-Fox and the cast of *Can-Can* were delegated to be his hosts.

A luncheon was held at which Sinatra acted as a kind of toastmaster. But Skouras decided it was a perfect opportunity to acquaint their guest with the fact that America and the capitalist system was the perfect way to run the world. Khrushchev had other ideas – and expressed them.

The Hollywood royalty present enjoyed the fun and the ever more flushed faces of the two protagonists. But Sinatra showed great courtesy to the Soviet visitors, displaying one of the redeeming sides of his character.

The film *Can-Can* offered one final bonus. Frank had fallen in love for the first time since Ava's departure from his life. He and Ms Prowse were an item.

I'M WALKING BEHIND YOU

Frank would later threaten her, but he was smitten. She was sassy with an elfin look, but the kind of long legs that seemed to end under her chin. They *were her* – all 5 ft 8 inches of her. Maybe she wasn't beautiful in the Gardner sense, but there was something very attractive about her. She had a wicked sense of humour. And her accent was, shall we say, a little faked. She spoke American – with a South African lilt. She also knew her own mind and wasn't willingly going to change her plans. That did not endear Frank quite so much to her. But there you had the story of his love affair with the dancer he met on the set of *Can-Can*.

There was no doubt that she was striking. Everybody around Sinatra at this time was constantly telling him so. But when they said they liked Juliet they were telling the truth – and if they weren't, there had to be something wrong with them. Not only was she spectacularly attractive in that elfin way, she was exceedingly intelligent.

In all those years since she and Frank first met, she kept her counsel about their romance. But then, shortly before her death and in a very long, taped session in her dressing room at Las Vegas, scene of so many of their trysts, for the first time she told me the story.

She was a member-by-adoption of the Clan. As soon as she was seen to be part of Sinatra's lifestyle, her association with old Rat Pack was assured. And her relationship with Frank began almost from the first moment they were seen talking animatedly.

Juliet had come to America because of *Can-Can*. It was the very first thing she ever did in show business. Hermes Pan, the choreographer on the film whose reputation was made by being Fred Astaire's dance arranger, had met her in Rome and decided, as she put it, 'to take a chance with me'.

The result was a sensation in two ways. Her performance in the ballet sequence was outstanding, and as the leading can-can dancer, it was she who had principally earned Comrade Khrushchev's rebuke. He called her performance, lifting her skirt and waggling her bottom, 'lascivious, disgusting and immoral'. She, for her part, admitted that 'it isn't exactly *Swan Lake*', had her photograph in every newspaper in America and was later seen smiling, shaking hands with the Soviet ruler. Both had seen the propaganda value of the occasion.

Her true meeting with Frank Sinatra came via the one scene they shared together. It was quite clearly the stuff of Hollywood. Frank did the singing, Juliet just looked. But it was the song and the way she looked that made it special. The number was called: 'It's the Wrong Time' and it sounded good the way he crooned, 'It's the wrong game with the wrong chips ... Though your lips are tempting, they're the wrong lips.' But they weren't.

When Frank had finished the song, he gallantly asked: 'Was that all right for you? Was that take all right for you?' Such courtesies were practically unknown, but a chemical reaction had been stirred. As she told me: 'It was a very good part. All I had to do was react and listen – and I'm very good at listening. It was a nice moment in the movie. And it sparked a little interest, you know.'

He asked her out for dinner – their first date. Actually, he asked her to accompany him to one of those Hollywood dinner parties she had at the time only dreamed of. The host was director Norman Goetz and she arrived at his Beverly Hills mansion knowing that most of the eyes at the party were going to be focused on her.

'There were also big eyes *from* me, too,' she told me, remembering the innocence of a youth fairly well spent. 'Gary Cooper was there, I think Kirk Douglas. How could you be so *blasé* as not to be impressed by seeing people like that? It was wonderful. Fabulous.'

She was undoubtedly more interested in the stars than in their wives. 'Because all they were interested in was their hairdresser, their manicurist. I remember thinking, how awful! It's their only interest in life. I had been around enough by then to know that I didn't want to be one of those people and be just a socialite.'

Being the centre of attraction among the stars was another matter entirely. It mitigated the fact of being somewhere she didn't feel entirely comfortable. 'I've never enjoyed being in a room with a group of people I don't know. I'm not a party person. I don't like being in a room and just talking about myself.' The best moments were when she was with Frank. 'He was always around, wanting to know if everything was all right for me. Then he'd disappear for a bit to go talking to his pals and I'd be with the girls, but he'd always come back to see if everything was fine. I don't remember if we sat next to each other. In those days, they used to like separating people – which I've never liked. I always like sitting with the people I came in with.'

Before long, they were in the midst of an affair, a more loving, cooler affair than most in which he had been involved. 'I mean, it was Frank wasn't it? Someone I had grown up with. Because I used to hear my mother play all his records at home. Someone you saw in the movies, almost someone you knew because you had seen him and heard him so much. And because he had an amazing charm – he really did, when he wanted to have it. And he was so nice to me.'

She thought she appealed to him because 'I was unspoilt. I was much younger than others he had been with. I am sure there were others who were as young as I was, but I was the youngest one he had taken time to form a relationship with.'

If she thought then that there was going to be a long, deep relationship with Frank she was in for a disappointment. It took four months before they came together and the affair would go on for another two years, with the sort of ups and downs which the other women in the Sinatra life would recognise – although he told her: 'You know, I never ever quarrelled or had a hard word with the women in my life.'

With her he was 'always amazingly kind and gentle. Maybe it was because I was closest to his daughter's age. Maybe he respected that more. I wasn't a woman who had run around a lot. I had never been married. And I remember him saying – he said that many times – that this was the most comfortable he ever felt in a relationship with anybody.'

They never lived together, but she would often take off for weekends or other short periods of time to stay with him. But from the beginning it was an incredibly domestic sort of relationship. 'We'd sit around the pool and I'd knit socks for him. He was wonderful. And when I had sore feet from dancing, he'd say, "You know, I've never known any married person who had sore feet."'

That statement, in the Sinatra codebook, was a proposal of marriage. He kept asking her to get married – 'and I was very iffy about it'. Sinatra was sure that Juliet was the one he wanted to spend the rest of his life with. She was less convinced – especially since there was a condition to the offer of marriage. Because of his experience with Ava, he wanted her to stop work and she didn't want to do so.

She asked: 'Stop what? Dancing altogether?' His reply was succinct:

'No. You can go to classes and whatever, but I don't want you to earn a living from it.'

What about children? He told her he didn't want any more. He had three already and he didn't want the complications of a second family. She wasn't sure. 'I was very torn because we had this wonderful relationship. On the other hand, too, I had an urge and a desire to work. It's something I loved doing. I've always loved performing – and to have to give it up when I was just starting a career, so to speak, I knew it would have interfered with us. Absolutely. It would have been disastrous. It's very hard to tell someone in our business that they've got to stop work.'

But for the moment, Frank lived in hope and Juliet enjoyed the relationship. It was, as far as anyone who called in at Sinatra's Los Angeles or Palm Springs homes was aware, a very pleasant sort of set-up. They seemed to be a happy couple. If, at forty-five, Frank *was* old enough be her father, such relationships weren't exactly unknown in the film town. 'I think I amused him in some way or other. He always found me funny and I saw him with a twinkle in his eye when he watched me go through my antics and things. And I think he actually genuinely liked me. I really do.'

But he didn't trust her. When she wasn't with him, he practically stalked her. 'One day he got so mad at me. He said, "I saw you the night before last, doing cartwheels down Wilshire Boulevard." And he was right. I was. I mean, I was in my young twenties and kids do those sort of things. I was with the young boy who was managing me.'

On other occasions, he stood on a street corner, watching her drive. 'He would say I was driving too fast. He would say, "Your whole life, you have to realise that the car is a weapon and it can kill you." He was really like a father-figure.'

He taught her a lot about the business – and about the two sides of his personality, the yin and the yang of the Sinatra persona. She saw the funny Frank. 'I remember once someone was very sick, a man who had had a very serious operation. Frank sent to his room some barbells and exercise equipment – stuff he knew the man could never use. But it was someone with that kind of humour whom he knew would enjoy it.'

On the other hand, there *was* the other Sinatra in her life, too. 'He could get terribly angry. He was never not nice to me, but I saw him being rude to people. One time we were in Palm Springs. We were out to dinner with some people – and it always happened, he had too much liquor under his belt and he got belligerent; most people do. They talk about happy drunks, but most drunks are belligerent. Frank would get a couple of drinks under him and become that way. I saw him give Jimmy Van Heusen the most horrendous dressing-down in a restaurant. I can't remember what it was all about. It was awful.'

I asked her if she was embarrassed. 'Oh yes. Very. And he would do things where he was rude. He would throw things on the floor if the service was not as he wanted it to be. You know, it's something I would find pretty amazing, and I never did that. It was not par for the course in my family.'

She didn't let it affect her relationship with him, however. 'I went out of my way not to have a confrontation and to calm things down. So I didn't like the things that were said when he got annoyed and had fights with people.'

The British journalist Robin Douglas-Home let the public benefit from his experience of Sinatra in a temper. 'I am not trying to white-wash Sinatra; he is quite capable of taking care of himself. I am merely stating the facts as I saw them.

'What usually happens is that some woman who has clearly had too much to drink comes over to Sinatra, uninvited, throws her arms around his neck and generally makes a nuisance of herself and a mess of him. On these occasions, in my experience, Sinatra himself has always behaved impeccably, in spite of the obvious difficulty of the situation and the provocation. It is not an easy situation for him to be in.

'What happens next is that the man escorting the intruding woman comes up in a jealous belligerent way and tries to pick a fight with Sinatra. With the woman looking happily on. And so . . .'

Sometimes, when he thought a fight was likely or the company was going to be unsuitable, he made sure Juliet was out of the way. 'He was very protective of me. I don't ever remember being with Giancana [the Mafia 'godfather' whose name would appear constantly in the Sinatra story] but he was often seen with these kind of people. I remember once when they were in his suite, he told me: "I'm going to send you back to Los Angeles."' She asked him why. 'He said, "Because I don't want you to be around these people." I said: "I'm a big girl and I can take care of myself," but he insisted I went.'

Some friends he *was* happy for Juliet to meet, like the man who was about to be elected President of the United States, John F. Kennedy.

Kennedy and Sinatra were very close at the time. Frank had taken it upon himself to collect an inventory of 'nice' jokes about the Kennedy election campaign in the way that Bob Hope's joke factory was building one up for Richard Nixon. He hired Mort Sahl, one of America's most trenchant comedians, to write them for him. Later, the friendship went sour. He invited Sahl to entertain at a Kennedy fundraiser and the comedian decided it was time to reassure old Joe Kennedy: 'You're not losing a son, you're gaining a country.' Joe regarded it as an impertinence and Frank said he did, too.

That was it. No more Sahl. Frank wanted to be sure that Kennedy would never be upset by anything he did. He was milking the friendship with the future president for all it was worth – and it was worth a great deal to anyone in 1960. Kennedy, for his part, was thoroughly enjoying the company of the Rat Pack, especially since he had had an 'in' with the group ever since his sister Pat married Peter Lawford. Lawford once said: 'Let's just say that the Kennedys are interested in the lively arts, and Sinatra is the liveliest art of all.'

It was Lawford who made the initial introductions. But the friendship was consolidated when Sinatra made introductions of his own. He and the young President shared women the way other men share golf partners. Peter Lawford also said, 'I was Frank's pimp and Frank was Jack's.' Before long, Marilyn Monroe would be in both their lives. Kennedy's long-term mistress, Judith Campbell-Exner, had previously had an affair with Sinatra. It was a complicated relationship. She said afterwards that she gave him up because he was 'kinky' in bed. To which Frank replied: 'Hell hath no fury like a hustler with a literary agent.'

There was another connection. Rumour had it that Ms Exner was still on very friendly terms with Sam Giancana who controlled as much of Chicago as Al Capone ever had and was also a 'sleeping partner' in the Cal-Neva Lodge at Lake Tahoe. This hotel had a complex relationship: it seems that Frank's close friend Hank Sanicola owned 16 per cent, Skinny D'Amato was in for 13 per cent and Dean Martin had a 3 per cent share. Sinatra owned 25 per cent. He was into property in a big way – 6 per cent of the Sands Hotel was his, although one of the places he wanted most, Ernie's, a much swankier establishment in San Francisco than the name indicated, didn't fall into his lap.

There were stories that Sanicola had also slept with Ava but he'd given her up because he thought she was mad. At about that time,

Jilly Rizzo, proprietor of Jilly's restaurant, Frank's favourite New York watering-hole and another close friend, tried to get Ava and Sinatra together again at his apartment. When that failed, Frank was all the more convinced that Juliet had to be the one to replace her.

Juliet met Kennedy at the time that he was in the midst of at least one other affair, with the actress Angie Dickinson. He hadn't yet become President and was in Las Vegas so that he could be with Angie in comparative privacy. 'It was at the Sands,' she recalled. 'I remember that he didn't come to the show, but was in Frank's suite.'

Soon, Frank would be working for Kennedy's campaign, giving what has since become the norm – a stamp of approval for a presidential candidate from the people of Hollywood. There had been a request for help from Joe Kennedy, the candidate's father, who would later be responsible breaking up the relationship between his son and Sinatra. The elder Kennedy also asked for help from Sam Giancana. He said that if the gang boss could deliver unions and sheriffs in West Virginia, he could prove that a Catholic could become President. The mobster engaged Skinny D'Amato – who owed Frank plenty – to use his influence and gained some 120,000 votes in the primary, to say nothing of a million or two dollars of trade union funds.

Giancana always said he was doing a favour for Sinatra and not for Kennedy, although that would come later. It is also true that if he helped Kennedy, he stood a good chance of relieving the pressure of the FBI, who were heightening their investigation into his activities.

After Kennedy won the nomination, Frank organised galas and went out of his way to try to raise funds for the Democrats – which he did by the million. All Juliet knew was that Kennedy and Sinatra seemed to be bosom pals when they were together. 'I think Kennedy liked Frank. It was a mutual admiration thing. Of course, Frank loves the power of politics, the power of those things which make things happen.'

It was one of the aspects of Frank that Juliet would have to think about.

— 21 —

DON'T BLAME ME

How close were Sinatra and Kennedy – and how much did Kennedy like the associations the public were drawing from their relationship?

There was no doubt that Frank was going to be useful to him, but were they as close as Sinatra liked to say? Not if the Clan's sworn enemy, the columnist Dorothy Kilgallen, was telling the truth. She quoted Kennedy as saying: 'He's no friend of mine, he's just a friend of Pat and Peter Lawford.' But he was sufficiently a friend for Frank to have a special phone line to the White House. The white telephone remained at the house in Palm Springs until the home was sold in the early 1990s.

Not many people believed either that Kennedy was no friend of Sinatra's or that Kennedy had actually made the statement. Particularly since Kilgallen added: 'So what? So last week the Democratic candidate for the presidency was guest of honour at a private little dinner given by Frank. No reason why he shouldn't, of course, but why try to kid the press?' Why indeed? The press didn't like Frank any more than Frank liked the press, but it didn't seem to have an effect on the numbers of people who bought records or tickets to his movies. And they were, almost twenty years after the bobbysox generation, voters.

When Peter Lawford threw a birthday party for his wife, Kennedy and the entire Clan were on the guest list. Kennedy was then still a senator but since he looked as if he were going to be more important than that, Frank occasionally found himself in trouble. In one instance, he was forced into making a public denial that he actually took instruction from the senator.

The problem arose when he decided to employ Albert Maltz to write the screenplay for the film he now wanted, more than anything else, to make: *The Execution of Private Slovik*, about the only United

States soldier in World War II to be shot for desertion. The choice was seen as a direct challenge to whatever was left of the Un-American Activities Committee because Mr Maltz had served a prison sentence for refusing to say whether or not he was a Communist. He was now seen as a red under Sinatra's bed. Maltz had been on the blacklist along with people like director Carl Foreman, the comedian Zero Mostel and a host of writers, notably Dalton Trumbo, and the assumption was that he was therefore a traitor.

At first, the Sinatra reaction was predictable. He told his lawyers and anyone else who chose to listen: 'No one is going to tell me who I hire. Albert is the best writer I know for this part and I want him.'

Frank took a full-page advertisement in *Daily Variety* and the *Hollywood Reporter*, declaring that he was not going to allow political intolerance to take over his professional life. He wrote:
'This statement is made by me so that the public will have all the facts before passing judgment in regard to my hiring Albert Maltz to write the screenplay of *The Execution of Private Slovik*. I bought the William Bradford Huie book which tells the true story of the only execution of a soldier by the United States Army since the Civil War. Since I will produce and direct the picture I am concerned that the screenplay reflects the true pro-American values of the story. This means that the picture must be an affirmative declaration in the best American tradition. I spoke to many screenwriters but it was not until I talked to Albert Maltz that I found a writer who saw the screenplay in exactly the terms I wanted. This is, the Army was right.'

[That was the first surprise to come out of the story – most people would have expected, especially from someone with Maltz's left-wing credentials, that the Army would be found guilty.]

'Under our Bill of Rights, I was taught that no one may prescribe what shall be orthodox in politics, religion or other matters of opinion. I am in complete accord with the statement made earlier this week by J. D. Nicola of the Catholic Legion of Decency, who said, "The Legion evaluates films on the basis of art, not the artist." As the producer of the film I and I alone will be responsible for it. I accept that responsibility. I ask only that judgment be deferred until the picture is seen.

'I would also like to comment on the attacks from certain quarters on Senator John Kennedy by connecting him with my decision on employing a screenwriter. This type of partisan politics is hitting below the belt ... I make movies. I do not ask the advice of Senator

Kennedy on whom I should hire. Senator Kennedy does not ask me how he should vote in the Senate.

'I am prepared to stand on my principles and to await the verdict of the American people when they see *The Execution of Private Slovik*.

'I repeat: In my role as a picture maker, I have – in my opinion – hired the best man to do the job.'

He was virtually challenging anyone to upset his arrangements. He didn't worry too much when General Motors withdrew sponsorship. There would be other sponsors, he believed. But the Kennedys were putting on pressure. They didn't like an association with a performer who once again was being made the subject of anti-Communist allegations in the Hearst press. Cardinal Spellman, the leader of New York's Catholics, was blunt about 'consorting with Communists'. John Wayne and he almost came to blows over the matter in a parking lot. Wayne thought that Frank was proving to be a 'Commie'. But Kennedy was the one who influenced him.

In the end, Frank had to decide: Be a pal of Albert Maltz or one of the Kennedy's old blue-eyed boys. Frank took the easier way out – and dumped Maltz and his project. He may have been influenced by the fact that his children, as Nancy, Jr. says in her book, were having problems at school with red-baiting children. The headline in the Los Angeles *Examiner* said it all: 'SINATRA OUSTS MALTZ AS WRITER'. The Hearst newspapers all carried the same banner: 'SINATRA FIRES MALTZ'.

Now he took another full-page advertisement, this time in the trade press. It ran:

'In view of the reaction of my family, my friends and the American public, I have instructed my attorneys to make a settlement with Albert Maltz. I had thought that the major consideration was whether or not the script would be in the best interests of the United States.'

'My conversations with Maltz indicate that he has an affirmative, pro-American approach to the story. But the American public has indicated it feels the morality of hiring Maltz is the more crucial matter and I will accept this majority opinion.'

Louella Parsons wrote: 'Knowing Frank as I do I am sure that the influence of his ex-wife Nancy and his daughter, Nancy, Jr., played a big part in his decision.'

Tina remembered that some of the girls at the Marymount Catholic School she attended called him a 'Commie' to her face. It made her cry. So Frank came to the school 'to prove he wasn't a monster'. Then he took her to the father–daughter square dance.

But was it just because of Frank's children that he dumped Maltz? Louella Parsons added in her piece: 'There may have also been influence brought to bear on him from some of his political friends.'

That was an understatement. The truth of the matter was that Sinatra wanted the same position in what would before long be called Camelot that Kennedy himself always had with the Clan. As it turned out, he was useful to the President, but was never going to be part of that gilded circle that he so craved. Yet whatever the administration or the family wanted – and at times it seemed as if the two were one and the same – he gave.

Maltz himself grew to be conciliatory to Sinatra. Shortly before his death in 1985, he said: 'Sinatra threw down the gauntlet against the blacklist. He was prepared to fight. Something had come from behind that caused him to change his position.'

Dorothy Kilgallen wrote in her column: 'Unquestionably anti-Communist, Dad Kennedy would have invited Frank to jump off the Jack Kennedy presidential bandwagon if he hadn't unloaded Mr Maltz.'

The Maltz affair was not an incident to bring any credit on the name of Frank Sinatra, although he would have been very brave indeed to have done anything else. And until this day, it rankles with people who expected him to go further to aid a brilliant writer. His standing with Kennedy, however, was now established.

Time magazine wondered about the wisdom of the Kennedy–Sinatra connection. It reported: 'Some of JFK's biggest headaches may well come from an ardently pro-Kennedy clique that is known variously as the Rat Pack or the Clan.' However, when Kennedy won his hair's-breadth victory over Richard Nixon in November 1960, both Juliet and Frank were cheering as loudly as anyone in the country. They knew there were rewards to come – and they did, quickly. The President confirmed that he wanted Frank to organise and host the big show he intended to hold as part of the inauguration celebrations.

Juliet was there, too, when Kennedy stayed at the Palm Springs house days after the victory in November 1960. Frank later put a bronze plate on the door of the President-elect's bedroom: 'John F. Kennedy Slept Here. November 6th and 7th 1960.'

As far as Sinatra the Public Person was concerned, this would be the biggest time of his life. He was stepping into the most powerful operation in the world. He knew there would be access to the White House whenever he wanted it, even if he wasn't exactly going to be a member of Kennedy's Cabinet.

For the inauguration Frank Sinatra was going to organise the greatest show on earth. So he had to look the part, too. It was not enough to get the best tailor in Hollywood to make him a new tuxedo – or even send his measurements to London for a little man in Savile Row to knock something up. He commissioned Don Loper, who was more used to designing gowns for the female stars whom Sinatra liked taking to dinner.

Loper admitted that Frank paid him a 'small fortune' to produce the outfit and that he himself was 'staking my reputation that Frank will be the most elegantly dressed guest at the inauguration. Furthermore, I believe he will revive a correctness in male dress that has been deplorably lacking since the thirties.'

He would wear white tie and tails with the latest British-style low top hat and an Inverness cape lined with rich, black satin. Loper even produced a chesterfield coat with velvet collar for day-wear and a bowler hat to go with that. Or rather, two chesterfield coats and two bowler hats, in case of disaster. In fact, there would be two of everything – two tailcoats and two sets of linen 'in case he spills anything'.

The inauguration was to be celebrated in a series of balls and other events, each more glorious than the next. The best champagne was going to be served to ladies in their finest gowns whose jewellery glittered under the most exquisite chandeliers. It all had a purpose – or two purposes: to thank the people who had supported the winner's campaign and to try to raise money to pay back the huge debts that had accrued during the months on the stomp.

Frank's contribution was a show to be written by Melville Shavelson and his partner Jack Rose. 'The Democratic party was three million dollars in the hole in the course of the campaign – a huge amount of money for 1961,' Shavelson told me. 'Sinatra knew about that and told Kennedy, "I'll get you out of debt in one night." That was when they decided to put on this gala with all of Hollywood's Democratic people – and in those days that was everybody in Hollywood – taking part or at least going.'

Sinatra was on the phone every day, sometimes a dozen times a day, to Kennedy and to his writers, Shavelson and Rose. Frequently they met at Sinatra's hideaway above Coldwater Canyon. All the artists and their guests received their invitations from Frank himself – inscribed on silver cigarette boxes. They stated: 'The inaugural committee requests the honour of your company to attend and participate in the inauguration of John Fitzgerald Kennedy, President of the United States of America, and Lyndon Baines Johnson, Vice President on Friday 20th January one thousand nine hundred and sixty-one in the city of Washington.'

Now, much-worn editions of the box (worth even more than the gold cuff-links and cigarette lighters that Sinatra enjoyed handing out to his buddies) can be found on selected desks and in the dens of various people who were Hollywood personalities at the time. The big, big affair would be held the night before the inauguration itself – the occasion when Kennedy called on his fellow citizens to ask not what their country could do for them but what they could do for their country.

One person was excluded from the line-up: Sammy Davis, Jr. He and Frank had not only made it up, but he had just married the blonde Mai Britt – with Frank acting as best man and also giving Davis a seven per cent share of the film they planned to make. But Joe Kennedy was on the phone again – it would upset people if this man involved in a mixed marriage were seen to be fêted. Frank agreed, but got Peter Lawford to break the news for him. Amazingly, Sammy said he understood. But it was all too reminiscent of how Sinatra had dumped Albert Maltz so recently.

On the night, Frank was made a fuss of by the President and his wife, Jackie, who, in a magnificent white gown, was escorted by Frank to the inaugural show. Shavelson told me: 'We all flew to Washington at Frank's expense. When we arrived, during that biggest snowstorm ever to hit Washington, we found that nobody could move along the streets to get to the convention centre. Finally, we got the stars there in a bus in order to do the show.

'The President and Jackie finally showed up at the National Guard armoury where the concert was going to be held – and we laid the egg of all time.' Only half the 12,000 seats were occupied (but 72 boxes were filled – people paid $10,000 for each of them) and only 60 of the 100-man orchestra was present. 'We had all the big stars. But nothing happened. Everybody was so cold and so angry and so tired, it was so late.'

Leonard Bernstein, America's most fashionable conductor, was primed to lead the 'Fanfare for Inauguration' but even he almost failed to arrive. He had to be rescued by a limousine sent by the White House. His own car, in which he was giving Bette Davis a lift, had been stranded. When he did appear, it was in a shirt two sizes too big. Ms Davis was in an ordinary dress, not the evening gown she had had specially made, and Ethel Merman, with whom Frank sang 'Let's Call the Whole Thing Off', appeared in a tweed coat.

'We had Sidney Poitier, with whom we rode in the bus along with his wife,' Shavelson recalled. 'We got stuck in the snow for half an hour and Poitier entertained us for half an hour. We had written sketches for all these people – and it just lay there.'

It was still an impressive, historic evening. Frank began the frozen celebrations by saying: 'Ladies and gentlemen, I hope nobody will think it presumptuous of some of us in the entertainment world who have come here to pay tribute to the President elect of the greatest nation in the world under the auspices of one of its great political organisations, the Democratic Party.' And then he told Kennedy jokes, mainly about the ages of the new incumbents (JFK was three years younger than Sinatra). One of them was about the White House security guard who shouted: 'Hey you kids – off the lawn. Oh, I'm sorry, Mr President.'

Frank commented on the quality of what was on offer – to say nothing of the risks to their reputations. 'We did not have too much rehearsal time because of the weather, but in four years' time we'll really have it in shape.' (This was a dream which, of course, would never happen. Kennedy would be assassinated before another election came round.)

The President was grateful enough. After the show he said: 'I first of all want to say I am proud to be a Democrat tonight because all of you are here. I am proud to be a Democrat because, since the time of Thomas Jefferson, the Democratic Party has been identified with the pursuit of excellence and we've seen excellence tonight.' This was a demonstration of the 'happy relationship between the arts and politics which has characterised our long history. [and] reached culmination tonight'.

He added: 'I know we're all indebted to a great friend, Frank Sinatra. Long before he could sing, he used to poll a Democratic precinct back in New Jersey. That precinct has grown to cover a country. But long after he has ceased to sing, he is going to be standing up and speaking for the Democratic Party and I thank him on behalf of all of you tonight. You cannot imagine the work he has done to make this show a success.'

Then the President made an announcement that had the place rocking. 'Two shows on Broadway closed down because the people are with us tonight.' Never before had show-people cheered the notion of Broadway theatres going 'dark'. But these were spectacular times, which the Kennedy family recognised immediately the proceedings were over.

There followed a celebration dinner for the cold, overworked performers. Sinatra sat with Juliet at a table with Sammy Cahn and his then wife Gloria. Mel Shavelson remembers: 'There was this big table – with caviar, champagne, everything, that Sinatra was going into a hole himself for. He was still paying off a lot of debts from the time when he was doing badly. Well, Peter Lawford comes in and says to Frank: "The President is downstairs at the inaugural ball and would like all the people involved in the show to come downstairs so that he can thank them individually and shake their hands".'

What happened next (until now never revealed) must rate as the most notable example of *chutzpah* in Hollywood history. Sinatra, says Shavelson, looked at Lawford and said: 'Tell him we are eating.'

Frank had snubbed the most important man in the Western world. 'Freddie March was at our table and Freddie says: "Listen, in ten minutes you're going to see one Wop nailed to that wall."' Instead, eventually (after finishing his dinner) Sinatra went down on his own to meet the President and returned ten minutes later – with Kennedy in tow. That was when the President made his apology: 'I didn't know you were eating.'

Later still, Joseph Kennedy took it upon himself to thank Frank and his guests for their work that night. He invited them all to a nightclub. 'Not me,' said Shavelson, 'I am a country boy from Hollywood and I don't stay up this late.' He and his wife Lucille went back to their hotel convinced that because of the weather, the inauguration ceremony itself would be called off. 'We switched on the TV and there was Kennedy making that great speech. We finally got out of the hotel and got there in time for the end.'

That night, Sinatra threw a dinner for everybody in the show at the Statler Hotel.

— 22 —

HEY, JEALOUS LOVER

When they returned to the West Coast, Frank and Juliet went on with their lives. Sinatra still hoped he would persuade Juliet to marry him, but she remained unsure. It did seem an idyllic relationship yet Juliet never became close to his children. 'I never knew Tina that well. I only knew Nancy superficially because she was married to Tommy Sands at the time, whom I knew. We had dinner once in New York – with Tommy, Nancy, Frank and me. Frank Junior I never knew very well at all. Except I knew Frank was a wonderful father to them. He called them every day; he would talk to them. I know that he was always on the phone with them, keeping contact. So many people did not do that in a divorce situation. But they knew there were always women on the scene. This had been happening since they were children. Dad was always with someone else.'

When Frank was with Juliet, he still saw other women. She knew that. She also knew who the one real love in his life was – in a way she could never be. 'Ava was the only one he ever spoke about. She was the big love in his life. Oh yes, definitely. She would just come up in conversation. I think until the very end [when Ava died] it was there probably. That happens in people's lives.'

Was that a problem for her? 'No – because you can't let something of the past come between you. If you still have a little thread going there, there is nothing you can do about it.'

Just as she was getting to know so much about the Sinatra life and lifestyle, so he became extremely friendly with Juliet's mother and step-father. They visited from their home outside Johannesburg and were treated like old Sinatra friends. 'My mother is a very classy lady, very well educated, and they got on very well. My stepdad, George Polty, was a great golfer and Frank gave him a gold putter. They played golf together with my brother, Clive, a doctor. They all got on great.

Anyone seeing Sinatra and Prowse together had to notice one thing about them: she brought a degree of quietude into his life. 'We had a very easy-going relationship. And I know the relationships he had prior to us, they were very traumatic. I think I was different, because I was not an American girl and had a very different attitude to life. I came from a very well-balanced family and a non-show-business family altogether. So I didn't have that behind me. I didn't have to follow in their footsteps, so to speak.'

But one night, things went badly awry. It's another story never told before.

'All the time we were going together,' she told me, 'I knew he was seeing other girls, that he wasn't just dating me. So I saw no reason why I shouldn't also go with this dancer, Nick Nevara. Well, he found out about it and came to my apartment at three o'clock in the morning, banging on my door. And I wouldn't answer the door because I had Nick with me inside. He then disappeared, screaming and yelling.'

Half an hour later, the phone rang. It was Sinatra's secretary, Gloria Lovell. She told Juliet: 'Get out of there quickly.' She passed on what she took to be a warning.

Juliet then called her manager Eddie Goldstone, the one who had been with her when she did her Wilshire Boulevard cartwheels. He came immediately and found Juliet and Nick Nevara sitting on the pavement outside the apartment building. He joined them in their 3.30 a.m. sit-in and waited. An hour later, Juliet decided to do something about it. 'That's when I got mad, thinking, "How dare he do this to my life?" Then I got *really* mad. I went inside and called him. I just read him the riot act, said I never wanted to see him again and he shouldn't try to get hold of me – and that was that.' She wrote to her mother about it.

They didn't speak for six months. In the meantime, people really did think Frank was seeing Marilyn Monroe – especially when she went to see his show at the Sands and was his date at a party given by Tony Curtis and Janet Leigh. But, it turned out, he had no romantic plans and was really trying to do a deal with her to star with him in a remake of the Judy Holliday classic, *Born Yesterday*. 'Then when I was in New York doing the Perry Como show,' Juliet continued, 'the phone rang and it was him. It was like we had just spoken yesterday. "How are you?" he wanted to know.'

The questions followed: 'What are you doing? When are you coming home?' When she said she would be back in Los Angeles in a couple of days, there were more questions: 'What plane are you catching? Is anyone meeting you at the airport?'

She told him that she didn't think that anyone was. 'Would you like me to pick you up?'

'Yes. If you want to.'

As she says: 'That stunned me. He came to LAX [Los Angeles Airport] all by himself. He was in his Italian Ghia. All by himself. I thought, "Wow!"'

He took no notice of the crowds who recognised him and may well have thought it was a scene from his next film – Frank Sinatra at an airport in his little hat with the wide ribbon.

'But he didn't care – and that was when he asked me to marry him – and after that whole six months of not seeing him, of not even talking to him.'

She didn't say yes straight away. 'I was always very iffy. As I said, I was very torn about the situation.' But before long, she did say yes – and he put a ring on her finger there and then (not at a party at Romanoff's, as the press reported). At the airport.

Juliet sat in the passenger seat, not knowing what had happened. Frank Sinatra was driving as though nothing had happened in the past six months. All she kept doing was looking at the third finger of her left hand and the 'beautiful' ten-carat, pear-shaped diamond and wondering what they were letting themselves in for.

As she told me: 'It was all a long old-fashioned time ago.'

Just how high the hopes were for a successful future between them is difficult now to say. Juliet wasn't sure even then, but she tried to hide her doubts as much as others tried to pretend it was all going to be a huge success. Ava sent Frank a telegram of congratulations. 'He showed it to me,' she recalled.

Once again Sinatra insisted that Juliet stop working and she told him she couldn't do so. But she didn't tell him to stop instead. 'How could I? He was the superstar. And our relationship had helped me a lot. I made two movies back to back: *Can-Can* was followed by *GI Blues* with Elvis. They didn't hurt at all.'

The relationship with Elvis actually did hurt. There was a short affair and Sinatra found out about it. 'Predictably, he was furious.' And it didn't show any signs of lasting. Neither did other people seem to know about it. But Frank went on with his dating of other women too. Dorothy Provine, who had a huge hit playing a girl called Lulu in the *Roaring Twenties* TV series, disappeared at the same time that

Frank went away from base without telling anyone and came back when he returned, too. This happened on a number of occasions.

Somehow, he was able to get about without being noticed, which was a big advantage. Juliet wondered at that as much as anybody else. 'I don't think he ever got sucked into the superstar syndrome, where because he knew he was so big, he was fussy about who he was with and where he was going. He wasn't like that. I remember once being with Engelbert Humperdinck in New York and he said he couldn't walk down the street without being mobbed by a crowd of people. I thought, "How awful." I mean, Frank would walk down New York city streets – and it never fazed him.'

But would he have been upset about not being recognised? Show-business history is littered with cases of stars who go places incognito so as not to be disturbed and then go into a depression when no one acknowledges them. 'I think he would have been upset if he had mentioned his name and someone didn't know who he was. There might just have been some places in Africa where they didn't know who he was. I couldn't think of anywhere else.'

Not that Juliet minded the publicity that she herself engendered. 'Well, it goes with the territory, doesn't it? How can you avoid it? You are in the public eye and you have to be aware of it. You have to be a performer and realise it's going to affect everyone and everything. I've always been lucky that I wasn't a superstar. It must have been very difficult for superstars and their big entourages and the death threats they get all the time.'

Sinatra, though, didn't get death threats and didn't have big entourages. 'We would go to places, just the two of us. Never anyone else.'

When he was performing in Chicago, she flew out there – just to join him on the train back. 'I think he chose the train because I never thought he liked flying particularly and it was a way of getting away and having some peace and quiet. I didn't even spend the night in Chicago. I just got there by plane and travelled back to LA in the train.'

They tried to have their quiet moments, he painting, she gardening. But these were all too few. He was usually away working and when he was, it was at places where the Mob were involved. And she knew the Mob were never far away when he was working. 'I never thought too much about it because they were so closely connected to Vegas, and the gambling operation was such that the Mob was just there. You expected them to be there before the corporations took over.

They ran that place. But he *never* wanted me to be involved with them.'

I asked her if she thought that he didn't really want to be involved with them himself, either. Kitty Kelley quoted Eddie Fisher as saying that Frank would rather have been the son of a don than President of the United States. 'It could be that he didn't want to be involved,' Juliet told me in that last interview. But then if you don't want to be involved with people like that, you get yourself out of it. Maybe he couldn't. I never pried into all that. It was not part of anything I wanted to know about.'

What she did want to know about – and more and more, as it turned out – was the continuation of her career. At the same time, he was increasingly convinced that they couldn't both be active in show business. He wanted a quiet little wife who would amuse him and provide the other comforts he sought. He didn't want to go into the kind of competition he had had with Ava.

In the end, it came to an ultimatum and she said no. 'I can't remember exactly what he said,' she told me. 'But you can't argue with someone when this happens. You can't try to talk them into it. I'd been going backward and forwards with this issue for at least six weeks. That on-again, off-again thing. Then I said I had had enough. No. I gave him back the ring – and it was over.' The farewell took place in Los Angeles. 'I think he kind of knew by then – because I had been so iffy for so many weeks. He was the one who wanted the answer and that was what made me decide.'

I wondered if he particularly wanted to get married – or just wanted to marry her. 'Oh, I think he wanted to get married.' Did he love her? 'Hmm ... hmm.' She was not prepared to commit herself. Did she love him? 'Oh, I don't think so, if I look back on it. No. I was really in awe of him and it was a pretty major experience in my life.'

Had she fallen in love with the image? 'Oh yes. Absolutely.' So no regrets. 'Oh no. None. Not for a second.'

A press release was issued: 'Juliet Prowse and Frank Sinatra today disclosed that they have called off their wedding plans.' The pair in a joint statement said: 'A conflict in career interests led us to make this decision. We both felt it wiser to make this move now rather than later.'

Her parents were a little disappointed. 'Especially my stepdad. I think he would have liked me to have been Mrs Frank Sinatra. But not my mother. She said, "Whatever you think is right for you, is what you have to do." My friends knew of the circumstances and thought it was wrong of Frank to ask me to stop. I don't thing any of them thought I was barmy.'

Predictably, after the split, her professional asking price went down. The girl who had been worth $500 a week to nightclub producers was at the time of the romance picking up $17,500 – a huge amount for the early sixties. When it had all died down, she was back to four figures again.

But Sinatra did remain solicitous for the first year or so. In the midst of the Cuban missile crisis in 1962, he rang Juliet when she was in New York and showed the kind of consideration and involvement she had always liked and resented when they were engaged. 'I don't know how he found out where I was, but he called me at my hotel and said: "I want you to get out of New York City because it's going to be blown apart.' He had prior warning of the impending crisis from Pierre Salinger, Kennedy's press adviser. She replied that she was going to stay put. 'You can't run for your life all the time,' she told him. As she said: 'It was kind of as though I was his daughter, you know, being very protective.'

She stayed in New York and wrote to her mother to tell her. Meanwhile, Frank's children had a similar warning and did heed it. They returned to the West Coast, where Sinatra told them of his own escape plans – he was stocking his private aircraft with everything they could possibly need for the next couple of months and he would fly from one airstrip to another until he found a safe port.

Juliet met Frank again when they were both working at CBS. 'He was in make-up and I popped in to see him and he was, not blunt, but very matter of fact. Then I went to see him performing in Las Vegas when he was dating Barbara [the present Mrs Sinatra] but I didn't go backstage. I didn't want her to feel uncomfortable.'

Meanwhile, Louella Parsons reported that the first Mrs Sinatra was still very much in love with Frank. 'It's as if, having given her heart when she was sixteen, she has never been able to take it back. Perhaps that's why she can understand other women falling in love with him – and they have.'

In a way, all that was true. When there were problems with any of the children, Nancy and Frank talked about it as though they still lived together. When Nancy, Sr., had a birthday, he bought her the most expensive mink coat in any Beverly Hills store window and a diamond bracelet to go with it.

One ex-lover said at this time: 'You have to take Frankie as he is.

When you invite him to a party, he may be an hour late or he may not show up at all. He gets involved and forgets even to telephone ... I think Frank treats a woman the way she deserves. He makes you feel like a woman, sometimes like a very wealthy woman.' An actress summed it all up: 'When Frank looks at you, a well of affection suddenly springs up and suddenly ... a Cadillac.'

— 23 —

SAME OLD SATURDAY
NIGHT

The time had come, the Chairman of the Board decided, to expand the activities of the Clan. Frank called a meeting, banged a gavel and ruled that it was about time they were put to work, or at least given the chance to earn a few thousand dollars. The result was *Ocean's Eleven*, a film about a heist of a casino in Las Vegas, which was typecasting of the kind the Clan members were interested in. Richard Conte joined them and they enjoyed having a real tough guy in their midst.

Jack Warner paid $50,000 for the script of what Frank would call, 'Not a great movie like *Gone With the Wind*, but something the public can enjoy. It's called entertainment.'

That was what he kept telling the veteran director, Lewis Milestone, too. In the old days of the Lower East Side of New York, they called it 'kibbitzing' – interfering in everything that goes on, whether it was any of his business or not. 'He wouldn't leave me alone,' Milestone, who first became famous with his epic movie of World War I, *All Quiet on the Western Front*, told me when we were preparing a BBC programme on Hollywood. It was the same experience that Frank Capra had found went hand in hand with working with Sinatra. He took over – to the extent of inventing characters for the film, so that buddies in need of a job could be paid for saying a line or two.

As Milestone recalled: 'When he wasn't actually acting himself, he would say, "Get him to do this" or "Make sure she does that". Ask me which was my least favourite film that I ever made and it has to be *Ocean's Eleven*.' But he couldn't afford to be choosy. The McCarthy blacklist had him as one of its victims and he was taking what work he could get.

Milestone had never before come across someone who, like Sinatra, demanded that scenes be rewritten as they were being filmed. Nor had he worked with an actor who had earned the nickname of One-Take Charlie. Where Milestone came from, it was the director who decided how many takes were to be shot.

None of that worried the Clan members who treated it as though it were a picnic. The New York *Post* had it about right when it said that the cast were 'performers who act as if a mere appearance would induce hysteria in the adoring public ... you wonder who is fooling whom.'

At the same time, the Clan were on stage at the Sands – in the most self-indulgent performance in which even they had ever been involved. The Vegas gamblers didn't seem to mind too much; they were content enough just to see Frank, Dean, Sammy and the rest while they sat drinking at their tables. The 'Summit Meeting' was unrehearsed and unplanned. No one could even be sure which members of the Clan would turn up for a show. In fact, advertisements for it actually asked: 'Which star will shine tonight?'

The group followed the *Ocean's* film, just over a year later in 1961, with their own version of Kipling's *Gunga Din*, adapted from India to the territory of Utah and from the British Army to the US Cavalry and now called *Sergeants Three*. The men catch Indians, have fun with girls – notably Ruta Lee playing the girl Peter Lawford was due to marry – and on the whole enjoy themselves more than did the audience.

Sometimes, the Clan filmed at the spot they had chosen in Kanab in the daytime, worked in Las Vegas at night and had about two hours' sleep between. Yet they loved it. At least, Ruta Lee thinks they did. And she was at the centre of it all. 'Every day, a helicopter would come to Kanab and pick me up.'

Sometimes, though, she would travel in Frank's private plane which had just been delivered. It was a custom-made jet with everything planned to the 'nth degree. 'I remember,' said Ruta Lee, 'sitting with him and talking about what colours would be right. The designers would come to his dressing room and he'd call, "Roots, what da ya think of this colour?"'

Orange was his favourite, along with other fruits like persimmon and canteloupe, all of which were incorporated in the décor. There was a piano on board, screwed to the floor, as well as sofas, chairs and a table.

From then on, it was Frank Sinatra's favourite means of transport.

When he invited friends to share the orange-coloured plane, said Ruta, you knew he was the boss. 'He provided the itineraries for everybody, decided where we should go.'

Sammy Cahn once told me: 'Travel with Frank and you discover that he's not just a great singer and actor, he is also the world's greatest travel agent. He will organise your luggage, have a car waiting to take you to and from the airport, have all the tickets you are likely to need.'

The flights between the film set in Utah and Vegas were frequent. 'They just happened,' said Ms Lee. 'It was all divinely done. One night, it was Frank performing, the next it was Dean. When one of them was on, the others would make a forty-minute flight to Vegas to see him – and, of course, join him on stage. We went for Frank's opening and we went down for Dean's opening and we went down to Sammy's opening and we went to parties in between.'

Back at the film, things were going much as usual. Frank was insisting on just one take. 'He'd say, "Print it because I'm not going to do it again." And unless it really hit the fan, he wouldn't. But he was very correct. He'd come in at eleven, but he'd say, "I'm giving you all the time in the world to set up the shot, I'll come in and do a walk-through. I don't want to hear after I've done a walk-through that there's a shadow here, that the sound isn't right there. Take all the time in the world, but when I walk in, I want it perfect."'

It didn't make him the easiest man in the world to work with. The cameramen and the technicians were petrified of him. 'Oh, absolutely,' she agreed. 'But on the other hand, he'd break up and do things on the set and then he'd have to do them again. So it lightened up. There was a lot of frivolity on the set. Everybody would be tight till he got there. Then things would lighten up.'

Dean had a birthday while working on the movie. Frank decided it was a cause for celebration, so threw a party for him – at Vegas, of course. All the cast were invited and flown out there in the plane. Ruta Lee had a wardrobe problem. 'We're talking about Kanab, which means we are talking about sage brush and pine trees and cow manure. Did I bring any pretty dresses? Well, of course not. I brought a little frock I could wear to play the dairy queen. Now, we're flying to Vegas every night and every night I've nothing to wear. And then there's this big fabulous birthday party that Frank's throwing with every star in the world there.

'Absolutely shimmering. Elizabeth Taylor who was this astounding beauty. And Marilyn Monroe, who had had her thing with Frank, was there and she was shimmering too. But he made me feel wonderful. He's a very sensuous man and he has the gift of looking you straight in the eye and there isn't another thing in this world that is of interest to him. And, oh boy, when his eyes look around the room, they're never seeing anything. He only sees you. Any man can rule the world if he is like that.'

Clearly, in the wide-open scrubland of Utah, sacred territory for the Mormons, it was party-time almost every day. 'It could not have been more wonderful,' says Ruta now, who agrees she was 'like the team mascot'. The men who were not exactly known for celibacy were given orders by Frank. 'He said, "Hands off Ruta, everybody!" There were always girls there. There were planes going up all the time and some of the pretty ladies from Vegas would come up and disappear a day later – that sort of thing. Frank made a rule – they could joke around, but "Nobody plays with Ruta. She is always walked home at night." Somebody always walked me to my room.'

In quieter moments, he would tell her about the early days of his life, about Hoboken, about the bobbysoxers – and, above all, about Ava. 'It was a long time after by then, but it still was a sad topic for him. He adored her.'

If feathers got ruffled, the rest of the gang were there to sort matters out. 'Sammy was so nice. If someone was upset, he'd go round and ask, "Are you all right"?'

One of the reasons why Sinatra was able to get away with all that he did was because he was protected by that coterie of hangers-on. 'As a rule,' said Ruta Lee, 'he was surrounded by family and if it wasn't his family, his extended family, his friends. I think he maybe needed to protect himself from the outside world. Maybe if you've got buddies, you've got people to play games with, without involving outside people, I don't know. It was a sense of confidence. After all, I suppose he enjoys being Pope.'

The interesting thing is that they let him be Pope. 'I think he just planned it better,' said Ms Lee. 'So they deferred to him. If Frank said, "We can all go and do it," they all went to do it.'

But he could also be very generous. He decided they had to say thank-you to the school that had allowed him to land his plane on their playing field. He asked for one of his pressmen to put together a list of the projects the school would like to have supported – but without telling them – so that he could decide which one to underwrite. Frank looked down the list – and ordered the whole lot to be paid for. The cost was $5,000, but he wasn't about to do things by half.

The Clan had a philosophy which Sinatra expressed a hundred times: 'You gotta love living. Dying's a pain in the ass.' That philosophy seemed to chime with film-making, so another project was lined up, *The Devil at 4 O'clock*, which was a much more significant venture. In this, Frank was one of three escaped convicts befriended by a priest played by Spencer Tracy. Here was another of those occasions when Sinatra was prepared to bend the knee to an old idol. Tracy, who looked much older than sixty-one, was already sick – he had another six years to live – but he appreciated how important a figure Sinatra was and the mutual admiration society was in full session throughout.

They both hosted a sixtieth birthday party for their director Mervyn Le Roy (renewing his association with Frank which began with *The House I Live In*). 'You've not only got to look sixty,' Tracy told his younger co-star, 'you've got to be sixty.' Frank, of course, still had fourteen years to go but it was a time when the generations really did seem to come together. If it were good enough for Frank to socialise and work with a man a generation older, there could be no reason not to reverse the situation, too. Elvis Presley, whose music Frank protested he hated so much and whose affair with Juliet had not improved matters, did a TV show with the Clan, wore a tuxedo – which suited him no more than spangles would fit the Sinatra persona – and sang 'Witchcraft' while Frank sang 'Love Me Tender'. He was paid £100,000 for his ten-minute appearance. But the real payment was the acceptance of 'the Pelvis' by a different generation, to say nothing of a different audience. Of the two, Frank's song sounded the more natural. But then, when you earned $4 million a year – an all-time record – anything could be made to sound right.

In 1961, Sinatra left Capitol Records, the seedbed of so much of his success. It wasn't that he was unhappy with the label that had brought him the *Songs for Swingin' Lovers* and *Come Fly With Me* triumphs and had been responsible for a new chart-topping album, *Sinatra's Swingin' Session*. There was a much better reason, as far as he was concerned. He was going into business on his own – with his own label, on which he would record all his friends, as well as his own LPs and singles. With the support of the music division of Warner Bros., he was in business, within months. Soon, he was not only recording himself but Bing Crosby, Danny Kaye, Ethel Merman, Dean Martin and Fred Astaire.

No one expected him to call the company Sinatra Records, but the title was surprising – Reprise. If you analysed it, it gave the impression of going backwards when everything about his career now seemed to be saying he was going forward. But it caught on.

When he wanted to call his new album, *Swing Along With Me* with music by Billy May, Capitol forced him to change the title to *Sinatra Swings*. They considered it was too similar to their own recent album, *Come Swing With Me* and Judge Gordon Files in the Los Angeles Superior Court called the case 'a classic example of unfair competition'.

To boost their own sales, Capitol offered dealers an additional 15 per cent discount; plainly, Sinatra was the winner – he took the lion's share of royalties on both albums. But these were nothing compared with the returns on his Reprise album, *Ring-a-Ding-Ding*. It was a huge success although, artistically, it didn't compare with the product of the following year, *All Alone*, which gave him a chance to sing some of the most poignant numbers in the popular music canon – Irving Berlin's title song and his 'When I Lost You' and the Al Jolson hit 'Are You Lonesome Tonight' which Presley made all his own.

Frank gave a contract to Nancy, who had for years wanted to follow in her father's footsteps. Now she recorded 'Cufflinks and a Tie Clip' and 'Not Just Your Friend' which had a country-and-western flavour – but certainly was not rock'n'roll. Daddy had banned Reprise from putting out any discs that sounded like R'n'R.

Nancy was the guest on his TV show. 'How long have you been in the business?' he asked her. She replied: 'Three days.' 'Well,' he replied, 'if you don't behave yourself, you'll have to go to bed without your Thunderbird.'

Sinatra ran Reprise like the big corporation he intended it to be. He gave pep talks to agents and dealers – or rather, he delivered speeches that Mike Shore, now very much a Sinatra adviser in the company, had written for him. Sinatra would later explain: 'In Capitol, I liked the people who ran it, we had a lot of fun. But I thought we should have our own record label so we could choose our own artists. I went round and spoke to all my friends before we set the company up, and we shook hands with those who were coming to the end of deals or didn't have deals. We started the company and we did very well.'

Reprise wasn't Sinatra's only business venture. There was still the Essex operation and now he also had Park Lake Enterprises, of which he was president, to run the Cal-Neva Lodge at Lake Tahoe, which, combined with his 9 per cent interest in the Sands Hotel, made him almost as big a hotel owner as he was entertainer. The inn bestrode the border between California and Nevada. As Frank joked at the time: 'This is the only place in America where you can walk across the lobby and get locked up for violating the Mann Act' (the law which prohibited the taking of people across the state line for 'immoral purposes').

An important new figure now joined Frank's team – Don Costa. It was with Stordahl that their first meeting took place. Sinatra had a concert in Boston and Stordahl was leading the orchestra, made up of Boston musicians. Costa was the guitarist. 'Terrified', was how Sinatra remembered him, but also great. Later, he would turn out to be Frank's favourite accompanist.

Sinatra would always say that while Stordahl was 'the daddy of them all', and Riddle more than reprised his talent a generation later, Costa 'never did realise he had great depth as a musician and as a writer. He would put himself down. I would shout at him and tell him to straighten up.' On another occasion, Frank said: 'Don could write jazz as well as anyone I know. He just hasn't got enough confidence in himself. He is one of the most talented musicians I know. But he's almost an amateur.' It wasn't intended to be an insult.

As he said, Costa could write down any sound that Sinatra wanted – and do it in fifteen minutes. The 1962 album, *Sinatra and Strings*, arranged and orchestrated by Don Costa, was pure Sinatra magic, one of the most important of his albums in a long list of 'most importants'. Frank sang the old standards, like 'Night and Day', 'It Might as Well Be Spring', and 'Prisoner of Love'. But they sounded newly-minted. 'Come Rain or Come Shine' has never been bettered – by anyone. It swings like a perfectly oiled shop sign – it tells you what it is all about and moves at the tempo governed by the surrounding circumstances; in this case, a Frank Sinatra with energy as well as fully controlled breathing, who wants you to know he really means he will love the girl of his dreams come rain, shine, or whatever the weather.

But the most remarkable feature of the disc is Sinatra's version of 'Star Dust'. Hoagy Carmichael's classic had never sounded like this before. For one thing, the phrasing has so much punch in it, every syllable counts. For another – and it is this that makes it unique – Sinatra just sings the verse; the much-better-known chorus is omitted completely. By doing this, Frank demonstrates not just his command of a lyric but also a firm belief that this is the more beautiful, much neglected part of a song that has much more to say. In effect, he recorded a brand-new song. Years before, he had recorded the chorus only. Putting them together makes an interesting experiment – and shows how much the Sinatra voice didn't just mature but took on a timbre no one has ever been able to emulate.

To those who remembered the amazing impact that had been made by the combination of Sinatra and Riddle, it almost seemed a kind of betrayal not to see Riddle's name on all the Sinatra records, no matter how glorious the sounds Frank was now making with Costa, Billy May and that veteran Gordon Jenkins, who had played for both Crosby and Jolson. 'It wasn't that I walked away from Nelson. I certainly didn't. He did the first single I did on Reprise.'

Sometimes, Frank would use both Riddle and Costa's talent for the same piece. His monumental 'All My Tomorrows', for instance, was recorded in both Nelson Riddle and Don Costa versions. The first was smoother, but there is little doubt that Costa's later interpretation was the one that became part of the archive.

One can never be certain how much of what Frank Sinatra did was done because it was Frank's good thinking, and how much was advice that he took. Certainly, he had good advisers but, above all, he had the ability to recognise just when that advice was right.

Frank's next hiring was of someone else who could provide good advice in abundance – Howard W. Koch. He was a television producer – *The Untouchables* was his main claim to fame – whom Frank had first taken a shine to when making *The Kissing Bandit*. Mike Rudin, Sinatra's lawyer, rang him one day and suggested a meeting. 'I want you to go to Frank's house. There's something I want to talk to you about.'

Koch asked what the important matter under discussion was. 'Trust me', was all he was told.

'When someone says "Trust me",' says Koch today, 'you should give him a kick in the face.' But he went to Frank's house where he was greeted by an ebullient Sinatra. 'Gee, Howard,' he said, 'I'm so glad that we're going to be working with you.'

'I didn't know what it was all about,' Koch told me. It turned out that Frank wanted him to produce his upcoming movie, *The Manchurian Candidate*. Koch was too canny a man to say merely 'Thank you – when do we start?' There had to be the courtship of big business.

'Jesus,' he replied. 'I've my own affairs to work on.'

Sinatra wasn't ready to accept any contrary arguments. 'Howard,' he replied, 'this is the greatest chance of your life.'

The producer came back: 'There are questions to ask.'

'You mean,' said Frank, 'salaries?'

'Yes. Salaries . . .'

'How much do you want?' As he told me, 'I had never been asked that before – and I had never made more than $40,000 before.'

Sinatra, who cased most deals before offering them, probably knew this. 'How about $100,000?' he asked, 'plus car and chauffeur.' They shook hands – and began a career of nine pictures together, with Koch acting as executive producer; in effect head of Sinatra's film business activities.

One of his first objectives, Koch told me, was to try to change the Sinatra image. 'He needed to be respected for his film-acting talent and not simply, as people were saying, as a rough hood. We talked for days about how we could get rid of that image. One of the first ideas was to try to forget about the Rat Pack.'

Another idea was simply to ensure that the parts Sinatra took were worthy of him. Taking the lead in *The Manchurian Candidate* early in 1962 was one of the cleverest things he had done since *The Man With the Golden Arm*. The movie was a deep, sometimes fantastic, always psychological story in which Frank plays a former prisoner of war in Korea who, along with his friend (played by Laurence Harvey), is brainwashed by his captors. Back in America, he realises that Harvey is being willed to assassinate a presidential nominee – by his mother, played by Angela Lansbury. Frank's was a highly powerful performance. 'I think I learned more from Sinatra about acting than from anyone with whom I ever worked,' Harvey told me for a BBC interview a few years later. He clearly agreed with Billy Wilder who once said: 'What Sinatra has is beyond talent. It's some sort of magnetism that goes in higher revolutions than that of anybody else.'

The President was planning a visit to Palm Springs and Sinatra issued the customary invitation for him to stay. Not just that, he also redecorated the house, brought in new furniture and literally had the red carpet laid out. But then John F. Kennedy announced that he was going to stay with Bing Crosby instead. This seemed like the supreme insult and a kick in the rear to the man who had done so much to foster his election chances – besides which, Crosby made no secret of the fact that he had voted for Nixon, which fitted perfectly into his Republican pedigree.

In the end, the Secret Service were invoked and confirmed that they wanted the President to stay in the Crosby house because it was less of a risk from the air. Robert Kennedy, then the Attorney-General, was always blamed by Sinatra for the change of plans, although there is some evidence to show that he, in fact, tried to buck the Secret Service decision because the President wanted him to. The advisers, however, thought it was just too easy to aim a gun from a helicopter. It is also a fact that he always denied the allegations of Mob connections – particularly with regard to the swapping of women between Frank, Kennedy and Giancana – which were worrying Bobby Kennedy tremendously.

The President telephoned Frank from the Crosby residence to apologise. But it was not enough to appease the insulted singer. Peter Lawford, who dared to appear smiling in one of the photographs with Bing and the President, then suffered the traditional night of the long knives for errant Clan members: he was out.

Frank might have forgiven the slight from the President, if something even worse didn't happen a little later. This was the real reason for the break-up between the two men, the President of the country and the king of the entertainment business. Melville Shavelson was let in on the secret by Sinatra himself:

'Frank and Dean Martin were vacationing in Monte Carlo when they heard that the Kennedy yacht was in harbour there. So they hired a launch to take them to the big boat.' They were convinced that they would be welcome, that old bygones would be old bygones. 'But Joe Kennedy wouldn't let them on the yacht because they hadn't been invited. Frank turned Republican immediately. The Kennedy thing was all over.'

Sinatra in fact remained a Democrat a few years more, and continued with an ambassadorial role of sorts – even though self-appointed. He launched himself in 1962 on what became known as the World Tour for Children, in which he went from Hong Kong to Italy demonstrating the fact that he as 'an over-privileged adult ought to help underprivileged children'. He visited hospitals, children's centres and homes as well as giving concerts in aid of the various young people's charities. Everywhere he went, he not only paid his own expenses, but those of his band and everyone else involved. In Israel, he met Prime Minister David Ben-Gurion and planted a tree in memory of his old friend Bert Allenberg, who had also been his agent. And he opened a youth centre in Nazareth for use both by Arab and Jewish youngsters.

The centre may have been for the joint use of the two peoples, but Arab nations were upset by the very fact that Sinatra was in Israel at all and saying nice things about the country to boot. They instantly put him on a blacklist held by the Arab League. Along with Coca-Cola and Hilton hotels, Sinatra films and records were banned in every Arab country.

France was less controversial. He played a show at the Lido in Paris and General De Gaulle awarded him the Order of Public Health, which sounds a strange sort of medal to give a singer. Maybe he thought that hearing Sinatra sing was enough to make people feel well.

In England, Howard Koch saw the tears run down Frank's face when he visited the Sunshine Home for Blind Babies. 'One little girl asked him, "What colour is the wind?" We all broke down. It was the most moving thing imaginable. Frank handled it beautifully, I remember. Fighting back those tears, he said: "It all goes so quickly, darling, you can't see if it does have any colour at all." '

There was one requirement: that he be given 50 tickets for his disposal at every performance he gave. Saul Chaplin remembered the concert at London's Royal Albert Hall. 'The lady in charge said that unfortunately she couldn't reserve fifty tickets for him. She could only find twelve. She hoped that would be all right.' It wasn't.

'Only twelve, really?' asked Sinatra. The woman said yes, twelve. 'Well,' said Frank, 'forget the concert.'

As Chaplin told me: 'The woman was beside herself because the concert was the very next night. She called the manager and he said, "Yes, we did promise fifty tickets for him." "Yes, I know," said the woman, "But it's a charity and I couldn't turn the money down." '

The next day, she told Frank that, yes, she had been able to get ten more tickets – 'from people who were willing to turn their tickets in for you. Will that be all right?' Frank said: 'Yes, I guess so.'

The woman was relieved, the manager was relieved, and the charity was relieved. 'As she left,' Chaplin said, 'Frank turned to his manager and said: "OK. Who are we going to invite?" He never even had a list, let alone needed fifty tickets.

'At a party that night,' Chaplin continued, 'someone was heard to say, "Do you want to go to the Sinatra show? I've just got some tickets from him." '

In Italy, Howard Koch helped him produce a TV special, which did not exactly go down in history as one of the great Sinatra performances. 'By then,' Koch remembered, 'Frank was getting a little weary.' He said, 'Let's get through this thing quickly. We recorded all seven numbers in fifteen minutes.' It sounded like it.

Frank sat on a stool to sing 'Witchcraft', closed his eyes and shrugged his shoulders. The songs were sung to Nelson Riddle arrangements, performed by a trio, the members of which didn't look any more comfortable than he did himself. He seemed to be missing a live audience – particularly when, in the middle of 'A Foggy Day', he pointed his finger at the camera, which just didn't respond the way the crowd at Vegas always did. There was one camera, a large cigar mike, and no production. When he added, after 'Chicago', 'in Illinois', it seemed like a plea for someone, somewhere to recognise him as much as the place he was singing about.

In Tokyo, he became the first American citizen to be awarded the key of the city. At the end of the trip, Sinatra was able to work out that in a tour that also took in Hong Kong, Greece and Morocco, he had raised more than a million dollars, a huge amount in 1962.

Despite the good work, not everyone seemed to like Sinatra. That year, the Ku Klux Klan burned him in effigy, with a note proclaiming, 'Death to Nigger Lover Number One'.

The allegations of a Mob connection were also beginning to bite now. Sam Giancana had been forbidden from entering the state of Nevada – yet he stayed at the Cal-Neva with Sinatra's full knowledge. Hank Sanicola was so anxious about this flouting of the law that he resigned from the business. Frank told him that the gangster was merely at the Lodge to visit his girlfriend, Phyllis McGuire, one of the famous McGuire Sisters, probably the most talented of the sister acts which had been so important in popular music for thirty years.

Giancana's relationship with Phyllis was the reason for the end of what might have seemed to be a much more precious friendship for Frank – that with Hank Sanicola. Sanicola hated any hint of gangland connections, real or imaginary. To Sinatra, saying that he was doing anything wrong was a kind of treason.

Soon after Hank expressed his views on the subject for the umpteenth time, Frank took him out for a ride in his car. The time had come, he said on the way, for their ways to part. He knew that he owed the other man a great deal in terms of friendship, so was making him a gift worth about $1 million. From now on, Sanicola would have control of Frank's music publishing interests. Before there was time to digest that statement, Sinatra stopped his car – in the middle of nowhere – told Sanicola to get out and to take his cases with him. Then he drove off, leaving his former friend to thumb a lift home. They never spoke again.

Frank himself would have said that was no more than a demonstration of the value he put on loyalty. Shortly afterwards, two other kinds of loyalty were being tested to the full.

Robert Kennedy, growing increasingly worried about the rumours then circulating about the relationship both he and his brother, the President, had with Marilyn Monroe, asked Frank to get her out of the way for them. Despite the previous rows, he did so willingly – by making a room available for her at the Cal-Neva Inn. By then she was a very sick woman indeed. Eyewitnesses speak about her wearing the same green dress the whole week she was there. Inn staff say that she was surrounded by bottles of pills and other drugs. Joe DiMaggio went to see her at the inn, but when he arrived was told she was not there. There are witnesses who say they saw him on the inn's perimeter watching Marilyn by the pool, gazing wistfully in her direction, but doing nothing about it.

The really sinister thing about the week in which, to all intents and purposes, Marilyn was held prisoner at the Cal-Neva was the presence of a man whom Frank's pilot, Dan Arney, said he knew as Dr Sam Mooney. Linda Leigh, a singer at the inn, said she knew him as Dr Formosa. The Nevada Gaming Board knew him as Sam Giancana – and they had banned him from entering the state. Frank always maintained he knew nothing about his presence there.

The mobster was sharing a room with Phyllis McGuire. But he also spent time there with Marilyn. It was a period recorded on camera. Frank knew that and decided to destroy the evidence. He handed a roll of film to his favourite photographer, Billy Woodfield, and asked him to develop it – specifying in no uncertain manner that there should be only one copy which he then had to hand to Sinatra. It was a degree of trust not lightly given.

Woodfield gave Frank the film – and then watched him burn it in his wastepaper basket. 'They are pretty sick, aren't they?' he said, looking at the pictures. Later, Woodfield would describe the shots he saw – of Marilyn Monroe 'wallowing and crawling around. Giancana was straddling her and lifting her up ... Obviously a lady in serious trouble and blasted out of her mind.'

Realising that, Frank made sure that she left the inn. At his request, Pat and Peter Lawford drove her to the airport – where she was seen running around barefoot. She went home to Los Angeles – to die.

Frank showed the required sympathy for her in the statements he made when Marilyn's body was found: 'She was a woman who knew she was normal, anxious, in need of love. But a star mustn't show weakness. The public killed her by demanding too much.' And she became just another one of the women in the Sinatra story.

Films still attracted Frank enormously. In the 1963 movie *Come Blow Your Horn*, he played the son of the actor he admired very much, Lee J. Cobb. Cobb was a manufacturer of artificial fruit. The Sinatra character couldn't have been more different – a womanising playboy, who showed no allegiance whatever to his old man's lifestyle and even less to those of his Yiddisher mama, played by Molly Picon. The director was the young Bud Yorkin, making his first feature film and renewing the association he had had with Sinatra when they worked on *The Dinah Shore Show*.

As Yorkin told me: 'He was terrific. I enjoyed working with him. He had retained all the qualities known to people working for him. He had a certain impatience, a certain desire to get moving.'

The 'certain impatience' was what directors had come to expect when working on a One-Take Charlie operation. Yorkin got to know about it early, indeed on the opening day on location. 'We were shooting the opening titles with Frank and Tony Bill walking down the street – Frank walking down Madison Avenue singing the title song.'

Now that can be a difficult thing to film at the best of times and for the best of experienced directors. That it was a challenge for the young and comparatively inexperienced Yorkin is putting it kindly. He had to watch Sinatra go through the kind of inconvenience he wouldn't wish on the most pliable young actor. 'I actually had Frank stashed in a store on Madison Avenue – because it's such a narrow street, you literally have sun at midday for forty-five minutes. After that, it's cast in deep shadows. In those days, films and lenses weren't as fast as they are today. You really had to wait for the light to be bright.' And that was what he had to tell Sinatra – who, unsurprisingly, didn't want to know about problems.

'We had cameras hanging out of the window on the second floor across the street. He had the music piped into his ear, so he could be mouthing the tune he was listening to. My assistant director was on a walkie-talkie talking to another assistant director. I kept hearing: "How soon are we going to go? How soon are we going to go?" '

It was the cameraman who had the say – and what he said didn't please either Yorkin or Sinatra. The director was patient, but his star was not. 'Knowing Frank, I kept pressing Bill Daniels, the cameraman. He kept answering, "It's not right yet. It's not right."

'I knew that these questions were coming from Frank to the other assistant director.'

So Yorkin had to do what he normally would never have done. He started nagging his cameraman, a cinematographer of great experience. 'We've got to really roll here,' he told him. Daniels was equally forceful. 'There's no point in getting to roll if I can't get you a picture. You tell that to Frank Sinatra!'

As Bud told me: 'It was because of the kind of feller that Sinatra was that I got such a senior cameraman like Billy. He was an older man, very staid in what he wanted, but he was a very wise choice. He actually would say: "Frank, the lighting wasn't right. I'm going to need another take." '

But it had to be said sparingly and the shoot on Madison Avenue wasn't the place. Finally, the word came: 'OK. We're ready to go.'

' "Great!" I said. "Action!" '

'We cued the music so that he could hear it in his earpiece as he came out of the door into the street. People were walking by and didn't realise it was Frank Sinatra, singing. He walked the block, stepped off the kerb, flagged the first taxi that came along – and was gone for the day. We didn't know whether we had the opening titles or not. We had one crack and that was it.'

Yorkin, then thirty-seven, had found the project and developed it, which also gave him the title of producer, although he shared it with Norman Lear. Yorkin had lots of ideas for the film, but even before the location shooting of *Come Blow Your Horn* he had difficulties with Frank. 'I was young and full of pep and vinegar. I suggested an idea.'

Frank reacted by putting on his hat and walking out of the studio. The next day, a dispirited Yorkin arrived at the studio to find a message waiting for him: 'Frank wants to see you in his dressing room.'

Sinatra was putting on his make-up. 'Sit down, pally,' he said to the younger man. 'Now let me ask you a question – did you ever hear that I was difficult to work with?'

The director–producer replied: 'Yeh, I've heard it.' There was plainly no point in beating around the bush. At which Frank put another question: 'Did you hear that I don't like to do a lot of takes? Did you hear that?'

Yorkin replied: 'Yeah, I've heard that.'

'And you've heard that come five o'clock, that's cocktail hour – and I don't like to work past that. Have you heard *that*?'

'Yeh. As a matter of fact I've heard *that*, too.'

'Well,' Sinatra answered in a tone of voice appropriate to a *coup de grâce*, 'if you've heard all that, why didn't you get Gordon MacCrea to play the part? He's a sweet guy. He'll cause you no problems.'

As Yorkin told me: 'Well, that got a big laugh and he said, "Come on, pal, let's get this thing over with." He broke the ice and we went ahead and did it. So, in a strange way, there are those good sides of him, which turn out to be better than those sonofabitch things.'

They had a lot in common. They talked about books they had read. 'He was a voracious reader, I suppose because he never slept much. There was never a book I used to talk to him about that he hadn't read.'

Later, Frank asked Yorkin to do his next picture. 'I said, "You and I are now friends. I would like it to stay that way." I knew that the second time around, there would be trouble. I didn't want to get into a pissing contest.'

Frank proved how good the friendship was at the opening-night celebrations for *Come Blow Your Horn*, held at one of his favourite watering-holes, Toots Shor's place. Yorkin's parents were there, too. Bud told him: 'I'd like you to meet my mother.' Frank found a photographer and went over to the senior Yorkins. He immediately struck up a friendship with the director's father, Morris. 'Hey Morris,' he said, 'your son's just great. What a genius! Let's get a picture together.'

Publicity for the movie was the responsibility of Mike Shore, who had been brought over from Reprise to handle the campaign. 'I came up with the slogan – "Art it ain't – Fun it is",' he recalled. But Sinatra wouldn't approve. He said: "I don't think you guys have enough respect for what you're doing." He wouldn't let us say it. I think that sort of complaint was a little far-fetched, but he didn't want to belittle what he did.'

Variety, however, had heard of the slogan and adopted it for its review. The paper said of the film: 'Art it ain't, fun it is ... a gas for the mass ... played with style by an attractive cast.'

Working with Cobb was the real delight for Sinatra while making the film. No matter how big he was, there was always something of the fan about him – a sense of idolatry for the people he respected. He certainly still felt that about Bing Crosby. In the summer of 1963 he and Crosby recorded their first single together, the first, that is, that did not come from a film soundtrack. With Dean Martin, they sang the hit from the film *Guys and Dolls*, 'The Oldest Established Permanent Floating Crap Game'.

Bing was going to succeed in the Reprise empire, taking Sinatra's advice all along the way. 'If you can't beat him, join him,' he said. 'Since 1960, my record albums have been a little slow. I mean, they haven't been selling like the man's. Then the man – Frank, I mean – asked me to sign up . . . It was what I needed to get my record career out of the doldrums. You see, no one knows as much about this business as Frank. If he handles you, you can't go wrong.' But there were those who thought Sinatra was doing too much.

Noël Coward braved him at Vegas at this time with what he thought was some sage advice from an older man: 'I'm worried about you, Frank,' he said. 'You're the finest singer since Al Jolson. But unless you follow a strict discipline your career won't keep going up. It's going to start running downhill.'

Frank decided to take the advice – and sometimes let his actions take unconventional paths. It was the year of the *Playboy* interview. That, too, involved Mike Shore.

At that time the magazine was regarded as the publication men didn't mind being seen reaching to the top shelf to buy. Everybody knew that Hugh Hefner's centrefold girls were the reason people bought *Playboy*. Since it was picked up and devoured – the advertisements alone were the most attractive in print; the cartoons better than those in the *New Yorker* – by men in government, by junior and senior executives alike, *Playboy* took its responsibilities seriously. It dealt with important issues like sex in the cinema, printed long articles on the medical advantages of free sex (it was a decade and a half before Aids) and, as its principal justification for being regarded as an intellectual magazine rather than a soft-porn sheet, included lengthy interviews. Cabinet members, ambassadors, business tycoons submitted themselves for interrogation – although to be fair, many of the questions were totally anodyne and so were the answers.

It was the writer Joe Hyams who suggested including Sinatra in the roster of celebrities featured in the ten-page interview spot. Frank wouldn't agree – it seemed unlikely at the time that he ever would.

Hyams told his friend Billy Woodfield about his quest. William Reed Woodfield was the one photographer Frank had not wanted to punch on the nose. In fact, not only had he proved a good friend during the years of the torment with Ava, he had been trusted with the Marilyn Monroe pictures.

Woodfield went to work on Frank, with the support of Chuck Moses, the man who had the hardest job in the Sinatra entourage: he was in charge of public relations. Moses thought it a wonderful idea. Frank's lawyer, Mickey Rudin, did not. He saw shelfloads of cans of worms about to be opened.

Eventually, Woodfield, who later became a writer and film director, got Frank's permission to work out a list of topics. Frank told him: 'OK. Shake it out. Make it controversial.' It was a Friday afternoon. As Woodfield left, Frank added: 'Let me see it on Monday.'

Woodfield agonised about it and started work at five thirty the following morning. At ten o'clock he rang Mike Shore. 'I can't get it off the ground,' he said. 'I don't know what to do with it.' Perhaps the man who was drumming up ideas and speeches for Sinatra's record company could get somewhere? Shore drove over to Woodfield's home in the San Fernando valley and tried to deal with the problem over the weekend – and came up not merely with Sinatra questions but also Sinatra answers.

Woodfield took the beautifully typed interview to Frank on Monday morning. Much to his and everybody else's amazement, Frank accepted it all and, again contrary to Rudin's advice, signed the piece.

It had captured Sinatra's speech pattern perfectly, which was perhaps only what might have been expected from the man who wrote his speeches. What was remarkable about it was that the 'interview' went far beyond the realm of show business. Frank Sinatra wanted an end to nuclear testing, for instance. He was keen on Red China getting a seat at the UN. And he was eloquent about religion. It was religion seen through the eyes of Mike Shore but sounding as if it came from the lips of Frank Sinatra.

As Shore told me: 'I have a thing about atheism.' Sinatra, the former altar boy whose mother owed not a little to the support of the Hoboken Catholic Church, was asked by Shore if he believed in God. Shore answered for himself: 'I believe in you and me. I'm like Albert Schweitzer and Bertrand Russell and Albert Einstein in that I have a respect for life – in any form. I believe in nature, in the birds, the sea, the sky, in everything I can see or that there is real evidence for. If these things are what you mean by God, then I believe in God, but I don't believe in a personal God to whom I look for comfort or for a natural on the next roll of the dice. I'm not unmindful of man's seeming need for faith; I'm for *anything* that gets you through the night, be it prayer, tranquillisers or a bottle of Jack Daniel's.'

It was dangerous stuff and immediately struck a chord in Frank. Even the last bit of that paragraph when he added: 'But to me religion is a deeply personal thing in which man and God go it alone together, without the witch doctor in the middle.'

Once Frank had signed the article, 'Mickey Rudin made me come in and sign a release.' The interview became the property and copyright of Frank Sinatra, who seemingly would have been the last person to say not just those things but anything at all for publication. 'I never dreamed it would happen,' said Shore. 'I never got paid for it. It was just good fun for me.'

He told Woodfield: 'Billy, they'll never let the magazine do it. I can see the American Legion complaining.'

Almost as dangerous as his views on religion were those about pacifism. The mail flooded in. Everyone concerned was delighted.

By now Reprise was producing more and more new Sinatra LPs with great regularity. Its list also included albums with Count Basie and others devoted to Broadway shows like *Kiss Me Kate*, *Finian's Rainbow*, *South Pacific* and *Guys and Dolls*. *The Concert Sinatra* was the first Reprise album featuring Nelson Riddle, who had to be brought over from Capitol, where he still had a contract. All sold well.

Trouble arrived in the late summer of 1963, in connection with the Cal-Neva Inn. The Nevada state gambling commission decided to investigate Sinatra and the commissioner Ed Olsen personally rang Frank to order him to appear before him. All Olsen would say was that he was investigating the matter of Giancana staying at the inn and had talked to 'the ownership and employees – so you can draw your own conclusion from that'.

The issue was that a gambling establishment had allowed access to someone included in the commission's famous 'black book'. Plainly, Giancana's name appeared on many pages of that book.

Soon, Olsen was threatening Frank with a subpoena – but Sinatra put the phone down on him. He didn't want anything which might be used to try and tie him in with the Mob. He told Olsen: 'You subpoena me and you're going to get a big fat, fucking surprise.'

Olsen retaliated in September by threatening to revoke Sinatra's gaming licence. As expected, the commission mentioned the name of Sam Giancana and the visit he had paid to the inn, the one that caused the break-up with Hank Sanicola.

Life magazine took that as an opportunity to bring up the alleged Sinatra–Giancana connection. 'How he got into his latest mess and how it could happen to Frank in the wide-open anything-goes state of Nevada is a tale that might make an interesting movie plot – though some of the dialogue would never get past the censors.' It was revealed that eleven undesirable names were connected with the casino – including that of Salvatore ('Momo') Giancana. The gentleman had been seen by an undercover agent to go into one of the chalets – no. 50, occupied by Phyllis McGuire – without taking the trouble to book in at the reception desk.

Olsen then took a telephone call from Mr Sinatra complaining about Giancana's treatment from the Board. Olsen said Sinatra's language in the conversation was 'vile, intemperate, base and indecent ... foul and repulsive ... venomous in the extreme.' As he also said: 'Frank called me every name in the book. I had never heard some of the things he called me.'

There was another incident at the inn. A pretty girl called Toni Anderson worked there after having an earlier affair with Frank. She was now married to Dick Anderson, a deputy sheriff. Anderson called for her at the inn one night as Sinatra was walking through the lobby. Frank ordered him out, only to be punched to the ground by the angry husband. A few nights later, Anderson was involved in an accident while driving his wife in their car. He was blinded by another vehicle, swerved and crashed into a tree. Dick Anderson was killed and Toni was seriously injured.

Before he could be called to give evidence to the Olsen investigation, Sinatra resigned his licence and his connections with Cal-Neva. By all accounts, it was Jack L. Warner who had forced the pace. Via Reprise which was partly financed by the company, Frank was about to take up a business interest in Warner Bros., one that would make him a top studio executive (he already owned a third of the stock of Warner Bros. Records). Jack, the last surviving Warner brother, insisted that if Frank wanted the deal to stay on the table, he had to disassociate himself completely from any Mob connections.

There were also rumours that Sinatra was about to vastly increase his interests in the studio. Jack Warner issued a statement: 'There is no evidence or reason for speculation that I am considering Mr Sinatra as my successor as President of Warner Bros. Pictures – or that Mr Sinatra desires to be my successor.' The notice was delivered in an official press announcement – which gives some idea of how worried Warner was at the prospect.

The Nevada Gaming Control Board did contact Frank. This time Mr Olsen declared that Sinatra had 'explained his philosophy to us in a very reasonable manner ... I asked him if he didn't feel that his association with Giancana and people of that notoriety, whether it be in Palm Springs or Chicago ... didn't reflect to his own discredit and also to the discredit of gambling in Nevada. Sinatra nodded at that and volunteered a commitment that he would not see Giancana or people of that type in Nevada but that he would continue to associate as he wished when he wasn't in Nevada. As he said: "This is a way of life and a man has to lead his own life."'

Plainly Mr Olsen's colleagues were pleased to hear of the changes in the inn's management, but revoked Frank's gaming licence anyway. Frank quipped at the time: 'Anyone want to buy a hot casino?' But nobody asked him any questions about his connections with members of the Mob.

Nancy said the reason her father gave up his licence so willingly was because of the danger it represented to the reputation of President Kennedy. Considering the way that relationship had been going, this was unlikely, although he probably did not want to lose the Kennedy connection.

He was a lot better off with the Clan, even if they didn't officially exist. When ABC offered him the opportunity to appear on a discussion programme about the Clan, he replied to David Susskind that his fee was $250,000 an hour. Susskind responded by telegram, assuming that that was the charge for 'a ring-a-ding-dinging with additional fillip of musical lyrics mounted on tele-prompter' and wanted to know his charge for a discussion. Sinatra came back by agreeing that, yes, that was his fee for 'my usual talent of song and dance. However, now that I understand the picture a little more clearly, I must change it to $750,000 for all parasitical programmes.'

Clan films continued. A spoof Western, *Four for Texas*, was more of the same, but *Robin and the Seven Hoods* was a little better, although not good enough considering the talent that was available. In many ways, it was one of the last real Hollywood musicals. It owed nothing to a Broadway show; instead, it was a fast moving gangster film with tunes by Sammy Cahn and Jimmy Van Heusen. There were Sinatra and Martin and the addition of a couple of co-options, Edward G. Robinson playing a cameo of his old Little Caesar role and Peter Falk, who hadn't yet established a reputation with his *Columbo* role. But, most important of all, Bing Crosby had a major part in this Clan caper.

In essence, the film introduced a 1920s twist to the old Robin Hood story. Frank played Robbo, who did a lot of taking from the rich and a little giving back to the poor; Falk was another gangster – Guy Gisborne – who regarded him as a kind of Al Capone about to raid his territory. The music included 'Mr Booze' and 'Style', good, sock-it-to-'em numbers. 'My Kind of Town' was a tribute to Chicago – and the best PR exercise in song to the windy city since the tune bearing the 'Chicago' name that Frank himself had sung in *The Joker Is Wild*. It fizzed its way through the two-hour movie and provided Sinatra with a new standard that would always be identified with him.

If only the movie itself had been quite as good as the fun enjoyed by the Clan, who were once more calling it a meeting of 'the summit'. Someone once asked how all these people could be paid, not in a film, but when Frank brought them into his nightclub performances. 'Nobody could and nobody did,' said Sammy Davis. 'We did it for love of Frank because he asked us to. If you dig Frank, you do things like that.'

Instead, and as usual, some people found filming an unhappy experience, including the director, Gene Kelly, who walked off the set. He was followed by his assistant, Saul Chaplin, who regretted the whole thing, but swears he saw it all coming from the moment Kelly told him he was going to do it – and then got sucked in.

When Kelly accepted the role of director, he phoned Saul. 'Listen,' he said, 'I'm doing a picture with Frank.'

'You've got to be joking,' Chaplin told me he replied.

'Why?'

'Because he won't rehearse.'

'No,' Kelly assured him, 'this is different. It's his picture. His company is going to do it. He's going to need to make it work.'

This sounded like a persuasive argument. 'I said OK, I'd do it, too,' said Chaplin. 'It *did* sound different. To cut a long story short, we all had a great time while Frank Sinatra wasn't in it. Then it got closer to recording time and he wouldn't show up for sketches or anything – and he was the producer. He wouldn't even make excuses. So Gene quit and, in essence, I became the producer. I knew then I didn't want to become the producer. I told Frank I wasn't well, which was partly true. So I quit too.' He never did tell Frank the reason.

Sammy Cahn always thought that the songs were just too good for the movie. 'Style' – 'You've either got or you haven't got style' – was, next to 'My Kind of Town', the best song in the film. Cahn was particularly unhappy that his own favourite, 'I Like to Lead When I Dance', was actually removed from the movie – an indignity rarely experienced by the man who had won so many Oscars, he had miniatures made to carry in his pocket. As he explained once: 'This was the song that was setting the whole film – she is feeding him the booze and coming over strong. Frank Sinatra liked that line, "I'm the one who's going to lead, I set the speed."'

Dean Martin did sing it, but Frank never filmed the number to his own recording – 'I think he was feeling a bit under the weather at the time,' said Cahn, expressing perfectly how everyone else concerned with the movie felt.

These weren't the only crises in Sinatra's life at that time. They seemed to pile up for him in direct proportion to the success of his career. In fact, it was all because of his success that he had those problems.

— 24 —

ILL WIND

Despite the cooling of their friendship, Sinatra mourned the death of John F. Kennedy. He was to say: 'I'm just one of the hundreds of millions of people who carry in our hearts a profound affection, respect and lasting sense of loss for John Fitzgerald Kennedy. I dearly wish I could find more ways to live those words of his: "Ask not what your country can do for you..."'

He went to church, privately and silently. He also decided it was time to enter the public arena and make a plea for all that he thought was still good about America – and about the state where the President was murdered. 'I have heard some unfortunate remarks about Texas,' he said over the loudspeakers on the set where they were still making *Robin and the Seven Hoods*. 'This indicates we are still not united, despite the terrible happenings of the past week. I beg of you not to generalise about people or make jokes about anyone from Texas. Or say anything that will keep us divided by malice or hatred.'

But worse was to follow. The kidnapping of Frank Sinatra, Jr., hit him like nothing he had ever experienced before. Like his sister Nancy, the younger Sinatra had embarked on a musical career. *Newsweek* had noted, early on: 'Frank Senior oozed innate musicality and phrasing and Junior, at least so far, oozes mainly mimicry.' Now, though, good notices were beginning to come. Ralph Pearl in the Las Vegas *Sun* had quoted 'Frankie's' manager, Tino Barsie: 'The old man would never let Junior get his feet wet in this business if he didn't think the kid has what it takes to make it on his own.' Pearl himself thought he could do with some 'beefing up'.

A series of articles about the uncanny resemblance the young 'Frankie' bore to his father appeared just before the kidnapping, with Frank saying that the boy needed experience: 'I mean he's got to learn to drink, carouse, and stay up all night.' Then, suddenly, the plot of a film Frank might well have made himself came springing to life: Son of wealthy entertainment figure hijacked. Ransom of a quarter of a million dollars demanded and paid, with the star making sure that the kidnappers are brought to justice.

It all happened in the second week of December 1963, and was the first story to take the repercussions of the Dallas shooting two weeks earlier off the front pages. (In later years, kidnappings would frequently be kept out of the media to avoid problems in settling arrangements between the kidnappers and the relatives; but no one was yet thinking along those lines.)

The younger Frank Sinatra was topping the bill at Harrah's Club at Lake Tahoe with what was publicised as the Tommy Dorsey Band – Dorsey himself had died seven years earlier – in an obvious attempt to recapture old times. He was just nineteen at the time. A gun was thrust into his ribs, he was blindfolded, and then bundled into a car. Also taken was his friend John Foss, a trumpet player who just happened to be in Frankie's dressing room at the time.

As he was taken out into the cold, damp night, John Foss managed to escape, undo both his blindfold and the tape on his wrist and telephone the police. While Frank, Jr., was being taken to a house at Canoga Park, the police and the FBI were already on the case. Roadblocks were up and the kidnappers were actually stopped by one. But they removed Frankie's blindfold and instructed him on pain of death (literally, they said) to pretend to be asleep.

Tino Barsie, phoned Nancy Senior's home at Bel Air, Los Angeles's most fashionable suburb, to tell her the news. Remarkably, she was able to compose herself sufficiently to ring her ex-husband in Palm Springs. Frank made it clear right from the beginning that he was not standing on ceremony. If money would get Frankie back, he would pay. 'I would give the world for my son,' he said and, cliché or not, he meant it.

He met Federal agents at Reno, Nevada. It was at the Mapes Hotel there that he received a call from the FBI's director, J. Edgar Hoover, which gives some idea of how seriously the Bureau was taking the whole affair. From that moment on, they supervised the operation. But Mickey Rudin remained on hand to make sure that his client's interests were never going to be compromised.

Frank himself took the calls from the kidnappers – although he had been advised by Hoover to 'keep your mouth shut' and talk only to his agents. Bobby Kennedy, still Attorney-General in those early days of the Lyndon Johnson administration, phoned, too. Peter Lawford had rung him and asked for his help. It was one of the few occasions on record when Kennedy and Hoover were of the same mind – although, by all accounts, Bobby's message was a lot more personal and sympathetic.

The kidnappers demanded $240,000 in used dollar bills. There was never any question that the victim's father was going to co-operate. He got the money immediately, while the FBI and Sinatra's bankers photographed every single note (they were all in small denominations).

Eventually, Frankie spoke to his father on the phone. Frank, Sr., had only two questions: 'Frankie, how are you? Are you warm enough?' The phone conversation had been recorded by the FBI and would later be played back in evidence. Then there were telephoned instructions about delivery: a courier had to go to a series of public phone boxes and use the name 'Patrick Henry'. It was an astonishing request. Usually, the last thing kidnappers ever wanted was to have a third person involved. But this was not a usual kidnap. Everybody knew who Frank Sinatra was and everyone also knew about the kidnapping.

Eventually, a 'drop' was arranged. Plainly, the courier had been watched as he made the trek from one gas station to another. Whether the kidnappers realised he was an FBI man nobody could be sure. They were sufficiently trustful to tell him to leave the money in an attaché case (Sinatra had to arrange for someone to go to Robinson's department store in Beverly Hills to spend $56 on a suitable container) between two parked school buses – and then to disappear. The message was that once the money had been checked and the kidnappers were sure they were not traced, Frankie would be set free.

He was, but only after more traumas. Frank went to pick up his son, as arranged, four hours later. He returned home alone, convinced that the gang had broken their word, killed the boy or were holding out for more cash. Tina was to say: 'Do you know what Dad's face looked like? I've never seen a face like that.'

The nineteen-year-old Sinatra was finally released at the Mulholland Drive exit of the San Diego Freeway. A security guard found him and at Frankie's suggestion, he climbed into the trunk of his car, to escape the attention of the press and the other crowds of people waiting for him.

After it was over and before the money was recovered, Frank asked a question of his financial advisers: Can a ransom be deducted for tax purposes? He was told 'any payment contrary to public policy' could not be deducted. But it was merely academic. The money and the people who took it were soon in FBI hands.

The kidnappers, Joseph Clyde Amsler, John W. Irwin and Barry W. Keenan, were found before they could dispose of the money. It was suggested that Frank, Sr., had had infra-red movies made of the pick-up. He later said: 'There was a lot of dangerous speculation throughout this thing. Anyone with a big mouth got their chance to use it, and they did.' Especially worrying, he thought, were criticisms he had heard of the FBI. 'Unwarranted,' he said. 'I think they did an amazing job.'

The kidnappers had spent $6,000 of the ransom, Keenan alone paid $600 for a share in a Honda motorcycle and spent another $1,000 on a car. However, most of that was recovered, too, and also a ring bearing the initials 'FS'.

It turned out that Keenan and Amsler were in the same class at University High School as Frankie's sister Nancy. They were on trial for six weeks and the question of a hoax and publicity stunt arose, but was dismissed in no uncertain terms by the judge.

Meanwhile, the younger Frank had come down with what would later be called the Pattie Hearst Syndrome – Pattie, the daughter of the newspaper magnate whose journals had conducted the big vendetta against Sinatra, was kidnapped and then joined her assailants in a bank robbery, saying she sympathised with all they did.

Frankie didn't go that far. But in court he admitted he had told them: 'I know you won't believe it, but I hope you guys get away with this. You guys have got guts.' It was on the record. His father's reaction was not, although the judge, William G. East, said he would consider issuing a subpoena enforcing his attendance at the hearing.

Amsler and Keenan were both sentenced to life imprisonment plus seventy-five years. Irwin was given sixteen years and eight months because he had been kind to his victim. Before long, all had their sentences reduced and they were made eligible for immediate parole.

In London, ITN news talked about the kidnap being thought of as a publicity stunt. Both Frank Sinatras sued for libel – and collected on behalf of the Sunshine Home for Blind Babies. Mr Justice Lawton said he needed to emphasise 'the gravity of the libel'.

Later, Frank sued the BBC for libelling him on two broadcasts: the television programme *24 Hours* and the radio programme *The World at One*. Both suits were later settled with Sinatra receiving 'substantial damages' and an apology for the suggestion that Sinatra had got his role in *From Here to Eternity* because of connections with the Mafia.

The principal victim of the incident was Frankie's own career. He had his gigs, sang on aeroplanes – it was a nice gimmick when the two-storey jumbo 747s were first introduced – and conducted the orchestra for his father's last concerts. But he was never allowed to be his own man. It was as though the kidnap brought on by his father's fame, and his rescue engineered by his father's wealth, had reconnected the umbilical cord between them, which could never again be broken. Certainly, as an entertainer, he now found it difficult to exist without the senior Sinatra's lifeline.

Frank himself needed one too. Warner Bros. and he were now in bed together as Jack Warner had promised: they had bought Reprise totally and given Frank the kind of movie-mogul office he loved, in addition to an unspecified number of million dollars, although he was not in charge of the films. One of his happiest moments, and one he was pleased to allow the photographers in to record, was when he was able to entertain Jack Warner himself in his sumptuous office in Burbank.

The Reprise label continued to take the best – and always Frank Sinatra was there to supervise both his own output and that of his pals. Perhaps the biggest satisfaction was knowing that his old idol, Bing Crosby, was aboard. There were the other artists, but it was Crosby's comment that must have pleased Sinatra most: 'Sinatra is a king. He's a very sharp operator, a keen record chief and has an appreciation of what the public wants.'

Now there was talk of the two, along with Dean Martin, starring in a film MGM had had on its stocks for years, *Say It With Music*, devoted to the melodies of Irving Berlin (the studio originally hoped to make a Berlin biography but the world's most prolific songwriter – 3,000 songs to his credit – always opposed that). But it never materialised. Nor did a plan for Sinatra to join Crosby and Bob Hope in a new *Road* film. He had made a brief cameo appearance in the 1962 *Road to Hong Kong*, but that was all. The new picture never happened.

Just the same, the old Sinatra was still very much in charge of his own work. When he recorded a new album for Reprise with Count Basie, the title wasn't just coincidental – *It Might as Well Be Swing*. 'Fly Me to the Moon' was the hit track and again it was added to the list of Sinatra standards.

Being a record company boss provided more than a deal of satisfaction. So why not also become a film director? It seemed a logical move. *None but the Brave* wasn't much of a war story and even less of a film, but it was a notably important milestone in Sinatra's professional life. He directed and starred in the movie about a group of American troops who crash-land on a Pacific island where an equally small band of Japanese soldiers has been stranded. They fight to the death – of the Japanese – after Frank, as a pharmacist, manages to amputate the leg of one of the enemy men. It was an interesting experiment. The director's role required, among other things, that he be nice to people and know all their names. The Japanese actors defeated him. He called them all 'Freddy'. He was actually running short of the famous Sinatra vocabulary. For reasons no one was able to explain, everything (and not just the 'broads') became 'bird'. As Frank said of one producer, 'He has a way of stepping on his bird.' The word fitted anything he wanted it to. When he recorded 'Mrs Robinson', he asked: 'How's your bird, Mrs Robinson . . .?'

Warner Bros. had had to be persuaded that letting Frank direct was such a good idea. Howard Koch was the one who put their minds at rest – at least, he talked them into it. The Warner executives were still not sure. 'We can hire a director for sixty grand,' said one of them. 'But Sinatra can do other things that are worth a fortune to us. So who needs him as a director?'

Variety wondered about it, too. 'Can Sinatra "Steady Down" To Direct?' it asked – and put the same question to Howard Koch. 'Let's wait and see,' he answered. 'He's got a chance to prove himself as a director. And you can't direct a picture unless you're there to prepare it. If he makes it, he'll be on his way. And I'm sure he'll make it. I really am.'

During the production, Frank was instrumental in saving Koch's wife from drowning. Ruth Koch decided to swim in the highly dangerous sea around the island of Kauai, close to Hawaii in the Pacific, where filming was taking place. While Frank sat on the beach watching, she was carried out for about a hundred yards by a massive wave. He immediately swam out to bring her back to safety – and was himself blown off-course by the intensely strong current. Both had to be saved. Actor Brad Dexter swam out to rescue them and was also sucked in by the undertow.

In what must be the bravest and least selfish statement by Sinatra on record, he called out: 'Save Ruth. I'm finished.' But he wasn't finished and both were saved, although a doctor who examined him said he thought Frank, now unconscious, was 'exhausted'. It was only later that everyone concerned realised how close to drowning they had both been. 'Remarkable man that Sinatra,' was how Koch put it to me. 'I think Frank would have accepted dying. He had done so much by then.'

Joey Bishop said he couldn't understand why Frank didn't do what everybody would have expected him to do: walk on water. The next day he was back at work on the set of *None But the Brave*.

A note of humour had begun to creep into his handling of the press. In February 1965, he spoke at a dinner in honour of Jim Bacon, an Associated Press veteran who had reported the Sinatra doings over the years. 'I believe, in certain quarters of the Hearst empire,' Frank told them, 'I am known as the Eichmann of song. Now, many of you might have heard that I have in the past been harmful and brutal to members of the fourth estate. These are lies, vicious rumours started by a few disgruntled reporters I happened to run down with my car.' It predictably brought the house down.

One of those people had been Bacon himself. He had been with the crowd of pressmen who had waited patiently at Los Angeles airport for Frank and Ava to return from Mexico. Bacon wrote in 1980: 'He took the wheel, stepped on the gas and the car swerved right at us. I can still feel that fender brushing my pants as we were pinned up against a fence.' A year after that incident, Frank spotted him at Romanoff's restaurant as the writer sat with Humphrey Bogart. 'I want to apologise for that thing at the airport,' Sinatra told him. 'I was madder than hell, naturally, because I thought [a] cripple had been planted there with the light shining in my face so I would take a poke at him.'

Bacon said that newsmen did set Sinatra up – willing him to take swipes at them. Frank remembered: 'I just wanted to get out of there in a hurry but the wheels were turned towards you guys. I would have gone right through that fence if I hadn't straightened them out.' As Bacon said: 'Well, I figured that if a guy is big enough to apologise then he's okay in my book. Since that day I have been with Frank drunk and sober and he's always been Charlie Charm despite the fact that I have printed things about him that have horrified his entourage.'

As he said, the way to make friends with Sinatra was simple: just treat him like any other God. Another time Bacon wrote: 'Frank is going to Rome where the Pope will make him a cardinal. That way, we will only have to kiss his ring.'

The improved atmosphere didn't prevent another bust-up with a photographer, Jimmy Jaye, who demanded $275,000 after Frank allegedly grabbed him by the throat for taking a picture of the singer with two blondes leaning over his shoulder. No one was sure that the girls hadn't tried to set him up (they hadn't been seen earlier in the evening) and there was a certain amount of sympathy for Frank's action in getting someone to grab the camera and expose the film. Nothing more was ever heard of the lawsuit.

He continued to play as hard as he worked and that, too, was why he got into so much trouble. In Rome, the paparazzi actually asked for protection – a complete turnaround from the usual battle between stars and photographers. They said they had been intimidated by Sinatra's bodyguards.

At the Del Monte Lodge at California's Pebble Beach, where Sinatra and Dean Martin were staying during the Bing Crosby golf tournament in 1965, he slugged the 185-pound socialite Richard Osborne and cut his eye. Osborne was president of the organisation running the inn. He was called in, very early on a Saturday morning, when Sinatra started complaining about the kitchen being closed. Osborne greeted his guests with a bottle of champagne. All Frank wanted to do was smash him with his fists. 'I guess I overestimated Sinatra's sense of humour,' Osborne said.

That September, in Malaga, where he was making the film *Von Ryan's Express*, Frank was himself at the receiving end of some unpleasant violence. At a restaurant in the Spanish city a Cuban actress threw a wineglass at him when he refused to pose for a photograph with her. His face was cut. Worse, he was fined $400, while the woman got off with just $40. 'How do you like that? I was the victim of this girl's attention and *I* get fined!'

Mickey Rudin, his lawyer, asked for an apology from the woman, but it never came. The explanation was that he was asked to go to a police station to make a statement and he refused – because he said it would take up a good portion of the $25,000-a-day it cost to make the film. As a result, thirty-five police ringed the hotel lobby and prevented his leaving. It took the American ambassador to persuade him to go to the police station. Brad Dexter said it was all part of a vicious anti-American campaign.

Von Ryan's Express was exceedingly pro-American. Sinatra played a prisoner of war of the Italians who in the course of escaping to Switzerland just happens to take over a German army train. It was a caper movie with Trevor Howard as another of the escapees and has a different claim to fame from most of the other Sinatra films: he dies at the end. The picture was a considerable success, which was a tribute to Sinatra's performance.

It was while making *Von Ryan* that Howard Koch had to go to Sinatra with the news that he was leaving. 'Not an easy thing to do,' he explained to me. 'No one ever quit on Frank before.' However, these were unusual circumstances. Koch had been invited to become head of Paramount studios, to sit in the chair of Adolph Zukor, one of the great Hollywood moguls.

Before he could tell Sinatra, Koch had to get things totally shored up. 'I kept phoning Los Angeles. I was, after all, frightened of upsetting Frank. Finally, I took a deep breath and approached him. He was dressed as a Nazi and two SS men were approaching him.' Can one imagine more intimidating conditions? 'The director said, "Cut" and I went up to Frank and said: "Gee Frank, you've really shot the crap out of that scene."'

He plainly thought that a little praise in Sinatra's vernacular was the way to his heart. Then he stumbled out the words: 'I've been made the head of Paramount. I'm afraid I'm going to have to leave.'

At which Sinatra looked at him and stopped all the action on the set. 'Hey,' he shouted out so that everyone could hear, 'my boy's just been made head of Paramount.' As Koch remembered: 'It was still very unofficial, but he shouted the news at the top of his voice so that everyone on the lot could hear.' It was, however, the best recipe for a continuing good relationship between them – and a chance to keep working together in other ways.

Sinatra's attention was soon turned to the work of the prize-winning author Clifford Odets, who had written stories like *Country Girl* and *The Big Knife* and, most notably, *Golden Boy*. Frank had read his newest work, *The Actor*, and wanted it for himself. Odets had agreed unofficially to write it for Frank, but then MGM took over the deal – but cancelled it before contracts could be signed for what they had agreed would be $200,000. Frank had accepted that *The Actor* would be part of a package. When MGM didn't want the package, Odets was out of pocket. Sinatra apologised and went on to other things.

Frank would never allow himself to be taken for any rides, but when he thought he needed to be generous, he always was. When a comedian called Soupy Sales launched a new TV programme – described by the UPI wire service as 'aimed for children – particularly those with a low IQ' – he appeared as a guest star, sang 'A Foggy Day', wearing an immaculate dinner suit – and caught a custard pie right in the face. He liked Soupy and simply thought he would do him a favour. Another time, a girl from a local Indian community wrote to ask for a toy for her baby brother. Sinatra waited a couple of days, went unshaven all that time, then donned the oldest clothes he had, put a hat over his eyes, and visited the child's home. It had nothing, the worst slum he had visited since his days in Hoboken. So he sent not just one but quantities of toys, as well as clothes and a massive box of groceries.

It was as though he regarded it all as part of the tax he paid to live in the superb house with its $100,000-kitchen at Wonder Palms Road, next to the 17th hole of the Tamarisk Country Club. This was his favourite home, the place he would helicopter to after a day's work in Hollywood. He preferred it to the pad he had in Beverly Hills or the apartment next to the East River in New York. At night he was sometimes spotted by one of his three servants sitting at the poolside wrapped in towels, attempting to assuage insomnia.

He was generous to people who didn't need help, too. Friends who would once upon a time get a cigarette lighter were now given $1,000-wristwatches. Others would find car stereos – a luxury in those days – they had never ordered delivered to their garages. But then this was a man who could indulge himself in everything he wished without feeling the effect on his bank balance. In December 1965 he could assess his good fortune. It was an important month in Sinatra's diary – his fiftieth birthday.

There was a party at Beverly Hills's prestigious Beverly Wilshire Hotel. The 150 guests at the olde-worlde hotel included Jack Benny playing his violin, Sammy Davis, Jr., singing 'He's My Kind of Guy' and Nancy, Jr., singing too. She told her father: 'Daddy, you're not going to like this.' She sang to the tune of 'Tit-Willow': 'The rug he once cut he now wears on his head, my daddy, my daddy, my daddy.'

Frank said: 'I look upon it as the halfway mark. I expect to swing for fifty more.'

Meanwhile, Hollywood offered him its supreme tribute – his footsteps in the cement forecourt of Grauman's Chinese Theatre on Hollywood Boulevard.

Billboard magazine published a 100-page section to pay tribute to him. There were hour-long shows on all three TV networks scheduled – and a standing offer of $100,000 for him to sing for just one night at New York's Madison Square Garden.

Life magazine devoted a massive feature to Sinatra entitled 'Me and My Music', in which he wrote in the first person about his early days in show business, his idol worship of Bing, his win with Major Bowes and then his time with Dorsey. And he paid tribute to the first Mrs Sinatra. 'Nancy is a noble woman; she's done a magnificent job of raising the kids.' Then he added: 'Divorce is not the end of the world. But it hurts.'

He had no plans to marry again. 'I don't say that marriage is impossible. But if I did marry, it would have to be somebody out of show business or somebody who will get out of the business.' He had finally learned his lesson. Or at least, he said he had. 'I feel I'm a fairly good provider. All I ask is that my wife looks after me and I'll see that she is looked after.'

He told his own version of the truth: 'I don't feel that I've ever been a demanding man, but in some respects I'm hard to live with. I live my life in certain ways that I could never change for a woman. I am a symmetrical man, almost to a fault. I demand everything in its place. My clothing must hang just so. And there are some things I can't stand in women. Strong colognes, for example, drive me out of the room. First of all I've got an allergy to them. I begin to sneeze – which is not very romantic.'

Life quoted one woman who agreed he was not altogether romantic. 'Frank is a very attentive man, but I don't understand him. He takes me out, then seems to spend most of the evening talking to the guys.' Sinatra agreed that he didn't have a Ph.D. on the subject of women. 'The truth is I've flunked more often than not.' He said he craved variety where women were concerned.

He gave his ideas on contemporary performers – and the way their audiences treated them. 'I get a kick out of reading what the kids today are doing to the Beatles. They seem a little more aggressive than they were a hundred years ago at the Paramount Theatre when the kids liked me.' It was possible that his memory was letting him down. 'As for the music, it wasn't nearly as good as it was ten or twenty years ago. But it's a whole new world. I have no complaint with the youngsters and their kind of music because we must stop and think that twenty-five years ago we made the music of our era.' And 'the era of cool jazz is gone. I think it's absolutely dead and buried.' How wrong he was to be.

He was forever optimistic. 'I get about 500 new songs a year sent to me and chances are 497 of them will be lousy ... There's always the chance one good one will come in over the transom.' That, he said, was how he got 'Witchcraft'.

As for competitors, 'For my money, Tony Bennett is the best singer in the business, the best exponent of a song. He excites me when I watch him. He moves me.' It was a mutual admiration society. But he had criticism, too. Technically, he said, Judy Garland and Ella Fitzgerald were 'two of the worst singers in the business. Every time I see Judy I fall down, and of course Ella is my all-time favourite, but they still sing wrong. I've heard Ella sing one word, then take a breath, then sing a word with two syllables in it and breathe in between the syllables. This violates all the rules of singing. Judy does the same thing. They forget they're telling the story in a song lyric.' That was quite an indictment, along with the compliments, and there were few people who would agree with it.

He thought that Peggy Lee was 'pretty good with lyrics'. Jo Stafford was even better. 'She can hold notes for sixteen bars if she has to.'

He felt able to make comments about other people because he had no worries about himself. 'At this stage of my career, I don't have any mountains left to climb.' The only thing he had never done was a Broadway show and he had 'absolutely no desire' to do one.

Frank did still want to make Hollywood films, though. His next movie was *Cast a Giant Shadow*, written, produced and directed by his old friend Melville Shavelson. It told the story of his own uncle, Mickey Marcus, an American officer who answers the plea of the Jewish underground movement, Hagana, to go to Palestine to help them set up their nascent army in time to fight the War of Independence in 1948.

The frustrations of making the film led Shavelson to write his legendary book, *How to Make a Jewish Movie*, the principal message of which appeared to be 'Don't', at least when the Israeli Army was providing the extras. As he told me: 'The cast itself immediately turned off the critics. I should have made *The Battle for Algiers*, which had been made before and had no stars in it. The stars were the war, and that was the truth. I, though, had to get Kirk Douglas, John Wayne, Yul Brynner and Frank Sinatra! United Artists said that with this cast they could make the telephone book and make a lot of money.

Well, they couldn't. They lost. But I think I was expiating my own Jewishness in it.'

He should perhaps have been warned. MGM were originally going to make the story, but backed down in the face of Arab opposition. Shavelson heard about it and decided to buy the project which he would then produce and probably direct himself. 'I didn't think I would write it because it wasn't my kind of movie.' He was more used to writing comedies for Bob Hope.

Paramount weren't particularly interested either. 'Who wants to see a movie about a Jewish general?' one of the company bosses, Jack Karp, asked.

Shavelson hired Sinatra as part of his policy of trying to 'unJewish' the film about Jews going to establish a Jewish state. He brought in John Wayne for the same reason. 'I told the story to Duke [Wayne] who said, "That's the most American story I ever heard! About an American general, who goes to help a little country."'

Wayne became the top American general who uses his influence to get President Harry Truman to recognise the infant State. 'I put in the Sinatra role, which was important,' Shavelson commented, 'but it might have been better with an unknown playing it. People might have believed it more. All of those things really happened. But having real movie stars in it, made people think it was all phoney and *nothing* was true, as if the war itself had never happened.'

Cast a Giant Shadow was filmed almost entirely in Israel and followed the story of Marcus, the fledgeling state's first 'Aluf', in effect the general who trained a group of irregulars and turned them into the army which won the war. Marcus, played by Kirk Douglas, was killed by one of his own men at the end of the film – because he couldn't understand the Hebrew for 'friend' or 'foe'. Sinatra's character had a more conventional ending, shot down by Arab gunfire as he flew the one plane the Israelis had, a string-and-canvas Piper Cub, and with just a series of soda siphons as 'bombs' – they whistled and made a huge bang as they landed and apparently had the Egyptians turning their tanks round in fright. 'His was a genuine character,' Shavelson told me. 'He really existed.'

Shavelson's agent, Hermon Citron – 'the best agent I ever had' – warned him against using Frank. As Mel Shavelson explained: 'He was becoming a real problem at that time for many people. I found that with most big stars – that was how they enjoyed their stardom, making problems. But I didn't think I was going to have any problems with a mere cameo, because it wasn't that important and if he delayed us it wouldn't be with anything important.'

Citron was for a time representing Sinatra, too – which Shavelson thought would be the perfect way of doing a deal. 'He cabled back to tell me: "You must be out of your mind. He'll never do it."'

But the next day came another cable: 'I don't know what happened. He'll do it.'

Shavelson was amazed. Sinatra was in Rome at the time, and the director–producer who had reluctantly agreed to write his own film script phoned to tell him that he'd make it easy for him and shoot his 'stuff' in the Italian capital.

Frank was not impressed. 'Unless I can go to Israel,' he replied, 'it's no deal.'

'I cabled back,' said Shavelson, ' "You've got your deal".'

Sinatra flew into Lod Airport, now Ben-Gurion, in his Lear jet, 'the only plane with a piano bar in it', Shavelson recalls.

The aircraft and surroundings used in the film were a lot less attractive. They shot Frank's main scene at the old Tel Aviv airport, now used for non-urgent military flights and internal journeys. He hoisted himself into the Piper Cub aircraft used for the scene and took delivery of the Seltzer bottles brought to him by a waiter. All that was in the camera and ready to be printed. Then Frank came up with the unexpected *pièce de résistance*. He told his director: 'You don't have to double me. I've got a pilot's licence. Let's do it all in one take and I'll take off.'

Shavelson continued: 'We photographed it. I panned the scene and then the plane came straight back.'

He asked what had happened. 'My insurance,' Frank replied. 'I forgot – it isn't any good over here.' So a double had to be brought in to do the flight after all.

Frank seemed to be happy with his part, and everyone else was certainly happy during the night scene, filmed after every one of the actors – 'all determined to out-Sinatra, Sinatra' – had been drinking toasts to each other in 180-proof Slivovitz.

As Shavelson said: 'Had they all exhaled at the same time, the flares would have ignited a fire bomb.'

The shoot over, Frank decided to hold a party – and asked a gofer working for Shavelson's production company to invite a 'few nice Jewish girls'. The man said he had only a nice Jewish wife, but an Israeli Army officer attached to the company agreed this was a matter of military importance. To him it was no more difficult than being asked to find a few dozen tanks to attack the Syrians. He achieved his objective brilliantly.

In another scene, Sinatra was to drive Kirk Douglas through crowds assembled especially for the purpose in the Tel Aviv suburb of Ramat Gan. Everyone expected that a few dozen people would answer an advertisement for extras published in the local newspaper. They didn't want the whole place to be busy, which was why they arranged for the square to be closed to all traffic. But an enormous crowd turned out. Twice as many as normal filled the square – including officials from the local Communist Party whose offices were there. They took it as a perfect opportunity to rain down leaflets upon the crowds, extolling the virtues of public ownership and the iniquity of American capitalists hijacking the story of one of the country's most historic events. Then they joined the rest of the throng, craning their necks with the best of them. Eventually, an area of the square had to be cleared so that the scene could be re-shot, and a dozen Communists were taken off to jail.

The Israelis later threw a party for the visiting capitalists who had, in the course of their wicked commercial endeavours, brought a great deal of currency into the country (and a nice amount of publicity at the same time) and gave each of the more senior participants a medal. Among those shaking hands and pinning on medals was one of the arrested Communists.

Finally, it dawned on Mel Shavelson that Sinatra's desire to go to Israel wasn't merely a gesture of solidarity with the country he himself had helped to establish – when he had ferried that satchel of money to the docks in New York eighteen years earlier. 'I found out why he wanted to come. They were opening the Frank Sinatra Arab–Israel Youth Foundation in Nazareth. No one knew there was such a thing, but he had been financing it since his last visit to Israel and it was going to have its opening the next day.'

Sinatra also ordered that his entire salary for the *Shadow* part should go to the centre, all $50,000 of it. He took his director along for the opening ceremony – and the show that went with it. 'It was all a big mistake,' Shavelson remembers. 'In the show, there suddenly appears this twelve-year-old monologuist who starts telling jokes in Hebrew. Frank nudges me and says, "Come on, let's get out of here."'

'I said, "Frankie, you can't do this, they've put on this show in your honour."'

'To hell with that,' said Sinatra. 'The Israeli Army have lined up two broads for us in Tel Aviv.' Frank was ready to leave but Shavelson was concerned about the consequences. 'You go,' he told him. 'One of us has to stay. I'm doing a picture here and I have to keep in with the Government.'

So Frank had his broad for the night and Shavelson kept in with the Government. But, back in the United States, there was more excitement concerning a woman. Frank announced that he had fallen in love with a twenty-year-old named Mia Farrow.

THE GIRL NEXT DOOR

Mia was thirty years younger than the fifty-year-old Frank Sinatra, but she appeared perfectly right for him. She was an actress who didn't seem too worried about making a big name for herself – although she had already done that in *Peyton Place*, the first TV soap opera to be aired on prime time and to be exported around the world.

Unlike Juliet Prowse and Ava, and certainly not at all like Nancy, she was a Hollywood babe. Lana Turner had come *from* Hollywood, of course. But Mia de Lourdes Villers Farrow was *of* the Hollywood film community, born into it, the daughter of a director named John Farrow and an actress called Maureen O'Sullivan, the 'me-Jane' girl of the *Tarzan* movies.

Dolly Sinatra, who would have liked nothing better than to have Ava living under Frank's roof once more – her proudest possession was a string of pearls her former daughter-in-law had given her – couldn't understand what all the fuss was about. 'My son is just helping this girl to become a star,' she said. 'How many times has Frank helped somebody to the top? This is what he is doing now. And he will do it again ... she is a nice little girl. And that's all. Remember, Frank's children are older than this girl.'

They met while Mia was working on *Peyton Place*, starring as Alison McKenzie, and Frank was busy on the next lot where they were shooting *Von Ryan's Express*. Unlike Juliet, when he said, 'Let's get married', she said 'Yes' immediately. Unlike Juliet, when he said: 'I want you to give up work,' she seems to have concurred.

The *Los Angeles Times* wrote: 'TV Starlet, Sinatra, 49, Near Altar'. It was wonderful old-fashioned stuff – the sort of headline used in a hundred backstage film musicals.

Nancy said that she and Tina had no problems with her. They were like 'three sisters, who shared each other's clothes and make-up' –

especially now that Nancy's marriage to Tommy Sands had failed and she was in the midst of a divorce.

'[The women in Frank's life] were really special ladies,' said Nancy. 'We were fast friends with Mia because we were close in age and had such a lot in common. And we had him in common. Actually, we lost him more to the guys – Monday night football or whatever it was – than to the women. He was definitely and still is a man's man.'

Mia and Frank embarked on a long courtship in which he hoped her career was going to wind down while his went from one success to another – most recently, a Grammy award for his album, *September of My Years*. Tracks included 'Come Rain or Come Shine', 'Night and Day' and 'A Nightingale Sang in Berkeley Square' which he had put on tape in London three years earlier. All gave the impression of being recorded with the same thought (and thought processes) that had gone into writing them, the finest tribute imaginable from a singer to a composer.

It was a perfect time for Sinatra to receive the award for best album – especially when the committee giving the prize decided he should also have their Lifetime Achievement Award. It was made 'for his continuing dedication to the highest of musical standards, both as a performer and as a recording executive and for his unswerving faith and devotion to the beauty of music'.

When Walter Cronkite hosted an hour-long documentary called *Sinatra: An American Original*, he was merely stating the obvious. The fact that this American original agreed to such a project showed a degree of taming of his reputation some people wouldn't have imagined possible.

But then he had no reason to complain. *Variety* commented: 'What was aired Tuesday night amounted to an almost unadulterated paean of praise for the singer–actor–producer.'

Sinatra now was so much more than just a singer or an actor or a performer. He had a staff of seventy-five to run his various business interests. They weren't only employed to manage his career or even his real-estate or record companies, they were helping *him* to run them. He was also involved in a small airline and a missile-parts firm.

The Cronkite television show was proof that TV companies were now showing Sinatra more respect. Then came the monumental, *A Man and His Music*, probably the best thing he ever did on television. The *Los Angeles Times* wrote on 25 November 1965: 'Frank Sinatra gave television a rare hour of excellence Wednesday night on NBC with a one-man performance that should have sent 90 per cent of the country's singers back to their vocal coaches.'

This celebration of what was billed as his twenty-five years in show business could not have been better marked – with the help of both Nelson Riddle and Gordon Jenkins. He covered his career with his songs, narrated the story that went along with it and picked up an Emmy for his trouble. Later, it became an album that has to be regarded as the definitive Sinatra double disc. Everything that he had ever done seemed to be included in this collection, and yet a second *Man and His Music* album followed in 1966.

But did the TV show represent the fifty-year-old Sinatra performing a swansong? To some it looked unpleasantly like it. Why else work so hard in reprising what had gone before? However, there was nothing to fear. He remained the busiest male vocalist of all time. He also had Brad Dexter installed in a luxury office, employed to search for new material.

He remained busy with movies, too, often of debatable quality, which seemed to roll off some kind of celluloid assembly line. *Assault on a Queen* was a weak film. *The Naked Runner*, about an American businessman in London involved in Cold War espionage, seemed to go some way towards salvaging his reputation.

The film was made in England, and the set was stormy. Frank was staying in central London, but the location was twenty miles away. He insisted on travelling every day by helicopter; a car would take too long. When his regular pilot was changed for someone else at the last minute, and the substitute neither knew where he had to go nor was able to navigate in the fog, it meant that a twenty-minute flight took at least twice as long. Mr Sinatra was not at all happy. When the helicopter finally touched down, he refused to work.

Sidney Furie, the director, responded angrily. When he couldn't bring Sinatra round, he drove away from the location site. 'I knew that sort of thing happens on every movie but I got pretty boiled up,' Furie told me. 'I still can't stand that sort of behaviour, even though it's my job to stand it. It's like I brought up six children and I still can't take that from them. As I got into my Jag, my new toy, I told him, "This is your company, your money – and it's your fault." '

Finally, Frank was brought round – with that emphasis on the fact that he was simply wasting his own money. Afterwards he and Furie made it up. 'That apart, he never wasted any time. There was nothing like stopping work to take calls in his trailer like with other stars. In fact, I don't remember his having a trailer.'

The initial row was a disappointment as much as anything. Furie had felt pretty sure that he and Sinatra would get on when they first met. He went round to Sinatra's Los Angeles home after he had finished shooting another picture. 'He was still wearing his shooting clothes. I thought then that he was a man still living in the past. Wearing a vest and jacket in his living room. I thought that was pretty weird.'

Sinatra had chosen Furie to make the film after seeing his previous magnum opus, *The Ipcress File*, starring Michael Caine. When the deal was done, Furie wondered what he had let himself in for. But his own parents were totally sure. As he said: 'Their Sidney Boy was directing Frankie Boy.'

But there were to be more troubles. Frank refused to do sound 'loops', re-recording certain dialogue. An engineer said to him: 'It's not in sync, Mr Sinatra.' 'That's your problem,' Frank replied.

The producer was Brad Dexter and Sinatra instructed him that the picture should be wrapped up in California where he had gone in the midst of production to aid the election campaign of the Democratic Governor, Pat Brown. Dexter said that he had contractual obligations and a budget to keep to and would be answerable to Warner Bros. He would finish the shoot in England and film the ending without Sinatra – some scenes shot earlier would have to suffice. Sinatra tried to fire him, but Dexter said he wasn't going. Eventually, he resigned and did without the $15,000 still owing him.

Sidney Furie, on the other hand, still has happy memories of the picture, and of Sinatra's kindness. 'We were shooting on the roof of the Playboy Club in Park Lane in London when he asked me what I was doing for lunch. I told him that I had my sixth-grade teacher from Toronto in town and I was taking her. "May I join you?" he asked. And he did – and made not just her day, but her life, having lunch with little Sidney and Frank Sinatra! I think he's very sensitive. There'll be five rights for every wrong. That's the key to this guy.'

This was the time when Frank decided the moment had come to regularise his relationship with Mia Farrow. Mia, however, now said she wasn't entirely happy with the idea of giving up her own work, even to marry the man she called Charlie. As she let slip at that time: 'I want a big career, a big man and a big life.' Frank was the big man and there was more than a mere promise of a big life.

Frank, for his part, was smitten. 'I think he was at his sweetest and gentlest with Mia,' Tina was to say.

When he took her for a cruise on the yacht he had chartered – the *Southern Breeze*, supposedly at a cost of $2,000 a day – it was an attempt to show her how much he cared. But it wasn't the get-away-from-it-all, quiet, smooth event he had hoped for. Two of the crew had overstayed their time onshore, took a dinghy back to the yacht, and were forced to swim for their lives when the dinghy collapsed. One of the two, 21-year-old Robert Goldfarb, was drowned.

The man's family visited the yacht soon afterwards – and announced that they were devastated that Sinatra didn't even bother to come out of his cabin to offer condolences. 'I think it's awful,' said Mr Irving Goldfarb. 'Even if Sinatra doesn't mean anything to me, I've lost my boy. I've lost half my life.'

Despite this, 1966 was a remarkable year for Frank, full of all the usual extremes: success as good as anything before in his work; apparent total happiness with a young 'broad'; all the usual kindnesses he told no one about (like the time he found a new home for a musician whose house was destroyed in a mudslide and sorted out the insurance problems and made up all the financial shortfalls); and a facility to get into arguments while sitting at bars.

Once he was sitting drinking surrounded by the kind of girls who wore sweaters to attract attention more than to keep warm. With them were their boyfriends, who, in London, would consider themselves part of the swinging sixties.

He was staring at the boots worn by one of the young men. 'Did you get them in Europe?' he asked. 'In England?'

'I don't know, man,' said the youngster.

'Well, I don't like 'em,' Frank replied. 'What do you do?'

'I'm a plumber,' he replied.

'No, he's not,' said a girl. 'He wrote *The Oscar*.'

'I saw it,' said Frank. 'It was a load of crap.'

Eventually, he was steered away before things got really nasty. At other times, his vicious temper was seen at its most volatile.

This was, in fact, the year when Frank himself was to wonder if he had gone too far … as he waited for news from the intensive care room in a Los Angeles hospital.

It all started when Frank took his pals Dean Martin, Jilly Rizzo (the blue Jew, as Frank delighted in calling him) and Richard Conte to the Polo Lounge at the world-famous Beverly Hills Hotel. The date was 8 June and Dean's birthday. There were three women with them and another three friends made up the party.

Now the Polo Lounge is where the greatest stars in Hollywood have always gathered to mark the big occasions, particularly when there were new contracts to toast. It is quite possible that Frederick R. Weisman and his friend Franklin H. Fox didn't realise they were in such exalted company when they were seated at a booth next to that occupied by the Sinatra party. They were only interested in the wedding being planned for their two children. They had decided to meet that night to firm up the final details of the nuptials about to be celebrated, and were in a good mood until Weisman decided he could no longer bear the noise from their neighbours. Indeed, they *were* noisy. They had a telephone by their table so that, if they chose to extend their circle, they could add others to the conversation. Sinatra in particular was in great form and didn't want any interruptions, especially from Mr Weisman who simply asked if they could lower their voices.

'You're out of line buddy,' he said.

Franklin Fox then said he heard some anti-Semitic remarks from Sinatra, which was totally out of character even if the temper was not. He also said Frank told him: 'I don't think you ought to be sitting there with your glasses on talking to me like that.'

Weisman stood up to complain and as he put his hands in front of his face, it was clear he was expecting some kind of violence. Fox later reported: 'My efforts were simply to keep Sinatra away from him and I did that by sidearming him. I was standing in front of Fred when Sinatra threw the telephone.'

Weisman's fears of violence were justified. He fell to the floor, deathly pale, unconscious and immovable.

An ambulance was called and he was taken to Mount Sinai Hospital. For forty-eight hours he was listed as in a critical condition. His family, his rabbi and other close relatives were at the bedside. Although not expected to live, he did recover – to the great relief of the family, and of Frank Sinatra who could have found himself arraigned before a Beverly Hills judge on a most serious charge.

Frank was beside himself. He said that he was provoked – and there was supporting evidence to show that he was. Sinatra said that Weisman was offensive in his language. He maintained the man told him: 'You talk too fucking loud and you have a bunch of loud-mouthed friends.'

As Frank later explained: 'I thought he was kidding; then I realised he wasn't. He hit me and at once another man jumped between us. The top of the cocktail table at which I was sitting was broken from its base as Weisman fell across the table and then to the floor. I at no time saw anyone hit him and I certainly did not. I looked behind me and as I left I saw a man on the floor.'

The *New York Times* reported that it was not known how Weisman had fallen. 'Police Captain John Hawkins speculated that he might have lost his balance and fallen.'

Oriana Fallaci, the Italian writer, said she heard a slightly different story from Frank. She reported him telling her: 'The cops came. We said we didn't know who did it and walked out. But we did, yeh.'

Weisman himself did not recover any memory of the incident.

Frank was frightened by it all, but Mia was a great comfort to him, simply by being there. She was too young to offer any words of wisdom but he was glad to know that she was his. In the summer of 1966, they announced their engagement. In July they were married – with Frank telling his daughter Nancy that he probably gave it no more than two years, but he was going to try.

— 26 —

LOVE ME OR LEAVE ME

He managed to keep the news of the event from everyone except the people he wanted informed. As far as the rest were concerned, when he boarded his private plane in New York on the morning of 19 July 1966, he was flying to London. Instead, in midair, the plane altered course and flew west – to Nevada. The wedding ceremony was held at the home of his Las Vegas friend, Jack Entratter; conducted by Judge William Crompton, it took five minutes.

There were the predictable comments from the comics. Joe E. Lewis said he couldn't understand Frank marrying someone so young. 'I'd want someone much more mature – a girl of twenty-two or twenty-three.' Sinatra's comedian friend Jack Leonard noted that Mia didn't drink or smoke. But how could she? 'She's still teething.'

They had a home in Bel Air. Mia had all the clothes she wanted – although they were not the kind of expensive furs and silks he was used to buying the ladies in his life; she looked like a teenager and dressed like one. Instead of pearls, she wore wooden beads. This was the era of the flower children and she was one of them.

But would it work? Columnists mentioned that they seemed to have so little in common. 'Now and then,' reported Dorothy Manners, 'she looks up and smiles at one of the regulars. She's a quiet girl who suddenly looks like a young boy with her sheared haircut and her slacks.' When the Sinatra crowd went in for dinner, she sat doing needlepoint. Frank wanted her to join them. 'There's no anger in his face. Just sort of blank patience, as if he had played this scene many times. "Are you going to join us?" he asks, "or are you going to eat that stool?"'

He wasn't beyond joking about her in his act, which she may or may not have appreciated. At the Sands Hotel, he confessed: 'Maybe you wondered why I finally got married. Well, I finally found a broad I can cheat on.'

There were some people who said that the only person to whom he was faithful was named Jack Daniels. The whiskey company were so grateful that they made a present to him of an acre of Kentucky soil where the barley for their product was grown.

People were always looking for signs that Mia might be exiled from his life. Unwisely, perhaps, his newest movie was called *Marriage on the Rocks*. This dreadful film, in which he co-starred with Deborah Kerr, had no significance of any kind and certainly didn't echo in the slightest the last film in which they had collaborated, *From Here to Eternity*. The best thing about it was that the cinematographer was the same Billy Daniels who had decided to stand for no Sinatra nonsense on *Come Blow Your Horn*.

Meanwhile, Frank went on making still more recordings. If Mia were going to be the perfect wife, she knew she had to cheer every opening, cosset every new album. She didn't have to walk far to know just how important her old man was. He played her his records at home incessantly and didn't take kindly to her request occasionally to hear something else; something that was swinging in the way San Francisco and London were swinging, not quite the way his albums were.

But the fact was that Sinatra was still very much part of the sixties himself. From every record store in New York and on virtually every music programme, Frank's hits could be heard. 'Strangers in the Night' was a chart topper such as Sinatra hadn't had for years. And that was its real significance, no matter how brilliant the number itself was.

The voice was deeper than a decade before. It didn't so much swing as canter along. The speed was lively. It seemed to say: 'I may be fifty but I don't have to sound it.' The record was bought everywhere and became yet another of those Sinatra standards that topped the list of the thousand titles he had by now recorded. It won the Grammy for best record of 1966 and his performance on the disc was judged the best male performance of the year. *A Man and His Music* was album of the year.

The very different 'That's Life' was much less melodic than 'Strangers' but, with its staccato philosophical stabbings, another indication of the way his singing was going to go.

He was top of the pops again. Until then, no matter how successful his albums had been, there had never been such competition, what with Presley, the rock groups and the Beatles. But Frank was supreme. For seventy-three weeks, the album was top of the charts – and enabled fans and people who had never bought a Sinatra disc or tape before to hear numbers like 'A Very Good Year for Girls' and 'Mrs Robinson', which nicely demonstrated how Sinatra was still very much in control of what he wanted to do.

Mia, meanwhile, was making what was to prove to be her most important movie, *Rosemary's Baby*, directed by Roman Polanski. Frank sent a note to Paramount Pictures – sack her. They refused, just as he ought to have expected them to do. A man's power was just so much, even Sinatra's.

This was also the year that a Sinatra connection was established with the continuing story of James Bond. Nancy was invited to perform the title song for the fifth in the series, *You Only Live Twice*. She came to London to record the number and enjoyed the hospitality of the Bond team, Sean Connery included. One night, the man who would shortly become Connery's agent, Dennis Selinger, invited the two Nancys, the singer and her mother, to his house for dinner. 'We were having a drink and there was a phone call from Las Vegas. God knows what time it was there. But Frank was on the phone from Vegas just to make sure they were *both* all right. That impressed me very greatly.'

There was a new command over audiences even for him now. When he performed live, he no longer just sang into a microphone, he held it in one hand and conducted himself with the other. Audiences could recognise the style, pushing down with one hand as he sang, as if to demonstrate to himself as much as to the orchestra the strength of what he was doing.

Walter Scharf, among others, thought that Sinatra ought to capitalise on his success and take on the role of a national institution, a singer laureate. 'I always wanted Frank to lead a national TV show on an American holiday, like the Fourth of July, Labor Day or anything like that. But he wouldn't do it. Crosby would, but Frank just couldn't be bothered.'

In other ways, however, it *was* a time for experimentation. He joined Antonio Carlos Jobim in an album and showed there was a velvet touch to his voice as well as to the instrumentation. Even the album sleeve had a restrained, soft quality about it, compared to the shouts of the swing LPs. It was an amazing performance – Sinatra swinging in perfect harmony with the smooth tones of Jobim's acoustic guitar. It took sense and sensitivity to do that, one as important as his own control of the phrasing.

Yet one other record possibly gave him even more satisfaction than most. 'Somethin' Stupid' was a duet with 25-year-old Nancy, whose own career had had a great send-off with 'These Boots Are Made for Walking' the year before, also on Reprise and also a number-one hit. The engineers told him he was singing too softly. 'You ought to sing louder, too,' he told his daughter. 'Yes, sir,' she replied, giving the appropriate degree of respect from a newcomer to an elder statesman professional. The public bought it – by the million.

If there were a novelty in making records that people in their masses wanted to buy, the novelty of being married to someone who was still waiting to be allowed to vote was wearing thin. Mia also seemed less content to hide her light under the bushel named Sinatra. They separated in November 1967. The marriage had lasted just fourteen months. They were divorced in Mexico in August 1968 on the grounds of incompatibility and 'intolerable arguments'.

Mia has since denied stories of Frank being cruel to her, even that there were rows. She says they broke up because of the difference in their ages, that she couldn't be enough of a friend to him, although their best times were when they were alone, eating spaghetti or doing crossword puzzles. Predictably, she says she still loves him.

Both went on to other things – and other people. Mia went to India to meditate with the Beatles' Maharishi ('Meditation is not a religion but a science of the mind'), then to London to marry André Previn. Woody Allen would come afterwards. As Mia was to say years later: 'I felt more at ease with Charlie than anybody my own age. People mostly think of him as "the man who has all the fights", but that is not Charlie at all.'

Frank was never short of female company. There were always beautiful girls around when he wanted them, even though, for the first time in his fifty-four years, the frame was beginning to spread and he needed a toupee whenever he was close to a camera or a lady he wanted to impress.

One of the girls he took to Vegas with him saw him being refused credit at the Sands Hotel. That was when he lost his teeth. 'I built this hotel from a heap of sand,' he declared – and was promptly punched in the mouth by the hotel vice-president, Carl Cohen, and lost the two teeth in the process.

But why was he refused credit? One of the reasons could have been that Frank made jokes about the Sands' current owner, Howard Hughes. 'You're wondering why I don't have a drink in my hand?' he just happened to say in his act at the Sands one night in 1967. 'Howard Hughes bought it.' The people in Las Vegas were even more strongly advised not to make jokes about Howard Hughes than they were about talking too loosely about Frank Sinatra.

Later, the Los Angeles District Attorney decided he wasn't that fond of Frank and pronounced: 'He will be run out of town if he doesn't stop behaving as if he owned it.' It just went to show how things had changed. The hotel later explained that the computer had cut off his credit after he had lost $200,000 – money owed via his 'markers'. He did not pay them cash. Frank, as a result, changed his loyalties to Caesar's Palace, where he appeared and where he now also gambled. But then his credit there was stopped, too.

What really happened was that the Internal Revenue Service had watched men they had decided were Sinatra employees cashing chips and then getting new ones on 'markers' which they were never seen to pay for.

Frank didn't take kindly to this ban either and had a row with an executive at Caesar's Palace, too. This was potentially more serious than losing teeth. The hotel man, Sanford Waterman, allegedly pulled out a gun and Frank grabbed him around the neck. Charges against him were subsequently dropped.

The Las Vegas sheriff, Ralph Lamb, declared: 'If Sinatra ever returns, he's coming downtown to get a work card. And if he gives me any more trouble he's going to jail. I'm tired of his intimidated waiters and waitresses. He gets away with too much. He's through picking on the little people of this town.'

Despite the divorce, or perhaps because of it, Frank became more family conscious than ever. The once-a-day telephone calls now became more frequent meetings. The 'Somethin' Stupid' record Frank made with Nancy was so successful, it seemed a perfect sounding board for the 1968 album, *The Sinatra Family Wish You a Merry Christmas*. Sammy Cahn wrote new words for the 'Twelve Days of Christmas'.

Sinatra was now entering the detective stage in his career. In three films on the trot he played an 'eye', two of them private, one public. *Tony Rome* in 1967 saw him as a private detective in Miami with so many good witty lines in his vocabulary you could afford to forget the story, with its Chandler overtones – rich men, missing jewels, daughters going astray. The following year, in *The Detective*, he worked for the police and was married to Lee Remick. But *Lady in Cement*, in which he co-starred with a nervous Raquel Welch, was the best of the three. He was Tony Rome again, the lines were less funny, but the story better – a search for buried treasure. It was not a monumental piece of work, but it was to be the last movie Frank Sinatra made that had any value at all. Others would follow, but he never really tried again. Why? Possibly because he himself had all the treasure he wanted.

Sometimes, though, he liked to see other people's treasures. He went to New York's Museum of Modern Art. As he studied the French Impressionists, he heard a woman say to her daughter: 'That's Frank Sinatra. I wonder what he's doing here.' The assumption he made was that the woman thought he was a philistine. It was four years before he could go to the place again.

While making *Lady in Cement*, he was once more double-dating professionally – filming during the day, performing cabaret at the Miami Beach Fontainebleau Hotel, where he had his suite, at night. The link with the Fontainebleau was to give him trouble. Immediately after being subpoenaed to testify to a federal grand jury in Las Vegas investigating the activities of the Mob, there was a subpoena from the *Miami Herald* who were being sued for libel by the hotel because the paper alleged Sinatra had agreed he met several mobsters there. In evidence, he said he didn't know Rocco Fischetti and that he had never stayed at the hotel at the same time as Giancana. He gave a deposition, but refused to appear 'live' at the hearing.

It was now election-time again. Lyndon Johnson had bowed out of a re-election campaign and Frank was busy trying to get Hubert Humphrey elected in his place – a fact that didn't altogether please Bobby Kennedy, who had put so much effort into getting young Frankie freed from his kidnappers. But Frank had had enough of seeking the Kennedy family's patronage and went to bat for the man with the reputation for being a top liberal, even though he was at the fulcrum of the Vietnam War effort. When Bobby was murdered, Frank went into isolation for days, as though he only wanted to remember the good things. He then supported Humphrey as never before.

When Hilly Elkins was putting together the Broadway March to Selma, an attempt at helping Martin Luther King's civil rights movement, his aim was to get the biggest stars to show their solidarity with the cause. Sinatra was among the first to be asked – and the first to say no.

Elkins told me, 'I said something bright and intelligent and well structured like, "Well, fuck him!" and Jilly [Rizzo], his close friend, stepped by to say that I was making a big mistake. Well, all this got back to Frank. I was told in no uncertain terms that Frank didn't like it. I said he must be joking. Jilly said No. I said, "Frank knows my relationship with a lot of his friends for a long time and it was frustrating because I was trying to do something worth while and I know where Frank's heart is. And I think his publicist, who was the one who said no to the march, was an asshole. Please apologise for me." And he did. When next I saw Frank he smiled and we shook hands.'

Now he says: 'To this day I don't know why he wouldn't do the march. It may be that he said, "I'm spending ten grand on good causes this month and we'll pass on it." What I said was silly, but there was nothing personal and I would have said it whoever it was. But Frank had a memory like an elephant. If he had a problem and someone had crossed him in some way, it was something he took with him for a very long time indeed – and we know the good things that he has done without any publicity.'

In spite of his refusal to march, the killing of Martin Luther King made Sinatra more enthusiastic than ever to back the black cause. He held meetings in his home. He even allowed the Black Panthers to be represented. The main objective was to get Humphrey elected, although he was also concerned with civil rights.

However the *Wall Street Journal* had printed a story alleging a link with organised crime and Humphrey decided he wanted no further connection with Sinatra. He severed his association with him and, to all intents and purposes, Frank Sinatra severed *his* links with the Democratic Party.

By then he had recorded the song that said it all – 'My Way'. It was to be his 'Pennies from Heaven', his 'Mammy', his 'I Left My Heart in San Francisco'. From that moment on, the opening chords of the number, adapted for him by Paul Anka from a French hit, were a more effective introduction than even the words, 'Ladies and gentlemen, Frank Sinatra'. He would never need those words again. He had had a hundred hits before, but 'My Way' was going to be bigger than any of them, perhaps bigger than all of them put together. It stayed in the charts for so long (120 weeks in Britain alone) that it virtually became the theme song for all the world's top-ten radio programmes.

It was a brave choice, even though Frank appreciated the beauty of the original François and Revaux number. Anka's words, '... and so I face the final curtain', were seen as symbolic but Frank said he took them no more seriously than anything else he ever sang. Usefully, the song fitted perfectly the Sinatra way of singing – always the lyrics in strings of four words – 'she-gets-too-hungry ...' 'Strangers-in-the-night ...' Now, there was 'the-end-is-near ...' and 'I-ate-it-up ... and-spat-it-out.'

People certainly took it as Frank's message of farewell – to show business, if not to life. He himself said: 'I was working in Vegas and Paul Anka came into town and said he had a song, a French song, and he had done a lyric. For some peculiar reason, people think it was written especially for me. Anyone could have sung this song. It had nothing to do with my life whatsoever. Any remarks are not my own, they are the words of the lyrics.'

But Frank fell in love with the piece – a love affair that would eventually fade, although the public's appreciation of it remained constant, like the money it brought. Within forty-eight hours of hearing it for the first time, Sinatra had got hold of Don Costa and the song was recorded. 'It just exploded.'

Three years after that great success, I met Paul Anka in Las Vegas and asked him if he really had thought it was a time when 'the end is near' for Sinatra? 'Absolutely not,' he told me. 'I wrote the words and then looked for someone to sing them. They had to be an elder statesman and Frank was ...' He didn't finish the sentence, but I knew what he meant.

The French connection was not entirely coincidental. 'My Way' was straight out of the tradition of chanson, a genre Frank would take to more and more in the years to come. Sinatra had found his *métier*, the kind of number that was going to dominate his repertoire, the dramatic song whose message would be longer-lasting than the melody.

'All My Tomorrows', recorded at about the same time, was perhaps the antidote to 'My Way'. Anyone who could think in terms of his tomorrows did not, after all, plan to dwell on his final curtain.

And elder statesmen tend to survive – and survive their opponents. That scourge of his existence, Dorothy Kilgallen, died in an accident.

He said: 'Dorothy Kilgallen is dead. Guess I'll have to change my nightclub routines.'

Sinatra meanwhile was going out of his way to show that if the curtain was coming down, it would only be for an intermission. And before any interval was due, he was going to make more hit records. 'A Very Good Year', 'Mrs Robinson' and 'Domani', all on the same *My Way* album, together with numbers like 'A Day in the Life of a Fool' and 'If You Go Away', were the guts of a new disc that rose to the heights, both on the sales charts and as definitive Sinatra material. 'All My Tomorrows', which he had first introduced in the movie *A Hole in the Head*, had never sounded so good.

The end was nigh, though, for another Mr Sinatra. Frank's father, Marty, was suffering from a severe heart aneurysm. Dr Michael DeBakey, the distinguished heart specialist, was treating the retired fire captain in his own hospital at Houston, Texas, but could do nothing to save him. Three thousand people attended the funeral at the Madonna Church in Fort Lee, New Jersey, in January 1969.

Frank without Marty was like a little boy. The towering presence of Dolly was still with him, but for the first time in his life he was without a parent and he felt every bit the orphan. Almost immediately after his father's death, Frank gave more than $800,000 to set up the Martin Anthony Sinatra Medical Education Center alongside the Desert Hospital at Palm Springs.

His new record title, 'A Man Alone', couldn't have been more appropriate. Rod McKuen wrote the lyrics and Don Costa arranged the music for what he would have liked to call a 'concept album' – a genre very much Sinatra's own since he had first introduced them with Capitol.

Frank's next album, *Watertown*, was the *Assault on a Queen* of the record business. The album, supposedly inspired by the small New York community of Watertown, was probably the first record mistake Frank had made since leaving Columbia. Almost nobody had heard of Watertown, New York, and even fewer got to know about the disc.

But by this time, the sophisticated Frank Sinatra could be forgiven for occasional lapses, especially when the jazz experimentation of which he was so fond was now taking hold. 'I've Got You Under My Skin', he insisted, was notable because it emphasised the talents of the people in the orchestra. He was invited to conduct the Billy May Orchestra on three albums – 'and', he would say, 'it's tasty. I'm proud. They've got the finest kind of music and I appreciate it.'

Others admitted they were copying Frank's style. Sarah Vaughan recorded 'Violets for Your Furs' and it sounded just the way Sinatra recorded it on his *Wee Small Hours* album.

But there were problems. Work was interrupted in December 1969 when Charles Manson was arrested for the murder of Sharon Tate and six others, and Frank's name was discovered – along with those of Elizabeth Taylor, Richard Burton, Steve McQueen and Tom Jones – on a list at Manson's home. Sinatra was reported to be out of his mind with worry.

On the other hand, his behaviour to other people couldn't have been more cavalier and selfish. Larry Adler knew the two sides of the Frank Sinatra who was about to face the new decade of the seventies. He met him in Singapore at about this time. 'I happened to walk into a shop and he was perfectly nice to me. On the other hand my brother had a totally different experience.'

Gerry Adler plays the mouth organ like his more famous brother and was playing with Sinatra at a series of concerts on the West Coast. Their last concert of this particular tour before flying off for the finale in Los Angeles was in San Francisco.

'On the way there,' Adler told me, 'Sinatra decided he wanted to go to Palm Springs. So they flew to Palm Springs. When they got there, it was too late for the pilot to fly back to Los Angeles, because in those days they would have turned off the airport lights at the small field they were using. So Sinatra just went home – and left the others sitting there at the airport. No consideration.'

Consideration in his other work had a great deal to do with his own perception of what was right for his career, at a time when he could now write cheques that had more noughts on them than any he had ever received. But it was also a time for consolidation. And for demonstrating what he regarded as friendship. He and his pals in the Clan were still taking Las Vegas to be their personal fiefdom. As he once said: 'I go there so often because I go to visit my money. I don't use money in LA. Just cards. I go to Crapsville.'

He recorded in Las Vegas, too. 'I've Got a Crush on You', accompanied by Count Basie and taped during a live performance there, was a spectacular demonstration of how brilliant he could be in an environment in which he felt wholly comfortable. When he sang the words 'a lovely cottage', the audience burst into laughter – the idea of Frank Sinatra living in a cottage was, after all, quite ridiculous. Frank took it in his stride, replying like a politician to a heckler at an election meeting: 'Do you want to meet Monday to pick out the furniture?'

Vegas was the scene of most of his business interests, but there were a few still in Los Angeles. He had an interest in the Bistro, the smartest watering-hole of the movie set. If you were seen there, the legend went, then you were on the way to being famous.

Las Vegas was always less pretentious, and Frank had more authority there. When Sammy Davis was at the Sands, he didn't have his own celebrity dressing room. Instead, he had a trailer at the back – a luxury trailer, it is true; a trailer with a bar, plush furniture and every conceivable frill that might make him happy – supplied to prevent his having to walk through the entrance lobby. No matter how big a draw he was on the stage, the owner Jack Entratter didn't want a black man to be seen anywhere else but there. Frank took matters into his own hands. If Sammy didn't get a celebrity dressing room – complete with his own steam room – there would be no more performances from any of the other Clan members.

Hilly Elkins, who was Davis's manager, told me: 'Sinatra made sure that next time Sammy played there, he had his own suite. Jack Entratter wasn't a racist. He wasn't going to march in Selma either. When it was brought to his attention that whatever the hotel policy was, this was bullshit and he'd have to stop, I don't think there was any moral dilemma. Sinatra made sure that there wasn't one.'

That was the kind of power he had there. As Ruta Lee told me: 'He really was Chairman of the Board. All the others would bend the knee to him. They were lazy and he found them work, fun, gambling opportunities and all that. After all, thanks to him they could sometimes sleep until about three in the afternoon. They they'd get up and go down to the steam room. They would order pound cake and root beer. A slice of pound cake, plus icy root beer. That was what they used to soak up the last night's booze. They'd have their massage, get ready for the show or for dinner and then start all over again.'

They kept their 'mascot' out of this. 'They wouldn't let me play, wouldn't let me play with any of the ladies who were around. There were always two kinds of women around him, the thinkers and the airheads. When I hear the stories of him and the women he was with, I think, well, he didn't treat them very well. But who asked them to get joined at the hip with Frank Sinatra?'

The fun at the Sands continued. 'May I say,' said Sammy one night, 'as Chairman of the Board, you're cooking tonight.' Davis at least recognised one of the titles sufficiently to use it from the stage.

To Dean, Frank could say: 'Be serious for once.'

'I tried to be serious, Frank,' said Martin, 'and all I could get was construction work. Do you know what a thrill it is to get a hernia at $62.50 a week?'

'I want to talk to you about your drinking,' said Sinatra.

'What happened? Did I miss a round?'

Sinatra was never any less interested in alcohol than was Dean Martin. But he didn't have the problem with it that Dino did. Not quite. There were moments when the tongue went out of control along with the fists, but he was never in the stupor that was so much a part of his pal's lifestyle. 'I know how much he liked his Jack Daniel's,' said Ruta Lee.

So did his audiences. 'I'm through,' he said one night, 'it's boozing-time.'

'One more,' a man called from the audience.

'One more what?' Frank asked. 'I'm going to the bar. I'll be saying that to the waiter. "One more."'

It had all seemed to come together at Vegas. Once Frank appeared at Caesar's Palace – to the predictably massive audience response – at the same time that Nancy was performing at the International Hotel there and Frankie was at the Frontier. The three also appeared on TV together in October 1969 – *Frank Sinatra, Jr., and His Family and Friends.*

Where Frank, Sr., didn't appear, however, was at a hearing of a committee in New Jersey investigating the Mob. He had been subpoenaed but refused to attend. Three months later, the state's Supreme Court would decide that he had no alternative but to go. But Frank thought there *was* an alternative. He could just decide not to visit New Jersey again. That would make things difficult when he wanted to see his mother or visit his father's grave. But he could solve those problems, too. He built a five-bedroomed house for Dolly in Palm Springs and said he was going to bring Marty's remains out west, too. Meanwhile, the New Jersey authorities issued an arrest warrant.

It was not an easy introduction to the 1970s. But then the seventies were not going to be altogether easy anyway.

— 27 —

SOMETHING STUPID

It was as though the change of decade changed everything for Frank Sinatra, too. You didn't have to be very observant to realise that the perfectionist who pronounced every syllable as though he were reading the Declaration of Independence, wasn't caring so much any more. Why else make *Dirty Dingus Magee*, which perhaps even he didn't remember much about once it was in the can? The 1970 movie had him playing a robber with a twinkle in his eye and gold in his heart, in a ridiculous story that was released by MGM, probably against their better judgment.

Bosley Crowther wrote in the *New York Times*: '... it is provoking – nay, disturbing and depressing beyond belief – to see this acute and awesome figure turning up time and again in strangely tricky and trashy motion pictures that add nothing to the social edification and encouragement of man. One after another of his pictures in the past several years has been a second- or third-rate achievement in dramatic content and cinema artistry, and the only thing to be said for a few of them is that they have galvanised and gratified some elements that prefer lurid action and bravado to solid commentary and sense.'

He was right, of course, but he could also have remembered *The Man With the Golden Arm* and *The Manchurian Candidate*, to say nothing of the Oscar-winning performance as Maggio. And Crowther did remember *Suddenly*, which he had praised at the time – so much so that Sinatra sent him a letter saying, 'Glad to have you on my team'. As the writer noted: 'That did it. I've had misgivings about Mr Sinatra ever since.'

There was talk now of Frank making a top new Hollywood musical called *The Little Prince*, based on a thirty-year-old French best-seller about a crashed aircraft pilot who is convinced by a nine-year-old boy that life is worth living. A score was in hand by Alan Jay Lerner and Frederick Loewe. But it all seemed like hard work, besides which,

Frank wasn't talking to Stanley Donen, who was due to direct. There was also the problem that Hollywood had stopped making new musicals in any real way.

He still appeared on TV because no one asked him to do more than sing the songs he enjoyed singing and it didn't require rehearsals. So was he relaxing, taking it easy before something big? Nobody had any real answers.

Neither could anyone now, any more than before, explain his bad temper. When he travelled and stayed at hotels he still took a whole floor. Once he got off on the wrong one and started shouting at everybody he saw walking around there. 'Get off my floor,' he commanded one poor matron and was about to launch into his usual vocabulary when the mistake was pointed out to him.

In Las Vegas, he was equally self-centred. A glass door at Caesar's Palace shattered when Frank, having some fun with one or other broad, charged into it in the golf cart he had been driving through the lobby. There were threats of more fists if anyone made any trouble.

The trouble with Frank Sinatra was that he seemed to need those fights, verbal as well as physical, as much as he needed to eat or drink. It wasn't just a violent streak. Much of it was the old insecurity that came from his Hoboken days. He was sure there was somebody out there who was not as impressed with him as he was himself.

The big things that pleased him now had nothing to do with his career, a word that no longer really seemed to apply. It was as though the guy who had pursued *From Here to Eternity* like another Ava Gardner had decided he had now done it all and if there were motions to go through, he would do so, but not much more. He taped TV programmes in London because he wanted to be in England. He flew in in his new private plane, *Sunbird*, and lived in the apartment he had now bought for himself close to the American Embassy in Grosvenor Square – he had painted it the same colour as his aeroplane; his favourite, orange – and was entertained at the residence of the Ambassador, Walter Annenberg.

His musical abilities were much less cause for challenge than his movies or his general behaviour. And when he sang now, even though the voice may have been less smooth and lyrical, he could compensate for the fact with an attack that was like a musical bulldozer; still in tune, but punching songs in a way he had never done before. He still phrased perfectly, never missing a note or a syllable, but made up for lost voice with new verve.

At his Royal Festival Hall concert, he was at his finest. He sang 'One for My Baby' – 'the daddy of all saloon songs' – and warned his band, 'I'm gonna make 'em cry a little'. Whether they actually cried because of his lyrics or because they knew they were watching a remarkable performance is hard to determine.

When it was all over, he went to New Jersey because he no longer had any alternative. He now faced the committee looking into organised crime. He agreed, when even Mickey Rudin saw no alternative, that he would give evidence to the state's investigation, but he would only do it at midnight. It was a ruse he had used before and for the same reason – because he didn't want any publicity.

Keeping the story of the New Jersey investigation out of the papers was, however, more than he could deal with. There were questions about Willie Moretti and Meyer Lansky – he admitted he had met them, but they weren't pals. Giancana and Skinny D'Amato? He agreed they knew each other, but that didn't mean he was in business with them in any definition of the term. Neither did he know anything about the Mafia or the Cosa Nostra. The committee decided there was no evidence of any Mafia involvement.

The final question he was asked was: 'Mr Sinatra, was that really you running for the train at the end of *Von Ryan's Express*?'

Rudin dismissed the whole appearance as 'a complete bullshit questioning session'. Nevertheless, there were headlines about Sinatra and the Mafia. And there were other headlines in the summer of 1970: 'SINATRA BACKS REPUBLICANS'.

The lifelong Democrat had switched allegiances and decided to support Ronald Reagan for Governor of California. He had earlier backed Reagan against the other Republican contender in the primaries, Jesse Unruh, and now, with the nomination secured for his fellow Hollywood actor, he was with him all the way in the main election. Sinatra said he supported the party platform on most things, except abortion, and hoped they would come closer to the centre of the political scene. But it was a very personal thing, stemming as much from his residual hatred for the snubs of the Kennedys as from his support for the man he was for the first time calling 'Ronnie'.

Shirley MacLaine said she thought it was just the way Frank was, changing his mind with 'alarming speed', as she put it in her autobiography. He hated Nixon, she said, 'with deep vitriol' but then before long would campaign for him. It was almost the same story with Reagan. 'A stupid bore who couldn't get a job in pictures,' was how she said Sinatra had described him. As for Nancy Reagan, 'a dumb broad with fat ankles who couldn't act'. Now, though, he was blowing the Reagan horn almost as loud as the Sinatra one.

In between the political exercises, however, he liked to show that he was still very much in evidence in his own profession. He might be taking other things at a slower speed now, but that didn't mean that his industry should forget all that he had done. In April 1971, the Academy of Motion Picture Arts and Sciences gave him their special Oscar – the Jean Hersholt Humanitarian Award. It had to be regarded as justified. Frank Sinatra may have slugged more people in real life than most stars signed genuine autographs, but he had also done more for those in need than anyone could contemplate.

Frank appreciated the award and used the presentation that Oscar night – which had none of the agony of waiting that had come with the award for *From Here to Eternity* – to be modest. He didn't see why you had to be well known to get an award for helping people. 'If your name is John Doe and you work night and day doing things for your helpless neighbours, what you get for your effort is tired. So Mr and Mrs Doe and all of you who give of yourselves to those who carry too big a burden to make it on their own, I want you to reach out and take your share of this because if I have earned it, so too have you.'

That Frank had earned this particular Oscar was very evident that year, a time when he still rallied to the side of people in need when others might think that any kind of intervention was unnecessary. About this time, he rang the veteran band leader and arranger Lennie Hayton, who was terminally ill. It was the usual convivial Sinatra voice which had a magic way of talking to people whom he knew were dealing with insuperable odds. He had a problem, Frank said. Could Hayton rewrite the arrangements for his hit, 'Something In The Way She Moves'? In fact, Sinatra didn't need new arrangements. 'It wasn't because he didn't like the one he had,' Hayton's wife Lena Horne recalled, 'but he knew how ill Lennie was and he wanted him to keep writing.'

When the musician was dying, Sinatra sent his plane to take Lena to the hospital more quickly than she would otherwise have been able to manage. 'At the time of his death, he was a wonderful friend. You don't forget.'

The Academy Award was as much as anything else for all those Lennie Haytons he had helped. But if the special Oscar was undoubt-edly well deserved, did it also mark a valediction? On 13 June 1971, at a benefit concert for the Motion Picture and Television Relief Fund in Hollywood, Frank Sinatra announced what had only been hinted at for the past six months: he was retiring. It was going to be his last show.

LITTLE WHITE LIES

The news, strangely enough, didn't shock. Frank Sinatra was fifty-five years old, looking maturer, but in good health (he vociferously denied that illness was the reason for his retirement) and singing almost as brilliantly as he ever had.

But people close to Frank had been expecting it for some time. Maybe all those poor-quality films were an indication of how much he needed a break. Yet with his music, there still seemed to be no reason at all to go. Those who only saw – and heard – Sinatra the singer imagined he was on top of the mountain still. There was no reason to quit. Every Sinatra appearance was, as far as they were concerned, still a moment to treasure.

True, he made love to the microphone differently now – with the round bauble at the top of the silver stalk close to his lips, his head bowed, his eyes closed. But what came out was vibrant and melodic. Slightly rough around the edges perhaps, more breathless (you could now hear the intake of air at the end of words), less swingy, but he had created a new singing style that was still unmistakably Sinatra and unmistakably great.

The records were coming less frequently, but in concert, he still sang pressing down with his hand as though there were a spring under it. This stage technique had been eased by an operation to release his hand which had become bent, almost claw-like. The surgery for Dupuyten's syndrome was successful, although he said it 'hurt like hell'. Now the hand was able to open normally, although a finger-joint continued to give a few problems.

Despite this minor handicap, you still got the impression that every gesture added to the seriousness of what he performed – as though it were all part of the phrasing. That was the secret of those concerts. As he said twenty years later, 'Performing live is the way I like to do it – nothing beats the electricity of a hot band and interplay between audience and vocalist.' Indeed, he had that interplay and the finest musicians at his disposal every time, particularly when Don Costa was fronting the orchestra. But in a way Frank himself was the only instrumentalist, equipped with the voice that sang the songs and also controlled the audience. For he didn't merely sing. He dominated. He controlled. He charmed. He manipulated. He used his *power*. And every time he made a record, he made it sound as if it wasn't just him and his orchestra, but him, the orchestra and an unseen crowd of millions still interplaying with him.

Don Costa had helped, almost as much as had Nelson Riddle or Axel Stordahl. Costa had the advantage of taking on an established superstar hit-maker. Riddle had had to create a new singer from a has-been; Stordahl had had to work to keep Frank and his record contract in partnership.

Frank said of Costa: 'He always added something to what the other boys missed or didn't realise.' But it was Sinatra who really counted and in those days he missed nothing.

When he sang, it was the old Sinatra way with words that might not have always impressed their creators, but seemed to excite the listeners every time. Sometimes they knew what he was going to say – the lady was still going to be a chick if she wasn't a broad – sometimes he would surprise. When audiences listening to 'It Happened in Monterey' first heard him sing about 'big fat lips as red as wine', they shrieked with delight.

'You know what ... you're a gasser,' he sang in the midst of 'I won't dance'. Fortunately, Oscar Hammerstein II was safely dead. 'Hey! Jealous Lover' had to include the words, 'oh the pizza's murder'. He hated the coffee he'd been given and complained about that, too – as part of the lyric.

Despite his antics with their lyrics, he took it as his duty to praise the men who gave him the words he mangled to such effect. 'A great song by Harold Arlen,' he would say and the crowd would shout and clap. They loved his rendition of 'My Funny Valentine' – and so did he. 'Isn't that a great song,' he'd say. 'I'd like a piece of that song. I'd like to have a piece of *me*!'

When he sang 'I Get a Kick Out of You', they knew he would sing about riding high with some chick in a plane. But they looked excitedly for variations. If he sang that 'the only exception I know is the case' he had to add, '... Case? Let's buy one.' And it was never 'Just one of those things'. It turned out to be 'one of those mothery nights ...' In

'South of the Border', he changed the dictionary. The smile was 'a-pon' her face, not 'upon'. But, then, that was the song in which he thought it superfluous to sing 'down Mexico way' when just '... Mexico way' was enough. Sometimes he turned old songs into totally brand-new ones. Eddie Cantor's opus, 'Yes Sir, That's My Baby' was re-scored and rephrased to become in effect a totally new number that its writer Walter Donaldson would probably never have recognised.

He would say he was going to sing the kind of thing he had in his *Wee Small Hours* album. The folks who still had dogeared copies of that record on their shelves stood up, clapped and whistled. But this wasn't going to be the stand-up-whistling kind of song. It was going to be 'quiet ... boy-girl music, smoochy stuff, necking kind of jazz ... I ain't about to bum-rap that kind of action either, you know. That's beau-oo-tiful.'

He asked for lights on Bill Miller, his pianist, who was a drinking man. He thought it would be useful for people to be able 'to see his complexion. Sometimes he gets so drunk I can hardly see him.'

They loved it. But did *he* still love it? There was the feeling abroad that he had had enough. All the old back-biting had got to him. Everyone knew he didn't want to get out of bed before most other people's lunch-time. Yet he was still at the very top, even if his record sales were only a fraction of what they had been. That was how he wanted to be remembered.

So he announced, via the columnist Suzy – the only female member of the journalistic profession to whom he would give a polite time of day – that he was giving it all up. 'I wish to announce, effective immediately, my retirement from the entertainment world and public life. For over three decades I have had the great and good fortune to enjoy a rich, rewarding and deeply satisfying career as an entertainer and public figure.

'Through the years people have been wonderfully warm and generous in their acceptance of my efforts. My work has taken me to almost every corner of the world and privileged me to learn by direct experience how alike all people really are – the common bonds that tie all men and women of whatever colour, creed, religion, age or social status to one another; the things mankind has in common that the language of music, perhaps more than any other, communicates and evokes.

'It has been a fruitful, busy, uptight, loose, sometimes boisterous, occasionally sad, but always exciting three decades.'

If more explanations were needed, he offered this: 'There has been little time for reflectional [the man with such respect for words still wasn't beyond making up a few of his own] reading, self-explanation, and that need every thinking man has for a fallow period, a long phase in which to seek a better understanding of the vast transforming changes now taking place everywhere in the world.'

The headline writers had never been happier. They used all the usual variants on 'Bye Bye Baby and Amen', 'Is it the final curtain?' and, most imaginatively, 'Come Cry with Me'. *Time* magazine headed its feature simply with the words, 'The Chairman Emeritus'. James Green in the London *Evening News* said it as well as anyone: 'Today the king abdicates'.

Indeed, the sort of publicity the occasion aroused was like that which would have greeted the decision of a more conventional monarch to give up his throne – and a good deal more than most kings would have received.

Green speculated that the retirement had something to do with the recent death of Jack Entratter, at the age of fifty-seven, when he was active and by all accounts in good health. True or not, the news was greeted with incredulity – not least in his favourite watering-holes. At Jilly's restaurant in New York, a waiter said how sad he was. 'A great entertainer – and a great tipper.'

As the New York *Daily News* reported on the day of the farewell concert in Los Angeles: 'A career that began in the early 1940s with bobbysoxers shrieking in New York's Paramount Theatre comes to a close tonight with the superstars of show business giving the accolade. It is his last performance. So says Frank Sinatra. Many doubt whether he can endure the tranquil life any more than the other great entertainers who have "retired" quite briefly in the past.' Could the career really have concluded for the man who had made fifty-eight films and recorded a hundred albums, nearly two thousand songs?

His retirement show was star-studded even by Hollywood standards. Princess Grace was patron. Vice-President Spiro Agnew and his wife were there, as was Henry Kissinger and the Reagans.

Danny Kaye was on the entertainers' list and so was Bob Hope, of course. Barbra Streisand was introduced by David Frost. Pearl Bailey sang 'Hello Dolly' and everybody knew she would rather have sung 'Hello Frankie' – except she knew that 'hello' wasn't appropriate that night.

Rosalind Russell hoped that she was speaking for the Sinatra fans when she said: 'He's worked long and hard for us with his head and his voice and especially his heart. But it's time to put back the Kleenex and stifle the sob, for we still have the man, we still have the blue eyes, those wonderful blue eyes, that smile. For one last time we have the man, the greatest entertainer of the twentieth century.'

Frank sang 'I've Got You Under My Skin' and all the other standards. He concluded with his favourite saloon song, 'Angel Eyes', and then pronounced his 'last words' – simply: 'Excuse me while I disappear.'

The lights went down and the audience was left standing, clapping in the darkness. Then the lights came up again – and he was gone.

— 29 —

NICE 'N' EASY

Perhaps that was the great secret of Sinatra's success, encapsulated in a single night: the man who hated journalists, had met mobsters, who hit people in restaurants was still considered to have so much talent that nothing could overshadow him.

Later, he told *TV Guide* that he had been forced to take the step of retiring. 'People were always spiritually peeking in my windows.' He said he planned to make it to the year 2000 at least and was going to spend a lot of time painting – which he did. He played golf, honoured friends at 'roasts' organised by the Friars Club and helped old entertainers to insult their contemporaries in the spirit of good fun.

Frank said that 'the time had come to take a breather' and that he was fortunate enough to be able to do so. There were suggestions that he was going to teach. Jim Mahoney, his press agent, said: 'I don't know of any professorship, but he may be open for one.'

The helicopter was still parked outside the pink-painted Palm Springs house. His private plane was at the airport. The doormat still invited visitors to 'Go Away' – a more polite message than he would have been likely to give in person. Another sign under the doorbell was even more charmingly Sinatraesque: 'If you haven't been invited, you had better have a damn good reason for ringing this bell.' People still knew to their cost that he meant it. More benignly, his Chinese chef was instructed to make the usual Italian dinner – there was no reason to alter certain habits of a lifetime.

He still went around having his affairs. At about this time I was researching a project on Harry Cohn. His widow Joan, recently divorced from the British actor Laurence Harvey, spoke freely, as we have seen, about *From Here to Eternity* but was feeling somewhat bruised the day we met. 'I've just rescued myself from Frank Sinatra,' she said. 'The bastard wanted to go to bed with me. I know what that would have meant – becoming his property. I wasn't going to do that. Harry

[Cohn] always let me have my own way. Frank? Never.'

Predictably, he was asked who he thought ought to play the lead in *The Godfather*. Unpredictably, he replied, 'Me'. The idea was never considered seriously, yet serious consideration was given to a Sinatra political connection – Sinatra, the Republican. Ruta Lee was among those who were amazed at the change. Speaking as a staunch Republican herself, she told me: 'Frank was a hell-bent-for-leather Democrat. There was just no way he was anything else and we used to argue, although I just wasn't wise enough to argue politics with him. He always seemed to know what he was saying. But when he made the switch it was very intriguing for me.'

This was a woman who was so well in with the Republican Establishment that she dated Henry Kissinger from time to time. Now, she was doing a lot of campaigning for the Nixon–Agnew team as they came up to the 1972 election, and was amazed to hear that Frank Sinatra was joining the set. It had a lot to do with his friendship with Vice-President Spiro Agnew.

'He was so close to Agnew,' said Ms Lee, 'that we started seeing a lot of each other in Palm Springs. Frank would say, "Come on over, we're doing dinner tonight and we're going to run a movie. Judy and Spiro are here ... So that was how *I* got to know the Agnews quite well.'

She has no doubt why Frank became a Republican. 'I think he was very, very hurt by the Kennedys. And underneath it all, I think that he's somewhat of a conservative even though he espoused a lot of Democrat causes. He recognised an old friend in Ronnie Reagan.'

Now, the old conversations about broads and booze changed to discussions about Republicanism, she remembered. 'I was an ongoing guest and I think he liked the fact that I could do something more than just look airheaded. It got to the point where, thanks to Frank, I debated with Warren Beatty and Dennis Weaver.'

Much of the switch did have to do with the fact that Sinatra never forgave his absences from the Kennedy White House, but there was also what happened afterwards. Lyndon B. Johnson was never a Sinatra fan. The doors of the mansion were firmly shut during the LBJ years. The President liked his entertainers to be western singers who would join him while he sat on the toilet and Frank who, despite it all, had thoroughly enjoyed the elegance of Camelot, drew the line there.

He liked the support of Reagan with whom he had never acted in

Hollywood, but who he knew was going to go further than the Californian state capital of Sacramento. When Reagan said: 'Frank, you are living proof that life does begin when you begin to serve,' it sounded like an invitation to big things to come.

The newly-elected Governor showed his appreciation by making a personal appearance of his own – when Frank and Dolly finally opened the Martin Anthony Sinatra Medical Education Center in Palm Springs. He and Nancy were guests of honour along with Agnew.

Spiro Agnew seemed to have become a permanent fixture in Sinatra's life. When the Vice-President was resident in the guest house at Palm Springs, all the towels and stationery were monogrammed with Agnew's initials. Frank serenaded the man he called 'Ted' (his second name was Theodore) with special Sammy Cahn lyrics to 'The Lady Is a Tramp' which became 'The Gentleman Is a Champ'. Agnew was no gentleman and Sinatra probably knew it (he also used nearly the same lyrics in tribute to David Sarnoff, head of RCA) but he did his bit to help Agnew's 1972 re-election campaign along with Nixon's. He made a huge fuss of the Vice-President at a gala organised by the State of Israel bonds drive. Speakers paid tribute to Agnew for helping Israel and Agnew paid tribute to Israel and its greatest friend in America, Frank Sinatra. To commemorate that friendship, Frank received a medal that night from Baron Eli de Rothschild.

What is undoubtedly true is that this scion of the New Jersey Democratic Party machine, who, as a young man, had sat at the feet of Franklin D. Roosevelt before becoming a devoted servant of John F. Kennedy, totally agreed with Agnew's right-wing policies and probably knew of the corruption which even before Watergate would force his resignation.

But by then, despite the honours and high-society connections, the shadow of the Mob had once again fallen upon him.

— 30 —

NOTHING IN COMMON

In London in 1972, Sinatra was told that a Washington committee was after him – and he promptly vanished from his suite at the Savoy. Rumours were put about that he had gone to Russia, as unlikely a situation as one could imagine. He was threatened with a subpoena to appear before the House Select Committee on Organised Crime – but his Democrat Senator friend John Tunny intervened to prevent it. Eventually, he said he would appear anyway – 'by invitation, but not by demand'.

When he turned up at the Washington hearings, he was asked about the $50,000 he had invested in the Massachusetts Berkshire Downs racetrack. Earlier, the Sinatra office had said that the deal had been handled by Mickey Rudin and that he himself had had little knowledge of it and had always rejected any moves to make him an officer of the racetrack or a director of the company. He wanted a private hearing now so that he could avoid 'unfair publicity'.

The hearing would not be held in private, but he would be allowed certain concessions. He protested that it was all unfair. Hearsay evidence had incriminated him. The committee agreed and again he left without an official stain on his character. Yes, he knew that the track was mainly owned by Raymond Patriarca who ran the Mafia in New England. Yes, it was also true that Tommy Lucchese who was not unknown to the fraternity in Manhattan also had something to do with it. Was either one of them a racketeer? 'That's his problem, not mine.'

Crowds assembled outside the Washington building where the inquiry was being held, on the steps and around the statues. Five hundred members of the public had got into the building. Another two hundred waited outside, including one woman who remembered fainting outside the Paramount. To her and to most of the others, this was another Sinatra show, except they knew that nothing would persuade him to sing.

There was a lot to answer to, he was told. Joe Barboiza, a mob hit man who revelled in the name of 'the Baron', had mentioned Sinatra's name and said he had hung out with Patriarca, who was to the Mafia in Boston what Corleone was to the families in *The Godfather*. 'There is no truth in it,' he declared firmly.

It was, he said, 'indecent . . . irresponsible to bandy my good name about'. Why, he asked the chairman, Claude Pepper, a Democrat from Florida and the oldest member in Congress, 'didn't you refute it?' And he asked the Committee angrily, 'Why didn't someone protect my position? Why didn't you just call in the press and tell them it was character assassination?'

To prove his point, there was a newspaper by his side. The headline 'WITNESS LINKS SINATRA WITH MAFIA' made his blood boil. 'That's charming, isn't it? Really charming. I'm asking someone to be fair about it. How do you repair the damage done to me?'

It was a fair assumption on his part that the Committee were involving him as a means of getting publicity for their actions. Congressmen and senators liked their constituents to know that they were busy people – and if they were strong enough to bring in Frank Sinatra, they must be worth voting for.

He finally said what he had wanted to say for a very long time. Every appearance before every committee of this kind linked him with the Mob. 'I won't have it,' he declared. 'I'm not a second-class citizen.' He also wrote a long letter to the *New York Times*, detailing his own impressions of the inquisition to which he had been submitted.

'The details of what happened that day have already appeared: the tedious questioning about a brief investment I made in a minor-league racetrack ten long years ago; whether or not I knew or had met certain characters alleged to be in the crime business; whether I had ever been an officer of the Berkshire Downs racetrack, etc. With my lawyer providing some details that had been lost in the passage of time, I answered all questions to the best of my ability. Assuming that the committee even needed the information, it was apparent to most people there that the whole matter could have been resolved in the privacy of a lawyer's office, without all the attendant hoop-la.'

But that was not enough to get off his chest. There were, he said, 'some larger questions raised by that appearance that have something to say to all of us. The most important is the rights of a private citizen in this country when faced with the huge machine of the central Government. In theory, Congressional investigating committees are fact-finding devices which are supposed to lead to legislation. In practice, as we learned during the ugly era of Joe McCarthy, they can become star chambers in which facts are confused with rumour, gossip and innuendo, and where reputations and character can be demolished in front of the largest possible audiences. In my case, a convicted murderer was allowed to throw my name around with abandon, while the TV cameras rolled on. His vicious little fantasy was sent into millions of American homes, including my own.

'Sure I was given a chance to refute it, but as we have all come to know, the accusation often remains longer in the public mind than the defence.'

It was a trenchant, highly articulate play against what he took to be a concerted, continuous attack on him. Whether he wrote it himself or used one of his various press agents to ghost it for him, it was the sort of thing Sinatra had been saying for a long time.

As he went on to say: 'Over the years I have acquired a certain fame and celebrity and that is one reason why so much gossip and speculation goes on about me. It happens to a lot of stars. But it is complicated in my case because my name ends in a vowel.'

Now that seemed to be hitting below the belt. Frank Sinatra, America's most successful ever popular singer, was charging racial discrimination, that he was being victimised because he had an Italian name. That had never been said before. Or was he saying that it was just assumed that someone whose family hailed from Sicily was expected to be a Mafia member?

He added: 'We might call this the politics of fantasy. Sitting at that table the other day, I wondered whether it was any accident that I had been called down to Washington during an election year, a year in which Congressmen have difficulty getting their names into the newspapers because of the tremendous concentration on the race for the Presidency...'

As he said, he hoped the time had come to 'start separating fantasy from reality and to bring this sort of nonsense to an end once and for all'.

He did not think of asking himself why he was still seen with mobsters, now that he knew all the trouble they brought him. Mud stuck, despite the adoration of show business and the welcome he was receiving in government circles.

And he was warmly welcomed. Possibly on Agnew's coattails, Sinatra was now back in favour at the White House. After his *Times* letter was published, President Richard Nixon phoned his congratulations – and said he would always be welcome in Washington. Even more ironically, when he did go there it was to welcome the Prime Minister of Italy, Giulio Andreotti, who would himself be indicted for Mafia connections. (Frank would before long be presented with the Grande Ufficiale Dell'Ordine Al Merito Della Republica Italiana, making him a 'great and meritorious official of the Republic of Italy.')

In introducing him, the President told the Italian Premier that he had invited Sinatra because 'in terms of entertainment, by all of his colleagues, he is considered to be what the Washington Monument is: he is the top.'

Sinatra sang 'The House I Live In' and Nixon then praised the man responsible for a rare event at the White House. 'Those of us who have had the privilege of being in this room have heard many great performances,' said the President. 'Once in a while, there is a moment when there is magic in the room, and a great singer, an entertainer, is able to capture it and move us all and Frank Sinatra has done that tonight.'

He *was* beginning to sing again – in private. Joe Masters, pianist at Palm Springs's Hotel Trinidad, would go round to his home and play for him till six o'clock in the morning. As he said: 'If this is retirement, then give me three weeks workout with a chain gang to catch up with my sleep.'

People – supposedly the President among them – were asking how long the nonsense of retirement was going to last. Nixon invited him to the inauguration celebrations in January 1973, but he said he would not perform. (He had been an honoured guest at the celebrations in Miami when Nixon was renominated by the party, but had said then, 'I'm just a visitor'.) He wavered for a moment, but when the security checks on Pat Henry, the comedian who accompanied him on his concert tours, couldn't be arranged in time, he backed out of being the MC.

There were other problems that inauguration night. Frank was accompanied by a new girlfriend, Barbara Marx, who had been married to the youngest of the Marx Brothers, Zeppo. Perhaps not surprisingly, Barbara was the centre of attraction. A new and – the public had been led to believe – serious Sinatra woman was not going to be allowed to escape their attention, retirement or not.

Barbara was approached by Maxine Cheshire of the *Washington Post*, another of those journalists against whom Frank had borne a grudge. In this case, he had never forgiven Ms Cheshire for interrupting the moment when he and the then Governor, Ronald Reagan, were stepping out of the state limousine and asking about his connections with the Mob: 'Mr Sinatra, do you think that your alleged association with the Mafia will prove to be the same embarrassment to Vice-President Agnew as it was to the Kennedy administration?'

Frank kept his cool on that occasion. Ms Cheshire's column was about to get national syndication; she would welcome any publicity she could get, and he didn't want to help her. Now he was thinking of Barbara. Before Ms Cheshire could ask any questions, he called the journalist a four-letter word beginning with 'c' and ending with 't' and declared: 'Get away from me, you scum. Go home and take a bath.'

He didn't leave it at that. He pushed two dollar bills into the woman's wineglass. 'You know what that means, don't you? You've been laying down for two dollars all your life.' The hard, tough reporter burst into tears. Frank was bursting, too. He took Barbara home without ever removing their coats.

Later, Ms Cheshire used lawyers to demand an apology. When it didn't come, she took the matter to court. But it didn't get very far. She was told that all the time she was suing Sinatra for slander she would have to keep quiet about him. That was more than a journalist could take. She withdrew the action and felt free to write what she liked, as before.

Henry Kissinger heard about the two dollar payment and told Frank: 'You overpaid.'

Scandal also dogged Spiro Agnew, who faced resignation in October 1973. Frank tried to persuade him to see it through and stay in office. 'Quit? Shit!' he said after the first charges of income-tax evasion against the Vice-President surfaced, 'that would be an admission of guilt.' Later, after Agnew did resign, Sinatra offered his friend support and said the man had been maligned. He asked Mickey Rudin to try to find a way to get him off the charges which included taking bribes and other underhand payments. But even Rudin would have to admit it was a lost cause. Nevertheless, there was a cheque for

Agnew with the Sinatra signature on it – for $30,000 towards both legal costs and an attempt at finding a new lifestyle for himself and his family.

Later, while plugging his book *The Canfield Decision*, Agnew told a reporter that he had only one real friend. 'Frank Sinatra – a gentleman and a true friend. I don't know how I would have survived without him.'

But there was no doubt that that friendship *had* been combined with ambition. The attempt to keep Agnew out of trouble was also a gesture of loyal disappointment. He had hoped that his friend would be President once Nixon had served his two terms of office. That meant Sinatra would have enjoyed open access to the Pennsylvania Avenue executive mansion. Now he was looking for another Republican candidate to go with. Or at least someone to seriously argue with.

That someone was again Sammy Davis, Jr. The unwitting source of the latest problem was his old pal Ruta Lee.

'It was truly nothing that I did,' she told me. 'But it was his perception of what I did.'

She ran an organisation with Debbie Reynolds called the Thalians – a group of young, very well-heeled and equally well-connected young people who, forty years ago, 'got tired of that young crowd who did nothing but smoke pot, hard drinking and sex and who never did anything good. They decided they could still have a good time and also work.'

As the years went by, Ruta Lee and Debbie Reynolds and the original members got older. But in that time, they had built a clinic for emotionally deprived children – partly through organising functions at smart places.

'Every year, we honoured someone in the industry who is not just a great entertainer, but also a great humanitarian. We had honoured Frank. We honoured Gene Kelly. This was Sammy's turn. I asked Frank to come to make the presentation to Sammy at the Beverly Hilton and to sing a song with special lyrics.'

It was a difficult time for Ruta. She told me the story for the first time. Her father had just been killed in a road accident and the funeral had been put off so that the dinner could go ahead. On top of that, she received a last-second message from Frank. 'He would not be attending. I don't know why. Not only have I lost a presenter (I also lost a date – but I wasn't worried about that). What am I supposed to do? It later turned out that the trouble over Spiro Agnew was still really hitting the fan and Frank was involved, but he didn't tell me. I asked him, "What do I say? What do I do? What am I to tell the press?" He never answered. Nothing.'

So Sammy didn't just get the honour that night, he also sang. 'He hit a high note – and then said, "Eat your heart out, Frank." Well, some of the people in the press picked up on that and thought it was a smartass attack against Frank. Others said that Frank had failed to honour his obligation and how could he do that to the Thalians.

'Well, he took umbrage with me – not me taking umbrage with Frank, which I thought I was quite entitled to do. He sent me an angry letter saying, "Next time you need help, why don't you turn to Rona Barrett and whoever else it was who had commented on my absence?"'

'I sent a long letter in return explaining what happened,' said Ms Lee. 'I don't know if he got it because I didn't get a reply.' As Shirley MacLaine had noted: 'Frank could never say "I'm sorry" or admit he was wrong. And the fear he aroused in others was sometimes stultifying.'

No contact with Ruta meant no friendship for someone who had been close to Sinatra's circle for a long time. 'I walked into a club one day and there's Frank sitting at the bar and as I walked in, I thought, "He's going to belt me." But instead he stood up, put his arms around me, gave me a hug. "Hey, Loudy," he said, "how are you?"'

'Loudy' was the nickname Dean Martin had dubbed her 'because there isn't a voice louder in the world. So I guess things passed in the night.' But it was months before Frank Sinatra spoke to Sammy Davis, Jr., again.

The Agnew friendship cost Frank other friendships. Shirley MacLaine was no longer the totally loyal friend she had been in the Clan days. She hated Frank for lining up with Nixon's Republicans – to say nothing of Agnew. It was, after all, the Watergate era.

But feelings towards others were as warm as ever. Sinatra defended Telly Savalas in the face of press criticism of a Las Vegas performance. One particular critic, Robert Hilburn, he said, should have been transferred to the comic pages. 'I don't know what Hilburn's problem is. But I gather it's being Hilburn. While it may be true that Telly is not the greatest singer in the world (for which I am personally grateful), that is not the point. The point is that people love him, are willing to wait in line to see him and leave some bread on the table for the privilege of enjoying one of the truly refreshing personalities of our time.'

He was even willing to help other non-singers to perform. He had heard that Kirk Douglas was singing in his latest film. 'If I'd known in time I could have been your coach. I coached Burt Lancaster, you know.' Then he added: 'No, on second thoughts that's not such a hot idea. Watching you making it as a singer might tempt me into going back to work.'

The retirement was still clearly on his mind, and on that of others, too. Gene Kelly said: 'Frank still has a lot to offer, he's too young to retire.'

In June 1973, he gave his answer, with a new LP with numbers ranging from 'Winners' and, poignantly, 'Let Me Try Again' to 'The Man Who Loved Cat Dancing'. The album was called *Ol' Blue Eyes Is Back*. It wasn't yet the ol' blue eyes his fans loved: only the really serious aficionados bought it. But it was the title that was the really significant thing about the album.

Nobody had called Frank Ol' Blue Eyes before. Now it became his trademark. It was used as frequently in association with his name as the words 'bobbysoxers' had been in the past.

The Chicago *Daily News* wrote about: 'Comeback by Sinatra – Greatest in Theatre History'.

'I was struggling,' he explained to Bill Boggs on the New York radio station WNEW, where he had done some of his very first broadcasts. He had been in the doldrums 'because when I quit, I let everything go. And it all fell down. It's like somebody who lifts weights and then stops for a while – a matter of consistency, you have to do it every day. The greatest training that any youngster can have if he really wants to become a pop singer is to sing all the time, every day.'

It was a moment of revelation for him – like Jolson before him, he needed to sing to be happy. But more than that, he needed his audience. Now he would get it again and, for the most part, that audience would be content. His voice wasn't as good as it had been before, and now that he had retired from being retired, people could hear the difference. The cloth that he always cut so perfectly for himself had more loose threads – even though the stagecraft, always one of his greatest assets, was perhaps going to be better than ever. But the advice he had given singers before – to keep practising the use of their vocal cords as though they were Stradivarius violins – was as valuable to himself as to anyone else. There was a lot of great material still to come, even though he could no longer claim to have the sweetest voice in show business.

In that *TV Guide* interview, he had said that it was 'worse than ever' in retirement. 'Some of the picayune stuff would cease, but there was always the press. I call them garbage collectors, the columnists without a conscience, the reporters who take long shots based on the idea that where there's smoke, there's fire ... They'd sell their mother out. Most of them have no guts at all. Even if you get a retraction, it's always on page 32.'

So if Ol' Blue Eyes really was back, what was to be seen? One event was a TV spectacular produced by Howard W. Koch, beamed appropriately from Paramount studios in Hollywood. The *New York Times* noted: 'Sinatra was in control and his instrument was music. The newspaper clippings became irrelevant. The focus stayed on the singer and his songs, which is hardly standard practice in TV music specials.' The music was 'startlingly moving ... the new material seems almost calculated to capture the new mellowness, the effective element of bittersweet maturity.' There were only two production numbers – one set in a saloon; the other in which he was accompanied by Gene Kelly.

He liked doing the show, but there wouldn't be many more, and very few movies, but a continuous line in new record sleeves. And a lot of continuing adoration for those he considered to be the greats of his business. When Jack Benny celebrated his eightieth birthday, there was only one place to hold the party – at Frank's Palm Springs pad, of course.

In March 1974, Frank was the host for a tribute to James Cagney – the presentation of the Life Achievement Award by the American Film Institute. I stood in the lobby of the Century Plaza Hotel and watched them come in – Governor Reagan, old tough guys from Cagney's Warner Bros. days like Pat O'Brien, as well as Groucho Marx, John Lennon, Bob Hope, Jack Lemmon – and Frank Sinatra. It was the second award of its kind and speaker after speaker came out and told how many times they had gone home repeating 'You dirty rat', which Cagney always denied ever actually saying. Frank went one better. He recalled how he had approached Cagney from the back of a restaurant and whispered the words, 'Ma's dead' – just like the convicts sitting at his table in *White Heat*, news that made the Cagney character go into a frenzy. Jimmy's only response was: 'Francis, that is the worst imitation I have heard in my whole life.'

But he recalled that he had, indeed, made a living of sorts doing Cagney impersonations before things worked out at the Rustic Cabin. 'I drove my mother crazy doing my impression of him in *Public Enemy*. I would ring the doorbell and fall forward on my face. Come to think of it, I still do a lot of that today.'

And, of course, he sang – a tribute to Cagney penned for him by Sammy Cahn. Inevitably, it was a variation on 'My Way' called 'His Way:

> 'James Cagney is
> The perfect whizz
> He did it . . . his way.'

Later Cagney sent a letter to Sammy Cahn: 'A belated note of thanks for the excellent lyric you put together for Francis. I think he did a helluva job with it and you are both to be congratulated.' So many people wanted a copy of the lyrics that he wanted to know if Cahn minded having them circulated. Of course, he didn't. He was in the business of making Sinatra sing parodies of great songs – like:

> There's not a ditty,
> He didn't make sound pretty,
> All the Way.
> Like Jolson, Crosby, Como
> He's still the major domo
> All the Way.

Being one of the presenters – along with people like Bing Crosby and Fred Astaire – of the MGM retrospective collection *That's Entertainment* was a similar sort of occasion. Frank was well paid for his appearance, but you had the feeling he would have done it for nothing, willingly – if everyone else did, too, of course.

But there were more pleasures to come. On 22 May 1974, Frank became a grandfather for the first time. Nancy gave birth to Angela Jennifer, forever afterwards known as AJ. He remarked at the time: 'I said a silent prayer that the world would be as good to this little angel as it's been to me. All I ask is that Nancy never lets the child grow up and see *The Kissing Bandit*.'

The family role was of great significance. As he said, 'I have perhaps been too much of a father from time to time. Not that the kids were spoilt. I was so crazy about them that I kind of crowded them, but they liked it and so did I and all three have turned out to be great kids and being a grandfather is something which is very difficult to explain. I wish I had more children.'

It seemed that Sinatra was on course for a new life: the funny, indulgent, loving grandfather. But the domestic interlude was short-lived. In the summer of that year, he went to Australia, didn't like the arrangements made for his tour and the work of his PR department and complained about 'bums, parasites, hookers and pimps', the journalists who did what no American reporter would dare to do – ask for interviews.

Journalists were roughed up and a TV camera was smashed. As a result, the unions refused to work for him. Things weren't helped when, uncharacteristically, Mickey Rudin stated: 'Mr Sinatra regretted the incidents, which have been blown out of proportion. We believe he has nothing to apologise for. Mr Sinatra was mistaken when he came, thinking Australia was a true, free country.'

It took four hours of negotiations led by Bob Hawke, who was to become the nation's Prime Minister, to diffuse the situation. At that time, he was the 45-year-old chief of Australia's Council of Trade Unions. Hawke told Frank: 'If you do not express regrets, your stay in Australia might be indefinite, unless you can walk across water.'

An apology did come – if grudgingly. There was no intention, it said, to offer any general reflection upon 'the moral character of working members of the Australian media'. But the statement added: 'He, of course, reserves his right to continue to comment upon the quality of the professional performance of those working members of the media whom he believes are subject to criticism on professional grounds.

'Frank Sinatra also expresses his regret for any physical injury suffered by persons as a result of attempts to ensure his personal safety.'

Then he went on TV and made love to the people down under. 'I like coming here,' he lied, but it saved the tour. 'And I like the people. I love your attitude, I love the booze and the beer and everything else. I like the way the country is going and it's a swinging place. So we come here and what happens? Gotta run all day long because of the parasites who chased us, with automobiles. Peace.'

Peace was what he needed most to continue what was the new part of the Sinatra routine. Concerts which had previously been the occasional luxury in between movies, TV spectaculars and, above all, appearances in Las Vegas, were now taking priority. He probably enjoyed them best of all. The only billing he bothered with said simply: 'He's Here.' When he appeared before a black-tie audience at the Pacific Amphitheatre in Costa Mesa near Los Angeles, there wasn't even that. People who had paid an outrageous sum for tickets just followed the car in front and got there. You didn't need to know where Sinatra was performing. You found it by compass. The concerts always needed the minimum of rehearsal. He was accompanied by the orchestras of his choice. He sang the songs he wanted to sing and there was practically no stage management – certainly nothing that affected him. He quickly mastered an art that would be copied by a thousand pop groups, sometimes with a great deal more public applause, but with none of the Sinatra finesse.

When he performed in the ring at Madison Square Garden in October 1974, with a Burberry raincoat over his shoulders like a boxer's dressing-gown, he was still the undisputed champ. It was an appropriate judgment of the man starring in what was billed as *The Main Event* and broadcast live on TV.

There were all the usual hits – if he hadn't sung 'My Way' now there would have been something like a riot – but also a few surprises. 'Angel Eyes', a song one might think would be better confined to one of his intimate parties in Palm Springs or to a reflective moment in a New York saloon, had the vast house gasping in the silence. The evening was televised, with the help of 350 technicians and a couple of dozen cameras (that was the way Sinatra did things). The *New York Times* said it was a 'superb' performance by 'the master of his generation'. Looking at many of the 20,000 people in the audience, it wasn't just his generation of which he was master.

The New York *Daily News*'s Kay Gardella, an old Sinatra fan, wrote: 'In a way, it's like a champ returning to defend his title. When Sinatra came out of retirement, he came out swinging. For a man who wanted a quiet place in the sun in Palm Springs in place of glaring spotlights, his turnabout rocked a musical world inundated with rock, young groups and new faces, but one that was not entirely ready to place Ol' Blue Eyes in the musical archives.'

At Carnegie Hall that year, people paid up to $900 for seats that were officially priced between $25 and $150 each. The proceeds were intended to go to Variety Clubs International and their work for children, although the ticket touts weren't exactly made poor by it, either. Sinatra himself benefited from dozens of standing ovations. It was almost like the old days at the Paramount.

When he occasionally forgot a lyric – he even came unstuck with

'My Way' – he had the perfect response: 'You probably don't know them either.' Actually, they probably did. They sang them all the time, which Sinatra himself had stopped doing a couple of years back. In 'The Tender Trap', he resorted to: 'la-di-dah-dah – It's been a long time since I sang this song.'

Not everyone was polite. 'Can't hear you,' someone shouted. 'Buy the record,' he snapped back. 'What do you want from me, I'm hollering.' The ones who could hear clapped, and did it loudly. But he added kindly: 'I'll try to be louder.'

The New York *Post*'s Jan Hodenfield wrote: 'Frank Sinatra was a religious event. If you were a believer, he kept the faith as Chairman of the Board of romantic balladeers. If you're not, he was a somewhat portly 58-year-old who had trouble staying in key.'

The Associated Press reported: 'Sinatra, in his first personal appearance in New York since 1957, showed Monday night he can still hit the notes he tries for and hold them as long as he tries to hold them.'

The note he touched at the 1975 Academy Award ceremony was more discordant. It soured his appearance at the Dorothy Chandler Pavilion that year, where he was one of the principal hosts of the evening, along with Hope, Sammy Davis, Jr., and Shirley Mac-Laine.

In 1975, the Vietnam War was still a highly-charged issue and matters became inflamed when the award for the best documentary feature went to a film devoted to the story of the conflict, *Hearts and Minds*. Everyone knew that the war was coming to an end, but Peter Davis, one of the movie's producers, hit a raw nerve by saying how ironic it was 'to get a prize for a war movie while the suffering in Vietnam continues'. He hoped his children would be able to live in 'a better atmosphere and better country'. Then the other producer, Bert Schneider, came on and spoke about his joy in knowing that Vietnam was about to be 'liberated'.

The Oscar ceremonies are legendary occasions for reading telegrams – usually notes of gratitude and congratulation from people who are unable to be present. This night in 1975, the telegram read by Bert Schneider was from somebody who would never in a million years have been invited to an Academy Award evening – the head of the Vietcong delegation at the current Paris peace talks.

'Please transmit to all our friends in America,' he wrote, 'our recognition of all they have done on behalf of peace and for the application of the Paris accords on Vietnam. These actions serve the legitimate interests of the American people and the Vietnamese people. Greetings of friendship to all American people.'

The gasps from the audience were drowned out by cries of 'Shame' and 'Disgusting' from John Wayne's table. Bob Hope needed no joke factory to help him express his indignation to the President of the Academy, who just happened to be Frank's old producer chum, Howard W. Koch. Backstage – while an award was being made to the French director Jean Renoir – Hope demanded that Koch come out and make an immediate disclaimer on behalf of the Academy.

Hope said it should come from Sinatra – who accepted the task. 'Don't you dare,' Shirley MacLaine screamed at him, but he was no more willing to let any other Clan member get the better of him on this occasion than before. He read a statement that he and Hope had given to Koch to approve, which he did as a matter of course. 'We are not responsible for any political references made on this programme,' the statement declared, 'and we are sorry they had to take place this evening.'

The discordant sounds heard earlier were repeated – except this time the reactions were reversed. The earlier booers now cheered and the ones who had applauded now booed. John Wayne poured out the invective against 'that Schneider guy, a pain in the ass and outta line and against the rules of the Academy'.

Only the director of *The Godfather Part II*, Francis Ford Coppola, was on the side of the film-maker. He said, 'In voting for that picture the Academy was sanctioning its message, which was in the spirit of Mr Schneider's remarks.'

Frank, before long, would join everyone else in condemning the Vietnam conflict and actually said later: 'Bob and Howard made me do it. They handed me this piece of paper and I read it.' Of course, the number of times when anyone forced Sinatra to do anything are strictly limited.

Schneider himself said: 'As a member of the Academy's Board of Governors, I resent Frank Sinatra taking this as an Academy point of view. He's a gutsy guy; why didn't he come out and say he helped write it and it was his point of view?'

Twenty years later, Howard Koch told me: 'I think that guy [Schneider] had no reason to do it. We got boos all over the place for what we did, but I think it was right.'

Frank's trip to Paris a couple of months later was less controversial.

Three thousand five hundred people filled the Palais de Congrès for the Sinatra concert there on 20 May. They clamoured for more tickets, even though the hall accepted only cash and tickets would not go on sale until the day before the show. The weather was terrible that night but there were still people queuing for any extra tickets when Frank flew in from Switzerland. People noted that he couldn't now reach notes that at one time had seemed to flow so easily, but few left the Palais feeling anything but ecstatic. Some even said that he was singing better than ever. It was, of course, an illusion. What was perhaps better than ever was the way he played to his audience. He no longer directed everyone – the audience included – as though he were a general in charge of a military operation; now he was courting them, saying, 'I want you to love this.'

It was the same story at the London Palladium when Sinatra made his second visit to the world's top variety theatre in November 1975. He was at his peak of maturity. No question now that the voice was not as it had been. English people could still satisfy themselves by seeing one of the really great performers of the age, singing their favourite songs with all the go and gusto at his command.

Within hours of the week-long show being announced, every ticket was sold. It was reminiscent of the sensational visits there by Danny Kaye, and the audience were as much in Sinatra's hands as they had been in Kaye's. He sipped a glass of whatever he found refreshing and told his adoring fans that he knew that *Kojak* star Telly Savalas had been there just recently. 'You've had Lollipops here,' he noted. 'And milk-drinking [Richard] Burton. But I'm here now and it's gonna be booze and broads and all that stuff.' They loved it.

Security had never been tougher, particularly backstage. There was a ban on anyone going behind the scenes without a special identity card. If a stagehand dared to pass by Frank's dressing room, a minion would come out to ask why. It didn't take long for the message to get through – no one was allowed even to pass his door. His arrival and departure was like the visit of a head of state. The Sinatra equivalent of secret servicemen got out of the car first, tore their way through the crowds and checked to make sure it was safe for their boss to leave or enter the theatre. There was an order to the musicians: Smoke at your peril. Frank had himself given up his old fifty-a-day habit and didn't want to smell fumes from anyone else.

When he marked his sixtieth birthday in December 1975, the tributes were not as fulsome as they had been when he had reached fifty. It was as though people were saying, 'So what?' They had heard it all when he retired and when he made his comeback. It was simpler just to list the work the old man had got through in the past twelve months, which included 140 performances before live audiences.

His film work was virtually confined to the memories of those of his own generation, but the Hollywood Foreign Press Association could think of no one they wanted more to honour with their famous Golden Globe award than the man they now called Ol' Blue Eyes.

At last, Frank had his mother close at hand when he was given these plaudits. Dolly had finally moved into the five-bedroomed mansion he had built for her in Palm Springs. She was also there to see her son married for the third time. He and Barbara Marx, after being together for three years, had decided to make it official. She was beautiful, blonde and, unlike the last Mrs Sinatra and his one-time fiancée Juliet Prowse, *almost* old enough to be Nancy's, Tina's and Frank's mother.

He professed undying love for her at the ceremony on 11 July 1976, held on the estate of the former American Ambassador, Walter Annenberg. Barbara wore a creation designed for her by Halston, who had achieved nation-wide fame by making clothes for Liza Minnelli.

Most of Frank's gang were there – Ronald Reagan, Gregory Peck, Kirk Douglas, Spiro Agnew (showing the old Sinatra loyalty was very much intact) and Michael DeBakey who had tried to save old Marty's life. (DeBakey said of Frank: 'Of all the people I've known he's the most unique human being I've ever met ... I saw the way he kissed his father.')

Others were noticeably absent. I remember having lunch with Sammy Cahn a week after the event. 'Were you at the wedding?' I asked. 'No,' he said, 'I loathe that whole area in the summer. It's stiflingly hot. And I knew Spiro Agnew was going to be there – and I detest that man.' Then he added: 'There was one other reason.'

'What's that?' I asked. 'I wasn't invited,' he replied.

For some reason that he couldn't understand, he had upset Frank, who showed his displeasure in the usual way: by freezing him out. 'It happens with Frank,' he told me. 'I don't understand why. No doubt, I'll be in favour again before long.' And he was. But the slight hurt.

If someone asked Frank what there was about these 'September years' that so appealed to him, the answer would probably be that he was *enjoying* himself. A lot of the old pressure was gone. He was still King of Las Vegas. He still did an ever-increasing number of mammoth concerts and he still cut records, but he did them now with a degree of ease he had never known before. 'I Love My Wife' was his latest recording. Not only was he having fun, he was enjoying being married.

When he did work, it was now always a grand occasion. Phil Ramone, who would later preside over one of the most important professional events in the late Sinatra career – his *Duets* recordings of the early 1990s – was introduced to the way Frank operated. There was a recording session set up at the Jefferson Memorial in Washington DC, as part of the 1976 United States Bicentennial celebrations, involving a huge orchestra and a choir. Open-air recording was always a huge risk. What if a plane flew overhead in the middle of a big number? 'That day it was very noisy out there. But you asked Frank about waiting for the planes and he said, "What planes?"'

The sound of a cannon was a different matter. In the song, 'The Cannon Roars', the director wanted a real gun to go off. 'It went off and Frank dropped the mike – into a thousand pieces. He wasn't expecting it. He's singing with his eyes closed and the heavenly choir behind him – and the cannon goes off. The director said, "You'd better get Frank to redo the ending."'

Ramone wasn't keen on that idea. 'I said, "Thanks a lot."'

'Frank said to me, "Don't say, 'Ready when you are, Mr De Mille.'"'

'"No," said the record producer, "But Frank, you dropped the goddamned mike. We have to redo the ending."

'Frank was mad because of the obvious idiocy of trying to be literal. I said, "Bar 86, please" and he was happy. Once you have shown him that you are not a jerk and you *are* prepared, it's all right.'

In January 1977, tragedy struck. Dolly Sinatra turned down the chance to fly to Las Vegas with her son because she had things to attend to – like moving some of her jewellery from Frank's safe to her own safe-deposit box. Yes, she'd still go to see her son at Caesar's Palace as usual, but she would travel via a small chartered plane a little later on.

The plane was arranged. A car came to pick her up from the new home in Palm Springs to take her to the airport. The flight would last about twenty minutes at the most, although there was a storm brewing, one of those dark, dismal storms which in January can make southern California look as though it has been hit by a plague of locusts.

The plane took off on time, but an hour later, there were calls to Frank's dressing room at Caesar's Palace to say that she had not arrived. There was good reason to fear the worst – the weather was terrible and all radio contact had been lost. No wreckage had yet been spotted, but there were mountain ranges on either side of the valley where Palm Springs airport was situated. The fog was heavy and the navigation equipment primitive on an aircraft like the one Dolly was using. It was all very ominous.

Frank knew what had happened. The plane had crashed. His mother was dead. But he went on at Caesar's just the same.

Among those with him that night was Dennis Selinger, one of the most important and successful theatrical agents in Britain, who was in Vegas to tie up a few deals. He was in Frank's dressing room with his client Michael Caine. 'Sinatra was totally shattered,' he told me, 'as if his life had come to an end. But he went on and did his act perfectly, didn't say anything about his mother or ask for any sympathy. Whatever else that could be said, he was a trouper. You would never know anything had happened.' He told me he came to a conclusion about Sinatra after that experience. 'I think that whatever their problem, the people who had difficulties with him were the ones who were not very good at their jobs.'

The next day, Frank went up in a helicopter to search for wreckage or some sign of what had happened. He found nothing. Meanwhile, a clairvoyant had been brought in. He pondered and thought and said, yes, he could 'see' the wreckage on Mount San Gogonio. At eleven thirty that night, a reconnaissance aircraft spotted the remains there of an aircraft and of the people who had been in it. It could only have been in the air for a couple of minutes before slamming into the mountain. (A few years later, the same mountain would claim the life of Dino, Dean Martin's son.)

They buried Dolly next to her husband in the cemetery at Palm Springs to which Marty's remains had been taken before she moved out west. There were simultaneous funeral services in California and at St Francis's Church, Hoboken – at the request of Frank Sinatra, who thought it was a necessary tribute to the woman who had done so much for Catholicism in her home town and who had been granted an audience with Pope Paul when she went to Rome shortly before her death.

Ruta Lee told me that Frank was distraught by his mother's death. 'He was devastated. He didn't want to see people.'

The last wish of Dolly Sinatra, the fragile old lady who had difficulty walking, had been that all her wealth be given to her grandson. She had told her maid and her gardener that as she made the journey to the airport, as though she knew something was going to go wrong.

But she wouldn't be remembered simply as the frail old woman who wore little boots to conceal her swollen ankles. She would linger in the memory as the woman who had always had her way; the feisty ward leader who had scared lesser politicians and not a few who were more powerful than she; the woman who could compete with Ava Gardner in using words not to be found in the dictionary; the saloon keeper-cum-abortionist who had guided her son's career no less than her husband's. To Frank, she would always be the big influence, the one who had bought the sound equipment that led him to the Hoboken Four and everything else that followed.

AROUND THE WORLD

To misquote one of the lovelier Frank Sinatra songs, 1977 was not a very good year.

On 6 July, the Mayor of Philadelphia, Frank Rizzo, presented Frank Sinatra with the city's highest award, the Freedom Medal. Philadelphia's newspaper, the *Inquirer*, asked its readers:

'Remember Frank Sinatra? He's the crooner who couldn't make it to Philly, to sing "The Star-spangled Banner" at the Bicentennial celebrations last year. This year, he flew in from New York, where he's making a movie, came in late, accepted the medal, spoke briefly to the ten thousand, some of whom had camped out on Independence Mall all night to see him, and jetted back to New York, skipping the official lunch.

'I've been glancing through our newsclippings file to find out how Frank Sinatra exemplified American ideals and perpetuated American heritage enough for him to win our Freedom Medal. I find that he was a high-school drop-out, that he was 4-F during World War Two, that by D-Day he was a millionaire from his recording and nightclub appearances, that he got a big piece of the action in Las Vegas, that the Nevada state gambling commission lifted his ownership of a casino in Lake Tahoe, that by 1960 he was introducing (a woman) to Sam Giancana, good friend of John Fitzgerald Kennedy, although by 1961 John Fitzgerald Kennedy was no longer his good friend, that he organised a group of slosh buddies whom he called the Rat Pack and who called him the Chairman of the Board, that he had a couple of highly publicised saloon fights, that he married four times, that he gives away money to good friends and tax-deductible charities, that he travels around the world with a pack of muscle-men, that he sings pretty good, but that one of his big songs [is] "I Did It My Way" (sic), which may be one of the most annoying songs ever written.

'As I say, it's tough to quarrel with other people's heroes. If the

Mayor figures Mr S. is tip-top in the American heritage sweeps ... so be it.'

That sour assessment didn't stop Frank continuing to receive invitations. The opera singer Robert Merrill was with him at Carnegie Hall that April at a concert in aid of the Lenox Hill Hospital and the Institute of Sports Medicine. More than $750,000 was raised. Walter Cronkite was MC. Also there were Governor Carey of New York, sports star Joe Namath and, most notably of all, Jacqueline Onassis. She complemented her stunningly elegant outfit with a pair of long white gloves. They caused as much of a stir as Frank Sinatra's singing. The next day, all the fashionable Manhattan stores sold out of long white gloves.

'Mr Sinatra,' said Enid Nemy in the *New York Times*, 'who sipped at what looked like a glass of wine, took over the hall as though he owned it and, indeed, for the second half of the evening, he did. Some of the younger members of the audience admitted later that their parents hadn't been all wrong in their idols.'

There was one song that proved the point. That year Liza Minnelli had made a not very good movie called *New York, New York* with Robert De Niro, which had a wonderful theme song, a crashing, rip-roaring, come-and-get-it kind of number that Al Jolson in his heyday would have taken over. Sinatra still had an eye and an ear for a song, but didn't like taking over someone else's tune. It smacked of unoriginality. It looked as though someone of hitherto great standing was making 'cover' versions. But Sinatra took the risk.

One of the reasons why he was able to do so was that he still had Don Costa behind him to orchestrate what Frank would later call his memorial. Like Minnelli, Frank sang the song as though he were in the ring at Madison Square Garden and punching for the title. He didn't just phrase it well, as everyone knew he would, he discovered a new voice – a voice that enabled him to bridge two bars in a way even he had never done before. He rasped the word 'and' and made it last for five or six seconds, the one word. It sounded wonderful.

This was to be his last big, all-alone number, and it more than eclipsed the perfectly fine song Leonard Bernstein had written for Sinatra and Gene Kelly in *On the Town*. The mere opening bars would from now on be enough to have thousands of people at a concert on their feet, cheering, before he sang a note. It was his only serious rival to 'My Way' and remains superior, always given in a superior performance, and a lot more positive in content.

For the first time in his life, Frank Sinatra now was being regarded as a performer for the older generation only. Youngsters might appreciate him as they would if educated in the warmth of a fine wine, but now he wasn't on their lists. It hadn't happened before. But it didn't stop him performing in top venues, before top celebrities. A concert at London's Royal Albert Hall, in aid of the NSPCC, was attended by Princess Anne and her aunt, Princess Margaret.

Meanwhile, a battle was developing between Barbara Sinatra and her husband's children. The three of them, Nancy, Frank, Jr., and Tina, had always got on well with their stepmothers. Ava at times seemed to love them more than she did their father; Mia had been a chum. Juliet, if she had ever married Frank, would have been a contemporary whose company they enjoyed. But Barbara they considered to be an interloper because she was closer to Frank's generation and a threat to their mother. Dolly, who didn't care much for her grandchildren's mother, had hated Barbara, too.

Frank appeared to be unconcerned by it all. Barbara was his wife and he showed her the consideration he believed she was due. One way of expressing it was with a new song – called 'There is Barbara'. She later said on a BBC radio programme: 'I didn't know about that song. He had kept it secret from me. He sang it on stage and I was a blithering idiot. Tears ran down my cheeks.'

By most accounts, they were in the midst of an idyllic marriage, exchanging his and her Rolls-Royces as presents. 'He's turned every single day into Christmas,' she said – and demonstrated the fact by displaying a gold choker made up of Roman coins.

Barbara made changes to the Palm Springs house – adding a new master bedroom, new bathrooms, new dressing rooms. She turned one room into Frank's private office, the walls to be lined with pictures from each of his films.

Nancy, Jr., Tina and Frankie continued to worry about Barbara's hold on their father, which made life difficult for Frank, who continued to dote on his offspring and still spoke to them on the phone every day. But matters reached a head when it was publicly announced that Frank would be seeking an annulment of his first marriage, to Nancy. This was the woman he still regularly contacted when he wanted to talk about their children and grandchildren, the woman to whom he still gave financial support and loving gifts like mink coats and diamond bracelets. Now, however, he and Barbara wanted to have a religious ceremony at St Patrick's Cathedral in New York, the place where John F. Kennedy's funeral had been held, which Frank thought suited his stature in the world. What was more, such a ceremony would help him cement his new-found relationship with the Catholic Church. He frequently attended Mass now and was convinced that a religious marriage would help him achieve respectability as a believer.

To Nancy, the idea was insulting, insensitive and inexplicable. She was the religious one, not he – even if the first thing he had done after Dolly's disappearance had been to have a private Mass celebrated. Their three children were deeply hurt, too, for their mother's sake and their own. They were not too pleased at the thought that suddenly, once they had grown up and had children of their own, they were to become illegitimate.

The annulment was announced, but it was premature. It never actually received papal confirmation, although Frank was later seen to be taking communion, which only an annulment would have allowed a divorcee to do. But then a question arose: 'Would one annulment be enough? Frank had had two further wives. The answer was a simple one – only the marriage to Nancy was recognised by the Church in the first place. Nancy, Jr., was to say: 'There was no annulment. It was talked about, but it was a sham.'

Frank was still grappling with investigations into the actions of the Mafia. For three years, grand juries had sat and pondered and heard his name mentioned. But there were never any charges against him. However, the press wanted to know why he appeared in a photograph with various known mobsters, taken in his dressing room at the Westchester Premier Theatre in 1976. There he was with James ('The Weasel') Fratianno, who had admitted murdering eleven people, and Carlo Gambiano, known as 'Capo di tutti' (Boss of Bosses), among others.

Frank said it was simply that the men came backstage and he was asked to pose with them, as he did with lots of people. But the photograph caused a huge stir. It was introduced as Exhibit 181 at the trial of eight Mafia members charged with racketeering, stock fraud and looting. Fratianno had been granted immunity to become the prosecution's key witness. Another gangster, Louis Pacella, later faced a grand jury inquiry on the same matter and was asked if he knew Sinatra. He decided to go to jail rather than answer the question. His lawyer explained: 'He was angry and offended at the Government's attempt to tarnish the name of Frank Sinatra.' That didn't stop the New York *Post* headlining its story: 'Mob Hit Man Is Tied to Sinatra'.

Fratianno alleged that Sinatra had used the Mafia to try to stop one of his former bodyguards writing a biography of Frank, after a series of protect-and-tell articles in the *National Enquirer.*

Pete Hamill, Frank's old pal at the rival *Daily News*, hit back by calling Fratianno 'this disgusting little cretin'. As Hamill wrote: 'He was a man who under oath was asked "to describe the inner workings of the Mob. He spent all of his life lying and murdering and we are supposed to believe what he says about Frank Sinatra."' Hamill was genuinely sympathetic to Sinatra, whom he called in an article in *New York* magazine, 'the most investigated American performer since John Wilkes Booth', the assassin of Lincoln.

Frank himself would say: 'Sure I knew some of these guys. I spent a lot of time working in saloons. And saloons are not run by the Christian Brothers. There were a lot of guys around and they came out of Prohibition and they ran pretty good saloons. I was a kid. I worked in the places that were open. They paid you and the cheques didn't bounce. I didn't meet any Nobel Prize-winners in saloons. But if Francis of Assisi was a singer and worked in saloons, he would've met the same guys. That doesn't make him part of something. They said hello. You said hello. They came backstage. They thanked you. You offered them a drink. That was it.'

There was no evidence introduced that Sinatra was involved in their activities.

Was there any evidence to show that he still had a movie career? Not much. In June 1977 he played a policeman in a three-hour movie for television, *Contract on Cherry Street*. The picture was made in the midst of the Big Manhattan Blackout – an event that people in New York now remember in the same way as the death of President Kennedy. For twenty-four hours, the whole of New York City was without electricity (fortunately it was during the summer). Frank had to walk down thirty-eight flights of stairs from his suite at the Waldorf Towers and then up eight flights to the studio at NBC. People working there at the time will remember it as the occasion they gave him a roar of applause when he turned up for work.

Working in New York always made Frank think of his past, the Paramount, the Copacabana, the radio stations. It also made him think of that little place across the water, Hoboken, where, in the same month of June, a collection of Sinatra memorabilia was to be inaugurated at the public library in Church Square Park. They hoped Frank would come for the ceremony, at which a portrait of Frank and Dolly (painted from a photograph) was going to be unveiled. Frank declined; however, he did send a telegram of apology which the Mayor Steve Cappiello read out. Cappiello said that Frank 'came off the streets punching to become the world's greatest entertainer. Hoboken, too, has been down and we have come off the canvas. Today we are America's urban contender.'

Jimmy Petrozelli and Fred Tamburro were there, recalling the days of the Hoboken Four. Tamburro finally admitted that he never sang as well as Sinatra. 'Naah,' he said, 'he always had something that we didn't have. There was always something about his voice.' Petrozelli said: 'He's a great guy and he lifted this town sky high.'

Sinatra, now friends again with Sammy Cahn, continued his search for new songs. The business, he reckoned, was producing 'kid's stuff' now, songs which he felt weren't worth the paper they were printed on. Cahn once told me: 'There really is no songwriting business any more – at least not since the rock bands started writing their own stuff, which they then own. If Sinatra were one of those new people in the business, I doubt if there would be a Sammy Cahn.'

The Beatles were good, Frank admitted. He liked Barry Manilow and appreciated the work of Jimmy Webb, who had produced 'By the Time I Get to Phoenix'. Frank described that as 'one of the great saloon songs of all time, as good as "One for My Baby".' He also wrote Sinatra's 'Didn't We?' and 'MacArthur Park'. But Webb, he said, was always escaping his clutches. Frank was sympathetic towards songwriters, but, agreeing with Sammy Cahn, he said: 'They don't have the openings that the composers and lyricists had years ago.'

In fact, songwriters of the time didn't send him material because they thought he wouldn't be interested. He was forced to read the trade press and send for numbers they said were good, in case any of them were suitable for him. Nancy, Jr., was also under instruction to keep looking for new tunes.

Barbara liked the things he did now better than most of his earlier material. 'He won't let me play his records when we have guests here. But when we are alone sometimes, I'd say, "There's something here I want you to hear" and he'll say, "That's pretty good phrasing, pretty good breath control." I can tell he's pleased with it.'

He liked classical music more than he once had. His favourite vocalist was the Italian opera star, Luciano Pavarotti, according to

Mrs Sinatra – although he rarely sang the kind of tunes Sinatra himself liked to sing. Actually, though, tunes weren't now what he was into. More than ever before, he was looking for new dramatic numbers that no one else would perform; lyrics that were poems, almost plays, set to three minutes of music – like 'See the Show Again'. It had been a long time since Frank sang of moons and Junes.

Only working for about five months of the year meant that he also had time to perfect his new 'career' as a cook, specialising in a dish his father had taught him: chicken in two different kinds of clam sauce. And he could indulge in foreign travel, too. He took a planeload of friends (and a huge supply of what Frank decided was an essential part of good living, like non-kosher frankfurters) with him when he went to Israel in April 1978. Gregory Peck was there with his wife and so was Ed McMahon, the second banana on the Johnny Carson show. They were part of a group known as the Sinatra Caravan, which had flown to Israel to underline his own friendship with the Friends of the Hebrew University. Now they were dedicating the Frank Sinatra International Student Centre at the University.

A total of 170 people with enough money to afford the multi-thousand-dollar contribution they were expected to make towards the youth centre were on the plane too. Some of them complained that all the time they were in the air, Sinatra didn't come to see them once, let alone thank them for participating. But they did attend the dedication ceremony. I was there that day and remember Tina, looking stunning, sitting with him on the platform during a succession of long speeches in Hebrew which he couldn't understand, but which he clapped politely and enthusiastically. When he himself spoke he took up the theme of one of the speakers who had addressed the group in English: that they were standing on one of the sites conquered by the Romans. 'I wish you had told me before about those Romans. They're my boys. I would have called the guys off.'

Later, he was invited to a ceremony when the Prime Minister, Menachem Begin, was to receive an honorary doctorate from the university. He turned down the invitation because he was invited as a member of the group, not as a guest of honour to sit at the top table. But the next day, he and Peck were invited to tea with the Prime Minister – who hugged him for his work smuggling the money that bought arms in 1948.

Gregory Peck and Cary Grant were now close Sinatra friends. They flew together frequently – in a plane provided by Fabergé for whom Grant was working – and became a group who on the surface couldn't have been more different from the Clan. This was a more restrained, more elegant group to fit in with the new, more elegant Frank Sinatra, the man who had now given up his toupee for the world's most publicised hair implant, giving him a greying crew cut which didn't altogether suit the now widening Sinatra girth.

On the afternoon that Frank and Peck went to see the Prime Minister, Sinatra wore a light-coloured ensemble while his friend had on the suit he had worn to play the US Ambassador in the movie, *The Omen*. Peck told me after that occasion: 'We both said to Mr Begin that we had a lot of time for what he was doing in Israel.' Frank said he thought the Prime Minister was a 'great person' but looked 'very tired. That's because he has so many problems.'

Peck celebrated his sixty-second birthday on the tour. Frank gave him a surprise dinner at the Gondola restaurant in Jerusalem – the lights went out and a huge cake with a single candle was brought into the darkened room. Peck was delighted. Frank was pleased, too, but the afternoon meeting with Begin was undoubtedly the highlight of the trip for him. Mixing with world leaders was one of the great pleasures of his life.

Eighteen months after the Israeli visit, in September 1979, Frank Sinatra, immaculate in his black dinner-jacket, performed in the shadow of the pyramids at Giza. It was he said, 'the biggest room I've ever played'.

Before the show he and Barbara were entertained to dinner by President Anwar Sadat and his wife, almost exactly a year before the Egyptian leader was assassinated. Sadat's thanks to Frank in a telegram became one of his most treasured possessions. It was, he said, an 'unforgettable experience' and the money brought in by the concert would help the children at the Wafa Wa Amal desert hospital. The words Wafa Wa Amal meant 'faith and hope'. 'You are both,' said the President.

He gave both those things to those to whom he was closest, even to the dead. When his friend Irwin Rubinstein died, and the grave-digger at the cemetery was off over the Thanksgiving weekend, Frank offered to pay all it took to bury him immediately in honour of Jewish custom 'going back to the time of Abraham'. If the cemetery superintendent had refused, Frank Jr. recalled for his sister's memoir, their father said he would 'punch that son of a bitch right in the nose and if he's too old, I'll punch his son in the nose'.

There were more compliments, mixed with jokes, when his pals gave Frank a 'roast' at the MGM Hotel in Las Vegas in February 1978.

Milton Berle quipped: 'This is a great crowd. But half of Frank's pals couldn't be here. Half didn't find the time and the other half are doing time.'

Dean Martin revealed that 'Frank loaned money to New York. When they didn't repay, he broke the Statue of Liberty's arms.' Then he added: 'Frank was an unwanted child. Now he's wanted in five states.'

Orson Welles, Don Rickles, Gene Kelly and George Burns were among those in attendance. Red Buttons paid the supreme tribute: 'We're here to honour Frank Sinatra – singer, swinger, actor, tycoon, businessman – and on the seventh day he rested.' Milton Berle couldn't be silenced. 'Frank calls Dial-a-Prayer to see if he has any messages.' Then he said: 'I'm glad you came out of retirement, Frank. Too bad your voice didn't join you.'

As he approached his sixty-fourth birthday, there was a special show at Caesar's Palace to mark Sinatra's forty years in show business. It was described as 'the biggest, most lavish, star-studded party in the history of Las Vegas'. To emphasise the peace that now ruled his life, both Begin and Sadat sent telegrams. President Jimmy Carter's mother, 'Miss Lillian', also spoke a few words of tribute.

Despite all the compliments, and the recognition of his efforts to do good all over the world, not everyone shared the enthusiasm. The Washington *Star* declared that the tributes at the televised celebrations were not love but 'obsequiousness. Some of the most celebrated men and women in entertainment marched across the stage – in Las Vegas, of course – in a parade of abjection. Has Mr Sinatra really accumulated so much wealth and influence that he can reduce Orson Welles, once a great actor and film maker, to a sycophantic blob?'

There were stories that he was taking singing lessons – from Robert Merrill at the Metropolitan Opera. When Merrill was a guest on my BBC radio programme at this time, he wouldn't confirm any such thing. All he remembered was that Frank had given a concert at the Met. 'A woman came up to him and asked how he had the audacity to perform there. He told her he sang a bit, very modestly. She was quite rude and he was very nice.'

The criticism didn't prevent Sinatra from giving a concert at New York's Metropolitan Opera House in October 1979 – *Sinatra at the Met*, which included a new look at *Guys and Dolls*. It raised more than $1 million for the Memorial Sloan-Kettering Cancer Center. He said from the stage: 'I am thrilled beyond words to have my notes bounce back to me from these hallowed walls. We meet here tonight to help our fellow man. But let's be honest about it, we're here for ourselves as well because it is only when cancer is down for the count that any of us can rest a little easier, a little more confident. I'm delighted to sing for such a great cause.'

At sixty-five, he was of pensionable age. Barbara was sending out invitations for a surprise party to the honoured few – the President, the Governor, a sprinkling of ambassadors and the greats of show business like Barbra Streisand and Bob Hope – with the words: 'Please keep this under your Stetson'.

When Ronald Reagan was nominated as the Republican candidate to fight President Jimmy Carter in 1980, Frank committed himself to this cause, too. He promised to raise millions for the California Governor's campaign. 'Why do I support Governor Reagan?' he asked. 'Because I think he's the proper man to be President of the United States. It's so screwed-up now, we need someone to straighten it out.'

Ronald Reagan was duly elected and Sinatra rejoiced. Robert Lindsey wrote in the *New York Times*: 'Frank Sinatra, who has had an off-and-on role as friend of politicians for twenty years, is re-establishing a relationship with the White House after Ronald Reagan's election as President.' But William Safire, the respected *New York Times* columnist, saw the black side of the liaison. He commented in print: 'The involvement with a man obviously . . . close to notorious hoodlums is the first deliberate affront to the propriety of the Reagan administration.'

Now Frank was planning the inauguration celebrations, bringing in friends like Bob Hope, Jimmy Stewart, Dean Martin, Sammy Cahn and Jule Styne. Joe Carrell, one of the Democrats' political consultants in Los Angeles, generously commented that Frank could raise more money for political events than anyone else; what was more, he guaranteed to bring Hollywood royalty with him. 'Usually in politics when you get somebody who's even slightly tainted, people avoid him like the plague. But not Sinatra. In fact, it may add to the mystique. And it doesn't cost you anything – just a phone call to him. He takes command of everything. There are no bills for the orchestra, no bills for limousines. He takes a block of tickets and pays for everything. People don't say anything. They jump up in the air when he calls.'

It was the success everyone expected. Frank sang a Sammy Cahn variant, of course. 'Nancy (with the Reagan Face)' contained the immortal lines: 'I'm so pleased that our First Lady's Nancy ... And I'm pleased that I'm a sort of chum. And the eight years ahead should be fancy ... As fancy as they come.'

Reagan said he could 'feel the magic of the Gala' long afterwards. He vowed he would never cease to be grateful for the Sinatra connection and the $4 million he raised for the Reagan campaign. But when Frank asked for tickets for Barbara and himself on the platform for the oath-taking ceremony, the request was politely turned down. Reagan had a hundred tickets at his disposal and he couldn't find another two. Frank still attended. He went up to an usher, told him he was Frank Sinatra (presumably the identification was not necessary) and was allowed on to the platform just the same.

This seemed to be the first suggestion that Reagan was getting a little embarrassed by his link with Sinatra. One member of the Reagan inner circle supposedly let it be known at this time: 'Anyone round here who talks about Sinatra and Reagan in the same breath is likely to lose his job. That's how touchy the issue is.' But the connection did continue, if less warmly than before.

As the 1980s got into their stride, Frank Sinatra had to consider where he was going now. For the first time he was seeking what could be described as 'respectability' with the Broadway Establishment. Since he had never appeared in a legitimate Broadway show, he felt left out of the theatrical scene. One way to remedy that was to join the New York theatrical club, the Players. One of its members, Jane Simon, told me: 'A lot of the Broadway people didn't want him and he only narrowly scraped in. But then when he came to the club, he insisted on not dining with the other members, but eating alone – which, as far as we could see, was a total negation of the idea of a club. Why did he want to join in the first place?'

He still performed, too, and sang as though he were creating numbers for the first time. 'Something in the Way She Moves' was almost of the quality of 'Strangers in the Night'. Appearing on television with Dinah Shore, they sang a medley that included 'They Can't Take That Away from Me', 'All of Me' and 'Day In, Day Out', one song segueing into another. 'Can't you see I'm just a mess without you?' Sinatra joked.

'Actually,' Dinah Shore told me in 1994, 'I think I would have been a mess without him. Nobody else could throw a medley together like Frank and make it sound like a brand-new number – a whole number.'

That was the mature Frank Sinatra – a whole number.

— 32 —

YOU MAKE ME FEEL SO
YOUNG

Frank Sinatra still behaved as though he were the world's greatest entertainer. That had been the title that Jolson had given himself. It appeared on all Jolson's movie posters and under his name on his record labels – and nobody objected. There is no question that Sinatra inherited the Jolson mantle, but by 1980 it was by way of being an honorary title, like calling a less active professor 'Emeritus' or, in England, receiving a peerage. The title was for services rendered in the past. Sinatra carried on as though he were the most popular figure in the entertainment world and as though his voice still had all the old swing and velvet. It didn't.

People still bought tickets for his concerts – but in many cases it was because Sinatra was still singing, still entertaining and perhaps they wanted to be able to tell their grandchildren that they had seen Frank Sinatra at work. However, when Reprise released a brand-new three-album record set called *Trilogy* in March 1980, it went to the top of the charts and won six Grammy nominations.

The triple album was the idea of Gordon Jenkins. Frank was overwhelmed when he heard the score and the ideas behind it. He spent months planning the mix. Some of the songs he'd recorded before. 'What we did was change the arrangements and I changed my versions so that they were little more fresh than what we did the first time.'

It was a strange compilation: three periods in Sinatra's life, his past, his present – and his future, which said a lot for his optimism. *The Past* did not necessarily include his big hits. Numbers, like 'The Song Is You', 'It Had to Be You' and 'Let's Face the Music and Dance' seem to have been chosen for their lack of Sinatra association as much as anything else. Billy May and his orchestra and chorus accompanied.

The Present was a less eclectic mix. 'New York, New York' was undoubtedly Sinatra. 'MacArthur Park' was his, too. The Beatles 'Something' had become his; Don Costa conducted this. The third volume, *The Future*, was bizarre. Its conductor was the man behind the project in the first place and the oldest of them all, Gordon Jenkins, master of the soaring strings, coming the closest anyone had yet come to the Axel Stordahl touch. Nevertheless, the songs, like 'What Time Does the Next Miracle Leave' and 'World War None', were strictly for the enthusiasts.

This was Sinatra's first new album recorded in a studio since 1973. He hadn't come to terms with the rock'n'roll era and most people had to be glad that he had not. But it would have been nice to hear him revisiting some of the old hits with new accompaniments and with that new voice – ragged around the edges, but still an effective weapon.

Instead, he made another of those terrible Frank Sinatra films. *The First Deadly Sin* was about a police lieutenant on the verge of retirement having to cope with a murder case, a new station boss, and being married to Faye Dunaway. It was a flop.

There were also rumours abroad that he and Barbara were heading for the divorce court. In 1982, after six eventful years, the Hollywood community was buzzing with the news. There had been a series of what could only be described as slamming matches in public. At one, he was heard to shout at her: 'You're the dumbest broad I ever met.' She called him 'an old drunk'.

Another time Barbara called Frank 'an old has-been', to which he replied: 'You'd be nobody without my name. I plucked you from obscurity and I can send you back there just as easily.'

But they patched things up. Barbara continued as wife, decorative hostess and sponsor of the $2 million Barbara Sinatra Children's Center which opened on the campus of the Eisenhower Medical Center at Rancho Mirage, the part of Palm Springs where the Sinatras now lived.

Frank too was his usual generous self when he heard children were in trouble. Hearing that four desperately poor Miami children were without Christmas presents when their home was ransacked, he sent them enough money to more than replace the lost gifts. At the same time, somehow, he seemed to be saying there were more serious things to worry about than money or even divorce – like the question of his friends, who seemed to be disappearing from his life at an alarming rate. 'You like people and they die on you,' he told the writer Peter Hamill, who wrote a kindly profile of Sinatra in the *New Yorker*. 'I go to too many goddamn funerals these days.'

Meanwhile, the audiences for his concert reached new peaks of enthusiasm. At Carnegie Hall it was standing room only for two weeks. Every seat was sold in one day, which was an all-time record.

The Songwriters Hall of Fame began 'inducting' Sinatra's records into their archive collection. In 1982 it was the 1940 recording of 'I'll Never Smile Again', two years later, his Capitol album, *In the Wee Small Hours*. It merely underlined his position in American popular music history.

The Clan were always threatening to make a comeback – rather like the Beatles. For the moment it was limited to a baseball game played in Atlantic City at three o'clock in the morning with two sides supposedly representing Frank and Dean Martin. Frank's team was called Ol' Blue Eyes. Dino's was Ol' Red Eyes. The players wore the names on their sweatshirts.

But the really exciting news of 1980 was not that he was making more concert appearances or that there was another TV special called *The Man and His Music* (selections from some of his most successful albums) but that he won back his licence to operate gaming casinos in Las Vegas. What clinched it was the backing of the President, who gave a personal recommendation.

The hearings at Las Vegas's City Hall had raised all sorts of things which Sinatra and his lawyers regarded as unpleasant. But he had prepared his case. Not only was there the reference from the President, but also, just before the hearings, Frank had had a cordial private meeting with Nevada's Governor, Bob List. The Governor heard that Frank wanted an assurance that 'we weren't going to poke him in the eye with a stick, and he got it. He felt that he didn't want to come in and have the Board or commission in an accusatory, hostile setting and I told him that's just not the way the board and commission work.'

Sinatra looked dapper if fatter, his hair weave in perfect place. Dale Askew, one of the three men sitting in judgment on him, declared: 'We will be examining Mr Sinatra's honesty, his integrity and his character.' Barbara was with Frank. So was Jilly Rizzo. Mickey Rudin, introduced rarely on this occasion as 'Milton Rudin', was representing him, as he always did.

The questions were probing, on all the issues he might have

expected to be raised – and much else, like Giancana's presence at the Cal-Neva. Frank replied: 'I never invited Mr Giancana to come to the Cal-Neva Lodge. I never entertained him and I never saw him.' It had never apparently occurred to him that he could be used as a 'front' for Giancana's operation.

Questions even came up about the use of Willie Moretti in putting the pressure on Tommy Dorsey to abandon his 'unfair' contract with Sinatra. Frank answered: 'Mr Moretti had absolutely nothing to do with my career.' He was just a neighbour whom he had known 'vaguely'.

One member of the commission asked him if he had 'skimmed profits' illegally from the Westchester theatre where he had been photographed with gang leaders, the same group whom a New York grand jury was now investigating. Sinatra was also asked whether he had taken $50,000 from concerts at the theatre, which federal prosecutors were charging was 'secretly hocked to hidden interests, including top levels of organised crime such as Carlo Gambiano'. Gambiano, the 'don of dons', was shot dead in 1976. Sinatra said: 'I have never in my life, sir, received any illegal moneys. I have had to work very hard for my money, thank you.'

Sinatra was never formally accused of any involvement. He was not afraid to address the problem of alleged Mob links. Yes, he had met mobsters. 'We don't seek them. They seek us out, our being celebrities. They are kind of star-struck.'

He had certainly never asked Jilly Rizzo, for instance, to 'break someone's legs'.

When he was asked if he would avoid 'undesirable social contacts' in future, he replied: 'By all means.'

Bob Hope sent an affidavit in praise of this famous man. There were character witness submissions, too, from Gregory Peck, Kirk Douglas and a Catholic priest. A university administrator from Nevada also spoke highly of Sinatra. So did Peter Pitchess, Sheriff of Los Angeles county. 'Mr Sinatra,' he declared as Frank beamed from one ear to the other, 'is a very good friend of mine. I feel I have spent a lifetime in inquiring and investigating Sinatra and at the same time enjoying a very close personal relationship with him. If Mr Sinatra is a member of the Mafia, then I am The Godfather.'

The chairman, a lawyer named Harry Reid, gave Sinatra – a man who had 'built orphanages ... orthopaedic hospitals ... blind centres' – back his gaming licence after six hours of hearings. It was granted without Sinatra even having to serve the customary six months' probation.

Reid told him: 'Eight days ago I had the preconceived notion that you were the type of person who should not be given a gaming licence. Now, having read all the testimony, I have to admit that I am a Frank Sinatra fan.'

Not just that, but another member of the commission investigating Sinatra, Carl Dodge, said: 'The record shows . . . conclusively that the allegations against Sinatra have been manufactured out of printer's ink . . . President Reagan, who contacted us through his lawyer, described Mr Sinatra as an honourable man, extremely loyal and charitable. Mr Sinatra has been maligned. He doesn't need the people who are involved in organised crime.'

Richard Bunker, the chairman of the Nevada Gaming Control Board, said finally: 'I am not suggesting he's a saint by any means, but in the areas we investigated we have not found any substantive reason why he shouldn't have a gaming licence.' This surprised everyone, who thought that Sinatra was finished as a casino operator. Now he was free to earn the $8,000 a week he had been promised to act as a consultant at Caesar's Palace. There was also talk of his becoming part-owner of the Dunes Hotel on the Strip at Vegas. Best of all, he was not only allowed back into the business, but was convinced that he was finally free from the Mafia charges.

He requested that the FBI hand over its files on him, which went back to the 1950s when he had appeared with Mrs Roosevelt. They revealed no evidence of any Mob connection. He was, after all, President Reagan's friend. When, in March 1981, Reagan was shot, Sinatra showed just what a friend he could be. He cancelled his show at Caesar's Palace and flew to Washington, staying with the President until he was sure he was going to recover.

The residents of the White House were not the only heads of state to show Sinatra friendship. When Princess Grace and Prince Rainier celebrated their twenty-fifth wedding anniversary in 1981, they chose to mark the silver occasion with Frank at Palm Springs. (The following year, Princess Grace was killed in a road accident. 'I feel as though the sword of suffering pierced my heart,' Frank wrote to Rainier.)

Frank also organised the entertainment when India's Prime Minister Indira Gandhi came to Washington. When the Queen and Prince Philip paid a state visit in 1983, he took it for granted that he would not only be received by Her Majesty but would be included in the party being entertained on the Royal Yacht, *Britannia*. The royals balked at this – but relented when Frank's friend Walter Annenberg made a personal request. Former ambassadors of super-friendly states were not usually turned down. Frank reciprocated by hosting a Vegas-type spectacular for the royal visitors.

But there were times when Sinatra's political touch was less sure. In August 1981, he went to what is now South Africa's own 'Vegas', Sun City, for a ten-day engagement. South Africa was then a pariah state and Sun City wasn't even situated – officially – within the country's borders. It was in Bophuthatswana – an enclave within the apartheid regime which was supposedly a 'Black homeland', in other words a client state set up to make the Botha regime look more sympathetic. Bophuthatswana was in every way a puppet state and not recognised by the world community, least of all by the United States.

The Reverend Jesse Jackson was among the first to complain. 'He came with us to Alabama in the sixties by identifying with the right cause and he simply shouldn't be trading his birthright for a mess of money now,' he declared.

Frank had been paid $2 million to do the concert. Elobe Braithe, who organised one of the numerous demonstrations against Frank's stand when he began his concert tour, said that the fee was 'blood money. It is money South Africa gets from the brutal system of apartheid.' The United Nations special committee on apartheid condemned Sinatra as a 'collaborator'. That was harsh language – not a good moment for the man who had once swiped the server at an army base canteen for not feeding a black musician. 'I play to all people of any colour, creed, drunk or sober,' he said – and then cherished the Order of the Leopard pinned on him by the Bophuthatswana President, Lucas Mangope, not one of the names that would enter the history of the period. The South African President told him he was the first white person to receive the award but that didn't make his critics feel any happier.

Indeed, later, in the summer of 1987, he had to cancel a tour to Scandinavia – because the Swedish Government said they were going to impose a special tax on him for appearing in South Africa. But that didn't stop his being given a Life Achievement Award from the Los Angeles branch of the National Association for the Advancement of Coloured People, also in 1987. The citation pointed to Sinatra's 'significant outcries against segregation, discrimination and bigotry'.

He had an equally good reception when he attended evenings commemorating the Holocaust. After one of these, the Nazi-hunter Simon Wiesenthal told me: 'I don't know of any other man who has shown such compassion for the survivors of that great tragedy as Frank Sinatra.') He also appeared on television to help free Poland, then at the height of its Solidarity fight. 'I'm not a politician,' declared Sinatra. 'I'm a singer, but when I see people being forced from their homeland to seek freedom someplace else, it makes me realise all over again how grateful I am for the freedom I have.' He sang a song in both English and Polish, 'Ever Homeward'.

Back in 1982, he conducted the orchestra for an album by the jazz artist Sylvia Syms. *Syms By Sinatra* may not have been the most notable recording the star made but it was certainly the most interesting – and emphasised her respect for Sinatra's art.

The year saw the deaths of several people in Frank's life, including Buddy Rich. Despite their distant falling-out, Frank was at the funeral and attended a tribute held at Universal's amphitheatre. Pat Henry, the comedian who used to start a number of the Sinatra shows, was another loss. Then there was Joe Louis, the former world heavyweight champion, whose entire hospital treatment (including the services of Dr Michael DeBakey) Frank had paid for and at whose funeral he gave the eulogy.

Hardest of all to accept was the death of Don Costa to whom he owed so much in recent years. The day Costa died, he was in the process of preparing a new orchestration that was to be used in Frank's next studio recording session. 'I was just a wreck for two weeks,' Sinatra said afterwards. 'His orchestration for "Come Rain, Come Shine" was a perfect example of his brilliance. "New York, New York" was his memorial.'

It was not a good time for Sinatra band leaders. Harry James died a matter of days later. If Frank mourned the loss of his latest collaborator, Harry James brought back memories of the days when he yearned to move beyond the Rustic Cabin. Another Sinatra 'contact' was also dead now: the Mafia 'godfather', Sam Giancana, was shot.

But there were good things, too. In December 1983, Frank was one of the performers decorated with the Kennedy Center Honor for Lifetime Achievement – along with James Stewart. Gene Kelly spoke on behalf of Sinatra: 'There is not the remotest possibility that he will have a successor.' With that, Mikhail Baryshnikov danced *The Sinatra Suite* with Elaine Kudo.

Undoubtedly, the 1984 movie *Cannonball Run II*, in which Frank made a brief appearance, was not one of his life achievements. But it is important in the Sinatra story because it was his very last film, and the last occasion on which the Clan got together publicly.

They had been talking about it for a long time. 'We love each other,' Sammy Davis told me, 'and we enjoy having fun.'

The film was supposedly about stunt riders, but really it was an opportunity for Sinatra, Sammy Davis, Dean Martin and Shirley MacLaine to assemble, while the real work was in the hands of the likes of Burt Reynolds, Telly Savalas and Dom DeLuise. Shirley MacLaine has described it as 'a disgrace'. She said: 'Frank worked only half a day and that was too long for him. He did one take and then left. It looked as though he were never there at all.'

The writer and director of the movie was Hal Needham, who has fonder memories of the occasion than does Shirley MacLaine. He remembers it as a time when Sinatra was still king. 'Even Burt kowtowed to him,' said Needham, who had first met Sinatra when he was a stunt man on *Four for Texas*, doubling for Charles Bronson. 'But he was very professional,' he told me. 'He had his make-up on time, in costume and ready to go. He did his shit and he was gone.'

It was a time for a new Sinatra enthusiasm: he now collected model trains. Needham had one installed in his dressing room, a gesture that was appreciated. 'I got along good with him because I gave him the respect he deserved. We liked the fact that he gave all the money he earned to charity.'

Actually, Sinatra's role was little more than a cameo. He only did one day's work, not the half-day that MacLaine remembers. The night before, he and Needham and their wives went out for dinner. Shirley Maclaine came too. 'It was like an old-time reunion. We had dinner and then said our adieus.'

He received honorary degrees and attended more White House functions and fundraising events – undoubtedly Reagan raised more when Sinatra attended the functions than when he was not there – but the most important events were when he was on the concert platform, although he did have another new album that year with Quincy Jones. *L.A. Is My Lady* was not vintage Sinatra, but it added to the catalogue and helped the demand for his live services, not just in America. The Mayor of Vienna invited him to perform at the Stadthalle and Frank gave all his take to children's charities.

He had a better reception there than he did in New Jersey the same year. In the midst of the 1984 election campaign, he finally went back to Hoboken – escorting the President to his old home town, as part of Reagan's campaign. They went to St Ann's Church in time for the seventy-fourth annual St Ann's Festival. Hoboken was excited by the first Sinatra visit since 1947 – at least, the first anyone knew about. At the public library they hoped that he would take advantage of his visit to see the Sinatra collection which was almost a shrine, but he didn't. In fact, he did little more than find time to shake hands and wave at the crowds. James Hans, the Hoboken historian, told me: 'It was amazing, though. He ignored Hoboken for a long time, but when he came back they loved him.' John Marotta put it into perspective when I asked him about the visit. 'When Frankie gets mad, he gets really mad, so he bypassed Hoboken for most of his life. Then when Ronald Reagan came here he behaved as if he loved the place more than anywhere else on earth and Hoboken decided it loved him, too. Strange.'

A little later on, he really upset his old home town by saying he had no plans to go back there again. 'I've got no reason to go back. I've no family there. I've no friends there. I don't know anybody there,' he declared.

Did that mean that the rumours were true? He and Hoboken didn't get along? 'I don't believe in rumours and speculation,' he said. As for his trip with the President: 'I was only there for about thirty minutes and I hardly recognised any of it. It's changed a lot.'

Later, Frank said that he wouldn't go back to play there ever – or anywhere else in the state of New Jersey. As far as he was concerned, America consisted of just forty-nine states.

The comment was made after a charge levelled by the state's Casino Control Commission vice-chairman, alleging that Sinatra had intimidated four workers at the Golden Nugget Hotel Casino in Atlantic City into breaking blackjack rules enforced in New Jersey. The hotel was subsequently fined a total of $25,000 for three violations when Frank and Dean Martin appeared together there. William B. Williams, who revelled in his reputation as the man who had first called Sinatra the 'Chairman of the Board', supported Frank's stand to boycott his old home state. 'I believe he made this decision because no one in New Jersey spoke up for him,' he said.

The next year, 1985, he was again performing at a Reagan inauguration. But a newspaper article published that day, which mentioned Sinatra's participation in the event, said that Reagan's advisers wanted him to sever all links with anybody who was alleged to have Mafia connections. The old story would not go away. Hours before the inaugural ball, a TV reporter named Barbara Howard stopped Frank to ask about it. He lost control. 'You're all dead,' he screamed at her. 'Every one of you. You're dead.' Ms Howard kindly absolved him of too much blame for the event. 'I think I incurred his wrath because I was the first person to fall under his gaze after he read the article,' she declared.

Despite his feelings for New Jersey, ten months after the Reagan visit he was back again – because the Stevens Institute of Technology made up for his not having achieved his ambition and become a student there by awarding him the consolation prize of an honorary doctorate.

It was not a popular decision. Cries went up of Sinatra short-circuiting educational convention simply because he was famous. There was a petition signed by present-day students at the Institute who were having to work for their degrees. They were not happy that he was getting for nothing what they were slaving over examinations to receive. It wasn't enough to say that every university in the world awards honorary degrees to celebrities. There was enough publicity for thirty-five news organisations to come along and record the event.

The citation made reference to Frank's singing style, his distinctive phrasing, his way of pausing and taking breaths. As far as the institute was concerned, that was engineering – engineering a song. As far as Frank was concerned, the honorary degree was one of the nicest things that had happened to him. He even finally graduated from high school. Dean Martin presented the belatedly-received certificate to him on television.

At the same time, he acknowledged the power of the education which he was always willing to accept had been denied him by setting up a Sinatra educational fund for Hoboken High School. But the biggest honour of all came just a couple of days later – at the White House again. President Reagan thanked him for all he had done for the United States by presenting him with America's highest civilian award, the Medal of Freedom.

Everyone was conscious that Frank's professional career was close to its end. Others tried to take the Sinatra baton. Michael Jackson came to a Sinatra recording. Frank showed the courtesy of agreeing to pose with the young star, but is not on record as saying anything about him. As far as he was concerned, there was still a little more to attend to – a new recording of 'Stormy Weather' for the *L.A. Is My Lady* album. It was not a remarkable performance. Now Frank was leaving those for his live concerts, which he usually finished by saying, 'May you all live to be four hundred years old and may the last voice you hear be mine.'

He was in London again in 1985. The British critic Dave Gelly wrote about his performance at the Royal Festival Hall: 'Every note, every word, fell precisely where it should ... Cole Porter could never have expected a more resonant embodiment of his idea then Sinatra's "In the Silence of My Lonely Room", which made "Night and Day" into what it was meant to be, a song of desperate longing.'

Then he went to the Royal Albert Hall. Hilary Bonner wrote in the *Mail on Sunday*: 'Nobody, not even his greatest enemy, has ever accused Sinatra of being ordinary or dull. He is a monument to romance. And despite the flaws of age, he makes sure he still looks the part. Women adore him, always will, and why not? His suits look a million dollars, which is probably only a little more than they cost. He sings about a way of life full of the kind of riches – material and emotional – few of us will ever find ... I agree that the miracle of a voice with which Sinatra was blessed is no longer an impeccable instrument. He does need a sheet of music nowadays to prompt him and almost everything written by the critics is true. But only the most soulless critic would suggest that we would be better off without this colour-splashed giant.'

It was seen as no more than justice for the entertainer who had stayed on top for so long – and who in December 1985 was seventy years old. It seemed unbelievable. The man who had had those bobbysoxers squealing was seventy? But he was beginning to look it. The paunch was more evident. The hair was silvery, more than it had ever been before.

Ava sent a message to say that she still loved him. 'I said "love", not "in love", there is a difference,' she said in London. Mia said she still adored the man she knew as Charlie. Nancy, above all, knew his faults and his qualities. 'Frank always treated me like a lady and insisted that everyone treated me that way,' she said, and there was a mountain of evidence to prove that to be true.

He reviewed his career. 'Throughout [it] if I have done anything, I have paid attention to every note and every word I sing. If I respect the song and if I cannot project it to the listener, I fail.'

His friends talked about him, too. One said: 'Get quoted anywhere and Frank's long arm will reach out and flick you off the tablecloth.' Another said: 'Frank seems to have come to some kind of contentment at long last. Mind you, don't go putting your hand in the tiger's cage. He still has a fearsome bite.'

Perhaps, though, after all, he had reason to do so. A newspaper story surfaced suggesting that the Mafia don Johnny Formosa had ordered Sam Giancana to take out a contract on the entire Rat Pack. A wiretap supposedly revealed Formosa saying: 'Let's show 'em ... these Hollywood fruit cakes. Let's hit Sinatra. Or I could whack out a couple of those other guys, Lawford and that Martin. Or I could take the nigger and put his other eye out.'

The information might have been useful at all those investigations to which Sinatra had been subjected. He was now 'revealed' as being on the other side of the Mob fence.

There were about seventy different concert bookings in 1986, but the early ones were overshadowed by yet another death – Nelson Riddle's in October 1985. It saddened Frank, although perhaps not as much as Kitty Kelley's monumental biography of Sinatra, *His Way*, published the following year. The family were ordered to pretend the book never existed, but Frank did go to his lawyers. Before long, it was apparent that America's First Amendment to the Constitution guaranteeing freedom of speech and freedom of the press would prevent any action being taken.

Nancy, Jr., in her own book, corrected a Kelley story – that Frank had pushed a woman through a plate-glass window at his house. Frank maintained that the woman was with a friend who called at the house. She was drunk and he ordered her out. It was when she was already *out* of the house that she fell through a plate-glass window *into* the building. Frank then himself drove her to the hospital, reported Nancy, and paid all her bills there.

It was one of those things Sinatra-watchers would almost have expected – the hard tough operator who takes on responsibilities far beyond the call of duty. Just as they would have anticipated the lashing he gave with his tongue to a photographer who dared to spot him on holiday in the snow at Gstaad in Switzerland with Barbara and with Roger Moore on hand, too.

Much less conventional for Sinatra was the lecture he gave in April 1986 at the Yale Law School. His subject: personal achievement. *Time* magazine thought it ought to have been considered to be the opening of a degree course for an Sh.D. (Doctor of Showbizology). He told four hundred students that he still wasn't apologising for going to South Africa. 'I'll go anywhere I want to go, any time I want to go.' He also told them: 'Keep working at it until it never fails you. I believe everything I was doing was right.'

One of the best ways of demonstrating the Sinatra achievements was to go back to the past. *The Columbia Years, 1943–52*, was one of the better retrospectives. The six-LP set recalled an era when a man named Sinatra made girls swoon and boys try to sing like him. It was a very attractive package, with each record showing a different Sinatra from those years. *Sinatra Standards* had a youngster with a quiff of greased hair over his forehead who sang 'Saturday Night Is the Lone-liest Night in the Week', 'Autumn in New York', 'April in Paris' and, for those with a nostalgic bent, 'Nancy (with the Laughing Face)'.

Love Songs showed him in tuxedo, plainly relaxing in the adoration of his fans. 'The Nearness of You' sounded wonderful. 'Someone to Watch Over Me' he would do better later on, but it was still outstanding.

Sinatra Swings – including 'Birth of the Blues', 'Blue Skies' and 'Mean to Me', wasn't exactly the Swinging Sinatra of the Riddle era, but the young Sinatra on the sleeve singing to a 1940s microphone looked racy enough. *Screen* – with 'The Continental' and 'The Brook-lyn Bridge' among the tracks – showed the pensive singer from *Higher and Higher*. *Sinatra Stage* had 'There's No Business Like Show Busi-ness' and 'Ol' Man River' with the adoring young man in a wide-lapelled sports jacket smiling benignly at the camera. The most mature Sinatra was the one on the *Saloon Songs* sleeve. Here was a man who liked to take a drink – as well as sing early versions of 'One for My Baby', 'I Should Care' and 'Why Try to Change Me Now'. It was all a wonderful relic of the days when The Voice was more melodic and more moving than anything else on offer. But it demonstrated for the 1980s public just how far his technique had come in the years since they were recorded.

In November 1986, Frank was admitted to the Eisenhower Medical Center for an operation to relieve what was officially diagnosed as diverticulitis. He had collapsed in the middle of a show at Atlantic

City and was taken to hospital on a stretcher, waving to his disappointed public as he went. Of course, the story was that he had bowel cancer, but there was never any confirmation of this, although some twelve inches of intestine were removed. He also had a colostomy bag fitted – temporarily, said a surgeon who had been told to say nothing. Ten months later, he had another operation that lasted eight hours.

But he recovered and, when he got better, he was off on the road again. In 1987, 1988 and 1989 he covered roughly the same number of engagements – about thirty each year. The difference was that the man standing at the podium which had been occupied so brilliantly by Don Costa and, before him, by Nelson Riddle and Billy May, was now Frank Sinatra, Jr., about whom Jonathan Schwartz wrote in *Esquire*: 'Junior has come to resemble his father by deftly removing himself from any chance of cordial encounter.' Frankie had decided to relinquish his ambitions as a pop singer and work with his father, which was His Way of both staying in the business and being close to his dad. The pianist would always be the white-haired Bill Miller, almost exactly Frank's own age.

In 1987, he appeared in a TV film, too, *Magnum PI*, with Tom Selleck, playing a private detective.

In 1988, a concert at which he and Liza Minnelli were due to perform was cancelled at fifteen minutes' notice. More than 19,000 people who had turned up for the event at the Meadowlands Area in East Rutherford near Chicago were turned away in ice-cold drizzle. The reason was that the sheet music for Frank's orchestra had got lost on the way from Los Angeles and they couldn't play without it.

Frank felt sorry for the people and he said he was sorry for the musicians. What was more, the man who had made a score of fortunes himself thought it time to look after others in the business, which was why he became head of the Performers Rights Society of America. The society wanted the same rights as members of ASCAP (the American Society of Composers, Authors and Publishers) when their work was performed.

Frank had for a long time been trying to encourage Dean Martin to join him, as in the old days. Finally, in May 1988, the singer–comedian agreed and began a tour with Sinatra, Shirley MacLaine and Sammy Davis, but he didn't last the trip. Ms MacLaine remembers him telling Frank: 'I just want to go to my room and watch TV and fall asleep.' By then, the death of his son in a plane that crashed into the same mountain that killed Dolly Sinatra, had broken him. 'I don't want to go, Dago,' he told Sinatra, who couldn't persuade him to last the length of the tour.

That is one side of the story. The other is that Sinatra got rid of him because he wasn't performing up to standard. 'Hell will freeze over before I speak to that drunken bum again,' he was overheard to say. Martin said that for once it wasn't drink that interfered with his work; he had kidney problems. Whatever the reason, he and Sinatra barely saw each other ever again.

The difference between them was that Martin had developed a reputation as a lush. Sinatra talked and sang about booze but usually looked in control. As Juliet Prowse told me: 'He was always a good drinker, even though when he knew he was going to do a gig or a recording, he'd go right off the sauce. Completely off it and he would get his voice back, the timbre of it.'

Now it needed more than laying off the sauce to bring that voice back properly. But the awards still tumbled in. He was both flattered and delighted when, in 1989, the Recording Academy presented him with their Grammy Legend Award 'to a man whose name defines the word Entertainer'. The award was made by the Irish singer Bono, from the U2 rock band: 'Rock'n'roll people know Frank Sinatra because Frank Sinatra has got what we want,' he said, 'swagger and attitude'. As Bono said, Frank was 'big on attitude, serious attitude, bad attitude. Frank Sinatra is Chairman of the Board. He's the boss, the boss of bosses, the man, the big bang of pop. I'm not going to mess with him. Are you? Frank walks like America, cocksure. The champ who would rather show you his scars than his medals. A man heavier than the Empire State ... living proof that God is a Catholic.'

But when Sinatra made his acceptance speech, he was interrupted after three minutes by commercials. The New York *Daily News* was furious. Eric Mink wrote: 'True, Frank had begun to play emotional free-association, but what the hell, it was live TV and one of the reasons we watch these things is the hope of seeing something unpredicted, the possibility that an icon might break character and accidentally reveal himself ... Cutting off Sinatra in mid-ramble looked rude, unkind and insulting to a guy being dubbed a legend by the business that he has helped transform into an industry over the last half-century.'

Mike Green, President of the National Academy of Recording Arts and Sciences, which controls the Grammy awards, said that Sinatra's own minders had ordered the cut made. If true, they were afraid of the 78-year-old Frank embarrassing himself. He couldn't remember what he was going to say next, which was why he was actually cut off in mid-sentence, paying tribute to Dean Martin after having asked the audience if anyone had appeared before him that night. He had asked Barbara to stand up twice in those three minutes he was allowed to talk, had told everyone how much he loved her, and said he loved New York. He was plainly floundering.

That kind of embarrassment was more and more familiar now. When, as often happened, Frank missed an entrance or let Frank, Jr., play more than the scheduled introduction, the audience knew he had gone wrong, but were glad to have him there at all. Such was the devotion that went with the legend. It no longer really mattered whether he was good any more. They weren't asking for good. They wanted Frank, however he wanted to play it.

The 1990s beckoned now and an opportunity to state his case – of which he was certain.

— 33 —

TOO CLOSE FOR COMFORT

The 1990s heralded Frank's eightieth birthday. It could have been a wonderful moment for retrospection. With that final curtain down on his career, he could retire, fabulously rich, marvellously endowed with memories. But that was not His Way. As far as Sinatra was concerned, this decade was going to be more of the same.

He had a full calendar, with tours abroad, concerts in Las Vegas, Atlantic City and places all over America, new records, articles: a mass of events that would show that nothing had altered.

As he had said all those years before, he was attending too many goddamned funerals for his liking. But now he began losing close friends, not just people he knew or with whom he had worked. The first, in May 1990, was Sammy Davis, Jr. The skinny, one-eyed black Jew had long since re-entered the Sinatra life, their various rows and feuds buried. Sammy was sixty-four, a victim of throat cancer, and his death came just six months after a celebration of his life on TV. Frank had taken part, along with people ranging from Michael Jackson and Richard Pryor to Shirley MacLaine and Gregory Peck.

Just a month later, Frank was in England, with a week of concerts at the London Arena, a huge soulless, cavernous auditorium which even Sinatra couldn't fill every night. The building, in what used to be the London Docks area was not the most salubrious, a fact reflected in the people who went there. The society audiences to which Frank Sinatra had been used in London were singularly absent.

That was enough evidence that things had changed. The night I was there, he forgot an occasional line, missed a vital note or two but, despite the dreadful atmosphere, you still had the feeling of being in the presence of a superstar. But the voice had lost even more of its timbre and there were words from songs that had once been as familiar to him as his children's names which now escaped him. At one point, he turned to the audience, an insecure expression on his face. 'Have I introduced the orchestra yet?' he asked. Yes, he had – five minutes before; the band conducted by Frank Sinatra, Jr., and each of the members of the outfit.

There were unanticipated clouds on the horizon now – when the old heavy hand was brought in, supposedly on Sinatra's behalf, and then thwarted for the most unexpected and unwelcome reasons. The Sinatras were guests at a party given by Billy Wilder for Sir Andrew Lloyd Webber, the Englishman who had adapted Wilder's film classic *Sunset Boulevard* into a hit stage musical. Someone asked Frank for an autograph. As quick as the old Sinatra might have said 'Ring-a-ding-ding', a bodyguard rounded on the maitre d' at Mortimer's restaurant, Steven Schrittweiser, and complained – somewhat unpleasantly. Why had the man allowed his staff to leak the fact that Frank was there? But that was not true, said the restaurateur, he hadn't done anything of the kind. 'None of our waiters even knows who Sinatra is,' he protested. 'They're too young.'

Frank still looked after the people whom he regarded as part of himself – not just his wife, his children and grandchildren, but also his musicians; caring for the needs of every one of them, asking people if they were comfortable as they sat on a transatlantic flight, taking them to yet another season of Sinatra concerts. Frank himself could never sit still on a plane. 'He's walking to Europe,' one of his grand-children said. As Sammy Cahn had said, he was the world's greatest travel agent, a travel agent who sometimes added a little sweetness to the lives of his passengers – in the form of candies and popcorn which he deposited in the shoes of the sleeping tourists. Just a Sinatra joke.

In 1989 the 74-year-old travel agent had booked his party for a tour that took in Glasgow and Stockholm. Two months later, he was touring with Don Rickles, a punishing schedule for a man half his age.

There were more awards, too, to decorate the walls of his Palm Springs home – including the Ella, the Society of Singers Lifetime Achievement Award named in honour of Ella Fitzgerald, of course. Ella sang to him at the ceremony before 1,200 people at the Beverly Hilton Hotel in Beverly Hills. 'There Will Never Be Another You' seemed a perfect title for her serenade. When they did a duet, it had to be 'The Lady Is a Tramp': 'She loves the cool knocked-out groovy cuckoo wind in her hair...'

If anyone doubted whether Sinatra should occupy himself with such exhausting shows, his reply was always that he had never felt better – which was why he was branching out into another business. He was marketing pasta sauces in three varieties – tomato, basil and parmesan; marinara with mushrooms; and marinara, Milan-style. The brand name was going to be Artanis (Sinatra spelt backwards) but by the time they were released at $14.99 each ($43.99 for a gift box of four varieties) he decided to call them 'Frank Sinatra's Gourmet Italian Foods'. The Sinatra name had to mean more to prospective customers. 'So Italian!' went the sales pitch. 'Gourmet restaurant taste at home!' They were backed by music boxes in stores – playing ten-second snatches of Sinatra songs like 'New York, New York'.

At the same time, he was branching out into what was called 'Frank Sinatra Legendary Neckwear' – a line in ties inspired by paintings Frank had done himself. It didn't tend to do anything for the image of Frank Sinatra, but he probably felt that was already well in place and if there were money to be made, why not?

When, in 1986, Kitty Kelley wrote her biography of Nancy Reagan and suggested there had been an affair between Sinatra and the former First Lady, Frank decided not to sue. His answer was that they were just good friends and that included the ex-President. Reagan was beginning to show signs of the Alzheimer's disease which before long would cripple him.

In December 1990, Sinatra was seventy-five years old. Patrick Pasculli, Mayor of Hoboken, made a proclamation in his honour. It was very, very American:

- 'Whereas, on 12 December 1915, Natalie and Martin Sinatra of Hoboken became parents of a son, Francis Albert Sinatra; and
- Whereas, young Francis Albert Sinatra, known as Frank, was reared and educated in his native city, learning on his way how to carry a tune; and
- Whereas, through his perseverance and faith in himself and an insatiable desire to entertain his fellow man, Frank Sinatra attained the highest accolades in the world of music; and
- Whereas no other vocalist in history has sung, swung, crooned and serenaded into the hearts of the young and old and all in between as this consummerate (sic) artist from Hoboken; and
- Whereas, all the World owes a great deal of gratitude to 'Ol'

Blue Eyes' for all the joy he has brought by his interpretation
of lyrics to all kinds of beats; and
- Whereas, the Town of his birth is proud of this great man,
once called Frankie.'

Hoboken took it all as if they had a personal franchise on the
birthday. Leo's Grandezvous sold all its pizzas at 75 cents, one cent
for each of the Sinatra years.

There was talk of Sinatra himself having trouble with his mental
capabilities, stories that were only enhanced by his forgetfulness. How
to counter them? Frank tried one way which he was sure would make
his intellectual powers unquestionable: he wrote a major article for
the *Los Angeles Times* on Independence Day 1991. 'I'm no angel,' it
said. 'I've had my moments. I've done a few things in my life of which
I'm not too proud, but I have never unloved a human being because
of race, creed or colour. And if you think this is a case of he who doth
protest too much, you're wrong. I couldn't live any other way.'

As he also wrote, he couldn't bear the people who declared: 'Some
of my best friends are Jewish.' He said: 'I don't envy their trails in the
next world ... For if we don't come to grips with this killer disease of
hatred, of bigotry and racism and anti-Semitism pretty soon, we will
destroy from within this blessed country.'

He went on: 'OK, I'm a saloon singer by self-definition. Even my
mirror would never accuse me of inventing wisdom. But I do claim
enough street smarts to know that hatred is a disease – a disease in
the body of freedom, eating its way from the inside out, infecting all
who come in contact with it, killing the dreams and hopes of millions
of innocents with words, as surely as if they were bullets.

'Who in the name of God are these people anyway, the ones who
elevate themselves above others? America is an immigrant country.
Maybe not you and me, but those whose love made our lives possible,
or their parents or grandparents. Those weren't tourists on the *May-
flower* – they were your families and mine, following dreams that
turned out to be possible dreams.'

He hoped that that Independence Day would be 'a day of love for
all Americans'. With that, he left for what he called his Diamond
Jubilee tour. The *Atlanta Journal* headed its review: 'SINATRA FAR
FROM BEING OVER THE HILL, THE CHAIRMAN OF THE BOARD
IS STILL KING OF IT'.

He also took his forty-strong orchestra to Europe again as part of a tour to mark sixty years in show business. Spain, Belgium, Italy, Norway, Sweden, France, Germany, Holland, Ireland – all heard Frank Sinatra live. Steve Lawrence and his long-time wife and partner Eydie Gorme accompanied him. They played in arenas, concert halls and among the ruins of Pompeii. He gave little cause for anyone to think that he was a ruin himself. In fact, he liked the tour so much – and received the old adoration in so many of the places on the way – that he said he would come back again the next year. He appeared on a Christmas album along with a number of jazz, country-and-western and pop singers including Barry Manilow, Willie Nelson and Dionne Warwick. To Frankie's accompaniment on the piano, he sang 'Silent Night'. Aside from the fact that the record benefited the Children's Hospital Foundation in San Diego, most of the real Sinatra fans would wish that he had passed that opportunity by. It was not the Sinatra people wanted to hear.

They did ask for new songs, but he said no – in an uncanny reprise of exactly what Jolson had said at the same point in his career: 'I don't do anything that's new because there's nothing new – and if it was new, I wouldn't understand a damn thing.'

Jilly Rizzo was dead now, killed in a car accident not far from Sinatra's home in Palm Springs. A month later, in June 1992, Frank was back on his European tour. One thing was obvious: if he were unsure of his work the previous year, it was much harder now. Prime Minister John Major came to see him at the Royal Albert Hall in London. But Frank had to be helped out on to the stage – a stage surrounded by auto-prompts. From almost any angle, audiences above stage-level saw the prompts on the TV screens. There was a sub-conscious urge to read along with him. Had it been one of the old vintage performances, you would have forgotten the prompts were there. This time, the Sinatra personality didn't obliterate the dis-tractions – especially now that he was even less able than before to follow all the lines. Having said that, the hardest number of all, the 'Soliloquy' from *Carousel*, was as perfect as it had ever been. But 'The Lady Is a Tramp' had none of the old verve. There were similar problems on other stages of the tour – in Spain, Portugal and Greece. Now, he was being advised publicly to give up – at last.

If he had, he wouldn't have suffered the indignity of a tour in October 1992 with Shirley MacLaine. He couldn't remember lines (and on one occasion couldn't remember her name) and entrances, or even read the monitors which showed whose turn to perform it was going to be. He refused to rehearse so they did whatever occurred to them, and as much as possible from a tape they had made beforehand. 'We're going to tear up the joint, baby,' he told her. But all that he really tore up was his reputation.

While performing, he still expected the trappings of greatness – like a 'technical rider' to his contract: three cans of Campbell's chicken and rice soup always had to be available, with a two-burner hot plate; bottles of vodka, Chivas Regal Scotch, Jack Daniel's, cognac and gin and a generous sprinkling of both red and white wine were essential, too. There had to be six bottles of Evian water, a large bottle of Perrier and twenty-four bottles of other assorted soft drinks (75 per cent of which had to be 'diet'). He also insisted on a siren-blasting police escort to take him to and from airports, even though there was not much traffic on the roads when he processed through places like Worcester, Massachusetts, at three o'clock in the morning.

In New Orleans he celebrated Shirley's birthday by singing 'Happy Birthday' to her. She said it was worth being a year older just to be personally serenaded that way. That night he thought the show had gone well and he was in a good mood. Other times he would say: 'The hell with it, I'm going to the races', and walk off. It was becoming increasingly clear that he should have packed up there and then.

But it was hard advice to take for someone who, if he didn't have any singing to do, had no purpose left in life. That was why Sinatra, looking old, along with Dean Martin, Steve Lawrence, Eydie Gorme, Liza Minnelli and Shirley MacLaine, all posed together at what was now known as the Stars' Desert Inn and Country Club in Las Vegas, where they had all agreed to play.

It was even harder to think of retirement when always there were more and more awards, like another for Distinguished Life Achievement coming from the American Cinema Awards and a Career Achievement Award at Palm Springs International Film Festival which said that the local boy had made good.

More surprising was the CBS five-hour mini-series, *Sinatra*, made in conjunction with Warner Bros., which was broadcast in November 1992. It was a remarkable production, not least because it was produced by Frank's younger daughter Tina, the one he always said was most like him. It was not great television or great drama. He would have preferred it to have been a feature film but the idea was abandoned when it became clear that it 'wasn't moving along'.

When it was first decided to turn the project into a mini-series, a ten-hour project was talked about. But that was in 1984. In the eight years that followed the first announcements, there were more discussions. Writers came and went, some succumbing to what the author of the series, Bill Mastrosimone, called 'the old, "Let's fly to Vegas, have another drink Sinatra" stuff'.

There was talk of Frank playing himself in the later years, but that idea was soon scotched. Sinatra wouldn't have wanted to rehearse and, frankly, his powers of memory were so bad now that it wouldn't have been possible even if the make-up men could have made the septuagenarian look a fifty-or sixty-year old. In the end, the go-ahead was given for the five-hour show.

Tina was responsible for casting. The man who played the young Sinatra, Philip Casnoff, wasn't all bad – even in lip-synching the Sinatra voice. The younger Sinatra was sung by Frank, Jr., whose own speaking voice was uncannily like his father's, and sometimes by the impressionist Tom Burlinson, who originally tested for the acting role and was found to be unsuitable. Casnoff mimed the songs the way that Larry Parks had done for Al Jolson forty-six years earlier. But this was no *Jolson Story* – it didn't have the same quality.

Marcia Gay Harden played Ava Gardner. She recalled her meetings with Tina: 'When she talked about Ava it was always positive, with understanding and compassion – not just taking her mother's side. She understood that her father needed to be with this woman in a more passionate sense. She wasn't trying to portray this diabolic bitch.' Nina Siemaszko played Mia Farrow. The story ends just before the meeting between Frank and Barbara.

The part of Dolly was one of the hardest to cast. Olympia Dukakis played her, after learning what she described as 'the Hoboken Italian accent'. She said that since she was pro-choice she had no problems with the idea of Dolly being an abortionist. Gina Gershon played the senior Nancy. It was a highly favourable interpretation, as one might expect with her 'daughter' in charge. Tina was to say: 'I'm viscerally connected to this woman. She comes to work and tells me, "You look thin. You're not eating." And I say, "You spoke to my mother last night, right?"'

Tina said that the hardest things to show on film were the scenes in which her parents were fighting. But when that problem was settled, she went to Hoboken to see the place for which her father still felt no affection. She found it a nostalgic experience, more than he would have done. 'I went to Garden Street and sat on the stoop [of] where he used to live.'

What was really remarkable about it was that Frank Sinatra of all people allowed it to happen. He himself would explain: 'I want it done when I'm alive. If they do it when I'm dead, they'll screw it up so I want to be around to see it's done right.'

'The more Frank thought it was impossible,' said Mastrosimone, 'the more Tina wanted to do it.' Sinatra read the final script and called his daughter. 'Hey, this guy was pretty tough on me,' he said. She replied, 'Oh shit, Dad. What part isn't true?' 'It's all true,' he admitted.

In the end, the man who hated any magazine articles about himself, and most journalists, agreed that the film could be made, mainly because it was produced by Tina. Even she said she was surprised by how 'candidly' he permitted himself to be portrayed. After all, it covered matters nobody could have thought possible, including the relationship with Sam Giancana, played by Rod Steiger, Sinatra's suicide attempt – implicitly admitted for the first time – and the moment Frank finally walked out on Nancy Sr.

Frank, however, made no attempt to censor the material on view. 'I think that was because he knew that I could see into his character very well,' said his daughter. 'It could have been only kin that could make this happen ... Frank wanted to tell his story as fully as he thought he needed to tell it ... He's not ashamed or regretful about his life'.

Nancy, Sr., was the first person outside the production team to see it. She was tactful, praised her daughter's brilliance and then said she would be glad when it was all over and forgotten. Frank saw the mini-series by himself, locked in his den, taking a break only to eat. He took more than a day to ring Tina – a hard, floor-pacing day for her – and pronounced that he was impressed.

Another huge loss occurred in January 1993, with the death of Sammy Cahn at the age of seventy-nine.

Later the same year, Columbia Records released a twelve-CD collection called *Frank Sinatra: the Columbia Years*, everything Frank had recorded between 1943 and 1952 for Columbia, a total of 285 sides in terms of the old 78s. It was so successful that Columbia experts rushed to the Library of Congress in Washington to find records that had been issued to the Armed Forces during the Second World War – on condition that they be returned and destroyed at the war's end (some chance!). These 'V-Discs' were exempt from all the tax restrictions then in force and from union requirements – they were even put out during a musicians' strike and all the artists performed without pay. Many of them were recordings taken at rehearsals or from radio broadcasts. Now they were available – in the kind of quality never heard before – to the general public on two Columbia CDs

In quick succession in 1990 there had also been *The Capitol Years* (containing some previously unreleased material including a stunning version of 'One for My Baby', recorded when he and Bill Miller and Miller's piano were in an otherwise empty studio) and *The Reprise Collection*. None of this involved Sinatra's active participation.

Yet he was still touring – with what could be described as the constant inconsistency that marked his performances these days. In June 1993, he was at the Westbury Music Fair in New York State for three days, where the lyrics were again lost in the mist of his occasional memory, while he stumbled from one video screen to the next. But two months later, at the Garden States Arts Center in New Jersey, he was, by all accounts, sensational.

'Right there,' wrote Ray Kerrison in the New York *Post*, 'the rich baritone voice boomed out with such power and verve that my startled wife turned and said: "This is unbelievable." It sure was. Right there, we knew we were in for a spectacular night. And before it was through, we saw things we would not have dreamed possible. Sinatra literally had 'em dancing in the aisles. Talk about star power.'

That October, a fundamentally important event occurred which none of the critics or the people who had been disappointed by recent Sinatra performances could have predicted: Sinatra made a new album and sounded *almost* like the Sinatra of old. *Duets* had Frank partnered by people ranging from Aretha Franklin and Barbra Streisand to Liza Minnelli and Charles Aznavour. None of them received any money for the project. They did it simply because they wanted to be part of a Sinatra adventure. And they all did it without seeing him. He recorded the songs alone on tape – and they then matched it with their contributions, wherever they were. But they didn't just sing to pre-recorded music, or the orchestra Sinatra had used. Spaces were made in the Sinatra recordings and the new music was added in what was not always the Sinatra key. You couldn't see the joins. As Phil Ramone, the producer, told me: 'You can't have these artists just sing eight bars. That's not a duet. You find a way for them to go. After all, girls don't sing in the same key as guys, so automatically you have to change keys in some places.'

The *Duets* album was historic for another reason: Frank's first return to Capitol since leaving the label for his own Reprise in 1959. Suddenly, those seven years at Capitol came flooding back, in which he could be heard singing some of the old songs to the old Nelson Riddle arrangements.

The idea for the album came from Phil Ramone, who had worked with him seventeen years earlier at that open-air Bicentennial celebration Washington in 1976 and then seven years later with Quincy Jones. It all took eighteen months to gestate, but Ramone kept begging, in between working on an album with Liza Minnelli. Begging? 'Begging,' Ramone told me, 'means saying, "Listen, we the group who make records, and the audiences, deserve to see and hear Sinatra as a mature artist. It is like people saw Chevalier, the people who talk about Jolson and any of the other legends like Crosby who worked till they passed away. To me he was the great artist of our time, if not of our own decades. We should really be able to honour him in this way." '

It was a paean which Elliot Weisman, Sinatra's manager, finally took to his client. Now, though, Ramone had to work out how to do the recordings if the miracle happened. One was to do a small intimate album with strings, a kind of updated *Songs for Swingin' Lovers*. If they did that, the recording could be made at a jazz club, like the Rainbow Room above Radio City, and the whole thing could be filmed. It was a grandiose plan. 'Lofty dreams,' said Ramone. The other idea was the duets.

No budget was set for the project. Whatever it cost, it would be worth it. In the end, it all came to about half a million dollars. But before those millions were spent, there were three problems: Sinatra's willingness to do the recordings – he hadn't made a new record in ten years – his ability to do it; his determination only to do concerts where he could feel the impact of the applause of a live audience.

He had made one trip to a recording studio and then abandoned the idea. He couldn't remember the lyrics. 'But,' said Ramone, 'he agreed to see me. We talked about the idea that he might like to lighten the load and sing with other people. We presented this as the youth of the world – young singers mostly who had come up in the last thirty years, people younger than that and people who loved him … That idea appealed to him.' In fact, the idea of youth was to be partially abandoned before long. How else to get Charles Aznavour and his hoped-for appearance by Ella Fitzgerald?

There was also an insurance policy. Don Rubin of Capitol told him: 'If this album doesn't go anywhere after we hear it, no one else will ever hear it. No one will ever know about it.' The conditions, therefore, were set up to make things comfortable for him. But not necessarily for the producers. 'We knew this could be a nightmare. On the other hand, I truly believed that he would do it. A lot of people didn't believe he did it – right up to the first night of recording.'

Then there was a problem. Frank showed up – and then left. As Ramone told me: 'He was uncomfortable. Part of that was the way it was all set up. We were pristine. We tried to set up the vocal so that there was a little isolation there. But he was too far from the band with these lofty great microphones and all the stuff that we used.'

So the studio set-up was changed. A small stage was arranged in the middle of the Capitol studios to make it feel like a concert platform. They lowered the lights. 'He turned around, he saw the guys, picked up his microphone and just before we started he put me through the test I knew was coming. I just didn't know when.'

Frank said: 'Why are we doing this?'

'We talked about this,' Ramone reminded him.

'Yes,' said Sinatra. 'But WHY? They've heard me singing this stuff for maybe fifty or sixty years.'

Ramone replied: 'There's a brand-new audience out there. There's an audience who don't know you exist.' Those were tough words that Sinatra might not have wanted to hear. 'Their parents might go to see you, but they don't. But if it doesn't work, we're out of here.'

'You mean we go to the bar?'

'Yes,' the producer assured him.

'You never saw so many nervous people in a control room', Ramone told me. 'Never. The crew of people like Al Schmidt the engineer. I said to people, "Just look at Al, look at me, and don't stop the tape machine. Just let it roll. There are two machines, an hour of tape on each." These guys are so used to stopping in between takes. I didn't want them to do this. I look at Frank and he's starting to snap his fingers. He blew it in the first four notes, but said, "Let's do it again." It was "Come Fly with Me", the number he usually opens up with in a show.'

There was a whole menu of songs. 'When we started going, he did the songs in two or three takes, sometimes just one. When we did it again, he didn't like his own performance. He said: "No, we can do better." We were one and one at that point. I knew that if people didn't like this, they didn't like ice-cream.'

Although none of the other singers worked with him on the record, he met them all. Gloria Estefan saw him in Florida before recording 'Come Rain or Come Shine'. On TV, he had watched Carly Simon, who was to sing 'Guess I'll Hang My Tears out to Dry' and 'The Wee Small Hours of the Morning'. Now he met her and the other artists in various parts of the country, wherever he happened to be at the time.

There was what Ramone called, a 'wish list' of about twenty people. Naturally, nobody turned them down. He knew Charles Aznavour and was delighted when he said yes to singing 'You Make Me Feel so Young'. His one regret was that he couldn't, after all, include Ella Fitzgerald in the list. She was just too ill. 'Where's Ella?' Frank asked. He had to be told: 'She's just not in the physical shape.'

There was also a cherished hope that Luciano Pavarotti would join him in 'My Way'. (He sang it when the Three Tenors – Pavarotti, Placido Domingo and José Carreras – had their monumental concert in Los Angeles in June 1994. Frank, there with Barbara and other assembled greats of Hollywood royalty, took a bow at that point.) But Pavarotti couldn't fit in time to do the recording.

The first artist to work on the record was Streisand. She sang 'I've Got a Crush on You' and asked Ramone if he could persuade Frank to include the line, 'I love you Barbra'. 'She said, "I'd love Frank to say that." He did. She then said, "I love you, Frank."'

The most unexpected coupling was Bono of U2 – proving just how much Sinatra did enjoy this singer from a different world and a different generation, who had said such nice things about him at the Grammy awards. 'Don't you know, Blue Eyes, you never can win,' he warbled in their recording of 'I've Got You under My Skin'.

There was even talk of releasing their joint number as a rock single, but nothing came of it.

The voice had little of its old power and the strains were obvious, but it was still wonderful to listen to. The idea of the duets was not only novel, it also allowed Frank to work without overstretching himself.

Billboard announced that the album, billed as 'The recording event of the decade', was being turned into 'the marketing event of the decade'. Capitol welcomed back their old star with a teaser campaign – posters and advertisements showing just two bar stools in a spotlight.

Sinatra's old hat was on one – and there was a boom microphone above. 'Start spreading the news,' said the ads. Every selling effort known to record producers was being brought into play – with just the results hoped for.

A Pittsburgh journalist wrote: 'Is Sinatra half the singer he was in 1942 or 1956? Actually he's about three-fifths of the singer he was – but that still makes him about twice the singer anyone else is.' The record buyers obviously agreed. Within six weeks the album had sold a million copies and *Billboard* now had it as their number one.

A year later, the second *Duets* album was released, not as big a success as the first, but it did get into the charts. Work began on it four months after the first was released. Ramone said, 'This was more interesting because you had more time. Once you've gone through this exercise it's like making a movie. In the second movie, you are more aware. We left all the Riddle, Costa and Billy May arrangements the way they were. I didn't want to alter them and we were not going to make them better. Nelson Riddle was so historic, it would be like taking a footprint away just to be a wise guy and that would have been stupid. The idea was to be able to sing with Frank Sinatra and his band. It *was* a moment for your history.'

There was a concession this time: Frank allowed a video of his own performance. But with restrictions. 'We only got some stuff. If the lights got hot and he was feeling the heat, he would say, "I don't want that …" When he took the lights out, it took out almost everything the director needed. But he said: "I don't want to see any cameras." I said: "You won't see any cameras at all." We hid them really out of the way.'

The new artists were, on the whole, ones who were on the original 'wish list' but for various reasons had had to be put on the reserve. Willie Nelson joined him in 'A Foggy Day', Lena Horne sang 'Embraceable You', and in a wonderful throwback to the important past, he sang 'The House I Live In' – with Neil Diamond. In 'Moonlight in Vermont' with Linda Ronstadt, he appeared to fail to hold a note and even a classy edit didn't quite work.

Frank was so bucked by the success of the first album that he embarked on a new series of concerts. He smoked in every one. That seemed to add atmosphere, but it didn't help his health. In March 1994, he collapsed on stage during a concert at the Mosque in Richmond, Virginia, in the middle of 'My Way'. As he fell, he hit his head on a monitor; the crack was heard throughout the auditorium. One of the spokespersons said he was out for about forty seconds. 'A chair,' he was heard to call. 'I need a chair. Get me a chair.'

For his fans, some of whom were weeping as he was taken away in a wheelchair, waving weakly, the end of the career was near indeed. Inevitably, journalists took it as yet another signal that he should cease work straight away.

'Were Sinatra a lesser artist,' wrote David Hinckley in the New York *Daily News*, 'he would very likely have followed the lead of most successful people his age and settled down by the pool. But when you're as revered and valuable a property as Frank Sinatra, who has a multi-million-selling record and a schedule of sold-out concerts, "retirement" is a trickier business. Did we ever think that when Father Time arrived, this guy would go quietly?'

And Mike Littwin wrote in the *Baltimore Sun*, 'If Mick Jagger can prance at fifty, Sinatra can perform at nearly eighty. After all these years, he's earned the right to go out any way he wants to.'

But the *Dallas Morning News's* Michael Corcoran, said: 'If Frank Sinatra's career were a prize fight, the referee would be stepping in about now. Last month, the 78-year-old legend even hit the canvas.'

Nevertheless, he went on – with Frank, Jr., conducting the orchestra, not always so happily.

Was there tension between father and son? It looked like it during a concert at New York's Radio City Music Hall in April 1994, when he called to the younger Sinatra: 'Sorry to wake you up.' But it was one of the better concerts. 'A class act all the way,' said Chip Defaa in the New York *Post*.

David Hinckley liked it, too. 'To hear Sinatra sing "One for My Baby" the way he did at Radio City Tuesday night is still worth paying money to see,' he wrote in the rival *Daily News*. 'But even if he didn't have a lifetime of nuance and affection to bring to his songs, it was clear how much he enjoyed singing them in New York. If he's done "Mack the Knife" and "Lady Is a Tramp" more times than he's called for a drink, he does them some nights like he's just plain happy to be alive. That's a feeling that spreads quickly.'

They plainly thought so too at the Foxwood Casino at Ledyard, Connecticut, after Sinatra played there in November 1994. From then on their gambling chips had Sinatra's face on the obverse. So the King had finally done it – his face on his own currency, his favourite currency.

In October he performed in Chicago. Howard Reich wrote in the

Chicago Tribune, 'Though he turns seventy-nine in less than two months, though he moves a bit more slowly than he once did, though he no longer attempts the high notes of his youth, Frank Sinatra showed a sell-out audience at the United Center on Saturday night what supreme swing-singing and sublime ballad-reading are all about...

'If Sinatra nowadays clips a note short where he might have held on to it in the past, if he uses silences and pauses as dramatically as he once used meticulous crescendos and decrescendos, the essential splendour of the performance remains. In other words, Sinatra, cunning interpreter that he is, knows how to turn disadvantage to advantage. When his voice sometimes reveals a harshness that comes with age, he simply uses that harshness for dramatic effect, making his staccato attacks all the more sharp and biting.' Tony Bennett, a mere sixty-seven, offered his own kind of encouragement: 'He's got a multimillion-dollar-selling album. If no one wanted to see him, I could maybe say, "Take a rest", but if you have that many people that love you, you should just keep doing it.'

There were some people who didn't love him but who, nevertheless, thought the time had come to make up. Jackie Onassis had never forgiven Frank for sharing Judith Campbell Exner with her first husband, President Kennedy, to say nothing of all the other things the Kennedy clan had against Sinatra. But just before her final illness in 1994, they were at New York's 21 Club at the same time. Frank invited her to his table. Jackie, then an editor for the Doubleday publishing firm, tried to persuade him to write his memoirs. They talked about the project and he later turned her down with a bouquet of exquisite flowers and the message: 'You are America's Queen. God bless you, always.' Soon afterwards, Ms Onassis was dead.

There were more shows in various parts of America. Some were wonderful. Some were embarrassing. At every one, the feeling was now the same: he wouldn't be going there any more, so make the most of the opportunity to see Frank Sinatra at work. It will be something to tell the grandchildren. In February 1995, he sang at a party coinciding with the end of the Frank Sinatra Desert Classic golf tournament. It resulted in almost $1 million being given to charity, including $400,000 to the Barbara Sinatra Children's Center.

It wasn't easy to get seats, even harder to get backstage (to do so, you needed a sticker on your shirt showing a picture of Frank wearing a baseball cap and holding a model train). Writing in *Esquire*, Jonathan Schwartz said of his 'I've Got the World on a String': 'Sinatra's voice is clear, tough, on the money. The lyric's last word, *love*, is held to the end with muscle and music.' But when, in July 1995, there was a series of concerts paying tribute to Frank Sinatra at New York's Carnegie Hall, he didn't appear himself. Rosemary Clooney, Vic Damone, Joe Williams, Linda Ronstadt and the songwriter Burton Lane who had given him 'That Old Devil Moon' performed instead. There was more disappointment when talk of Frank coming to Hoboken to launch a Sinatra museum, came to nothing.

Howard W. Koch hoped he would take part in a celebration marking the seventieth birthday of the Hillcrest Country Club, but he didn't. Frank gave a party in January 1996 for George Burns's hundredth birthday (just weeks before the comedian's death). But Burns wasn't well enough to attend and Frank wasn't up to singing. The Voice's singing days were finally over.

— 34 —

ALL THE WAY

It would be nice now to think of Frank Sinatra finally putting those feet up by his pool and letting the records sing for themselves. What songs they were! Songs of unrequited love, of course, of drinks set up at the bar, certainly, but songs that helped him to swing easily with the kind of commitment to a lover whom he had under his skin. But old age was not sitting well with him.

He had given up his home in Palm Springs and moved to Beverly Hills, just five blocks away from where Nancy, Jr., lived. On a good night, he'd stay in with Barbara and play Sinatra records. Her favourite was the little-known 'Here Is that Rainy Day'.

People paid him more and more honours. After all, it was extremely rare for a star who had become the world's greatest entertainer to reach the age of eighty. When he did celebrate his eightieth birthday in December 1995, there were huge spreads in the world's newspapers and a massive television festival of praise to him and to his career from the great stars of the age. Radio programmes put out nothing but Sinatra tributes. In Britain, the BBC's Radio 2 station included a Sinatra spot in every single show. In New York, there was now one radio station playing nothing but Sinatra records every day of the week, one Saturday morning featuring no fewer than five versions of 'Witchcraft' on the trot.

In Hoboken, River Drive had long since become Frank Sinatra Drive ('The signs to the Drive were always disappearing and it so happened that one fell in here,' said Joe Spaccavento in Piccolo's restaurant) and they were still hoping for a Frank Sinatra museum in the town. The local newspaper published a map showing 'Sinatra Landmarks'. At Piccolo's and at Leo's Grandezvous, complete sections of the establishments were given over to photographs of the local boy who made good.

The City Hall became a Frank Sinatra shrine with the entrance

421

hall and the first floor of this bastion of civic probity turned into a showplace for Sinatra photographs, records, posters and other archives. 'It's a kind of olive branch,' McKevin Shaughnessy, who organised the display, told me.

How much did Frank himself know of all this? The *National Enquirer* revealed in April 1996 that he was suffering from microangiopathy of the brain – a disease which caused the network of tiny blood vessels in the brain to wither and the brain itself to shrink.

Shirley MacLaine told Juliet Prowse shortly before the dancer's death from cancer in 1996 how shocked she had been by Frank's appearance. Juliet told me in that last interview so close to her own death, that Ms MacLaine 'could swear he had Alzheimers. I think it was drink, too.' Now, according to Shirley, he had barely recognised her.

Dean Martin died in December 1995, just a few days after Frank's birthday. Sinatra was distraught. 'He was my brother,' he kept saying between the tears. 'Not through blood but through choice. Our friendship travelled down many roads over the years and there will always be a special place in my heart and soul for Dean.'

Friends reported that he was eaten up with remorse – because they had not behaved like brothers in the last few years. In fact, they had barely spoken since Dean left the reunion tour in 1988. He had sent a message to Sinatra: 'Tell Frank, if we don't meet now, it's going to be too late.' Frank allegedly replied: 'I'll have to think about it.' Dean couldn't understand why he hadn't been invited to take part in the eightieth birthday celebration. Martin died alone on Christmas Day with just a housemaid, a private security guard and a nurse for company.

'The fight has gone out of him,' said one of the Sinatra team, now employed to keep people away – and from asking when Frank would be singing again; everyone now knew that he would never do that again. Was he suffering from Alzheimer's disease? Nancy, Jr., admitted on a radio programme that she didn't quite know. Even the old anger had gone – along with the gait and the enthusiasm. He shuffled when he walked. His eyesight and his hearing were deteriorating rapidly.

When he had appeared at a music industry benefit in 1994, Morton Gould, president of ASCAP, had had to help him on to the platform. Gould was even older than Sinatra. A few months before his own death, he told me: 'As I helped him slowly walk up to the rostrum, he said: "Are you taking me to the old people's home?"' Worst of all, he had a wispy white beard circling his face that made him look like some latter-day Captain Ahab or an Amish elder.

Occasionally, he thought he *would* sing again. He took a trip to a recording studio that had been alerted to the possibility of new Sinatra songs, but when he got before the microphone, no voice would come out. He didn't remember the words. It was no good giving him cue cards, he couldn't read them. He didn't even know to which song they referred. He spent days at home not getting out of his pyjamas.

One report said that the superstar of 1996, Michael Jackson, so cared for what had happened to his idol that he had sent him an $80,000 'hyperbaric' oxygen chamber which he was sure would rejuvenate him. Frank, who was determined to live to be a hundred, was grateful and said he would try everything.

In November 1996, he was taken to the Cedars Sinai Hospital in Los Angeles with what was described as a pinched nerve. Later that week, it was revealed that he had had a mild heart attack and a stroke. Newspapers and television stations all over the world dusted off their obituary columns – until he left the hospital and went home. In January 1997, he was back again. He had had another heart attack.

His declining health was a big cloud on his horizon, but there was another one: the continuing feud between Barbara and his children. Nancy was quoted as saying that Barbara wanted to keep her and her siblings away from his eightieth birthday celebrations. However, Frank himself said he couldn't rest in peace without their making up.

Yet there is so much to be thankful for – for them and for his public. The family knows that he was never the perfect father. Certainly, he was never a wonderful husband, yet what he showed them all was a profound kind of love. In a way that was what he showed his audiences, too.

The ice-cold world of business has had its own pounds of flesh from Frank, along with the ones he extracted for himself. They took everything he could give them – and, when he made another million or two with his *Duets* album, accepted their cuts avidly. They know that even now there are more discs in record stores marked 'Frank Sinatra' than by anyone else, living or dead. They also know that there were a lot of words eaten by the Warner records man who, less than twenty years before, had said, 'There's just not enough of Frank's people around any more to make him a monster record-seller. He's not Fleetwood Mac. He's not Pink Floyd.'

But he made the big mistake of carrying on too long. As Melville

Shavelson remarked to me: 'The prime example is Cary Grant. When he saw the picture up there on the screen and didn't like what he saw, he quit. Sinatra should have done it, too.'

Juliet Prowse, in that last interview, thought he had become rather like Nureyev in his last years. 'He danced against twenty-year-olds who made him look pathetic. That was Sinatra when I saw him work last.'

To some people he was like Eddie Cantor in 1964, remembered but no longer important. That could never be true.

In the early summer of 1997, Nancy Jr., rang up her father's friend Jerry Lewis. 'She wanted to have as many of his friends around or to ring him because she knew that there wasn't all that long to go,' Lewis told me. He said he was pleased that Frank, though weak, was feeling better and knew what was happening around him.

Bud Yorkin has seen the more recent changes: 'In the last couple of years, he has not been what he was, but up to then he was always fun. At Christmas a year ago,' he told me in 1995, 'Mo Wasserman and I walked up to him at a party. He didn't recognise either one of us. I was with him at a dinner party a couple of months ago. He said to the person he was sitting next to, "I'm sitting here and I wonder what I am doing here. Who are these people?" He knows he just can't deal with it.'

Walter Scharf told me of the disappointment when he saw him at Mattheo's restaurant – a place where he would have his spaghetti with a glass of wine, followed by a Jack Daniel's, before going into the kitchen to smoke – 'I saw him recently and he didn't know me. He said, "Who are you?" He was speaking in dribbles, in the corner over there with a lot of people around him.'

But Scharf, like everyone else, knew that given a chance and a return of the voice and the memory, he would go on singing still. 'It's that confidence he had – the most confidence of any human being that I know outside of Barbra Streisand. When he stepped in front of an orchestra, it was like he was up in heaven and surrounded by all his saints.' Sinatra was rarely surrounded by saints; nevertheless, he *could* always say with truth: 'Whatever else has been said about me personally is unimportant. When I sing I believe I'm honest.'

The fascination with Sinatra continues unabated. In late 1996 Martin Scorsese announced his full-length feature film on the Sinatra story – at last, the thing that wasn't thought possible when the mini-series was made, was going to happen. It would be one more memorial and if he knew anything about it, Frank couldn't object to that. 'I just hope,' he had said, 'that if I leave anything behind, it might be the fact that I've tried constantly to have taste in what I did. I tried to pick the best material. I tried to enunciate words so that listeners would know what I was saying and that I understood the lyrics before they even heard them, so that it might continue with other kids as they grow older now, singers in the business who might catch on to some of those things. I hope they do. It might be a nice thing for me to remember.'

He was not just a great entertainer, but a marvellous singer, even a dangerous personality, someone who could tear up conventions simply by changing a word in a song and, as a result, have the people out front licking his hands in adoration. The grandmothers – and some of them great-grandmothers – who stood in line at the old Paramount can testify to that. Others have just one or two words for what he was and what he did. He was a musician. He was an artist. And whether he now likes to hear it or not, he always did it His Way – All the Way.

PUBLISHER'S NOTE

On May 15, 1998, the world awakened to the news that Francis Albert Sinatra was dead. He had died the previous night of a heart attack in Los Angeles. He was eighty-two years old.

As with that of other legends who have lived long and complete lives, Sinatra's death was heralded not just as the passing of a man but the passing of an era. An era that was a time that Frank Sinatra helped define and powerfully shape by the simplest of instruments—his magnificent voice. That voice will sing forever.

INDEX

Titles of films and albums are listed in the main sequence; those of songs are in a sequence under Sinatra, Frank: **songs**.

INDEX

MGM contract 101–2, 131–2, 146,
152
trouble with 162–3
punishment for FS 169–70
contract ended 171
Miami Herald 338
microphones 40–1
Milestone, Lewis 287–8
Miller, Ann 88, 146, 155–6, 158
Miller, Bill, pianist 352, 402, 413
Miller, Glenn 51
Miller, Mitch 167–9, 245–6
Mills Brothers 29, 147
Minnelli, Liza 378, 402, 410, 413
Minnelli, Vincente 256
The Miracle of the Bells (film) 143–4,
146
Mitchell, Guy 168
Mitchum, Robert 166, 212, 224
Mob, the 44, 71, 132, 134–5, 138–9,
178, 182, 269, 283–4, 298–9,
339
and Kefauver Committee 179–80
and *From Here to Eternity* 188–9
Giancana's club 206, 207
New Jersey Committee 344, 347
Washington Committee 358–60
Mafia trial 380–1
La Vegas hearings 391–3
enmity towards FS 400
Mocambo Club 243–4
Monroe, Marilyn 214
the Wrong Door Raid 233–5
and the Rat Pack 241
Kennedy and FS 270
and FS 281, 289–90
at Cal-Neva Lodge 299
death 300
'Mooney, Dr Sam' (i.e. Giancana)
299
Moore, Roger 400
Mooring, W.H. 105–6
Moretti, Quarico 'Willie Moore' 71,
166, 347, 392
Morgan, Michele 90
Morris (William) Agency 213, 248
Morrison, Charles, death 243–4
Mortimer, Lee 95, 111, 132
war on, by FS 134–8, 139, 142
Moses, Chuck 304
Mostel, Zero 273
Munshin, Jules 155
Musicians Union 33, 37, 83
My Way (album) 341

The Naked Runner (film) 328, 334
Namath, Joe 378
National Academy of Recording Arts
403–4
National Association for the
Advancement of Colored
People,
award 394
National Enquirer 381, 422
NBC radio 58, 71–2, 215
NBC TV 227
Needham, Hal 396
Nellis, Joseph 179–80

Nelson, Willie 409, 417
Nemy, Enid 378
Nevada Gaming Commission 207
Nevada Gaming Control Board 307
Nevara, Nick 281
Never So Few (film) 258, 259
New Jersey state, on FS's black list
397
New Jersey *Observer* 18–19, 140
New York magazine 381
New York *Daily Mirror* 134
New York *Daily News* 137, 353, 369,
381, 403, 418
New York Herald Tribune 71
New York *Mirror* 95
New York Philharmonic 89
New York *Post* 200–1, 288, 370, 380,
413, 418
New York Times 227, 359, 366, 369,
378, 386
New Yorker 391
Newman, Paul 227
Newsweek 225, 310
Nicola, J.D. 273
The Night Club (film) 29
Niven, David 226, 235
Nixon, Richard, President 270, 275,
296, 347, 356, 361
None but the Brave (film) 315
Not as a Stranger (film) 224, 236
Novak, Kim 227, 228, 236, 247
The Nuggets 204

O'Brien, Margaret 100–1
'O'Brien, Marty' (i.e. Marty Sinatra)
6
O'Brien, Pat 366
Ocean's Eleven (film) 287–8
Odets, Clifford 318
O'Hara, John 248
Oklahoma! 82, 103, 123
Ol' Blue Eyes Is Back (album) 365
Old Gold cigarettes 130, 139
Oliver, Sy 51, 56, 74
Olsen, Ed 305–6, 307
On the Town (film) 131, 152, 155–8,
169
On the Waterfront (film), and
Hoboken 4, 213
Onassis, Jacqueline Kennedy *see*
Kennedy, Jacqueline
Only the Lonely (album) 257
Oppenheimer, Per J. 231
Osborne, Richard 317
Oscars:
The House I Live In 127
From Here to Eternity 201
nomination, *The Man with the
Golden Arm* 228
The Joker Is Wild 251
O'Sullivan, Maureen 326
Our Town (TV) 227
Oval Bar, Hoboken 20

Pacella, Louis 380
Pacht, Isaac and N. Joseph Ross,
lawyers 137
Pal Joey (film) 247

Palisades Park, Hoboken 20
Pan, Hermes 265
paparazzi, Roman 317
Paramount music theater, New York
75, 81, 85, 99
return flop 184
Park Lake Enterprises 292
Parker, Eleanor 227
Parker, Sol 65
Parks, Larry 88
Parsons, Louella 126, 131–2, 160,
219, 259, 274, 275, 285
Pasculli, Patrick 407–8
Pasternak, Joe 102–3, 104, 146
Pastor, Tony 67
Patriarca, Raymond 358–9
Pavarotti, Luciano 382, 416
Payne, Frank 47
Pearl, Ralph 310
Pearson, Al 136
Peck, Gregory 373, 383–4, 392, 405
Pegler, Westbrook 110–11, 181–2
Peikov, Assen, sculptor 223
Pepper, Claude 359
Perfectly Frank (radio) 202
Peformers Rights Society, FS head of
402
Petrozelli, James *see* Skelly, Jimmy
Phair, George 88–9
Philadelphia, presentation of
Freedom Medal to FS 377–8
Philadelphia Orchestra 158
Philadelphia Philharmonic 86
Philip, Prince, Duke of Edinburgh
181, 393–4
Piccolo's Restaurant, Hoboken 9
Picon, Molly 300
Picturegoer 105–6
Pidgeon, Walter 159
Pied Pipers 54, 56, 58
Pink Tights (film) 214
Pionbino, Nick 20
Pitchess, Peter 392
Pius XII, Pope, FS audience with
121–2
Playboy interview with FS 303–5
Players (theatrical club), New York
387
Poems in Colour (LP record) 228
Poitier, Sidney 278
Poland 395
Polanski, Roman 335
Porter, Cole 39–40, 57, 113–14, 261
'Don't Fence Me In' 113
High Society 229, 230
Powell, Eleanor 58, 59
Preminger, Otto 227–8, 236
Presley, Elvis 215, 242, 250, 261,
291, 292
affair with Juliet Prowse 282
press, and FS 95–6, 110–11, 129,
177–8, 179, 217, 225–6, 316–
17
Australian 368
Roman 317
Previn, André 130, 166, 228, 336
The Pride and the Passion (film) 235–
6